SAP PRESS e-books

Print or e-book, Kindle or iPad, workplace or airplane: Choose where and how to read your SAP PRESS books! You can now get all our titles as e-books, too:

- By download and online access
- For all popular devices
- And, of course, DRM-free

Convinced? Then go to www.sap-press.com and get your e-book today.

SAP S/4HANA® Finance: The Reference Guide to What's New

SAP PRESS

SAP PRESS is a joint initiative of SAP and Rheinwerk Publishing. The know-how offered by SAP specialists combined with the expertise of Rheinwerk Publishing offers the reader expert books in the field. SAP PRESS features first-hand information and expert advice, and provides useful skills for professional decision-making.

SAP PRESS offers a variety of books on technical and business-related topics for the SAP user. For further information, please visit our website: *www.sap-press.com*.

Mehta, Aijaz, Duncan, Parikh
SAP S/4HANA Finance: An Introduction
2019, 397 pages, hardcover and e-book
www.sap-press.com/4784

Anup Maheshwari
Implementing SAP S/4HANA Finance (2nd Edition)
2018, 570 pages, hardcover and e-book
www.sap-press.com/4525

Hilker, Awan, Delvat
Central Finance and SAP S/4HANA
2018, 458 pages, hardcover and e-book
www.sap-press.com/4667

Bardhan, Baumgartl, Choi, Dudgeon, Lahiri, Meijerink, Worsley-Tonks
SAP S/4HANA: An Introduction (3rd Edition)
2019, 647 pages, hardcover and e-book
www.sap-press.com/4782

Janet Salmon, Michel Haesendonckx

SAP S/4HANA® Finance: The Reference Guide to What's New

Rheinwerk
Publishing

Editor Emily Nicholls
Copyeditor Melinda Rankin
Cover Design Graham Geary
Photo Credit iStockphoto.com/964064950/©akinbostanci
Layout Design Vera Brauner
Production Hannah Lane
Typesetting III-satz, Husby (Germany)
Printed and bound in the United States of America, on paper from sustainable sources

ISBN 978-1-4932-1805-9
© 2019 by Rheinwerk Publishing, Inc., Boston (MA)
1st edition 2019

Library of Congress Cataloging-in-Publication Data
Names: Salmon, Janet, author. | Haesendonckx, Michel, author.
Title: SAP S/4HANA finance : the reference guide to what's new / Janet
    Salmon, Michel Haesendonckx.
Description: 1st edition. | Bonn ; Boston : Rheinwerk Publishing, [2019] |
    Includes index.
Identifiers: LCCN 2019000949 (print) | LCCN 2019004018 (ebook) | ISBN
    9781493218066 (ebook) | ISBN 9781493218059 (alk. paper)
Subjects: LCSH: SAP HANA (Electronic resource) |
    Corporations--Accounting--Data processing. | Corporations--Finance--Data
    processing. | Business enterprises--Data processing.
Classification: LCC HF5686.C7 (ebook) | LCC HF5686.C7 S2664 2019 (print) |
    DDC 657.0285/53--dc23

LC record available at https://lccn.loc.gov/2019000949

Contents at a Glance

Dear Reader,

For many SAP customers, the arrival of SAP S/4HANA signals the renovation of long-standing finance processes.

However, in the last four years I've discovered that what often accompanies industry excitement ranges from insatiable curiosity to professional skepticism. For savvy finance practitioners, the question isn't "What can the new suite do?" but "What can the new suite do that my current system can't, and why?" and "How do the changes in SAP S/4HANA impact me?"

But as I considered practitioners' search for details, I concluded that existing book concepts aren't well suited for this line of inquiry. High-level introductions paint the big picture in broad strokes, and implementation guides and business user handbooks are too deep. A new kind of book was needed.

Enter the first SAP PRESS "change guide," a practitioner's nitty-gritty look at SAP S/4HANA Finance that focuses only on the areas where new ground has been broken. Here finance experts Janet Salmon and Michel Haesendonckx direct your attention to the difference between the two systems, digging into the true technical and functional advances until they reach ones, zeroes, and your bottom line. If you're looking for the SAP S/4HANA Finance delta, then this change guide is for you.

What did you think about *SAP S/4HANA Finance: The Reference Guide to What's New*? Your comments and suggestions are the most useful tools to help us improve our books. Please reach out and share any praise or criticism you may have.

Thank you for purchasing a book from SAP PRESS!

Emily Nicholls
Editor, SAP PRESS

emilyn@rheinwerk-publishing.com
www.sap-press.com
Rheinwerk Publishing · Boston, MA

Contents

1 The Universal Journal: Designing a Steering Model for the Business — 49

6   Key Figures for Operational Reporting: Measuring Financial Performance   223

7   Real-Time Financial Close: Providing Timely Information   247

11 Inventory Accounting: Simplifying Material Valuation, Production Cost Analysis, and Actual Costing

12 Group Reporting: Producing Consolidated Financial Statements

15 Cloud Extensions and Connectivity: Looking Beyond the Core

453

Foreword

With business models constantly changing and decision-makers becoming increasingly hungry for up-to-date, relevant information, finance departments must adopt new technologies to stay competitive. SAP S/4HANA Finance (formerly SAP Simple Finance) is a comprehensive finance solution, using an SAP HANA in-memory database that covers financial planning and analysis, financial accounting and closing, and treasury and risk financial management.

SAP S/4HANA simplifies finance in ERP. It grew from a project initiated in 2006 by Professor Hasso Plattner, a member of SAP's supervisory board and one of the founders of SAP, to build an in-memory database that could combine transactional and analytical data. This new technology provided the cornerstone for a radical simplification of the data model and a drastic improvement in query response time. Fixed aggregates and indexes could be removed, and the new Universal Journal merges financial and management accounting and the other subledgers in finance. This simplified architecture allows further innovations to steer the business.

Since 2016, I have been responsible for the software development in finance. The finance product portfolio covers accounting, controlling, planning, group reporting, and treasury management. I have been working for SAP for almost 10 years in various roles in software development and finance business. The design and development of the Universal Journal was one of SAP's key innovations delivered during this period. This book was written by two finance experts in SAP product development and solution management, and I would like to thank them for their commitment and dedication to writing this book.

I am pleased that you are interested in learning more about SAP S/4HANA Finance use cases and their innovative functions. This book will illuminate the value of SAP S/4HANA Finance in your daily work.

Matthias Grabellus
Head of Software Development, Finance
SAP SE

Preface

SAP S/4HANA Finance was released in March 2015. Already there are plenty of books on the market explaining what it is, how to implement it, and how to migrate your existing system to bring your existing accounting documents into the new structures. White papers make the case for a finance transformation, and blogs describe successful implementations and migrations. The message is out: SAP S/4HANA Finance brings significant change.

However, for many finance professionals, knowing that significant change has arrived isn't enough. To find out more, you can download a thousand-page simplification list from the internet or search for SAP Notes with "S4TWL" in the header, but these tell you *what* changed, not *why* SAP made the change and the implications for your organization.

This is where our reference guide comes into the picture. Our aim is to take you behind the scenes and help you understand why we think the world of finance has evolved and how SAP S/4HANA can help you navigate the winds of change.

Objective of This Book

We talk to SAP customers and prospective customers almost daily.

Some are looking to reduce the cost of finance and provide better decision support to their businesses. Some find that the business world in which they operated at the time of their initial implementation isn't the world in which they operate today. Some have inherited a heterogeneous system landscape with multiple systems set up using very different implementation principles. Some are evaluating a move from an on-premise to a cloud deployment. Some are looking ahead to the end of mainstream maintenance for SAP ERP on December 31, 2025. Whatever the starting point for the conversation, we try to explain what's changed and why SAP S/4HANA can potentially help them going forward.

The contents of this reference guide grew out of these conversations. To help articulate the key areas where SAP S/4HANA has changed finance, we selected what we think are the 15 most important technical and functional changes in the new system and tried to explain them in business terms. For example, you've probably already heard of the Universal Journal, but in this book we'll explain how to design a steering model for your business around this giant pivot table, and show how the same data model is used as a basis for planning and consolidation. You've probably already seen examples of SAP Fiori, but we'll explain the fundamental differences compared to existing transactions and reports and discuss what it means to work with live data rather than data that has been moved to a data warehouse. We'll also explain how SAP S/4HANA can change your close processes and provide forward-looking information to steer your business by using predictive accounting. We'll look at what's changed in asset accounting, product costing, cash management, and tax reporting, and discuss when you might use other products to extend the digital core. We'll give you our honest assessment of where SAP stands on each of these topics.

We wanted to write a book that would explain the business impact of the functional and technological changes, rather than a function and feature description of the SAP S/4HANA product. Our aim is to provide insight for the office of the chief financial officer (CFO) and the finance leadership team. Finance professionals—from financial consultants to accounting and controlling managers to business process owners and key users—will find explanations that offer a mix of business, IT, and accounting information, depending on the nature of the change described.

We wanted this book to be neither a business user guide (it's not about a user's daily work, but about how their general working environment will change) nor an implementation guide (though we will show configuration settings when they make sense); rather, we seek to effectively occupy the middle ground between the finance transformation white paper and the thousand-page simplification list and to deliver information that finance professionals depend on.

This is your guide to the key finance areas in which SAP S/4HANA is different from SAP ERP and to the big topics that you should consider to be ready for the future.

How to Read This Book

Although you can start at the beginning and read to the end of this book, we know that most of our readers may prefer to go straight to their topic of choice, so we've designed the book so that you can dip in and out. Chapter titles are structured around the key change (e.g., "The Universal Journal") and its strategic importance or impact (e.g., "Designing a Steering Model for the Business"). We recommend that you read in the order that you see fit and use the index as well as the chapter titles to find what interests you.

Let's walk through the book, chapter by chapter.

Introduction

The introduction looks at the impact of digital technology on finance and how finance departments must transform to deliver insights to a demanding business. We'll look at changes within the finance organization in terms of people's roles and ways of working as finance professionals become system-savvy and as millennials with little desire to learn a list of transaction codes enter the workforce.

In the introduction, we'll also begin to weave in our SAP focus. To give more context to the current situation for many SAP-run businesses, we'll tell the story of SAP from its very first customer to the present-day multinationals; we'll introduce the application components and the basic integration points between logistics and finance in SAP R/3, then look at changes that occurred in implementation approaches as organizations became more global. This introduction charts the rise of the data warehouse in the late 1990s, along with the shift to SAP ERP and the introduction of industry solutions, before looking at the technological shift that became possible with SAP HANA and how this allowed SAP to redesign the finance solution.

The Universal Journal: Designing a Steering Model for the Business

Even before opening **Chapter 1**, every finance professional knows that the steering model is the set of financial data that allows an organization to set its future direction and the key reporting dimensions within that model.

Every organization has a steering model, though the elements will be different depending on the industry and the maturity of the market. Before SAP S/4HANA, the components in SAP ERP spread the reporting dimensions in this steering model across several tables, meaning that finance professionals spent a significant amount of time reconciling the legal figures with the management figures in the past. With SAP S/4HANA, all financial data moves into a single table so that the legal and management views are simply different aggregations of the same basic data. (This announcement is often a source of relief for customers accustomed to reconciliation!) Chapter 1 discusses the reporting dimensions in the Universal Journal, how they relate to the entities available in SAP ERP, and how to extend and change the steering model if required.

Local and Global Controlling: Changing Organizational Structures to Satisfy Various Sets of Requirements

Many multinationals use data warehouses as a corporate umbrella to combine financial data from the various local systems and convert it into a common data model for global steering. To report on live data, organizations need to remove this transformation layer and use the same steering model to meet local legal reporting requirements and corporate steering requirements in a single system. Of course, the Universal Journal helps, but as you'll see in **Chapter 2**, design decisions in your original SAP ERP implementation might stand in the way of your achieving a global view of your finance data. This chapter explains how to use the different ledger and currency settings in SAP S/4HANA to provide a global view of your supply chain that is independent of the transfer prices set for intercompany business transactions.

From Products to Services: Unifying Approaches to Controlling and Financial Operations

When SAP introduced its industry solutions, it distinguished between the product-related industries and the service industries, as if its customers fit into either one or the other.

Now these distinctions are blurring, as organizations introduce new business models that combine physical products and services, from providing after-sales support to offering a completely new way of delivering and charging for use of a product. **Chapter 3** discusses the various industry solutions and shows how the industry-to-core approach in SAP S/4HANA is making some industry changes available for everybody; it then discusses how the principle of one is driving the compulsory use of the business partner. It explains how controlling and financial operations are changing as business models shift and illustrates the various approaches to controlling and financial operations using SAP Fiori applications.

Financial Process Optimization: Standardizing and Automating Processes

The need to reduce the cost of finance is forcing organizations to rethink their business processes. **Chapter 4** looks at simplification in terms of automation, process guidance, and flexible collaboration, as well as the impact of moving to a shared service environment or implementing Central Finance. It explains how cloud thinking can help to standardize processes and introduces machine learning, giving examples of managing cash and reconciling goods receipts and invoice receipts and of redesigning applications for allocations, intercompany reconciliation, and accrual management.

SAP Fiori and Live Data: Merging Transactional and Analytical Data

Chapter 5 explains what SAP Fiori is and uses examples from cash management, financial operations, and accounting to introduce various types of applications. It explains how SAP uses compatibility views to support existing reports but delivers a new virtual data model to provide embedded analytics that modernize the reporting experience and rely on live data. It also describes how to handle hierarchies when reporting in SAP S/4HANA and provides a vision of reporting in the intelligent enterprise.

Key Figures for Operational Reporting: Measuring Financial Performance

Chapter 6 introduces the SAP Fiori overview pages as a way of delivering actionable insight to business users, starting from the operational key figures associated with their roles. It then goes behind the scenes to explain how to use semantic tags to select the appropriate accounts to deliver these key figures and how to introduce additional quantities for volume reporting. It explains how to go beyond traditional P&L-based reporting to calculate key figures for balance sheet entities.

Real-Time Financial Close: Providing Timely Information

Chapter 7 explains how to improve both the entity close and the group close and how to orchestrate the close more effectively using SAP S/4HANA Cloud for advanced financial closing. It then looks at new initiatives to support a soft close for commercial projects by immediately assigning profitability segments, performing revenue recognition in real time, and enhancing resource-related intercompany billing. The chapter then discusses how SAP is extending this vision for production controlling.

Predictive Accounting: Providing Forward-Looking Insights

Chapter 8 explains how predictive accounting uses existing forward-looking information in the system to steer the business. It provides specific examples of predictive accounting by looking at accounting for incoming sales orders, statistical sales conditions, and purchasing commitments.

Unified Planning Model: Moving from Financial Budgeting to Driver-Based Forecasting

Chapter 9 picks up the idea of the Universal Journal and explains how the same steering model and reporting dimensions are needed for planning. We look at how to create and manage plans using SAP Analytics Cloud for planning and SAP BPC for SAP S/4HANA, and at how to capture plan data from other SAP applications, including commercial projects, capital expense projects, and production orders.

Asset Accounting: Making Real-Time Postings for Multiple Accounting Principles

Asset accounting was traditionally a subledger with integration into the general ledger, but in SAP S/4HANA the asset accounting data is part of the Universal Journal.

In Chapter 10, we look at the link between depreciation areas and the handling of assets according to different accounting principles. We introduce SAP Fiori applications to display the key figures used in asset accounting, explain the link to controlling to value assets under construction, and show how changes to the maintenance order improve cost transparency.

Inventory Accounting: Simplifying Material Valuation, Production Cost Analysis, and Actual Costing

Inventory accounting was traditionally separate from the general ledger, but in SAP S/4HANA the inventory accounting data is included in the Universal Journal and the use of the material ledger becomes compulsory. As we'll discuss in Chapter 11, the move to an account-based model also has an impact on the handling of the cost of goods sold. In this chapter, we'll explain how to split costs to separate accounts, settle production variances, report costs by work center, and perform actual costing in SAP S/4HANA.

Group Reporting: Producing Consolidated Financial Statements

Group reporting traditionally required a data warehouse to combine the financial statements from each local entity into a central model before eliminating intercompany payables/receivables and intercompany profits. Chapter 12 picks up the idea of the Universal Journal as the central steering model and shows how to leverage the same data for the purposes of consolidation using SAP S/4HANA for group reporting.

It shows how to acquire the data for consolidation either directly from the Universal Journal or indirectly by bringing financial data first into Central Finance.

Cash Management: Improving Cash Operations

SAP S/4HANA includes new cash management functionality. **Chapter 13** explains how cash-relevant transactions are brought into the One Exposure table. It explains how to manage bank accounts, perform cash operations, and manage and plan liquidity in the new environment.

Tax and Legal Reporting: Ensuring Compliance with Key Requirements

Chapter 14 looks at the ever-changing tax regulations across the world and introduces two solutions—SAP S/4HANA for advanced compliance reporting and SAP Localization Hub, tax service—as a way to successfully manage tax requirements.

Cloud Extensions and Connectivity: Looking beyond the Core

Chapter 15 explains the requirements to run SAP S/4HANA as the digital core and how its scope can be extended using additional finance-related solutions and extensions available through the SAP Cloud Platform.

Looking Ahead with SAP S/4HANA

This summary outlines the SAP S/4HANA roadmap for finance in the next two to three years and recommends additional resources to readers.

Acknowledgments

For their help in answering the many questions that arose during the writing of this book, I would like to thank my colleagues: Michael Conrad, Manfred Crumbach, Marei Dornick, Ralf Dinkel, Georg Dopf, Holger Faber, Mick Hohendorf, Ralf Ille, Sasa Markovic, Uwe Mayer, Birgit Oettinger, Judith Pistor, Eva Wang, and Stefan Walz.

For the many hours spent discussing and writing the book, a huge thank-you to my co-author, Michel, and to Emily Nicholls and the SAP PRESS team.

And as always, a big thank-you to my husband, Nick, and children, Martin and Lucy.

Janet Salmon

While being an author outside working hours has been an enriching experience, it also meant sacrificing quite a lot of quality time with my family and friends. That is why I'd like to take the opportunity to especially thank you—Ilse, Sofie, and Maxim—for your flexibility, understanding, and tremendous support. I'd also like to thank my colleagues for their input, and in particular to thank Janet, with whom it was an absolute pleasure to co-write this book.

Michel Haesendonckx

Introduction

Before we introduce SAP S/4HANA, let's begin by examining the functional drivers that necessitate it. To understand the technological evolution toward SAP S/4HANA, in this introduction we'll also examine the history of SAP's ERP software.

Business is currently undergoing a digital transformation, with new technologies being introduced in all areas, resulting in fundamental changes to how businesses operate and how they deliver value to customers. For the end consumer, this means a completely transformed buying experience. For the finance department, this means a shift from transactional work—delivering reports to support the business and a lot of manual work in spreadsheets—to a new way of working.

If the business as a whole is focused on supporting the end customer, then the finance department as a subset is supporting the business as its customer. As finance departments are discovering, the business can be as demanding as its own customers; leadership is no longer prepared to wait for numbers but instead wants immediate access to key figures to determine whether the business is performing to plan or whether corrective action is needed. To meet these requirements, finance departments must embrace technology to deliver the key figures that support the business, a planning process that can operate with a minimum of human impact, and predictions that show where the business is heading.

There has been a generation change. Whereas twenty years ago, CFOs brought accounting skills to the table and focused on producing and analyzing financial statements, now the accounting function has been computerized, so today's CFOs must understand IT systems. This isn't to say that most CFOs have a programming or data science background, but they certainly understand the technology enough to drive conversations with IT about what they want and what's feasible—and to be active participants in implementing a software system that can achieve those goals.

So as an introduction to *SAP S/4HANA Finance: The Reference Guide to What's New*, we'll discuss the changing role of finance and the expectations of the business today in the The Changing Role of Finance section.

Many readers may be somewhat familiar with SAP systems already; perhaps you're running one now or have implemented it for many years. In either case, you know that design decisions made when your organization implemented SAP affect what information you can get out of your system today. In the Finance with SAP section, we'll look at the history of SAP, because understanding the SAP story in the context of finance will help you understand why your organization might be doing things a certain way. Only if you understand where you're coming from can you shape where you want to go tomorrow. Our goal is not to advocate change for the sake of it but to take a long, hard look at the way finance is operating today and how it can be improved.

The Changing Role of Finance

The role of finance once was simply to produce and analyze financial statements, but those days are gone. Let's take a look at three key trends impacting the way the role of finance is changing: the expectation for finance to act increasingly as a strategic business partner; the fact that CFOs are becoming more system-savvy and are partnering with IT to put an entire management system in place, not only close the books but also to enable finance to assume a more strategic business partner role; and the movement toward finance operations being increasingly mobile.

Finance as a Strategic Business Partner

If you've been around business and IT long enough, you've surely heard claims that the finance organization should become an active rather than supportive partner for the business. This is often accompanied by excited discussions of "finance transformation" and "digital finance."

Wherever they are on their finance transformation journey, many finance organizations are rethinking their role in the greater organization, their purpose and their internal organization, the skills their personnel require, and the type of system landscape needed to support them. What does this mean practically?

To understand how finance is changing, consider Figure 1. We'll discuss three key finance duties: running the business, delivering insights, and supporting strategy.

Running Finance Operations

Historically, finance's main concern has been to ensure that required operational tasks are executed so that the business keeps on running. In other words, finance makes sure that the bills get paid and the lights stay on so that the revenue-generating functions of the business can continue.

And surely business functions like payables management and tax reporting are still critical, both today and tomorrow. However, this is no longer enough. Instead of just concentrating on keeping the finance factory running (as cost-effectively as possible, of course!), we're seeing an increased focus on delivering business insights continuously and a shift toward prioritizing tasks and activities that *create value* for the organization.

To free up time for these value-creating activities, operational tasks can't just be abandoned (as illustrated on the left side of Figure 1). They need to be executed, but in a much more efficient way—and this is exactly where modern technology plays an important role. In classic enterprise resource planning (ERP) systems, a lot of automation was based on establishing a set of rules and then automating their execution. Although this has introduced some efficiency improvements, rule-based automation has its limits, simply because the real business world will never conform perfectly to any set of rules. Think about the order-to-cash process: if the world *did* run on a set of rules, then every business partner you invoice would pay the amount due exactly within the limits of the agreed-upon payment terms, which would result in days sales outstanding being zero. Unfortunately, few if any organizations in real life are in this situation, which illustrates that rule-based thinking can't be the answer to everything.

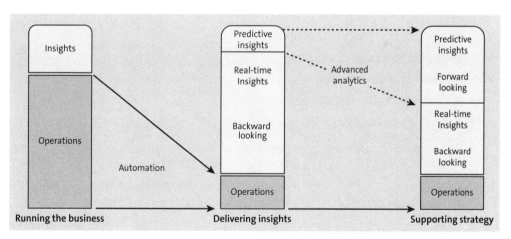

Figure 1 Reducing Operational Finance to Deliver Better and Forward-Looking Insights

Therefore, SAP has been working to introduce an unprecedented level of automation, based on and including the following ingredients:

- Leveraging analytical capabilities to guide finance users to the critical tasks that should be concentrated on, instead of going through the same routine every day. For example, you'd never need to look at your open item list if a KPI showed you that all due open items had been paid. Having access to this type of information from your home screen allows you to immediately focus on areas requiring attention.

- Introducing experience-based learning instead of rules-based learning. This mimics the way we learn as human beings, and is what we refer to as *machine learning*.

- Collaborating with different people, within or across departments. Similar to Alexa or Siri, digital assistants such as SAP CoPilot can help ensure better communication and collaboration.

This subset of capabilities both supports operational processes in general and enables you to transform the modeling and execution of finance processes specifically.

Delivering Forward-Looking Insights and Supporting Strategy Execution

In the past, the automation of operational finance tasks often was intended to reduce headcount (thereby lowering the cost of finance operations), but today this vision has changed. Although the cost of finance should still be kept as low as possible, much more attention is given to the *value* that the finance department brings to the organization. So instead of operational automation being about getting rid of the headcount, it's much more about eliminating non-value-adding jobs to make room for new, innovative, and valuable roles, such as the following:

- Big data analysts or data scientists
- Market observers and analysts
- New business modelers
- Simulation and prediction experts
- Business strategy experts

The automation of finance goes much further than just delivering month-end reporting for both external and internal purposes. Which brings us to the second key area, next to efficient finance operations: ensuring finance has the time and ability to deliver insights to support the business in its decision-making process.

Looking into how many finance organizations handle decision support today, we see a lot of room for improvement, particularly in the following areas:

- **Timeliness of availability of management information**
  Management information often is only available after month-end close; organizations require quicker access to financial management information for it to be useful.

Think about the classical periodic closing process, which delivers both external and internal information only after the periodic close has been finalized. For some organizations, this information is coming far too late for business decisions that need to be made mid-month, for instance. To bring this information to the table at the right moment in time, the notion of continuous accounting or soft close is gaining a lot of interest. The purpose of continuous accounting is not to execute a hard close at any moment during a period, but instead to deliver materially correct information to the business that is complete and detailed enough to drive decision-making on an ongoing basis.

- **Automation of report generation**
  Creating business insights is a highly manual process, but automation enables organizations to focus on actual improvement actions.

  The efficiency of delivering the right information to the business can be vastly improved. Microsoft Excel is probably still the most-used application for reporting purposes, and though it's very flexible, it has several downsides, such as data consistency and the need to manually slice and dice data to get the right answers.

  What if we could automate a lot of the report generation *and* make it more flexible so that any user could access the necessary information directly or even get it pushed to them proactively? Or even go a step further and have the system proactively provide the root cause of a deviation in the financial performance of a particular business line, for instance?

  In many cases, existing data warehouses cover some of these requirements—but they result in time delays, and most require a certain level of aggregation, therefore losing details that are potentially important to really understand the root cause. In fact, the use of data warehouses is the source of additional reconciliation efforts (i.e., different sources of truth). But enabling the delivery of insights directly within the operational ERP system makes it possible to not only base insights on transactional information but also ensure a single source of truth because everyone automatically looks at the same data.

  This doesn't mean that data warehouses or business intelligence architectures are a thing of the past. They surely offer many advantages, including the ability to bring together data from different sources.

- **Replacement of backward-looking reporting processes**
  Management reporting mainly analyzes past performance; moving forward, organizations want to invest in forward-looking insights to support the business.

Past performance can only tell us so much about optimizing future situations. Consequently, many organizations are seeking more forward-looking insights to support the business. Organizations are moving away from classic budgeting exercises and toward driver-based forecasting based on their understanding of the underlying business drivers for financial performance. Moving beyond spreadsheet-based planning models, advanced planning and forecasting applications are a big step forward.

However, yet another step would be to integrate this forward-looking information in the same single source of truth, not eliminating reconciliation issues but ensuring that forecasts can be based on real-time actuals.

On top, predictive modeling can help automate processes and bring forward-looking insights to a higher level. As you'll see in Chapter 8, this doesn't necessarily mean that everyone needs to be a statistics expert.

Automating a lot of the existing manual reporting work, ensuring availability of insights within a period at any moment needed, and extending actuals information by including forward-looking insights are key elements in enabling finance to become the strategic business partner within the organization that it's expected to be. Throughout this book, you'll see how SAP S/4HANA supports these elements, based on a single source of truth.

System-Savvy CFOs

Chief financial officers are the heads of their organizations' finance departments. Historically, their responsibilities have been to manage both the financial accounting (external) and management accounting (internal) finance functions.

However, we see that in recent years the required skillset of CFO candidates is expanding beyond a mastery of financials topics to include a better understanding of finance software systems as well. This is because new technologies offer critical opportunities for finance transformation—but the only way to realize these benefits is to embed the use of technology in the functionally driven finance transformation process.

So to ensure we make a clear link between the finance function and technology in this book, let's start by taking a look at the core finance, which is made up of two processes:

- The record-to-report (R2R) process focuses on the legal accounting function. It involves recording all entries that could come from multiple operational systems and then performing financial accounting, financial close, and financial reporting.

- The plan-to-optimize (P2O) process focuses more on the internal financial planning and analysis function. The emphasis here is to plan and predict, run management accounting, perform margin analysis, and simulate and optimize a company's financials.

These two bundles of financials processes are related, often interdependent, and woven together in the financial sequence in Figure 2.

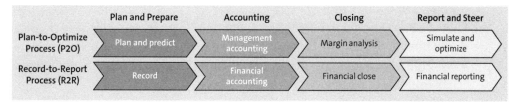

Figure 2 Core Finance Processes

> ## Treasury and Compliance
>
> Note that our diagram doesn't represent *all* aspects of finance. For example, though treasury activities are a crucial component, we'll limit ourselves to cash management only here. Similarly, regarding the broad topic of compliance and risk management, we'll limit ourselves to the evolution in SAP S/4HANA regarding legal reporting and taxes. Addressing treasury or compliance in more detail requires a complete book of its own!

Plan and Predict

The starting point of any organization is to create and operationalize a business plan and then to create a forecast or prediction for the upcoming period to determine the success (or failure!) of that plan.

This planning and forecasting exercise is, in certain cases, a purely financial one. In line with the changing role of finance, aiming at becoming a strategic business partner, more and more forward-looking views are being set up based on key internal (e.g., decisions about product mix or geographical focus) *and* external (e.g., changing market conditions) business drivers. These driver-based forecasts are being developed to be used as steering instruments for organizations that can translate both strategy objectives and tactical and operational goals. To allow for variance analyses later (as part of business steering), it's important to be able to generate these projected financial results based not only on the current but also on the future organizational structure.

Challenges finance typically needs to address at this stage of the finance process include the following:

- How can we make the planning process more agile and less labor-intensive?
- Can we achieve flexible planning, including top-down and bottom-up planning, long- and short-term planning, and the inclusion of predictive capabilities?
- How can we move away from the classic standalone financial budgeting model and toward a driver-based planning approach?
- How can we integrate operational and financial planning while maintaining a central overview of the process?

Record

When a plan is made, the purpose surely is to execute it—largely through nonfinancial activities such as procurement, manufacturing, sales, and so on that might be managed in different applications. Bringing all this information together can be a challenge by itself.

Financial and Management Accounting

In the end, finance is responsible for accurately recording all business activities in accounting and delivering a comprehensive view of all these activities aligned with (inter)national accounting principles and tax regulations. This is usually the purview of *financial accounting*.

Apart from this externally driven requirement, let's not overlook the internal view, known as *management accounting*. This includes correctly valuating products in inventory (based on economic valuation principles), providing transparency into revenues and direct cost, and tracing allocated costs on the level of each division or department or down to the specific customer, product, or service.

Questions the finance team might ask to improve in this respect include the following:

- How can we make these core finance processes both more reliable and less manual to ensure a low-cost finance function?
- Focusing on the internal or management accounting part and supporting business decisions requires information to be available within the period at the right

moment rather than just at month end. How can we move toward such continuous insights?

- How can we embed proactive compliance checks instead of reactive controls?
- Much time is lost because of a lack of agreement among finance, sales, and marketing on revenue/margin definition. Reconciliation issues between internal and external accounting information also can produce delays. So how can this single source of truth across the entire finance process be achieved?

Financial Close

After the accounting information has been accurately recorded, the next step is the financial close. Although financial departments operate continuously, it's critical to identify a specific moment when the books for a given period (a month, a quarter, or a year) are officially closed for legal reporting purposes. Before looking at some of the typical challenges in this area, let's consider the importance of closing from the controlling perspective.

Margin Analysis

A cutoff process is a requirement for margin analysis purposes as well, but it should be set on a more regular basis because getting access to continuous information is a key to ongoing (and instant) decision-making. Another big consideration for financials departments is the high, concentrated effort right after period-end to perform the closing tasks.

As a result, it's critical to reexamine closing processes to make them more efficient and carefully schedule and prioritize closing-related steps; for example, some closing tasks required for legal reasons may be omitted for internal reporting

Then again, whereas regulatory and tax reporting is often related to the level of the individual legal entity, business decisions are often made on the level of a business unit or even on the group level. It therefore becomes increasingly important to execute the entity (individual profit center), divisional (subconsolidation), and even group (consolidation) closing process multiple times within a single period if required.

To make the right decision, often an end-to-end, reconciled view of intercompany financials is required. This holistic view of financial close as one process rather than two (entity close and group close) is a quite recent change, and raises a few questions:

- How can we eliminate manual effort and get rid of decentral closing processes across entities to shorten closing times, lower the risk of errors, reduce the cost of finance, and increase visibility?

- How can we decrease closing effort and spread operational tasks more evenly across a period?
- How can we optimize group-wide business steering (and financial performance) through faster availability of decision-support information on the business unit or group level?

Financial Reporting

When closing has been performed, the last major step within the end-to-end finance process is to provide the right reporting and insights.

From a legal perspective, this means the correct representation and disclosure of financial statements according to (inter)national accounting principles, delivery of insights into tax liability, and alignment to tax regulations. How can we address fast-changing legal and tax regulations across different geographies? That's only one of the challenges to be addressed.

Simulate and Optimize

From an internal steering perspective, financial reporting is all about providing the right groupwide steering information to support the business in its decision-making process. This is not limited to P&L information, but surely includes an end-to-end view of product and customer profitability, including simulation capabilities to consider the impact of potential decisions on the cost structure. Steering the business, in our view, goes further than providing detailed reporting because the final goal is not to deliver the right insights but rather to ensure an optimization of the organization's financial performance. Related challenges to be addressed include the following:

- From an internal steering perspective, everyone can produce a P&L. But what about margin insights by customer or product? How can we identify the all-in cost of a specific business activity or provide full cost transparency in cross-charges, cost of support services, and so on?
- How can we flexibly access information without a lot of manual work? How can we ensure everyone uses the same single source of truth as a basis so that the focus is kept on making the right decisions rather than discussing who has the right figures?

As you can see, many challenges must be addressed to ensure finance lives up to the expectations from the business. To make their finance transformations a success, we are convinced that today's CFOs need to understand how technology can support this transformation. Simply stated, two broad areas of understanding can be identified:

- An understanding of technology—and more specifically, the impact technology can have on the automation of finance processes. Understanding how new technologies can drastically change the way processes are automated also impacts CFOs' ability to design finance processes within their organizations.

- An understanding of data—not only how data can be retrieved and accessed, but also how an intelligent use of data can drive an organization's performance.

In this book, we'll address how SAP S/4HANA can improve the finance department's day-to-day life by addressing the different parts of and challenges associated with the finance process just described.

Mobile Finance

One additional important aspect to address when discussing the changing role of finance is related to the way we work.

When we entered the workplace over twenty years ago, hardly anyone had mobile phones or even laptops. Today's workplace is a stark contrast: many people, including finance professionals, carry mobile devices and have new expectations about mobility. Now that most consumers have access to all kinds of information in our private lives (e.g., reviewing recent expenses and paying bills instantly from our personal mobile devices), similar expectations have arisen about how to perform our day-to-day jobs (e.g., reviewing product margin information and approving company payments while not in the office).

One consequence is the demand for a flexible user interface that's accessible from any place at any moment on any device. Although SAP historically hasn't been known for its user interfaces, this is one area in which SAP S/4HANA makes significant strides—both with the introduction of SAP Fiori with SAP S/4HANA and through more advanced ways of interacting with the SAP S/4HANA environment. For example, natural language processing (NLP) capabilities make it possible to interact with the system using human language instead of transaction codes, not only by typing but also by using your voice or handwriting.

Let's look at an example. If you still think that managing accounts receivable is all about entering transaction codes, filling out complex selection screens, and wading through endless result lists, consider the Supervise Collections Worklist app (SAP Fiori ID F2375) shown in Figure 3. This combines familiar elements (such as the list of

customers from whom receivables are to be collected and the days in arrears key figure) with innovative ways of selecting data for display. Clicking the bars and dough-
nuts in the upper part of the screen changes the data shown in the worklist graphics
and result lists. Every new selection by the user triggers a new selection from the
database, making for a highly interactive experience that is always as up to date as
the data captured in the system.

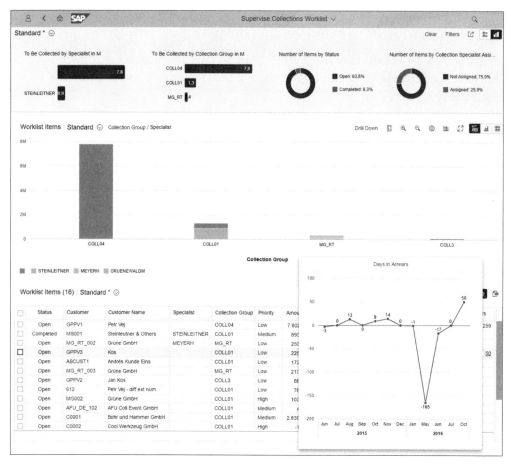

Figure 3 The Supervise Collections Worklist App

So far in this introduction, we've discussed how finance has changed and examined its
evolving requirements. Before we take a deep dive over the next 15 chapters into what

we consider the 15 key functional and technical changes in SAP S/4HANA compared to SAP ERP, we should consider how SAP itself has evolved and how its customers' interactions with the key systems and technologies have changed, too.

Finance with SAP

The SAP story begins with its first customer: a nylon factory that needed an IT system to handle its financial accounting, materials management, purchasing, and invoice verification tasks.

In 1972, such systems were typically mainframe-based and custom-made, but the founders of SAP had different ideas. With a handful of employees, the five founders built a system for one company that would be used by many others. With this, the notion of *standard software* was born. By 1974, forty other companies were running SAP. By 1976, the nylon factory was handling 40,000 transactions per month; the notion of *real-time business*—in the sense that the values associated with the goods movements were being recorded immediately in financial accounting rather than in nightly batch loads—had arrived.

Fast-forward to 2019, when SAP S/4HANA claims to offer real-time business (again). Unlike in the 1970s, or even the 1990s, the corridors are now free of paper, and everybody carries a smartphone and a tablet. Reinventing finance isn't simply a matter of converting paper lists to make them searchable on a smartphone, but rather of providing information to steer the business in an easy-to-consume way, as you saw in Figure 3. Of course, users from the 1970s would still recognize the fundamental business issues being handled, but instead of a long paper list of open receivables, they're now working with an application that gives an immediate impression of how the task is progressing and which customers have particularly long-standing open items.

In this section, we'll tell the unofficial SAP story as it relates to finance, explaining what changed with SAP R/3 and SAP ERP, considering where the goal of real-time finance was made ever more difficult because of heterogeneous system landscapes and accounting structures, and introducing the architectural change that enabled the development of SAP S/4HANA. We'll also talk about the fundamental changes in the approach to an SAP implementation, from one company in southern Germany operating in one factory using one currency, to the multinationals with global supply chains, international rollouts, and distributed system landscapes.

SAP R/2, SAP R/3, and SAP ERP

As the 1970s continued, SAP would add sales and distribution functionality, gain its first international customers, and be available in translation in French, English, and Dutch. With the 1980s came a redesign of the core to deliver SAP R/2. Further components were added, including Controlling, Production Planning, Human Resources, and the first industry solution to support billing in the utilities industry.

Along came SAP R/3 in 1992, which held at its heart the notion of real-time integration among sales and distribution, production planning, purchasing, materials management, finance, and controlling.

Let's take a trip down memory lane. Presentations in this era would begin by explaining how these components were designed to operate in sync, before going into the specifics of each application. Figure 4 is a graphic from the late 1990s that displays the core functions needed to run a factory (sales and distribution, materials management, production planning, quality management, plant maintenance, and human resources) on the left and the finance functions (financial accounting, controlling, fixed asset management, and project system) on the right.

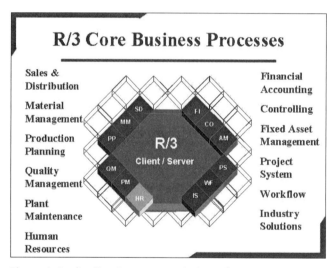

Figure 4 Application Components in SAP R/3

Figure 5 is a slide from the same era showing Treasury (TR), Financial Accounting (FI), and Controlling (CO) as the three pillars of operational accounting, with Enterprise Controlling (EC) across the top and Investment Management (FI-IM) along the bottom.

For an organization operating on a single instance of SAP R/3, Enterprise Controlling supported corporate reporting and planning and consolidation, and Investment Management allowed the management of capital expense projects.

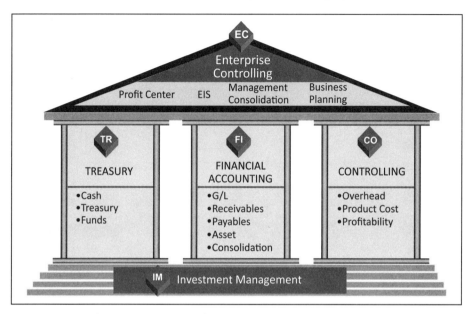

Figure 5 Pillars of Accounting in SAP R/3

Figure 6 provides a sense of the integration among the components that is the heart of the design of SAP R/2 and SAP R/3. We see that the operational processes for procurement, production, transportation, sales, and billing update the appropriate accounts in Financial Accounting (FI), are transformed into cost elements and flow through Cost Center Accounting and Product Cost Controlling (CO-PC) to Profitability Analysis (CO-PA), and Profit Center Accounting records the same values by profit center to provide a basis for divisional reporting.

But though the value flows are taking place in real time, the slide shows clearly that finance at the time comprised three distinct boxes: Financial Accounting, Controlling, and Profit Center Accounting. Each of the three boxes has its own structure (accounts and company codes in Financial Accounting, cost elements and cost objects in Controlling, and profit centers and accounts/cost elements in Profit Center Accounting) and approach to segmenting financial transactions for analysis. The result was that there were three different ways of looking at the same numbers.

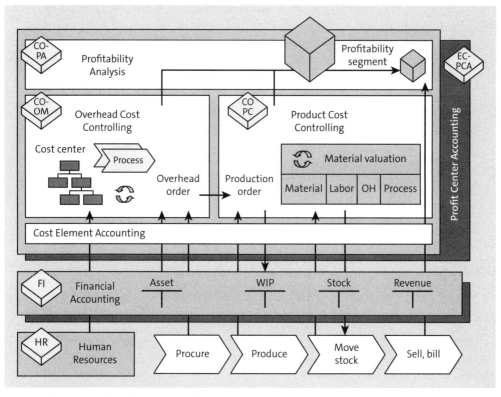

Figure 6 Value Flows in SAP R/3

What changed in SAP R/3, with a few exceptions, was not the business approach, but the shift away from expensive mainframe computers to the then-new *client/server architecture*. The client/server architecture was comprised of three layers:

- **The database layer**
  Customers could choose their preferred database (and new databases were being certified constantly).

- **The application layer**
  This layer contained the code for the various software applications for materials management, production planning, financial accounting, and so on.

- **The presentation layer**
  This layer provided a graphical user interface. (Remember that before the arrival of the internet and consumer websites, the GUI delivered with SAP R/3 was considered

more attractive and easier to use than many of the mainframe interfaces in use at the time!)

As the decade passed and globalization advanced, the SAP system became available in more languages and with more local versions to handle the very different accounting standards in different countries. With the core functionality represented in Figure 4, you can also see the introduction of more and more industry-specific options alongside local versions of the software.

By the end of the 1990s, there was also a shift in the understanding of finance in SAP. In the early part of the decade, most SAP implementations started with one factory (according to one set of accounting principles in one currency) and moved onto the next, with no real attempt to build consistent data models or any understanding of how a common structure could support global reporting. Common symptoms of this very local focus during the implementation were multiple controlling areas, operating concerns, and charts of accounts, a topic that we will return to in Chapter 2.

As the decade continued, the first *template implementations* were made that put certain key structures into place, such as a central chart of accounts or profit center structure, to make it easier to benchmark businesses against one another. These implementations might run on separate system instances, but the data had a common structure. This more global approach also drove developments including transfer pricing and group valuation, topics that we will return to in Chapter 2 when we look at what's needed to achieve a global accounting approach.

When SAP R/3 was replatformed and renamed SAP ERP in 2004, the heart of the product remained largely unchanged. From a functional point of view, the innovations were typically industry-driven. Although industries such as chemicals and consumer products were able to work with functions carried over from SAP R/3, dedicated *industry solutions* were built on top for retail, public sector businesses, banking and financial services, and many others in SAP ERP. In total, SAP ERP became available for 25 industries.

In many cases, these industry solutions are associated with switches that are selected when the system is set up. These switches control whether certain menus and customizing sections are displayed or not. Of course, these switches can be used in combination; an automobile manufacturer might both use the automotive solution and use the banking solution to allow its customers to finance their car purchases. We'll look at the finance challenges in some of these industries along with how the industry segmentation is changing in Chapter 3.

In addition, a substantial shift was afoot in the underlying SAP NetWeaver stack. This allowed the ERP system to communicate via *web services* with other applications such as SAP Customer Relationship Management (SAP CRM) and SAP Supplier Relationship Management (SAP SRM) using standard protocols. It also allowed significant changes to the user interface: new web applications (e.g., for manager or employee self-services) could be built and delivered in the SAP NetWeaver Enterprise Portal.

Organizations always wanted real-time business, but multinationals struggled to store the data they needed to run their business in a single SAP ERP instance. Sometime in the late 1990s, many companies started to work with dedicated management information systems, data warehouses, and data marts. These systems were designed to make the vast amounts of data being captured in the companies' various operations easy to query and report on. SAP's eponymous business warehouse, SAP Business Warehouse, offered online analytical processing (OLAP), as did many other products on the market. The result was that each night, huge amounts of data would be loaded from SAP ERP, SAP CRM, SAP SRM, and other systems into the data warehouse to support multidimensional reporting.

At its simplest, this meant putting the data associated with an invoice or an order into a multidimensional data model to allow multidimensional reporting on the customers served and the products sold in the relevant regions. In many cases, it also involved significant data cleansing to solve underlying master data issues and transforming the data records to assign them to a group chart of accounts, a group profit center structure, and so on.

For example, Figure 7 shows the basic architecture for a data warehouse taking feeds from multiple SAP ERP systems, each running CO-PA. From a business point of view, it's important to understand that each SAP ERP system was potentially using a different operating concern, with different reporting dimensions (characteristics) and measures (key figures). The methods of deriving the characteristics were often different in each system, as were the calculations affecting the key figures. This made it extremely difficult to compare apples to apples—or, in finance terms, to compare the same dimensions or measures across multiple systems.

At the time, multinational organizations needed a data warehouse to handle the volumes of data generated in their operations, but they found themselves paying a high price for the flexibility of their management information systems in terms of the timeliness of their data. Most of the information available for reporting was at least a day old; consolidation processes loaded the financial statements from the local subsidiaries only once a month.

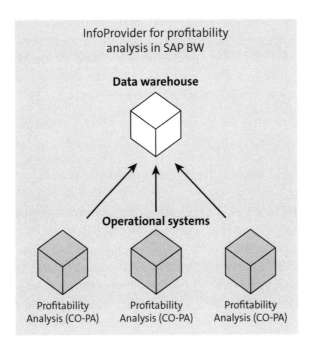

Figure 7 Using SAP BW to Merge Data from Several SAP ERP Installations

This wasn't just a problem of data latency, however. Any transformation requires reconciliation and manual confirmation that the invoices that left the SAP ERP system arrived in SAP BW correctly. There is more to corporate reporting than aggregating the financial statements submitted by each of the subsidiaries. Corporate finance users will inherently view many transactions differently from local accountants:

- From the point of view of the local system, many of the invoices loaded are to external customers and vendors. However, from a corporate point of view many of these customers and vendors are simply *affiliated companies* in the same group. The value flows link up, and values in these intercompany invoices need to be eliminated from a consolidation point of view.

- From a local point of view, the cost of the goods sold can be derived from the bill of material and the routing for the product manufactured. However, from a corporate point of view, the raw materials in one plant are the products of the preceding plant. When both plants are in the SAP ERP system, product costing can be configured to pull cost estimates across plants. From a corporate point of view, there is often a break in the value chain that needs to be fixed in the reporting system to understand the product cost flow.

- Allocations to assign heating costs to the shop floor can work perfectly in the local system. However, there are many other allocations that assign research and development costs or marketing costs that are incurred centrally to legal entities all over the world. We start to find the data warehouse being used not just to aggregate data for reporting but also to perform allocations across systems.

With this quest for a corporate view, we're clearly now a long way from a single factory in southern Germany.

SAP S/4HANA

In 2011, Hasso Plattner, one of the founders of SAP, published his book, *In-Memory Data Management*. In it he described the architecture of SAP's new database, SAP HANA, and imagined a management meeting of the future in which, instead of participants arriving with a set of briefing books that tried to anticipate every possible question and that were by their nature outdated by the time of the meeting, managers would have instant access to *real-time business information* and could spend the meeting simulating the effect of various assumptions on their bottom lines before agreeing on the actions to follow.

SAP HANA evolved from Hasso Plattner's work with his students at the Hasso Plattner Institute (*http://hpi.de/en.html*) in Potsdam, Germany. From a database point of view, the radical change is that all data is kept in main memory rather than on a hard disk, which significantly accelerates data processing. From a finance point of view, the big change is the shift from row stores to column stores. This may not sound like something that anybody in finance should get excited about, but think of what happens to select data for profitability analysis. In a *row store*, the system must read every line of data to determine whether the record refers to the region or product group to be included in the selection. In a *column store*, there are as many lines in the column as there are regions or product groups. That quite simply means faster data access and more timely reporting.

Once the SAP HANA database was available, SAP set out to redevelop many of the functions delivered with SAP S/4HANA, beginning in finance but quickly moving into other areas, such as inventory management. SAP S/4HANA, however, is not simply a replatformed SAP ERP; it's an ERP system with several key elements:

- The database has been architected to create the ultimate pivot table that brings together all the reporting dimensions needed to steer an organization. We'll look at the implications of this Universal Journal in Chapter 1.

- The user interface was rebuilt to support mobile devices and provide instant access to relevant steering information. We'll look at this new approach to reporting in Chapter 5 and Chapter 6.

- The solution was designed to be available on premise and in the cloud. This book mainly describes the finance functions from an on-premise perspective, but where relevant we'll highlight key design decisions behind SAP S/4HANA Cloud so that you can see the direction in which SAP is moving.

Let's look closer at two key considerations: functionality and implementation.

Simplifications

With the new product comes a long list of areas where the product has been rewritten. These are called *simplifications*. You can familiarize yourself with the implications of these changes by reviewing SAP Notes; look for those that begin with "S4TWL" for the application components that you're interested in. The complete simplification list for SAP S/4HANA 1809 includes the following SAP Notes and many more:

- S4TWL: Data Model Changes in FIN (SAP Note 2270333)
- S4TWL: General Ledger (SAP Note 2270339)
- S4TWL: Technical Changes in Controlling (SAP Note 2270404)
- S4TWL: Profitability Analysis (SAP Note 2349278)
- S4TWL: Material Ledger Obligatory for Material Valuation (SAP Note 2267834)
- S4TWL: Material Valuation Data Model Simplification (SAP Note 2337383)
- S4TWL: Asset Accounting—Changes to Data Structure (SAP Note 2270387)
- S4TWL: Data Setup Guide for SAP Cash Management (SAP Note 2233405)

To make sense of the impact of the changes on your organization, be sure to focus not just on the core but also on any industry solutions you may be using and any localizations that you have in place. The full list is over a thousand pages long, but there's a common pattern in the contents of many of the SAP Notes:

- *Totals tables* have been removed, so the system is no longer aggregating data into period blocks in financial accounting, controlling, accounts payable, accounts receivable, and inventory valuation. Instead, whenever such data is needed to run a report or perform an allocation, it's aggregated on the fly. This approach speeds up the process of capturing transactions because it's no longer necessary to lock the totals table to include the latest update.

- *Index tables* have been removed, so the system is no longer using a separate index table to select data records in financial accounting, accounts payable, accounts receivable, and inventory valuation.

- *Summarization tables* have been removed, so you'll find summarization hierarchies aggregating data on the fly rather than reading it from tables that have been filled using a data collection run. This removes steps from the period close.

Of course, the scale of such simplification can sound frightening. It's all very well for SAP to start rewriting its code—but what happens to all the partner solutions and modifications that customers have been running for years?

The trick here is the use of the *compatibility view*. Whenever a table has been removed, it has almost always been replaced by a view; so long as the program is only trying to read data, you won't notice the change. When programs are writing data, SAP has delivered tools to help you to identify the points in the code at which the program will no longer run.

Implementation and Deployment

Let's consider implementation for moment.

In general, there are two types of SAP S/4HANA implementations: greenfield projects that start from scratch, and brownfield projects that function more like upgrades of existing SAP ERP systems.

If you're running a greenfield project, then simplification details won't concern you because you'll be using a brand-new system and will start with business partners instead of separate customer/vendors, long material numbers, merged accounts and cost elements, and the Universal Journal as the heart of your steering model.

If you're running a brownfield project, then SAP offers conversion tools to help you migrate your data from the old structures to the new. This can either be a one-stop shift from SAP ERP directly to SAP S/4HANA or a conversion first to the SAP HANA database and then to SAP S/4HANA.

Before you embark on your journey, it makes sense to have your IT department run the *readiness checks* described in SAP Note 2290622 and to discuss the results with your implementation partner. The readiness checks cover the following topics:

- Identification of relevant simplification items based on your existing system setup

- Custom code impact

- SAP S/4HANA sizing
- Suggested SAP Fiori apps to replace existing transactions
- Business process analytics
- Data volume management
- Business warehouse extraction

To make sense of the different SAP S/4HANA versions, you'll need to understand the new product naming conventions. The SAP S/4HANA version nomenclature now includes the month and year of the release: for example, SAP S/4HANA 1511 was released in November 2015, SAP S/4HANA 1610 in October 2016, and so on. An on-premise edition is delivered once a year, so at the time of publication (spring 2019), the current on-premise release is SAP S/4HANA 1809.

A cloud edition of SAP S/4HANA is released once per quarter. The cloud editions in 2018 are SAP S/4HANA Cloud 1802, 1805, 1808, and 1811. A cloud edition provides not just coding, but also preconfigured content for the new functions and best-practice documentation that walks you through all aspects of its use. Cloud releases offer a restricted feature scope compared with the on-premise editions, so as you read product roadmaps, be aware that some of the topics are genuine new features that didn't previously exist in on-premise SAP S/4HANA, and some are features that have already been enabled for use in the cloud, such as actual costing in SAP S/4HANA Cloud 1811. What we're describing here is the SAP S/4HANA Cloud multitenant edition (formerly known as the "public" cloud version). In the course of the book, we'll explain what is available in SAP S/4HANA Cloud to describe the restricted scope delivered with the multitenant edition, such as the use of a single controlling area.

SAP also offers the SAP S/4HANA Cloud single-tenant edition (formerly known as the "private" cloud version). This edition receives updates twice a year and gives you more flexibility in terms of configuration and features while moving you into a cloud-based mindset. It allows you to configure functions and industry approaches not currently delivered as best practices in the multitenant edition. We won't specifically refer to it during the book, since from a functional perspective it can be configured like the on-premise version of SAP S/4HANA.

In this book, we've chosen not to write separate chapters for cloud and on-premise features. Instead, we'll identify features that are offered only in SAP S/4HANA Cloud under the assumption that the cloud-first approach means that these features will reach the on-premise edition at some time in the future. We'll also describe restrictions underlying the use of SAP S/4HANA Cloud to help you to understand the differences.

The implementation approach is not black and white, and we expect that many organizations will run a mixture of on-premise SAP S/4HANA and SAP S/4HANA Cloud, depending on the needs of the headquarters and the local subsidiaries, as shown in Figure 8. This is known as the *two-tier approach*, the idea being that the headquarters requires a tier-one system, but some subsidiaries can live with the restrictions of a tier-two system that's available at a lower cost.

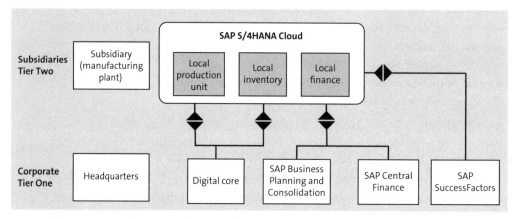

Figure 8 Two-Tier Approach to SAP S/4HANA Implementation

Summary

In this introduction, we discussed the modern business climate and the key players in finance, and we explained at a very high level how finance departments and their supporting systems have evolved. We've looked at the very different skillsets and expectations that finance professionals bring to the table today, and at how the systems have evolved from working for a single nylon factory in southern Germany to meeting the needs of multinationals with multiple system landscapes. We've given you a hint of the changes inherent in SAP S/4HANA, but this was just the introduction.

Now let's start our detailed coverage of the key innovations in SAP S/4HANA with the most fundamental change for finance: the introduction of the Universal Journal as the new business steering model.

Chapter 1

The Universal Journal: Designing a Steering Model for the Business

For organizations, steering models are sets of financial and nonfinancial indicators that support them in determining their future directions. This chapter dives into what is needed to steer an organization from the point of view of different stakeholders and shows how SAP S/4HANA— and more specifically the Universal Journal—supports this.

What is the profit margin generated by a specific product line? What is the total cost to serve a specific customer? Which is the region in the world contributing most to the overall profit of the organization?

Many organizations have been struggling to come up with the correct answers to these and many other questions that are crucial to understanding where the value of the organization is created—or destroyed. The answers deliver key information to make the right decisions for the future.

But finding the answers can be a challenge. Which indicators should be included? Which dimensions should be reported on? What level of detail is required? And, in the end (although this is surely not the initial concern), what should the visualization of the report be?

To answer these questions correctly, start by ensuring there is a common understanding of and alignment to the organization's strategic goals and how they create value. Based on this, the key value drivers, sometimes known as *leading indicators*, can then be identified. Without this step, you can't define key reporting requirements for your various functional leaders in sales, procurement, and so on.

And once these key reporting requirements are defined on paper, the next hurdle is to implement an information model with the relevant combinations of measures and dimensions in a system environment. Or in other words: the setup of the company's steering model is what ensures that all functional departments "speak the same language" and base their insights and decisions on a single, shared source of truth. This model must have a unique definition of each business partner, cost center, or product but a common definition of measures like revenue, margin, or sales volume.

This chapter explains how SAP S/4HANA's Universal Journal provides a mechanism for a modern steering model. We'll start the chapter by looking at where most organizations are coming from, discussing current accounting models and their limitations in Section 1.1. We'll then introduce the Universal Journal as SAP's new steering model and explain how it can help you to steer your business more effectively in Section 1.2. Next, we'll look at the various reporting dimensions to help you understand how to transition from SAP ERP to the new SAP S/4HANA world in Section 1.3. We'll end the chapter by explaining the different ways of extending the steering model (Section 1.4) and changing it as your own organization evolves to keep pace with a dynamic business climate (Section 1.5).

1.1   Designing a Steering Model for Your Business

Let's start by focusing on the financial single source of truth. What does it look like? How can you use it to steer your business? Typically, you incorporate dimensions like organizational characteristics, your products and services, and your customer segments. These dimensions usually come with a certain hierarchy so that detailed analyses roll up into an aggregated picture.

But that's not always enough. Perhaps you'd like to incorporate certain views along different currency and valuation approaches or various data categories besides actuals (e.g., plan, prediction, simulation, and consolidated views). Maybe you need the steering model to work on different levels, at least on the operational and group levels. But is all information centrally stored like this in what could be seen as the equivalent of an *enterprise pivot table*? This giant pivot table is what allows you to slice and dice the business information that determines whether your organization will be successful or not; it is the key to steering your business and providing the appropriate reports to all relevant stakeholders.

1.1.1   From Legacy Accounting Models to Multidimensional Steering

When many organizations embarked on their first SAP implementation, their accounting model was worlds away from this enterprise pivot table. Some SAP customers had literally *two* dimensions in their accounting model (the account and the cost center), which carried all the accounting information they needed for reporting. Over time, they added even more accounts and cost centers, and they embedded even more logic into these structures, until the two dimensions and the associated hierarchies had become completely unwieldy. In many cases, these SAP customers structured their systems this way simply because that's how their pre–SAP ERP legacy systems were organized. With the move to SAP S/4HANA, the time has come to ask whether the legacy approach can still deliver the information required for the key stakeholders to steer the organization.

Other organizations worked with the delivered SAP account assignments (cost center, order, work breakdown structure [WBS] element, etc.) and the derived reporting dimensions (profit center, functional area, trading partner, etc.), but still struggled to get the reports they needed out of their SAP ERP system. The challenge for these organizations often was found in the fact that the reports were spread across many applications (e.g., for financial accounting, profit center accounting, special ledger, cost center accounting, product cost controlling, and profitability analysis), each with its own way of interpreting and presenting the data. Individual cost center managers or plant managers might have been happy with the data they were presented with, but corporate accountants looking at the business across several applications tended to struggle to steer the organization using the information at their disposal. Recall from the introduction that the applications were integrated in such a way that sharing data was easy, but it was difficult to explain the financial position of the company using the delivered reports for each ledger and application. Many organizations were still taking weeks to close their books and spending time on non-value-adding reconciliation tasks rather than making recommendations that would help drive the business.

Let's take a closer look at how the data model in SAP ERP could impede financial reporting and consider SAP customers' requirements to move toward multidimensional financial reporting.

1.1.2   The Structure of the Data Model in SAP ERP

If we look at how data is stored within a classic SAP R/3 or SAP ERP environment, we see that different subsets of information are stored in separate tables. General ledger, fixed assets, inventory, overhead cost controlling, product cost controlling, and profitability information data was all stored in separate tables, each with different key fields, as shown in Figure 1.1. Moreover, profit center accounting and special ledgers also were used to store aggregated views of financial information. Here we clearly can see that each application has its own fields and ways of structuring financial information for its purpose. Notice that neither the company code nor the account is included in every table. The management accounting and profitability tables do not include the company code; they both transform the accounts and assign them to cost elements and value fields.

Sometimes this information is simply an aggregation of the underlying business data, but you also could create separate profit center documents and special ledger documents to make management adjustments or reclassify postings. Then it becomes very difficult to compare results because you should understand which entries were derived from the business transactions and which were created as higher-level adjustments.

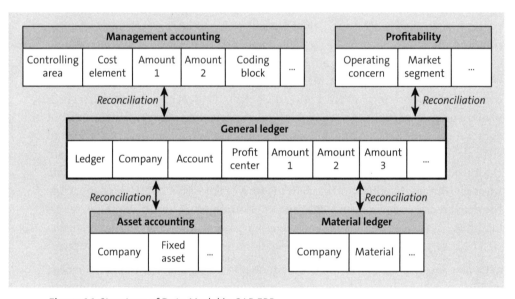

Figure 1.1 Structure of Data Model in SAP ERP

Storing financial-related information in such a way results in several challenges, including the following:

- There is no single source of truth. If you only look at assets or inventory, you may not worry unduly, but you will encounter challenges as you cross these applications. The "truth" needs to be constructed by reconciling and combining the content of these different tables. This puts an unnecessary burden on corporate finance teams and is not an activity that adds value for the business.

- In certain cases, data even needs to be moved from one table to another to ensure it can be reported on appropriately. Consider, for example, allocations and settlements in the area of profitability analysis. This transformation is needed to go from cost by nature to cost by function, but it brings its own challenges of reconciliation, since not all costs become cost of goods sold (COGS) by the end of the period.

- Not all financial information is stored on the most granular level. Different levels of detail are stored in their respective tables. For each application shown in Figure 1.1, there is both a line item and a totals table—again, requiring reconciliation to ensure that the totals really are the sums of the line items.

- Components also are structured differently. For example, fields and entities differ between the different components: Financial Accounting (FI) has its accounts, Controlling (CO) has its cost elements, and the account is not contained in either the asset or the inventory tables. As a result, the applications cannot always be reconciled easily.

- Different capabilities are available in isolated components: multiple currencies in FI tables are not available on the CO side, multi-GAAP valuations are not treated in a harmonized way (think of the depreciation areas in asset accounting), and so on.

Although this way of storing data in the SAP ERP environment was implemented partly due to the computing power constraints of the 1990s and 2000s, it was never an ideal starting point from which to create a single source of *financial* truth.

This complexity becomes even clearer when looking at the multitude of SAP BW extractors that were needed to combine all financial information from each of the applications in a single data model and enrich the data with further attributes for reporting.

1.1.3 Toward a Multidimensional Steering Model

The complexity that results from the classic storage of financial information in SAP ERP results in a set of additional restrictions that are not in line with the multidimensional steering model that today's business users require.

In an ideal financial and management accounting system based on a centralized financial steering model, these restrictions must be overcome and new capabilities must be delivered to answer the following business requirements:

- Think of the combination of actuals and forward-looking information for decision-making. Actuals are interesting to understand the past, but don't necessarily tell us a lot about the future. Therefore, getting access to forecasting information or having the option to simulate different scenarios (or even use predictive capabilities to simulate the future) is becoming more important. We'll return to these topics when we look at predictive accounting in Chapter 8 and the new planning model in Chapter 9.

- Sometimes the devil is in the details. Having access to the most granular data possible (i.e., the individual transactions) is the key to enabling fully multidimensional analyses. This is especially relevant for management reporting, in which managers can be associated with each order, project, cost center, and so on (rather than legal financial reporting, which typically is arranged by legal entity). In Chapter 2, we'll look at the challenges of combining local legal requirements and corporate reporting requirements in the same data model and how organizational units such as multiple controlling areas and operating concerns can blur the picture.

- Related to the level of granularity, depending on the organization's industry, an extension to the steering model design may be required that keeps the single source of truth intact. Of course, this doesn't mean that every controller can start adding his own fields to the steering model, but instead that the organization can decide that it needs an extra view. We'll explain how to do so later in this chapter.

- For many organizations, having information available only after month-end close is just not good enough. Decisions need to be made at any moment in time, which means that relevant insights should be delivered also throughout the month. We'll come back to this topic in detail when we look at the move toward a real-time financial close in Chapter 7.

- When asking yourself at what organizational level decisions are made, consider that the answer will depend mostly on the specific decision that needs to be made. Certain strategic decisions typically are made at the group level, whereas others are made on the level of an individual legal entity. But many decisions are made at the level of a specific business unit or division. This business requirement is one we can translate into the need to produce both unconsolidated and consolidated views on financial results that, linking to the previous point, also should be made available in real time. We'll look at these challenges in detail in Chapter 2 and when we look at group reporting in Chapter 12.

- Alongside the challenge of the entity structure and the various business units that typically cross multiple entities, many organizations struggle with the currency challenges associated with trying to manage finances in the local legal currency and yet have a common currency for the business units and the group as a whole. Transactional, local legal, and group currencies are needed at a minimum. But what if you need more? Imagine a US-based organization, the group currency of which would be USD. But for its European activities, the regional head of the group would like to see the results of the European region in euros alongside the dollar values. This is a simple example of how multicurrency reporting is increasingly relevant and should be provided flexibly, rather than being added as an enrichment when postings are moved to a data warehouse.

- In classic SAP ERP, manual reconciliation was a must. When we combine this with the ever-increasing amounts of data being put at our disposal (thanks to initiatives such as the internet of things), it's clear that data redundancy should be avoided at all times. A future-proof financial steering model therefore should be one without data redundancy and, as a result, can be reconciled by design with a full audit trail.

Now that we've explained the challenges faced by organizations reporting in SAP ERP, let's introduce the Universal Journal, a key element to facilitate financial reporting in SAP S/4HANA. We'll look at how the various fields have become dimensions in the Universal Journal and start to explain how to derive the appropriate measures and reports from the posting lines captured.

1.2   The Universal Journal

In SAP S/4HANA, the Universal Journal provides the basis for what is essentially an enterprise-wide pivot table. But before we discuss the individual reporting dimensions, let's take a high-level look at why it's needed and how it relates to the structures you know from SAP ERP.

1.2.1   Reporting Dimensions

When conceiving its next-generation enterprise application, it was clear that SAP needed to change the classic data model structure as it exists in SAP ERP. The new central financial steering model is the architectural cornerstone of SAP S/4HANA, used to ensure that this ERP system delivers a financial single source of truth for an organization. This steering model or single source of truth is what we call the *Universal Journal*.

How does the Universal Journal manage to be the single source of truth for an organization? It captures line-item details in a first layer, which we refer to as table ACDOCA. The Universal Journal is structured along the typical business dimensions, like company code, profit center and other organizational dimensions, customer, product, and so on. This is the place to retrieve all the details of a transaction with the highest granularity of data available. Table 1.1 lists some of the reporting dimensions across different categories included in the Universal Journal.

Organization	Product and services	Customer
■ Unit	■ Product	■ Customer industry
■ Region	■ Portfolio category	■ Customer segment
■ Market unit	■ Service model	■ Distribution channel
■ Company	■ And others	■ And others
■ And others		

Table 1.1 Reporting Dimensions in the Universal Journal

The Universal Journal is the common line-item persistence option within SAP S/4HANA for all finance data. It combines transactional line items from different functional subdomains:

- General ledger
- Profit center accounting
- Fixed asset accounting
- Material ledger
- Controlling
- Profitability analysis

This means that the classic split between the legal accounting and management accounting worlds no longer applies, and all financial information is stored centrally in a single table.

This does *not* mean that all different "fields" or dimensions are always filled in the Universal Journal. Dimensions such as the general ledger account, the company code, the ledger, the document number, the record type, the period, and the fiscal year will be filled in for every posting, but—as illustrated in Figure 1.2—different fields are filled in depending on the type of financial journal entry. In the case of an asset-relevant posting, the asset number will be filled in, but there will be no customer unless the journal entry represents the sale of an asset. In the case of a payroll posting, there will be neither asset nor customer, but only a cost center.

Technically, this is known as a *sparsely filled matrix*. Some columns are always filled in, but many, including the asset, customer, and material fields, will be filled in only for certain transaction types. In classic databases, this made data selection difficult, but in a columnar database like SAP HANA, the system selects data by column rather than by row. So when a user searches for a customer, for example, any lines that do not contain a customer are simply ignored.

We can use an example of asset acquisition to imagine how the posting string shown in Figure 1.2 is filled. The asset acquisition will obviously result in the update of the asset field and of the associated general ledger account. These updates fill in what used to be the asset subledger and the general ledger. The asset also is assigned to a cost center; this will be updated, too, filling in what used to be the controlling table but is now simply an additional reporting dimension in the Universal Journal. The cost center is also assigned to a profit center and a functional area. Again, this used to result in an update to a separate profit center ledger and COGS ledger, but both are now simply further reporting dimensions in the Universal Journal. The result is a single document for the asset acquisition that combines data previously spread across multiple applications.

The posting logic hasn't changed, so you won't need to adjust your business processes, change field status groups, or modify the way you derive your profit centers when you move to SAP S/4HANA. However, you do need to understand that data relating to a single business transaction is no longer chopped up and stored in different application tables but instead stored as a single, richer journal entry.

1.2.2   Measures and Reports

Figure 1.2 focuses on the multidimensionality of the journal entry, but it's also important to understand what the different boxes mean. They represent the various measures and reports that can be built using the data collected in the Universal Journal to satisfy the needs of the different stakeholders. You can see that the financial statements are an aggregation of all the posting lines for one or more company codes:

- To see an asset history sheet, you would select only the asset-related lines and show the company code with the relevant asset dimensions. An asset accountant sees only those posting lines relating to assets.

- To see inventory balances, you would select only the material-related lines and show the company code with the related inventory dimensions. An inventory accountant sees only those posting lines relating to inventory.

- To analyze profitability, you would select the lines relating to the revenue and COGS, along with the relevant market segments (products, customers, regions, etc.). A sales accountant sees only those lines that determine the contribution margin.

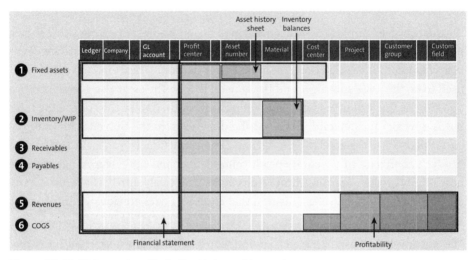

Figure 1.2 Multidimensionality in the Universal Journal

We'll explain how to calculate the relevant measures in Chapter 5 and Chapter 6. In this context, we also have to think about how the accounting data is segregated.

The *ledger* is a key element in the Universal Journal; it's used to separate documents that support different accounting principles. This allows you to represent each measure (revenue, operating expense, capital expense, etc.) in accordance with different accounting principles. This allows corporate accountants to see all values according to a common accounting principle, such as IFRS, and local accountants to see the values for their entities according to Russian GAAP, Brazilian GAAP, and so on. We'll look at these differences in more detail when we look at local reporting requirements in Chapter 2 and how to handle different valuations for asset reporting in Chapter 10 and inventory reporting in Chapter 11.

Currency is also a key element; any posting line may include several currencies. Any document in the Universal Journal will be available in a local currency (currency type 10) and a global currency (currency type 30). Other currency types can be added per ledger as required. We'll look at these settings in more detail in Chapter 2, but for now note that different stakeholders focus on different currencies—so a plant controller or a local accountant uses reports that mainly show the values in the local currency, whereas a corporate accountant looks at the same business transactions in the global currency. What's important is that the currency conversion from transaction currency to local and group currency takes place in real time, rather than after the fact when the documents are loaded into a data warehouse.

1.2.3 Measures for Actuals and Other Values

If you read the technical SAP Notes and blogs about SAP S/4HANA, you will learn that the Universal Journal combines information from the general ledger (table GLT0 or FAGLFLEX), any special ledgers, controlling (table COEP), asset accounting (table ANEP), and the material ledger (table MLIT). In other words, all the tables related to actual data are being moved into a single journal entry.

But that's not the full story: table ACDOCP is designed to extend the Universal Journal to store *plan* data. It is structurally designed in the same way as table ACDOCA, but with the purpose of incorporating all plan data so that you can run actual-plan comparisons. What's important is that if you add fields to the Universal Journal, they are included in the planning table automatically if they are part of the relevant include structure. This makes it very easy to build reports that compare plan and actual data.

A third table, table ACDOCU, holds all *consolidation* relevant information—again, coming structurally with the same data model. The consolidation table is essentially an aggregation of the entries in the Universal Journal: it will include the legal entities that act as trading partners and the various management dimensions used for matrix consolidation, but it won't include every order and network from the operational processes like the Universal Journal. These details are simply aggregated and do not appear in the consolidation table.

We'll look at the planning table in more detail in Chapter 9 and the consolidation table in Chapter 12.

1.2.4 The Universal Journal and Items in Table BSEG

One myth we've encountered is that table BSEG disappears with SAP S/4HANA because all financial journal entry items posted in an SAP S/4HANA environment are recorded in table ACDOCA as the single source of financial data.

Figure 1.3 shows the structure of the accounting entries in SAP S/4HANA. The familiar tables BKPF (journal entry header) and BSEG (journal entry line item) from the SAP ERP world continue to exist in the context of SAP S/4HANA. Table BSEG is still relevant for specific operational finance processes, including open item management.

So how does this relate to table ACDOCA? There is still the classical link between the header and line item tables, as expected, but in the end, table ACDOCA contains all the details of the financial document and stores all fields relevant for accounting processes and reporting.

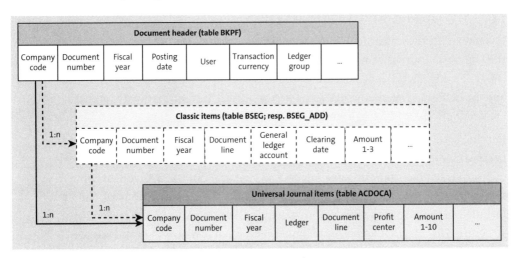

Figure 1.3 Data Model for Journal Entries in SAP S/4HANA

Figure 1.4 illustrates the interdependencies between tables BSEG and ACDOCA. The BSEG line items have been highly summarized so that we are left with a receivables line, a tax line, and a revenue line (three separate accounts). In table ACDOCA, we see many more line items for the same business transaction. We summarized the revenue line in table BSEG to remove the customer and product in the invoice and the derived profit center, but we can see the separate customers, products, and profit centers in table ACDOCA. The tax and receivable lines were captured by company code, but we've used document splitting to break out the tax and receivable lines to represent the three separate profit centers in the revenue line.

When you think about sizing your accounting system, it's important to look at whether your table BSEG has been highly summarized and how the number of table ACDOCA lines will grow if you did not previously use document splitting. One of the major headaches of table BSEG was that the number of posting lines per document could not exceed three digits. Because table BSEG now generally will be summarized, this should cease to be a problem. The maximum number of posting lines in table ACDOCA is 999,999.

With that high-level view of the Universal Journal in place, we'll now dive into the details and explain how each of the new reporting dimensions relate to the structures you know from SAP ERP so that you can understand the impact of a move to SAP S/4HANA.

Table BSEG		
001	Receivables	$ 900.-
002	Tax	$ 100.-
003	Revenues	$ 800.-

Table ACDOCA							
Ledger 1	000001	Receivables	$ 225.-	Profit center 1	Product A	Customer X	...
Ledger 1	000002	Receivables	$ 225.-	Profit center 2	Product B	Customer X	...
Ledger 1	000003	Receivables	$ 450.-	Profit center 3	Product C	Customer X	...
Ledger 1	000004	Tax	$ 25.-	Profit center 1	Product A	Customer X	...
Ledger 1	000005	Tax	$ 25.-	Profit center 2	Product B	Customer X	...
Ledger 1	000006	Tax	$ 50.-	Profit center 3	Product C	Customer X	...
Ledger 1	000007	Revenues	$ 200.-	Profit center 1	Product A	Customer X	...
Ledger 1	000008	Revenues	$ 200.-	Profit center 2	Product B	Customer X	...
Ledger 1	000009	Revenues	$ 400.-	Profit center 3	Product C	Customer X	...

Figure 1.4 Comparing Billing Documents in Tables BSEG and ACDOCA

1.3   Reporting Dimensions in Detail

Let's dive into more detail on the different dimensions and financial views embedded in the Universal Journal, not forgetting that the actual master data definitions of accounts, cost centers, and other business dimensions are stored in separate master data tables. We'll look at how the views work to bring the master data tables back together with the line item table when we look at the new options for reporting in Chapter 5 and Chapter 6.

We'll begin with the merge of the general ledger accounts and cost elements, which comes as a direct result of bringing the FI and CO components together. We'll then look at the company codes and trading partners and explain what you should think about to ensure that the Universal Journal can be used reliably to build a base layer for your consolidation processes. Moving into what was the domain of the CO component in SAP ERP, we'll look at the changes to the way costs are updated for cost centers, orders, projects, and so on, before looking at the reporting dimensions that are derived from this master data (i.e., profit centers, functional areas, and segments). Finally, we'll look at the case for moving the profitability segments into the Universal Journal rather than using costing-based CO-PA as a separate application. We'll then wrap up the section with a review of the reporting dimensions and how the different applications fold into the Universal Journal.

1.3.1   Accounts and Cost Elements

The first dimension to focus on is the account and its associated cost elements.

The general ledger account needs no further introduction: any financial posting or journal entry will always be associated with an account. Knowing that legal and management accounting information is stored in a single place now, we no longer require the cost element as the vehicle for moving information from FI to CO in an SAP ERP context.

This has prompted a change in the data structure such that all postings, in both financial accounting and controlling, are posted with reference to an account. If you use the new SAP Fiori–based reports, you'll only see the term *account* on the user interface. (If you continue to use the legacy Report Writer reports in cost center accounting, order accounting, and so on, you'll still see the old cost elements. This is because these reports use compatibility views to convert the new data structures back into the old structures and ensure that all legacy programs and reports continue to work as before.)

Transaction KA01 (Create Primary Cost Element), Transaction KA06 (Create Secondary Cost Element), Transaction KA02 (Change Cost Element), and Transaction KA03 (Display Cost Element) have been removed from the SAP Easy Menu in SAP S/4HANA; if you do call these transactions, you will be redirected to Transaction FS00 (Display G/L Account Centrally; shown in Figure 1.5). Behind the scenes, the master data tables for the cost elements continue to exist; they are still read when you create an assessment cycle, a settlement rule, or a costing sheet, or when you perform any of the other configuration steps that need to check the availability of the cost element.

What changes in SAP S/4HANA is the use of account types to distinguish pure accounts and account/cost elements. Figure 1.5 shows the different account types available in SAP S/4HANA. In SAP ERP, the only distinction was between balance sheet accounts (type X) and profit and loss (P&L) accounts (type blank). Balance sheet accounts continue to be used largely as in SAP ERP, though we will look at some changes for event-based revenue recognition and work in process in Chapter 7.

In SAP ERP, some P&L accounts only existed in the FI component, but most had a "sister" cost element in CO. These were the primary cost elements used for wages, salaries, materials, and so on. In SAP S/4HANA, we distinguish between P&L accounts that are used only in financial accounting (nonoperating expense or income, or type N) and those with a sister cost element in controlling (primary costs or revenue, or type P). Nonoperating expense and revenue accounts are used for postings that do not affect controlling, such as gains and losses in the treasury, and are never linked with an account assignment in controlling. Primary cost elements and revenue accounts, by contrast, are always linked with an account assignment in controlling.

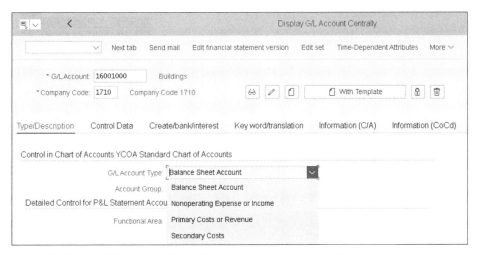

Figure 1.5 Display G/L Account Centrally: Showing New Account Types

During the technical conversion from SAP ERP to SAP S/4HANA, the system will check whether the P&L account has a sister cost element and, if it does, include the control data for the cost element in the account. The old posting logic still applies, so any costs assigned to a primary cost element or a revenue cost element also must be assigned to a cost center, order, WBS element, or profitability segment. You can still use substitution and validation to switch among and check the account assignments as before. You will potentially lose two features in the move:

- The cost element was time-dependent, whereas the account isn't. When the cost element becomes part of the account, it loses its time dependency.

- In SAP ERP, you could enter a default account assignment (cost center or internal order) in the cost element. In SAP S/4HANA, you have to use the configuration available in the IMG under **Controlling • Cost Center Accounting • Actual Postings • Manual Actual Postings • Edit Account Assignment** (or Transaction OKB9) to maintain these default account assignments.

In the CO component in SAP ERP, secondary cost elements were used to move costs from cost center to cost center or from cost center to order and so on using assessment cycles, direct and indirect activity allocation, overhead calculation, settlement, and the like. In SAP S/4HANA, the processes to move costs from the sender to the receiver haven't changed, so you'll still find yourself running assessment cycles and settlements and calculating overhead at period close. One of the key differences in SAP S/4HANA is that the secondary cost elements, under which these cost flows are recorded, also become P&L accounts of the secondary costs account type (see Figure 1.5).

You might already be familiar with drawing T-accounts for the balance sheet and P&L postings in FI, but it's worth taking a minute to imagine the postings for an assessment or settlement in CO. Figure 1.6 shows a simple assessment cycle with a single cost center as the sender and four profitability segments as the receivers. When the assessment cycle runs, the cost center is credited and the four profitability segments are debited under the same secondary cost element. You'll see the same basic picture for all direct and indirect activity allocations, overhead calculations, and settlements. The secondary cost element always has a balance of zero from an accounting perspective, with the change visible in the different account assignments as values flow from the sender(s) to the receiver(s) in CO. What changes in SAP S/4HANA is not the sender-receiver relationship, but the fact that all five posting lines will be visible in accounting and not just in controlling.

Another key difference that comes with the move to SAP S/4HANA is that these new P&L accounts for secondary costs replace the reconciliation accounts that used to be updated either in the reconciliation ledger when you ran Transaction KALC at period close or in the SAP ERP General Ledger to move costs between company codes in real time. This is a significant change to the posting logic, but it means that you will never again have to reconcile controlling and financial accounting; however, if you are feeding account-related information to a data warehouse or consolidation system, be aware that such costs will now be stored as accounts/secondary cost elements rather than the reconciliation accounts in SAP ERP and include this change in your project plan. The only substitutions and validations that won't work anymore are those that check the reconciliation ledger (table COFI), which has been removed in SAP S/4HANA.

We'll return to the idea that all postings to the Universal Journal are double-sided when we look at the journal entries for incoming sales orders and statistical conditions in Section 1.3.5 and at predictive accounting in Chapter 8. Historically, these postings were one-sided in SAP ERP and only contained the assignment to the profitability segment (the P&L side), not to the receivables item (the balance sheet side).

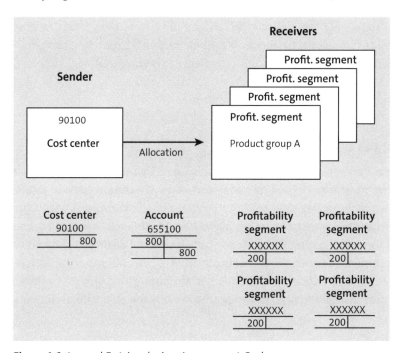

Figure 1.6 Journal Entries during Assessment Cycle

That explanation of how controlling and financial accounting merge might seem a little limited for some controllers, because it only focuses on actual costs and revenues—so let's take a minute to discuss what happens to *statistical postings* in the Universal Journal. It's easy enough to draw T-accounts for the direct postings to cost centers, orders, projects, and so on, and then have these costs allocate to other objects in controlling. However, many organizations also use statistical orders and projects in addition to the real cost assignment to provide a finer cost assignment. This raises the question of whether statistical postings continue to be supported and, if so, which account assignment "wins" in the Universal Journal.

In the merge of financial accounting and controlling, SAP revisited the idea of the controlling object and introduced two new fields—ACCAS (account assignment) and ACCASTY (object type) —to the Universal Journal. The real posting will always update the account assignment with the correct object type. So, if the real posting is to a cost center, you'll see the cost center number as the account assignment and KS (for cost center) as the object type. The statistical posting will also update the order or WBS element field (depending on the account assignment), but not the account assignment and object type fields. Drilldowns in the trial balance, profit center reporting, and other areas will show only the real account assignment—in our example, the cost center. To see the costs assigned to the statistical objects, you'll have to call up the relevant cost center, order, or project reports and select the **Is Statistical** flag. As before, you will be able to include real costs only in an allocation or a settlement. Statistical postings stay wherever they were originally captured.

1.3.2   Legal Entities and Trading Partners

When you look at how reporting dimensions are filled in Figure 1.3, it's obvious that all journal entries must be assigned to a company code. We cannot acquire assets, post goods movements, or pay salaries without reference to a company code as the legal entity in which the transaction takes place. Because financial accounting and controlling will always be in sync, the company code is checked during all postings to an account assignment in controlling. This means that in SAP S/4HANA, it's no longer possible to remove the **CoCd Validation** flag in the controlling area. In this way, the system ensures that all financial postings are always associated with a company code.

As you run assessment cycles, indirect activity allocation cycles, settlements, and so on, you may inadvertently cross company codes. Some organizations try to block such postings by setting up validations to prevent cross-company allocations. Others allow such postings, but then use the reconciliation ledger in SAP ERP to understand how costs flow from company code A to company code B and issue invoices after the fact. In SAP S/4HANA, if you allow such postings, they will update an intercompany clearing account.

As you design the reporting dimensions to be included in your steering model, don't forget to take the requirements for group reporting and consolidation into account, even if you aren't necessarily using an SAP consolidation tool. Make sure you are clear about how the trading partners are derived for customers, vendors, and company codes and that you understand which entities are required for matrix consolidation (profit center, business unit, cost center, and so on). We'll return to this topic when we look at how the reporting dimensions in the Universal Journal are selected for group reporting in Chapter 12.

1.3.3   Cost Centers, Internal Orders, and Projects

The way in which cost centers, internal orders, and projects are handled in SAP S/4HANA is almost the same as in SAP ERP, with the important difference that all these responsibility accounting dimensions are included as individual reporting dimensions in the Universal Journal instead of in different tables. With the move to SAP S/4HANA, the old controlling object is unpacked, and the data stored in the cost center, internal order, WBS element, business process, and other fields. This makes it much easier to build reports to analyze the various dimensions and to perform drill-downs, as we'll discuss in Chapter 5.

In SAP S/4HANA, the purpose and use of management accounting dimensions including cost centers, internal orders, and projects remain the same as in the SAP ERP environment. What changes is that these different dimensions become reporting dimensions in the Universal Journal and have financial postings linked to them directly or after applying allocation logic; this enables an organization to report on a specific area of responsibility.

Cost centers are the responsibility accounting object typically used when focusing on the structural or organizational setup. You can identify cost centers in the Universal Journal by the object type KS. In many cases, cost centers supply services to the organization in the form of production activities, maintenance activities, sales activities, and so on. The activity type (object type KL) also moves into the Universal Journal, and you'll still find the old functions for splitting cost-center-related costs to the relevant activity types. If you currently work with target costs or calculate variances in the Cost Center Accounting subcomponent of SAP ERP, note that these are not part of the Universal Journal but still use the legacy tables. For this reason, you may still need to use legacy reports to meet some of your reporting requirements.

Internal orders and projects largely serve a similar purpose: grouping together P&L information related to a particular activity or topic that is temporary in nature (e.g., a marketing action or an investment project). As a guiding principle, internal orders are applicable for straightforward structures, whereas a project is more applicable if the activity is comprised of subcategories for which costs and revenues should be tracked. You can identify orders by object type OR. Order items (for joint production) and operations are also supported if you work with operation-level costing in maintenance. The individual elements of a project are known as WBS elements; these find their place in the Universal Journal along with networks and network activities.

Projects in SAP S/4HANA Cloud

As of SAP S/4HANA Cloud 1802, internal orders are no longer supported. Instead, simple projects that comprise a project definition and one work package should be used.

If you are using make-to-order production, note that the sales order item is still supported as an account assignment in SAP S/4HANA. If you work with activity-based costing, the business process is still supported as an account assignment. Only the cost object and cost object hierarchy are no longer supported in SAP S/4HANA; SAP is advising customers to take alternative approaches as part of their conversion projects.

It's worth noting that the cost centers, orders, and WBS elements are recorded in the Universal Journal, along with the partner cost centers, partner orders, and so on. However, cost center hierarchies, order groups, cost element groups, and so on remain separate. We'll look at how to build and report on these hierarchies in Chapter 5 when we look at how to work with SAP Fiori and report on live data. We'll also look at new options for managing hierarchies in SAP S/4HANA in that chapter.

1.3.4   Profit Centers, Segments, and Functional Areas

Let's consider profit centers, segments, and functional areas. When moving toward the analytical reporting dimensions, their basic purposes remain the same in SAP S/4HANA as compared with SAP ERP. The difference, of course, is that all dimensions and all partner reporting dimensions are part of the Universal Journal, rather than separate table structures.

If you've worked with the SAP ERP General Ledger (formerly known as the "new" General Ledger), then you may recall that the profit center, segment, and functional area were already part of table FAGLFLEX for multidimensional reporting in the General Ledger. However, many organizations are moving to SAP S/4HANA from the classic (or "old") General Ledger, where there were separate ledgers for profit center accounting, cost of sales reporting, consolidation preparation, and so on. It's technically still possible to run all of these applications as separate special ledgers for a transition period, but the recommendation is to move into the Universal Journal.

Profit centers can be implemented as a simple reporting dimension—similar to cost centers, but with the purpose of representing a margin-generating part of the organization. They also can be used to set transfer prices between divisions within an organization, something we'll come back to in Chapter 2.

As we look at profit center accounting and the principle of the single source of truth in SAP S/4HANA, consider that the use of profit centers as an analytical dimension and the setup of profit center accounting is embedded in the Universal Journal. This does not mean that profit center accounting (or, more generally speaking, special ledgers) can't be set up anymore. The functionality is still supported in the on-premise edition, but there are two caveats:

- The special ledger itself has not received innovations like the new intuitive UI, the removal of aggregates, or general process acceleration.

- Because the Universal Journal covers almost all prior use cases of the special ledger, SAP recommends that you consider switching all (or most) special ledgers to be part of the Universal Journal.

When organizations with systems based on the special ledger are considering whether to integrate all management accounting views into the Universal Journal, they should develop a clear understanding of what exactly it's possible to integrate or not. Let's start with the reasons that organizations would set up a special ledger and compare against what's covered by the Universal Journal:

- One common use case is the requirement of an additional standard dimensionality (profit center, cost center, order, etc.) in the ledger. This is included in the Universal Journal, which has 350-plus dimensions by default and can be extended further as required.

- Closely related is the requirement to add customer-defined dimensionality in the ledger. The Universal Journal can be extended easily during setup. We'll return to this topic and explain how to add fields and create the derivation logic to fill them in Section 1.4.2.

- Special ledgers can be set up as parallel ledgers for statutory reporting (local/group GAAP). Now the preferred approach is to implement parallel ledgers within the Universal Journal. We'll return to this topic in Chapter 2.

- Special ledgers can be set up as parallel ledgers for management accounting, tax, or other perspectives. Here the question is whether a full ledger is required within the Universal Journal or whether to explore the concept of an extension ledger, which contains only the delta postings.

So in general, only a few scenarios (e.g., if a customer changed mandatory SAP logic in its special ledger) may not be suited for the Universal Journal and should continue to use the special ledger.

Special Ledgers in SAP S/4HANA Cloud

In SAP S/4HANA Cloud, it isn't possible to use separate special ledgers, profit center accounting, or COGS accounting. These reporting dimensions are only available as part of the Universal Journal.

When moving to the Universal Journal, there is no change in the way profit centers are derived. It's also possible to set up rules for substitution and validation as before. Figure 1.7 illustrates the main difference between the SAP ERP approach (which relies on a general ledger and one or more special ledgers) and the SAP S/4HANA approach. In the latter, the *standard ledger* is a full ledger that contains all financial postings for a given valuation approach. Any valuation-specific changes are posted manually in the *extension ledger*, which sits on top of the standard ledger and is always analyzed in combination with the standard ledger underneath. The SAP ERP setup resulted in high data redundancy because the management view had 95% of the same data as the legal view, plus 5% adjustments; in contrast, the SAP S/4HANA setup results in no data redundancy and the separation of management data from legal data.

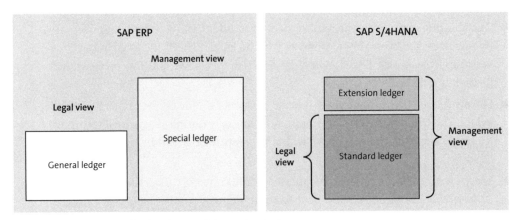

Figure 1.7 Standard Ledger and Extension Ledger

One practical use case for such an extension ledger is when you require a reclassification of profit centers. When profit center accounting was a separate special ledger, it was easy to create profit center documents to make such corrections as the organization required. These sat alongside the profit center documents that were derived from the operational business transactions. Now, with SAP S/4HANA, all operational business transactions will be assigned to a profit center in the standard ledger. If a reclassification is needed, these special postings are created manually in the extension ledger. We'll look at further use cases for the extension ledger when we look at predictive accounting in Chapter 8.

1.3.5   Profitability Analysis

Now that we've described the dimensions related to legal and management accounting in the context of the Universal Journal, in which both worlds have become one, the missing piece that we'll address next relates to profitability analysis. In SAP ERP, this was typically done in the CO-PA subcomponent.

Recall that the goal of the Universal Journal is to act as the single source of truth for financial information. This means integrating profitability analysis data with all relevant profitability dimensions into the same table.

The first thing to know about profitability analysis in the Universal Journal is that the characteristics used are the same as for costing-based CO-PA. At the time of publication (spring 2019), this means that you can still use a maximum of sixty characteristics (including those delivered by SAP) to form your profitability segments. When you post a journal entry or create an invoice, you are posting to a combination of characteristics and using derivation logic to fill in the product group from the product, the customer group from the customer, and so on. There is no change to the derivation logic in SAP S/4HANA (though we will look at new options to derive profitability segments for cost centers, orders, and projects in Chapter 7).

In Section 1.3.1, we looked at how the account is a key dimension in the Universal Journal. All postings to profitability analysis are made to an account/cost element. If we compare this to the "classic" CO-PA approach in SAP ERP, it becomes clear that the only way to have profitability analysis data reconciled with P&L accounts by design is to use the account-based approach so that the P&L statement and profitability reports naturally line up. Historically, this was not the way to deliver margin information on the level of a customer, product, or service—or any other relevant business dimensions. Although account-based CO-PA was introduced in the mid-1990s, it was generally recommended *not* to include the product or customer as market segments for performance reasons; consequently, to deliver margin insights by profitability segment, most organizations chose to set up costing-based CO-PA in SAP ERP.

Today, with the column-based database SAP HANA, storing profitability segments for customers, products, and so on is no longer a problem, and you can easily use the same profitability segments in both account-based and costing-based profitability analysis. During system conversion to SAP S/4HANA, the system creates a column in the Universal Journal for every characteristic in the operating concern.

If you are considering a move from costing-based CO-PA toward profitability analysis integrated in the Universal Journal, bear in mind that all revenue accounts to which you will be posting invoices must be set up as primary cost elements, as must all accounts for COGS. If you use assessment cycles, settlements, and so on, consider that the secondary cost elements used to clear the cost centers and orders/projects will show up in your profitability reporting. If you clear all assessments under a single cost element, you might want to add more secondary cost elements to give more transparency to the sales and administration costs that you are allocating.

It's still possible to use costing-based profitability analysis in SAP S/4HANA, but there are some drawbacks:

- It requires setting up a separate data model because there is no direct link to an account. In other words, profitability insights are not part of the single source of truth. Instead, you'll work with a key figure model that assigns all postings to value fields. Nevertheless, you may wish to keep costing-based profitability analysis running for an interim period while you build up historical data that is assigned to an account.

- As a result, this approach leads to challenges when reconciling profitability information with general ledger information. The value fields rarely match the account/cost elements one to one, and some postings to costing-based profitability analysis do not have an equivalent accounting document.

- This approach delivers insights into the contribution margins from sales, sales deductions, and COGS during a period. However, to derive contribution margins that include overhead, you have to wait until month-end close. There are new options to derive profitability analysis dimensions immediately when you post to cost centers, orders, and projects, which we'll discuss when we look at the new options for real-time closing in Chapter 7.

These drawbacks can be removed by taking advantage of the Universal Journal-based architecture, which is the recommended approach. The direct integration of profitability analysis into the Universal Journal ensures both real-time information and the reconciliation with financials by design.

Profitability Analysis in SAP S/4HANA Cloud

Only profitability analysis in the Universal Journal is supported in SAP S/4HANA Cloud. It isn't possible to activate costing-based profitability analysis separately.

To get a clear understanding of what capabilities are available and possible reasons to stay with costing-based CO-PA (and therefore a separate data model), consider the comparisons in Table 1.2.

Capability	Example	Profitability Analysis in SAP S/4HANA	Costing-Based Profitability Analysis
Reconciliation	Reconciliation of legal and management accounting—for example, by profit center.	From version 1503	No
Drilldown from income statement	Drill down to product and customer-related characteristics within income statement report.	From version 1503	No
Profitability characteristics on balance sheet items	For unbilled revenues or WIP, a customer wants to see the project, region, or customer category.	From version 1610	No
Top-down distribution	Distribute high-level costs to the relevant market segments.	From version 1503	Yes
Realignment	If profitability characteristics such as the assigned division are changed, it's possible to derive new values for historic data.	From version 1610 (realignment report from version 1709)	Yes
COGS splitting	Breakdown of COGS into fixed and variable costs, and breakdown by cost component, such as material, overhead, or production.	From version 1503 (actual costing scenario from version 1809)	Yes
Splitting of production variances	Distinguish variances in costs of manufacturing materials by price, quantity, or scrap variances.	From version 1503	Yes

Table 1.2 Capabilities of Profitability Analysis

Capability	Example	Profitability Analysis in SAP S/4HANA	Costing-Based Profitability Analysis
Statistical sales conditions	Sales conditions can be used to calculate contribution margin level, such as sales commissions, calculated freight, or discounts, which are not posted in the general ledger.	From version 1809	Yes
Incoming sales orders	Creation of a sales order item generates expected revenue and COGS entry in profitability.	From version 1809 (predictive accounting)	Yes

Table 1.2 Capabilities of Profitability Analysis (Cont.)

The initial conclusion from looking at this comparison table is that all margin insights that could be delivered with a standalone costing-based approach are also covered by the profitability analysis integrated into the Universal Journal. Let's take a more detailed look at some of the key items.

First, there is the question of the showing the split of the COGS within your margin reporting. This is a key topic for any production organization interested in isolating different parts of the COGS into separate reporting lines to isolate material- and labor-related costs. We'll return to this example in more detail in Chapter 11, but we'll focus on the business side here.

As illustrated in Figure 1.8, initially COGS entries all end up in a single P&L account. If no additional details are picked up from the product cost estimate, which is linked to the production order of the material being analyzed, then only one total COGS amount is displayed in the margin analysis report. By picking up the product costing details (from the product cost estimate mentioned) and clustering these (e.g., in a separate material and labor category), this distinction can be included in margin reporting.

Splitting the COGS to enable clear margin reporting (e.g., including information for labor and material costs separately) follows the same logic in the integrated profitability analysis approach as in the costing-based approach. The only difference is that when you're using profitability analysis integrated in the Universal Journal, the different COGS captions are defined as separate P&L accounts.

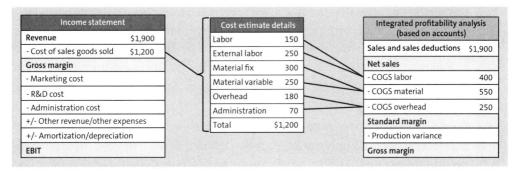

Figure 1.8 Splitting the Cost of Goods Sold

This example applies not only in case of organizations using a standard cost; these insights also can be delivered when actual costing is used within the product costing context. When the product costs and inventory valuation are calculated based on the actual costing logic, you need to ensure that the COGS revaluation based on the actual costs at period end is represented in your profitability reporting as well—in other words, including the split into material, labor cost, and other COGS categories. We'll look at the detailed postings generated here in Chapter 11.

The addition of this split logic, including the actual cost-based revaluation, was introduced with SAP S/4HANA 1809. Now all the different product costing scenarios can be covered, presenting the COGS split in a correct way within the margin reporting without the need for reconciliation.

The new approach is adequate so long as you don't need an additional *alternative* product cost valuation method, like a second standard. The main gap in this area is that it's not possible to include different assumptions concerning the COGS. We can choose standard costs and correct them using the actual costs, but we can't bring in multiple cost estimates to represent different assumptions concerning the standard costs.

When considering *production variances*, a similar note can be made about splitting production variances into different categories, such as input price variances, quantity variances, and scrap. Like the COGS information, variances between the actual cost and target cost of a production order are initially posted to a single P&L account. To see these variances presented in different nodes in the margin analysis, details are picked up in product costing and recorded in separate accounts. We'll look at the detailed postings generated here in Chapter 11.

Apart from these margin insights specifically relevant for production-oriented organizations, another key topic to address is related to volume discounts (which are not completely known at the time of margin analysis) or transportation costs related to a particular sold product (the incoming invoice was not received yet). These and other types of *statistical sales conditions* are required to get an accurate view of the contribution margin. This is achieved by marking specific statistical conditions as relevant for accounting, which triggers a financial posting for, for instance, the statistical discounts or transportation cost.

Does this mean that these statistical costs are then just added to the financial statements? (This would surely not be in line with financial regulations!) These postings need to be isolated. As illustrated in Figure 1.9, this is done through an existing mechanism available within SAP S/4HANA: the extension ledger (recall Figure 1.7). An extension ledger is used to capture a specific subset of postings, and it sits on top of a base ledger (e.g., the leading ledger). We'll look at this topic in more detail in Chapter 8.

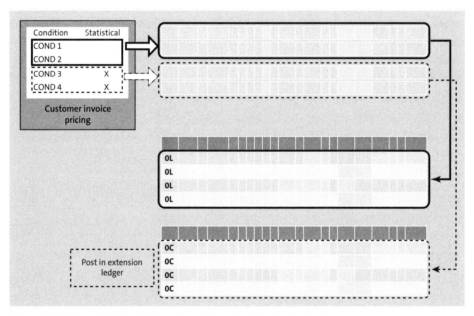

Figure 1.9 Using Statistical Sales Conditions for Margin Analysis

In addition to the statistical sales conditions, another topic to address in some more detail is the treatment of incoming sales orders. This is another type of non-GAAP-relevant transaction that should be translated into financial postings, to both include the statistical postings in our margin reporting and generate a complete view of all related revenues and costs within a specific period.

Whereas these incoming sales orders can be captured under a separate record type in costing-based CO-PA, in the integrated profitability analysis approach all items need to end up in the Universal Journal as postings to a specific general ledger account. This comes down to simulating financial postings before the sales order has been delivered and billed and is known as *predictive accounting*, an approach that will be described in more detail in Chapter 8.

1.3.6   Reviewing the Steering Model

As we said at the beginning of the chapter, the easiest way to picture the Universal Journal is as a huge pivot table with the information in the old applications (FI, CO, FI-AA, ML, CO-PA, the industry-specific fields, and any extensions) folding together into a single structure. Figure 1.10 shows the Universal Journal line item table, with the **Ledger**, **Company Code**, **Fiscal Year**, **Account Number**, and **Document Number** fields, plus several include structures that contain the fields in the old application tables. By viewing the fields in the separate include structures, we reach the 350-plus fields that are part of the Universal Journal.

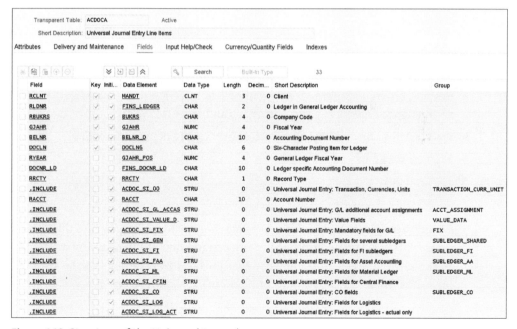

Figure 1.10 Structure of the Universal Journal

All postings will be assigned to a company code, a ledger, and an account; the P&L accounts are effectively a combination of accounts and cost elements. We'll look at where group accounts fit into the picture in Chapter 2 and Chapter 12.

The subledgers section (ACDOC_SI_FI) carry the following reporting dimensions, which are derived from the master data in controlling:

- Profit center and partner profit center
- Segment and partner segment
- Functional area and partner functional area (for COGS reporting)
- Business unit and partner business unit (on-premise SAP S/4HANA only)
- Trading partner and partner trading partner (for consolidation/group reporting)

Asset-related postings will update the fields that used to be considered part of the asset subledger (section ACDOC_SI_FAA). We'll look at these fields in more detail in Chapter 10.

Material-related postings will update the fields that used to be considered part of the material ledger (section ACDOC_SI_ML). We'll look at these fields in more detail in Chapter 11.

Controlling-related postings (section ACDOC_SI_CO) are supported for the following reporting dimensions:

- Cost centers and activity types
- Internal orders (on-premise only), all orders from logistics (production orders, maintenance orders, etc.), and operations and order items
- Project definition and WBS elements, networks, and network activities
- Sales orders items
- Business processes
- Profitability segments

This section explained how to move the data model you have today into the Universal Journal. However, you also need to understand how the accounting model has been extended for the various industry solutions and what options will be available in the future. Therefore, let's now look at how to extend the steering model.

1.4   Extending the Steering Model

In our experience, the adjective that most organizations use to talk about the FI and CO components in SAP ERP is *robust*.

Of course, customers could make changes, but it wasn't easy and was usually expensive. Over the years, many of the industry solutions have added their own fields to the accounting model, so if you work with, say, joint venture accounting in the oil and gas or mining industries, then you'll be familiar with the use of fields such as **Equity Group** and **Recovery Indicator** in your financial processes. If you work in the public sector, you're probably using fields such as **Fund** and **Grant** in your financial processes to indicate a source of funding. Likewise, there are additional fields for real estate management.

If a field wasn't already available, most customers simply used the field that was nearest to their requirements to avoid changing the data model. A Norwegian fishing company once represented each of its boats as water-based plants that delivered to land-based plants when the boat docked and unloaded its catch, and it treated ocean freight being shipped between continents as a project that was complete once a ship delivered its cargo to its destination.

Changing the accounting model was expensive in SAP ERP because of the complex layering of financial information. The SAP ERP structure was more complicated than the Universal Journal in SAP S/4HANA because each of the applications had not only its own line item tables, but also *totals tables* that summarized the line item information by period. In many cases, fields were included in the line items that were not available in the totals. Adding a field meant extending the line item table and understanding which other aggregations had been built on top of that table.

With SAP S/4HANA, these totals tables have been removed, along with the associated index tables. We'll look at what this means for reporting in more detail in Chapter 5, but for now, having one table—the Universal Journal—also means having only one place that needs to be extended to meet additional reporting requirements. This means that extending the steering model just got easier. We'll now look at what SAP has done to include new fields from logistics in the steering model and what you can do to extend the reporting dimensions to meet the reporting requirements in your organization.

1.4.1   Financial Dimensions in Logistics

If you worked with maintenance and service orders in SAP ERP, you might have used an optional business function for operation-level costing that changed the accounting logic; instead of assigning the costs to the headers of the maintenance orders, they were assigned to the operations within those orders. This business function, introduced in Enhancement Package 5 for SAP ERP 6.0, essentially changed the data model and posting logic to provide better cost transparency for maintenance orders by focusing on the costs per operation.

SAP ERP customers sought the same transparency for production orders, process orders, and so on. Figure 1.11 shows the data available in Production Planning (PP) in SAP ERP. The material components are included in a bill of material (BOM). When a BOM is issued for the production order, the materials will always be included in the posting document. The various operations are listed in the routing. When the operation is confirmed on the shop floor, this confirmation is recorded at the work center in PP—but *only* at the level of the cost center assigned to the work center in CO. In Figure 1.11, work is performed in four operations, but we would only see two cost centers and two activity types in CO. In SAP ERP, customers who wanted cost detail per work center would create hundreds of cost centers to represent the associated work centers.

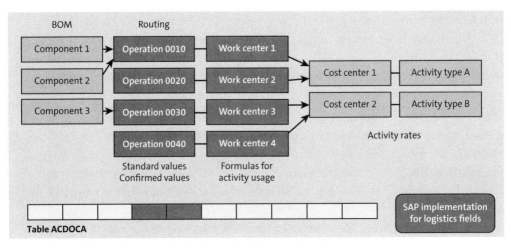

Figure 1.11 Adding Logistics Fields to the Steering Model

In SAP S/4HANA, the Universal Journal is extended to include both the operation and the work center so that you will now see all four operations and work centers in the accounting document. We'll look at how these fields are included in the planning model in Chapter 9 and how they provide the basis for improved variance reporting in Chapter 11. For now, it's enough to understand that you can now analyze the costs of each work center to make decisions based on the cost inputs to that work center—a degree of detail that was not available in SAP ERP. New fields also have been added from maintenance to enable the analysis of the costs by equipment, functional area, functional location, assembly, planned work, suboperation, and so on.

Of course, the ability to add fields to the accounting model is only one part of the challenge. Many organizations have tried to implement a factory dashboard to show plant-related costs in SAP ERP. This is relatively straightforward in Profitability Analysis and Product Cost Controlling, for which the plant is available in all transactions. However, cost centers and activity types have no direct link with a plant (or only have such a link in the sense that the activity types are linked with a work center). Delivering plant-specific cost rates would require significant rework of the accounting model and is not yet available in SAP S/4HANA.

1.4.2 Adding Your Own Dimensions

It was possible to extend the data model in SAP ERP. Customers could add their own characteristics to the operating concern in CO-PA and extend the coding block using CI_COBL. In SAP S/4HANA, these options are still available, but so are a few others, as we'll explain in this section.

Figure 1.12 shows the two options to extend the general ledger in SAP S/4HANA. The first option is to use the coding block extension. It was possible to extend the coding block in SAP ERP, and if you migrate to SAP S/4HANA any fields previously included in the coding block extension (CI_COBL) automatically will be included in the Universal Journal and will behave as before. If you explore the new extension options, you'll find that this option continues to exist as the **Coding Block** business context. This approach should be used for fields that are filled in by users during document entry when an invoice or accounting document is created; these fields then are transported by the business process into the Universal Journal.

The other option to extend the accounting document shown in Figure 1.12 is known as the "inside ACDOCA extension," or the new extension option with the **Journal Entry Item** business context. This field is always filled in using the contents of another field in the Universal Journal or a master data attribute by means of a derivation.

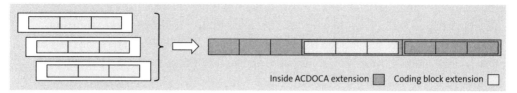

Figure 1.12 Adding Fields for Accounting

CO-PA in SAP ERP is always based on a flexible data structure. SAP delivers a fixed set of characteristics (including material, material group, plant, industry, customer, customer group, sales district, sales office, sales group, country, billing type, sales organization, distribution channel, division, sales order, sales order item, WBS element, internal order, and cost center). Organizations can add their own characteristics, up to a maximum of sixty (including the SAP-delivered characteristics), by adding fields to the operating concern. These are filled in using derivation rules defined in Customizing. During a migration to SAP S/4HANA, columns are created in the Universal Journal for all characteristics in the operating concern.

Figure 1.13 shows the new option to use fields for profitability analysis in the Universal Journal. The existing operating concern tables for the characteristics continue to exist as table CE4 and can be extended using the existing configuration options available in SAP ERP and on-premise SAP S/4HANA. However, a new option is being developed in SAP S/4HANA Cloud to add additional fields to the Universal Journal using the **Market Segment** business context. These are already available in reporting in planning, and work is under way to include the added fields in assessment cycles, top-down distribution, realignment, and all other profitability analysis applications. However, it will take several editions to completely replace the generic functionality associated with the operating concern with the new approach.

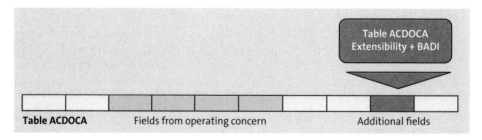

Figure 1.13 Adding Fields for Profitability Analysis

For reporting purposes, it's also important to be able to extend the master data to include your own attributes. In SAP S/4HANA 1809, the master data for cost centers, profit centers, assets, and so on contains an `include` structure to hold any fields that an organization adds. If you add fields to the master data, they are added to the `include` structure in the relevant master data and to all SAP Fiori applications and Core Data Services (CDS) views that read that master data. You then can use these fields to build hierarchies to aggregate the transactional data associated with your cost centers and profit centers, as you will see in Chapter 5 when we discuss the use of flexible hierarchies.

At the time of publication (spring 2019), this also represents a new way to segment your business based on the underlying master data. In the future, we expect that SAP will build applications that not only report on these fields but also use them in applications, such as division- or group-wide cost estimates, in which such segmentations can be used to explain the whole value flow across the corporation.

You've now seen how to extend the steering model. In today's volatile business world, it also often can be important to change your steering model to handle new business models.

1.5   Changing the Steering Model

We started the last section by stating that most organizations consider the FI and CO components in SAP ERP to be robust. Some of its users might go even further and declare it *rigid*. Changing data models is expensive, but time to change also is rapidly becoming one of the measures used to judge the efficiency of finance departments. Nobody wants to hear that restructuring the profit centers will take not months, but years.

If we go back to the simple two-dimensional model that we talked about at the start of the chapter, change appears easy: you simply add more accounts and cost centers as needed. A merger or a carve-out was relatively straightforward, so long as you could segregate the affected legal entities. As the steering model is extended to include more dimensions with the introduction of Profit Center Accounting in SAP ERP and complete multidimensionality in SAP S/4HANA, we have to be very clear about what can be changed after the fact and what can't. We are considering a set of accounting documents, so we can't change company codes, accounts, segments, profit centers—indeed, anything that is relevant for external reporting—after the fact. However, the Universal Journal also includes the profitability segments, and reporting dimensions such as sales districts and customer groups are notoriously volatile, requiring changes with alarming regularity. Since SAP S/4HANA 1610, it has been possible to realign profitability analysis characteristics to reflect changes to the sales structures and the like, in the same way that was possible using Transaction KEND in SAP ERP.

In this section, we'll explain the challenges associated with finding the connections among the various reporting dimensions. We'll then show how to perform realignments in profitability analysis and reorganize profit centers.

1.5.1   Finding the Connections

In Section 1.3, we explained which reporting dimensions were entered directly in the business transaction (company code, account, cost center, etc.) and which were derived to fill further reporting dimensions (profit center, functional area, segment, and characteristics). These derivations are as good as the assignments in the master data used to drive the derivation rules—so clearly one of the first requirements of a good financial steering model is that the master data is clean; otherwise, you'll discover that the data shown for the aggregated dimensions (profit center, functional area, etc.) isn't reliable. Many organizations have implemented master data governance solutions to help them achieve clean master data, particularly if they are working with multiple ERP systems.

It's also worth noting that assets, profit centers, cost centers, and activity types allow you to maintain *time-dependent* fields. This means that you effectively have data slices for the same cost center, so a single cost center might have the following data slices:

- From 01.01.2015 to 31.12.2017, assigned to profit center 1000
- From 01.01.2018 to 31.12.2019, assigned to profit center 2000
- From 01.03.2018 to 31.12.9999, assigned to new manager

Other master data, including accounts, materials, internal orders, and WBS elements, is not time-dependent. Internal orders and WBS elements will ultimately reach the end of their lifecycles and be closed, but this can be a problem for general ledger accounts and materials.

So if you have to make changes, it's important to understand whether you are changing an assignment that impacts only the P&L statement or one that also impacts the balance sheet. When you realign data in profitability analysis, you are creating a structure that is valid from that day forward because the P&L statement is time-based. When you change a profit center, then you will be impacting the P&L statement, the open items in accounts payable and accounts receivable, and the values of assets and inventory. Because the balance sheet is always a summary view on a key date, any shifts in the structure of the data are much more problematic and require a reposting to document the move of values from one profit center to another.

One thing that is starting to happen in SAP S/4HANA is that SAP is delivering where-used lists for financial master data. We'll look at the first examples when we look at SAP Fiori in Chapter 5. The idea is that when you look at a cost center, you can quickly understand the value flow that it's part of and know which allocation cycles, settlement rules, and so on use it before you initiate any change.

1.5.2 Realigning Profitability Analysis Data

As we discussed in Section 1.3.5, profitability analysis is part of the Universal Journal in SAP S/4HANA. This means that all the invoices, cost of sales postings, assessments, settlements, and so on are accounting documents and can't simply be changed to meet the whims of the next reorganization.

Figure 1.14 shows the impact of the new data model. For the purposes of realignment, we must separate external reporting dimensions that *cannot* be adjusted once posted from internal reporting dimensions that *can* be adjusted to deliver management reports in accordance with the new structures. Although you are allowed to make changes to the internal reporting dimensions after posting, the changes are documented in a separate table and the impact of the structural change reported on.

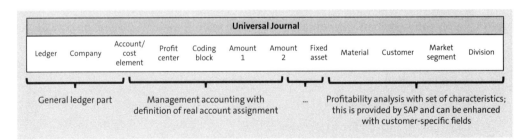

Figure 1.14 Realignment of Profitability Analysis in the Universal Journal

The first use case for a realignment is quite simply a change to the sales structure, product groups, or customer groups. It's easy to imagine that any changes here always will be driven by internal requirements, but customer segmentations also can be external. If your customer is a chain of supermarkets, then you may have to adjust your internal structures if the supermarket chain reorganizes. One lesson here is that some organizations realign their CO-PA characteristics in SAP ERP regularly (sometimes as often as once a month), whereas others rarely touch them in SAP ERP and do all their realignments in their data warehouse.

It also can be necessary to perform a realignment when master data has become outdated and inconsistent. Whenever you post to profitability analysis, derivation rules are used to derive the product group from the material, the customer group from the customer, the sales district from the sales organization, and so on. If the master data has not been kept up to date, the wrong assignments may be stored in profitability analysis; you'll need to use realignment to perform a new derivation to correct the assignments.

In both cases, you need to perform a *realignment* to change the characteristics based on the new master data assignments. CO-PA in SAP ERP offers two views of the data: the **As Posted** view, which contains the assignments at the time of posting, and the **Read According to Current Structure** view, which shows the latest data assignments.

What changes with SAP S/4HANA is that there is no longer a separation of FI and CO components; as you have seen, the former CO-PA characteristics are simply part of the accounting document. Nevertheless, journal entries must continue to follow the guidelines of the standard accounting principles. Realignment can be performed only on the fields that do not contain general ledger-relevant information; you are only allowed to change a subset of the CO-PA characteristics using realignment, but cannot change profit centers, functional areas, accounts, and so on.

The normal reporting applications that we'll discuss in Chapter 5 will always show the latest assignments to reflect what is shown in the Universal Journal. If you perform a realignment, there is a new report to explain the difference between the data structures at the time of posting and after realignment. At the time of realignment, the system will update a separate table to document what changes have been made during realignment.

1.5.3   Reorganizing Profit Centers

Reorganizing profit centers is more problematic than realigning profitability segments because it's possible to have a balance sheet sorted by profit center.

Let's walk through the basic flow of such a reorganization. The first step is to identify what will change as a result of the reorganization (such as the split of an existing profit center into two). The next is to identify which objects are assigned to the profit center and decide what the new assignment should be. Although the profit center structure is typically set at the corporate level because of the integration with group reporting, the objects themselves (cost centers, materials, assets, etc.) are generally local in scope and often managed at the plant level. For this reason, a reorganization typically involves a dialog between corporate and local accountants to determine how the shift to the new organization will be executed. Both master data and transactional data will be affected because the profit center usually will be part of existing purchase orders, production orders, projects, sales orders, and so on. Finally, adjustment postings are needed to move the balance sheet items to the new structures, and it is these adjustment postings that represent the critical difference between changes to the profit center structures and changes in profitability analysis.

The reorganization process is supported by a set of tools that allows you to generate worklists that list all the objects that are assigned to a profit center and will be affected by a change. These include materials, assets, purchase orders, sales orders, projects, production orders, and so on. These worklists can be shared with the relevant stakeholders so that they can then specify, for example, which materials will belong to profit center A and which to profit center B in the future. It is then possible to schedule the changes as a series of automated steps that will switch the master data and generate repostings to move balance sheet-related items from one profit center to another.

1.6 Summary

This chapter introduced the Universal Journal as the basis for a new steering model. Its arrival represents one of the most fundamental changes in SAP since the move from SAP R/2 to SAP R/3 in the early 1990s. We looked at the new data structures and how they support multidimensional reporting and then explained the impact on the different reporting dimensions in detail. We explained how to extend the steering model to meet industry requirements, the need for more transparency in logistics, and how to handle your own specific requirements. We ended by explaining what happens when you need to change your model to meet new business requirements.

In Chapter 2, we'll look at the challenge of using the Universal Journal to support both management reporting and local legal reporting according to different accounting principles.

Chapter 2

Local and Global Accounting: Changing Organizational Structures to Satisfy Various Requirements

In this chapter, we'll explain how the organizational structures you chose previously in SAP ERP can stand in the way of your common steering model. We'll discuss how SAP S/4HANA can help satisfy two very different sets of requirements in one accounting system.

From the moment that data warehouses appeared on the scene in the late 1990s, large organizations often have chosen to handle their corporate reporting requirements in a separate data warehouse from their operational accounting systems. This data warehouse acts as a corporate umbrella, combining financial data from the various local systems in which the business transactions are recorded and converting them into a common data model designed for corporate decision making.

Although the process of extracting and loading the data is generally in the hands of the IT department, the business focus is on the transformation of this data to provide a common steering model. The aim is generally to assign the disparate financial data to a common chart of accounts—with harmonized profit centers, cost centers, trading partners, and so on—and to clean up the various customers, vendors, and materials created in the field with the goal of delivering the financial insights needed to run the business.

In this chapter, we'll look at what happens when we try to remove this transformation layer and design a system that supports local reporting requirements and global reporting requirements *using the same steering model* to leverage the full benefits of running SAP S/4HANA in a single system. The range of challenges is illustrated in Figure 2.1, in which you can see the local requirements concerning compliance excellence on the left, the more global requirements for steering the organization on the right, and the need to synchronize the two very different sets of requirements in the middle.

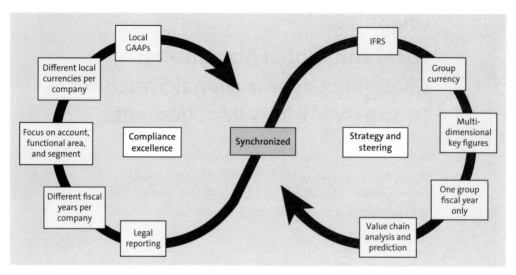

Figure 2.1 Differing Requirements for Local Compliance and Global Strategy and Steering

Organizations are approaching SAP S/4HANA implementations with a view to combine the requirements of financial accounting and controlling in a single system. This chapter looks at what must be in place to support a global controlling approach across the whole organization, while still handling the local legal requirements in each country where that organization operates. As organizations combine SAP system instances in the move to SAP S/4HANA, it is important to clearly separate the global view that may have already been achieved using a template implementation from the local views, where each system may be structured very differently in terms of its financial steering model.

In Section 2.1, we'll look at the key settings that will affect whether you can achieve a single global view to steer your organization in one system, and we'll explain the impact of the controlling area, the operating concern, and your profit center structure on your ability to report globally. In Section 2.2, we'll look at what can get in the way of that goal from a local perspective, in terms of different accounting principles, local currency reporting requirements, different reporting calendars, and the structural challenges required to achieve a global view in the same system that handles the local legal reporting requirements. Finally, in Section 2.3, we'll introduce new functions that support global supply chains and the reporting requirements associated with these value chains.

As we look at what needs to happen in SAP S/4HANA to allow transactional and analytical data to sit comfortably alongside one another in the Universal Journal, take the time to look critically at the SAP ERP design that you have been living with since your initial implementation. Ask yourself whether you will simply migrate it to the SAP S/4HANA world and continue much as before, but with your financial data in the Universal Journal—or whether you should change the existing steering model and start afresh with a greenfield implementation or perhaps transfer data from multiple different systems into one Central Finance system. We'll also introduce the key settings in SAP S/4HANA Cloud to meet best practices in this context.

2.1   Controlling and Global Business Management

In Chapter 1, we looked at the various reporting entities used for business management and explained how these entities are now captured in a single table, the Universal Journal.

From a controlling point of view, it's important to understand the roles of the controlling area, the operating concern, and the profit center structure, which will determine to what extent you are able to achieve consistent global business management within SAP S/4HANA. Many organizations have been coping with multiple instances of SAP ERP and so previously had to use a data warehouse to achieve the global view. As they move to a single instance, these key configuration settings can stand in the way of global business management, unless you enforced consistent structures as a guiding principle of your initial SAP ERP implementation.

2.1.1   The Single Controlling Area

Let's start by looking at the implications of the settings for the controlling area.

The *controlling area* is the business entity for which you perform your controlling tasks. Ideally it represents your whole corporate group, so in a perfect world, you would have a single controlling entity to which all your company codes, profit centers, and cost centers are assigned. However, for many organizations, the ideal world is just that: a hard-to-achieve ideal. Having more than one controlling area won't stop you from migrating to SAP S/4HANA, but it will mean that your controlling transactions are segregated by controlling area and that you won't be able to perform allocations between company codes in different controlling areas. This can be a problem if you want to charge central costs from headquarters to each local subsidiary.

If you look at the settings associated with the controlling area in Figure 2.2, you can start to understand where the problems lie in terms of global business management.

The controlling area controls your global currency, your global chart of accounts, and your global calendar. If your original SAP ERP implementation team didn't "think global" from the start, you may have inherited many controlling areas, each with different settings, and have little chance of establishing a global structure that spans your entire organization. So take the time to think about how your current controlling area(s) relate to your current company codes and how these come together for the purposes of consolidation.

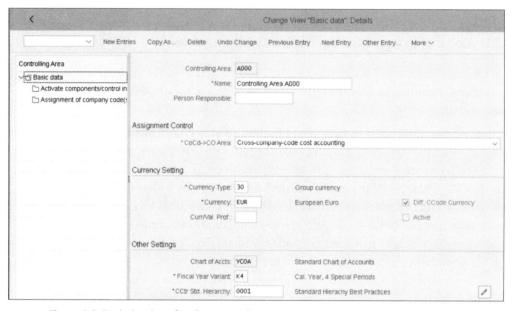

Figure 2.2 Basic Settings for the Controlling Area

Controlling Areas in SAP S/4HANA Cloud

If you are considering a move to SAP S/4HANA Cloud, bear in mind that only one controlling area is supported there, so make your design decisions accordingly.

We'll now look at the implications of the settings for the controlling area to understand how they affect global business management. We'll start by explaining the need to perform cross-company cost accounting in general; then we'll discuss the implications of the settings for the global currency, the operational chart of accounts, and the fiscal year variants, which have often resulted in fragmented reporting structures.

Cross-Company Cost Accounting

The first setting that is important for global business management is **CoCd • CO Area** (in the **Assignment Control** section), which determines whether multiple company codes can be assigned to one controlling area.

In Figure 2.2, we chose **Cross-Company-Code Cost Accounting**, meaning that multiple company codes (i.e., legal entities) are linked to a single controlling area. But in the 1990s, many organizations ignored this setting and created as many controlling areas as they had company codes; in extreme cases, this resulted in a different controlling area for every legal entity. This not only led to highly fragmented reporting and budgeting structures (because all tasks in Controlling are performed within a single controlling area), but also prevented allocations of costs from one legal entity to another because allocations are only allowed within a single controlling area.

As organizations set up shared service centers to handle operations for multiple legal entities in low-wage countries, it proved impossible to allocate costs from these shared service centers to the countries that they served in SAP ERP. One "simple" configuration setting resulted in their data warehouses being used not just as a reporting environment but also for cost allocations. Specialist software packages for cost allocations and service charging entered the market and flourished where organizations had set up their controlling areas without thinking about the need for intercompany allocations. Bear in mind, however, that though it is possible to set up allocations to charge costs to every cost center in a single controlling area, there are no facilities to invoice the various legal entities, requiring manual workarounds for compliance purposes.

Later implementations used a single controlling area to allow for cross-company code reporting and allocations. Although this setup has benefits, there are also challenges, such as managing the period close; the close tasks are locked not by company code, but by business transaction. This means that you cannot lock postings in Asia but keep them open on the West Coast in the United States, because everybody is working to the same schedule.

Currency Settings

The next key setting for the controlling area is the currency type. In Figure 2.2, we entered **30** (**Group Currency**) into the **Currency Type** field and defined this currency as the **Euro**. We also have allowed different currency settings for the associated company codes (**Diff. CCode Currency**). This means that you also can have company codes operating in British pounds and Norwegian kroner (the local currencies) assigned to the euro headquarters.

Figure 2.3 shows the delivered currency types in an SAP S/4HANA system. You can access these by choosing **Financial Accounting • Financial Accounting Global Settings • Ledgers • Ledger • Define Settings for Ledgers and Currency Types** in the IMG. The delivered currency types are the same as in SAP ERP, so you are probably already familiar with the concept of the transaction or document currency, the company code currency, the group currency, and country-specifics such as the hard currency or index-based currency.

Note the **New Entries** button in SAP S/4HANA, which allows you to create additional currency types. You might add a new type for the functional currency or a presentation currency as needed and then include it in the ledger settings for the relevant company code. You should create new currency types in the customer namespace (e.g., Y1) and not change the delivered settings. In the **Settings Def. Level** column, note that some of the currency types shown are global and some are company code dependent. This means that you can define company code-specific conversion rates for some currencies as needed.

Also note the **Valuation View** column. We'll return to these settings in more detail in Section 2.3.1, but for now be aware that some currencies are associated with legal valuation for local tax purposes and some with group or profit center valuation to provide a basis for global business management by group or division.

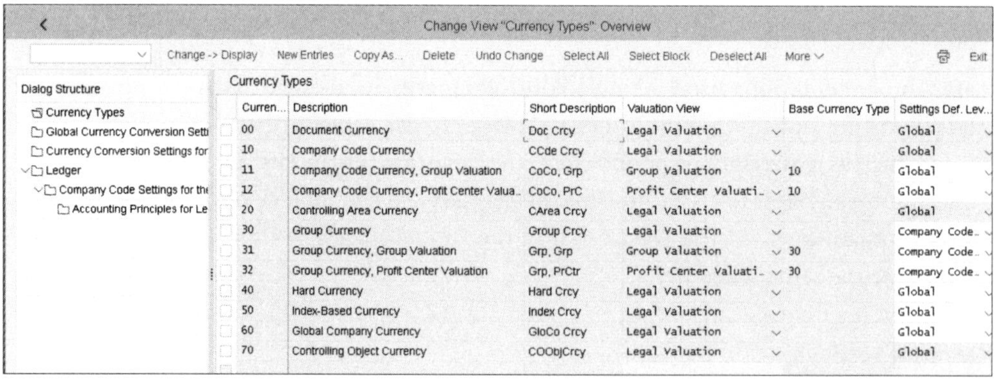

Figure 2.3 Currency Types

In the context of the single controlling area, let's consider your options to set a group currency. If you are headquartered in the United States, the group currency will almost certainly be US dollars, and if you are headquartered in one of the countries in the European Economic and Monetary Union, it will almost certainly be euros. This setting sounds like a no-brainer that can be decided based on the location of your headquarters, but that's not always the case.

The currency challenge is that in SAP ERP, the Financial Accounting (FI) component could handle *three* currencies, so it was possible to set up the group currency as US dollars, set the local currency as the currency required by the individual country, and enter a third currency as the index currency or whatever other country-specific currency requirement prevailed. These same settings could be used for asset accounting and actual costing in the Material Ledger subcomponent. However, the SAP ERP Controlling (CO) component could only handle *two* currencies.

To understand the implications of this requirement, let's look at some specific examples:

- If your organization is a US organization but has a Mexican plant that trades mostly with the United States, then you are required to record all financial transactions in Mexican pesos and in US dollars (the functional currency for the Mexican plant). The CO component can cope with this requirement because you can handle the Mexican pesos as the object currency and the US dollars as the controlling area currency in SAP ERP. When we move to the Universal Journal, the object currency becomes the company code currency (10) and the controlling area currency the global currency (30), and every financial transaction is recorded in these two currencies.

- If your organization is a European organization with the same Mexican plant that trades predominantly with the United States, then you need to accommodate Mexican pesos, US dollars, and euros as the group currency for the headquarters. What often happens in such a scenario is that instead of the global currency being set up to capture euros, the controlling area currency was used to represent the functional currency (US dollars). Such organizations then find themselves with controlling areas that reflect the currency buckets required for their functional currency requirements, have a dozen or so controlling areas in SAP ERP, and only achieve a common currency in their data warehouses and consolidation systems.

With SAP S/4 HANA, the currency settings have been extended such that it is now possible to record each journal entry in up to ten different currencies. These settings were introduced with SAP S/4HANA 1610 and can be accessed by following **Financial Accounting • Financial Accounting Global Settings • Ledgers • Ledger • Define Settings for Ledgers and Currency Types** and then **Ledger • Company Code Settings for the Ledger** in the IMG.

Figure 2.4 shows the new settings. You can see that all journal entries are recorded in the **Local Currency Type** column (currency type **10**) and in the **Global Currency Type** column (currency type **30**) and that additional columns are available for the additional currencies, depending on the company code. This means that you can easily add an index or hard currency that is used only in South America or define a new currency to represent the functional currency that you assign to Mexico (for the purposes of our example). The virtual data model that converts these settings to fill the various financial reports uses the labels *local currency* and *global currency*. The meaning of any additional currencies will depend on your system configuration, so as you add currencies to this view, we recommend establishing rules such that the third currency column is used for the for local legal currency requirements, the fourth for the functional currency, and so on, because there are no dynamic labels for the other currencies in the SAP Fiori reports.

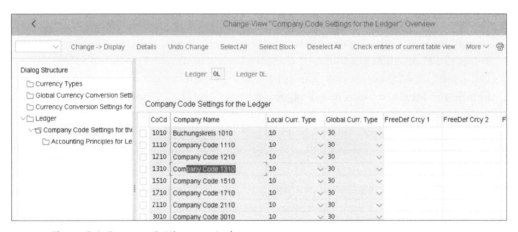

Figure 2.4 Currency Settings per Ledger

Work is now under way in SAP S/4HANA to extend controlling, asset accounting, and the material ledger to handle all the currencies in the ledger settings. To understand what this means, let's consider a simple example in the CO component in SAP ERP.

During one accounting period, a cost center has collected costs in many different transactional currencies because employees have bought goods and incurred travel costs in several different currencies (the **Document Currency** in Figure 2.3). These costs have been converted into the company code currency for the legal entity to which the cost center is assigned at the time of posting and the controlling area currency (which is the same for every cost center taking part in an allocation). Cost allocation is based on the controlling area currency, so cost centers with different local currencies (such as Canadian dollars or British pounds) can receive costs from that cost center, and the ratio of the costs to be shared will be calculated in the group currency and then converted into the local currency. You can also allocate in the local currency, but only if all participating company codes work with the same currency. Any additional currencies defined in Figure 2.4 will be converted only at the time of posting, leading to inaccuracies if there is significant volatility in the exchange rates between the involved currencies.

Chart of Accounts Settings

The next key setting for the controlling area is the *chart of accounts*.

Because many countries and industries have their own requirements for the structure of the chart of accounts, you may find that the entry in your controlling area contains the chart of accounts required for local legal reporting—so a French chart of accounts in France, an Italian chart of accounts in Italy, and so on. This also may be the case if you have multiple industry solutions on the same instance of SAP ERP. In many cases, this approach also has resulted in a proliferation of controlling areas, with the only options to merge the chart of accounts being in the data warehouse and in consolidation.

The preferred option is to have an *operational chart of accounts* that is consistent for all the company codes assigned to the controlling area and then to assign a country chart of accounts at the level of the company code. Figure 2.5 shows the global settings for the company code, with the **YCOA** chart of accounts, which is the same as in the controlling area, and an additional chart of accounts, **YIKR**, which is used only in the German company code.

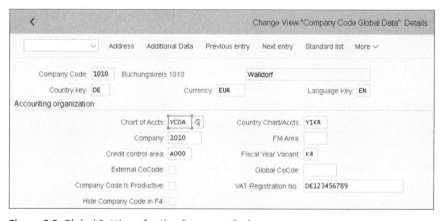

Figure 2.5 Global Settings for the Company Code

The operational accounts don't have to be the same as the group accounts. Figure 2.6 shows the settings for a sample general ledger account and for the assignment to a group account number and, if necessary, to the trading partner for consolidation. You can check these settings by using Transaction FS00 or selecting **Accounting • Financial Accounting • General Ledger • Master Records • G/L Accounts • Individual Processing • Centrally** and entering a general ledger account and a company code.

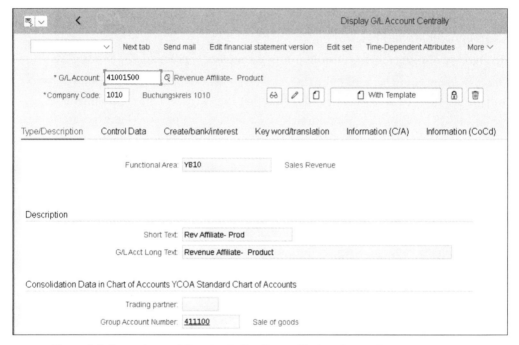

Figure 2.6 Group Account Number in the General Ledger Account

The more elegant way to handle local charts of accounts is not as separate charts of accounts, but as alternative accounts that are mapped to the main accounts, as shown in Figure 2.7, using the **Alternative Account No.** field. To access the company code-specific settings for the general ledger account, choose the **Control Data** tab in Figure 2.6. With the move to SAP S/4HANA, the option of setting up alternative accounts is also available for cost elements.

Remember as you go through the exercise of setting up the chart of accounts that the *financial statement version* controls how the accounts are displayed in the financial accounting reports.

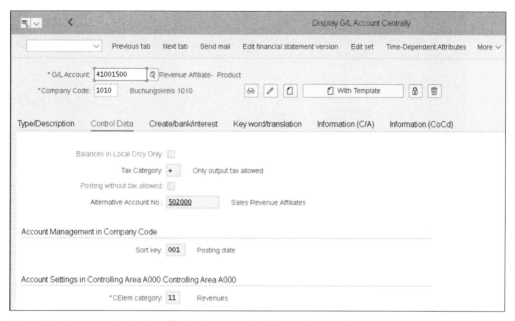

Figure 2.7 Company Code-Specific Settings for the General Ledger Account

Figure 2.8 shows a sample financial statement version that structures the P&L-related accounts for margin reporting. You can continue to have multiple financial statement versions for each of the countries you operate in and a central one for corporate reporting because the financial statement version is a selection parameter in SAP Fiori applications and reports. Check your existing financial statement versions by going to **Financial Accounting • General Ledger Accounting • Master Data • G/L Accounts • Define Financial Statement Versions** or running Transaction FSE2. We'll look at new options for maintaining your financial statement versions when we discuss global accounting hierarchies in Chapter 5.

Although the chart of accounts and accounting principles aren't linked directly, it's worth considering whether you already have a common accounting principle, such as IFRS if you are headquartered in Europe or US-GAAP if you are headquartered in the United States, for all your legal entities. What this means is that every legal entity in your organization will be delivering values according to a common accounting principle in addition to the local requirements of the relevant legal entity. This is one way of ensuring that the values submitted by each legal entity are comparable at the corporate level, and it can greatly speed up the group close.

Figure 2.8 Financial Statement Version

Fiscal Year Variant

Another key setting that can lead to a proliferation of controlling areas is the fiscal year variant.

In SAP ERP, the fiscal year variant controlled the structure of the totals tables and thus the periods available in the FI and CO components. Although the totals tables have vanished in SAP S/4HANA, the fiscal year variant continues to determine the start and finish of the fiscal year and the number of accounting periods and special periods. Many fiscal years run from January to January, but it's also common to have a different starting period in the southern hemisphere, with reporting calendars running from April to April, for example. Some organizations in the manufacturing industry require a completely different periodicity from the calendar, such as 4-4-5 (i.e., quarters comprising two four-week months and one five-week month), and some industries, such as retail, prefer a weekly calendar to a monthly calendar.

In some organizations, the requirements of the headquarters have dominated the design and you'll find everybody working to the same period structure, with any differences being handled in special ledgers or using manual journal entries. In other organizations, you'll find that the number of controlling areas has been driven by the

different reporting calendars and that they have as many controlling areas as they
have fiscal year variants.

2.1.2   The Single Operating Concern

If choices associated with the controlling area represent the biggest challenge in terms
of reporting requirements, the design of the operating concern is often the next biggest. Compared to the use of costing-based CO-PA in SAP ERP, profitability analysis
in the Universal Journal inherits the settings from the controlling area, so you will
have the same currencies, chart of accounts, and so on as for all other controlling
transactions.

In Chapter 1, we looked at how to include the characteristics for account-based profitability analysis as columns in the Universal Journal. Some fields, such as **Material** and
Customer, are always part of the Universal Journal, whereas others are added during
the configuration process to set up the operating concern, along with the derivation
logic to fill these fields. Figure 2.9 shows the characteristics in a sample operating concern and the fields used to derive them. Those beginning with "WW" are specific to
that installation. When you convert to SAP S/4HANA, the system will generate a column in the Universal Journal for each of the characteristics listed here.

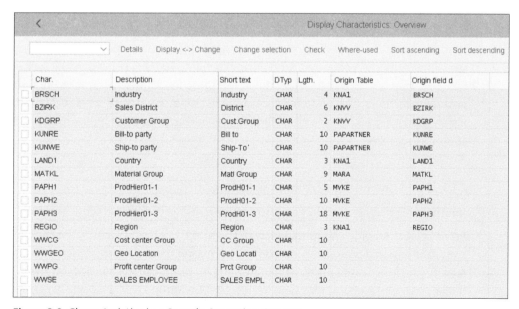

Char.	Description	Short text	DTyp	Lgth.	Origin Table	Origin field d
BRSCH	Industry	Industry	CHAR	4	KNA1	BRSCH
BZIRK	Sales District	District	CHAR	6	KNVV	BZIRK
KDGRP	Customer Group	Cust.Group	CHAR	2	KNVV	KDGRP
KUNRE	Bill-to party	Bill to	CHAR	10	PAPARTNER	KUNRE
KUNWE	Ship-to party	Ship-To'	CHAR	10	PAPARTNER	KUNWE
LAND1	Country	Country	CHAR	3	KNA1	LAND1
MATKL	Material Group	Matl Group	CHAR	9	MARA	MATKL
PAPH1	ProdHier01-1	ProdH01-1	CHAR	5	MVKE	PAPH1
PAPH2	ProdHier01-2	ProdH01-2	CHAR	10	MVKE	PAPH2
PAPH3	ProdHier01-3	ProdH01-3	CHAR	18	MVKE	PAPH3
REGIO	Region	Region	CHAR	3	KNA1	REGIO
WWCG	Cost center Group	CC Group	CHAR	10		
WWGEO	Geo Location	Geo Locati	CHAR	10		
WWPG	Profit center Group	Prct Group	CHAR	10		
WWSE	SALES EMPLOYEE	SALES EMPL	CHAR	10		

Figure 2.9 Characteristics in a Sample Operating Concern

Having several different operating concerns won't stop you from converting to the Universal Journal. However, each journal entry may result in different customer-specific fields being filled in, because only the characteristics available in that operating concern can be filled in. Of course, if you work for an oil company with a retail business supplying various gas stations and a chemical business converting the oil into the products that can be sold at those gas stations, this may not be a problem, because you want to manage those two businesses quite differently. But if you work for a consumer products company that has set up a different operating concern for each region that you operate in, then this may well be a problem: your different operating concerns will effectively stop you from comparing apples to apples in terms of the different characteristics in the various markets. In this context, it's worth looking not just at the characteristics in your existing operating concerns but also at the derivation logic used to fill them to ensure that there are no inconsistencies.

Operating Concerns in SAP S/4HANA Cloud

If you are considering a move to SAP S/4HANA Cloud, bear in mind that only one operating concern is supported and make your design decisions accordingly. Market segment extensibility becomes more critical in the cloud; the first developments became available with SAP S/4HANA Cloud 1805, and enhancements being added in every subsequent edition.

If you have been using costing-based CO-PA until now, it also makes sense to analyze the value fields that you are currently using in your operating concern. We'll look at how to set up key figures for operational reporting in Chapter 6, but take the time now to understand whether you have a common set of key figures for global reporting in place or whether your key figures are currently as heterogeneous as your account structures.

2.1.3   Profit Centers for Divisional Reporting

Another area to look at as you move to SAP S/4HANA is your use of profit centers.

Profit centers provide an internal view of the profit and loss structure; they are derived from the assignments in the controlling master data, as we discussed in Chapter 1. If you've activated document splitting, then profit centers can also give you a management view of your payables, receivables, inventory, and so on. Profit centers can be used to represent divisions within a corporation and to provide a management reporting level above the legal entity, but below the group. When you consolidate, the profit center generally is one of the entities that you will want to include in the consolidation process to look at the flow of values from the profit center to partner profit center.

Ideally, your profit centers will already give you a divisional view of your organization. The default substitution rules essentially give you a product-centric view of your organization. As goods are traded between these divisions, you can use the profit center valuation to apply transfer prices to these flows. We'll return to this topic in Section 2.3.1.

Figure 2.10 shows a sample profit center hierarchy that is largely product-driven with the aim of assigning all costs to each product served. You can check your existing profit center structures using Transaction KCH6N or by going to **Controlling • Profit Center Accounting • Master Data • Standard Hierarchy • Display**.

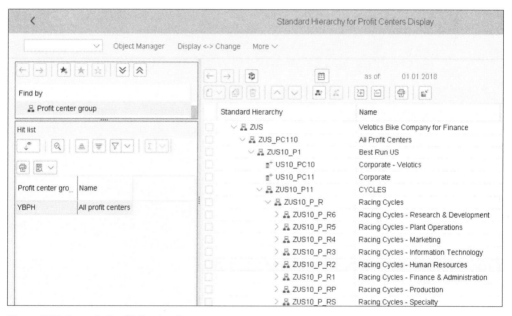

Figure 2.10 Sample Profit Center Groups

Many organizations have made design decisions that have resulted in a proliferation of profit centers. Some have a one-to-one relationship between their cost centers and profit centers, as well as many different profit center groups that try to split your business according to different viewpoints. In the context of the Universal Journal this isn't necessary because having the same cost center and profit center in a single journal entry stands in the way of multidimensional reporting.

Other organizations effectively have used profit centers instead of profitability segments and multiplied combinations of product and market views in their profit center structure. This isn't wrong, necessarily, but having a lot of profit centers generally means that every organizational change will result in the need for new profit centers and a reorganization. By comparison, adding a new product line or region in profitability analysis will not require you to change your operating concern.

Organizational changes can be painful with such profit center designs because profit center structures tend to evolve and change over the years. This can be the result of internal changes, acquisitions, and carve-outs that eliminate existing profit centers.

In this section, we focused on controlling and the preferred structures to support global business management. But every global organization has to handle local legal reporting requirements in accounting; we'll look at handling these differences in the next section.

2.2   Accounting and Local Business Management

Whatever your corporate reporting requirements in SAP S/4HANA, the company code continues to control your *local* reporting requirements, as you saw in Figure 2.5 when we discussed the use of the **Country Chart of Account** field. Note also that the company code is assigned to the country key, a local currency, and the company for consolidation (the trading partner).

In this section, we'll focus on the typical settings that vary locally, looking beyond the local currency and the local chart of accounts to discuss the things that typically vary in each country that you operate in. These include different accounting principles, different currency requirements, and different reporting calendars.

2.2.1   Multiple Accounting Principles

One of the challenges of running a local business is the need to deliver financial statements in accordance with the local accounting principles, alongside your corporate accounting principle. If your headquarters are in the United States, then you will most likely be using US-GAAP for your corporate accounting principle, which means that to compare financial results across entities, you will want *all* company codes to report according to US-GAAP, rather than just the US entities. If your headquarters are in Europe, then your corporate accounting principle is likely to be IFRS.

Because **Ledger** is a key field in the Universal Journal, the preferred way to handle the corporate accounting principle is to set up a ledger for your corporate reporting in SAP S/4HANA and assign all company codes to that ledger. In SAP ERP, this ledger was considered the *leading ledger* (the **Leading** column in Figure 2.11). You can check your ledger settings by choosing **Financial Accounting • Financial Accounting Global Settings • Global Parameters for Company Code • Enter Global Parameters** and then **Ledger** in the IMG.

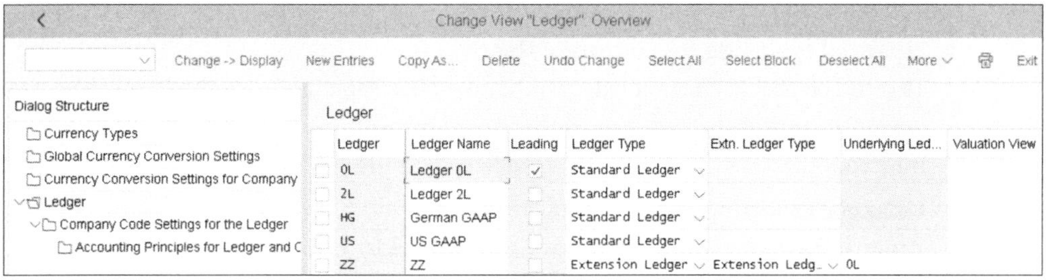

Figure 2.11 Ledger Settings

Then you would set up a second ledger to accommodate those legal entities with additional reporting requirements (e.g., Brazilian GAAP, Russian GAAP, and so on) and assign the relevant company codes to this ledger. You don't need to set up a separate ledger for each noncorporate accounting principle because the valuation takes place for the combination of ledger and company code, so you could record Brazilian GAAP and Russian GAAP in the same ledger, separated by the company codes for Brazil and Russia. Notice in the menu structure in Figure 2.11 that you can assign multiple accounting principles to the same ledger.

The settings for each valuation approach are handled within the various applications, so each country might have different requirements concerning inventory valuation, asset accounting, revenue recognition, and so on. These generally are set up for the combination of company code and accounting principle and then assigned to the ledger. We'll return to the specific settings when we discuss asset accounting in Chapter 10 and inventory accounting in Chapter 11.

Notice also the new **Valuation View** field for the ledger. If you have migrated values in group or profit center valuation to SAP S/4HANA, then all values will be in the same ledger. In a greenfield approach, you can choose to set up separate ledgers for group or profit center valuation.

As you draw up your ledger design, be careful to distinguish the following approaches to financial reporting:

- **Financial reporting according to the group accounting principle**
  This approach covers all company codes and values assets, inventory, revenue, and so on in accordance with one *common* accounting principle, such as IFRS.

- **Financial reporting according to the local accounting principle**
  This approach covers all company codes but values assets, inventory, and so on *differently* depending on the accounting principle used in the relevant legal entity.

- **Financial reporting for corporate steering**
  This can be part of the first ledger or handled in a separate ledger but uses the *group valuation* approach. This means that intercompany profits are eliminated and all intercompany goods movements are based on the costs of goods manufactured.

- **Financial reporting for divisional steering**
  This can be part of the first ledger or handled in a separate ledger but uses the *profit center valuation* approach. This means that profit centers trade with one another using transfer prices.

2.2.2   Multiple Currencies

We discussed the currency requirements for corporate reporting in Section 2.1.1, but we'll return to them here to look at the local requirements.

One leftover from the SAP ERP settings is the notion of the first, second, and third FI currency, as shown in Figure 2.12 (the BSEG currencies). You can access this view by choosing **Company Code Settings in the Ledger** (check the left side of Figure 2.11) and then selecting the line for one ledger/company code combination.

These used to be currencies in table BSEG that were used for open item management and the like. Although it's now compulsory to set the **1st FI Currency** as currency type **10** (**Local Currency**) and the **2nd FI Currency** as currency type **30** (**Group Currency**), you choose what currency is the **3rd FI Currency**. This currency will be used to clear open items alongside the local and group currencies.

The Universal Journal allows you to use up to eight freely defined currencies. The additional currencies shown in Figure 2.4 and Figure 2.12 are currently *reporting currencies* that are derived from either the document currency or the company code currency and can be used to handle requirements such as the need for a functional currency. They can be viewed in all the SAP Fiori apps for finance users. We expect

SAP to extend the use of these currencies to carry them through controlling, asset accounting, and actual costing in a consistent way across SAP S/4HANA.

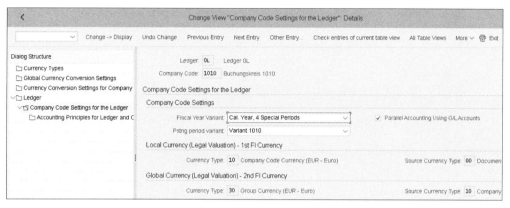

Figure 2.12 Currency Settings for the Ledger and Company Code

Many organizations have been relatively conservative in their use of currencies in their accounting systems—often using only one or two—and have performed all other conversions in their data warehouses. If you are setting up an SAP S/4HANA system from scratch, it therefore makes sense to look at what other currencies are currently being used for group reporting and convert them on the fly in the Universal Journal, rather than waiting for the data load at period close.

New Currencies in SAP S/4HANA

Note that at the time of publication (spring 2019), it's possible to add new currencies to the ledger settings in the general ledger once you have financial data in your system, but not for the subledgers or controlling.

2.2.3   Multiple Reporting Calendars

Figure 2.13 shows sample settings for the periods within a fiscal year running from July to June. You can check whether all your company codes use the same fiscal year variants by choosing **Financial Accounting • Financial Accounting Global Settings • Fiscal Year and Posting Periods • Assign Fiscal Year Variants to Company Code** in the IMG. Then check the individual settings by choosing **Maintain Fiscal Year Variants**. This setting can affect functions in asset accounting, controlling, and actual costing because it means that the period buckets may potentially be different in each company code.

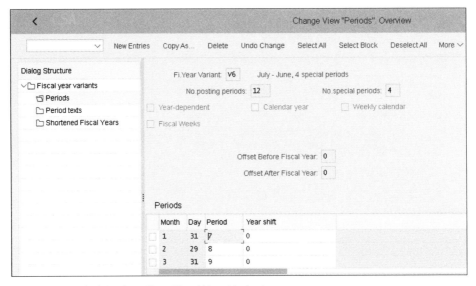

Figure 2.13 Period Settings for a Fiscal Year Variant

In this section we looked at which financial settings can be different for each legal entity in a corporate group. We'll now return to the group view and discuss how to reflect global value chains in reporting.

2.3   Global Value Chains and Local Reporting

In the introduction to this book, we explained how many early SAP implementations were local in their scope rather than global.

If your organization is essentially a holding company, then it can still make perfect sense to run each business locally and then combine financial data in your consolidation system because there's generally a relatively small amount of intercompany business. However, if you have a global supply chain that moves goods around the world and holds them in various distribution centers before final sale, it makes sense to rethink your approach and take a more global view within your operational accounting system. There are many examples in which one affiliated company will trade with another; the chains involved have become ever more complex as tax considerations as much as supply chain logistics have driven the shape of these flows.

As we'll discuss in Section 2.3.1, every legal entity in the supply chain buys and sells from its respective partners, so these intercompany payables and receivables need to be eliminated as part of the consolidation process. The *transfer prices* used to record the sales between affiliated companies are essentially political (i.e., they are set by the organization rather than driven by the external market) and result in profits being recognized in the selling entities in the supply chain rather than only in the entity that makes the final sale to the end customer. These intercompany profits need to be identified and eliminated as part of the consolidation process. Given that the goods do not flow instantaneously through the supply chain, you also will inevitably be holding inventory and in-transit stocks that include the intercompany markup from the selling company, and the intercompany profit needs to be eliminated from these inventories; we'll cover this topic in Section 2.3.2.

Even if you don't have a physical supply chain, you'll often find that company codes are performing services for each other that must be correctly accounted for. We'll look at this process in Chapter 7, in which we'll show some examples of how professional service companies use SAP S/4HANA to improve their internal charging processes for intercompany services.

2.3.1   Group Reporting and Intercompany Transfer Prices

The notion of intercompany transfer prices is hardly new. From the perspective of the selling plant, they are the prices agreed on with the buying plant as if that plant were an external customer. You will often hear this process referred to as *arm's length trading*; in other words, you're trading with the buying plant as if it were an external customer and not simply the next leg in your supply chain. To this extent, the price conditions are just like those that might be used with an external customer, though they are typically based on notions such as resale minus or cost plus. These prices have been coming under more intense scrutiny in recent years following moves by the Organisation for Economic Co-operation and Development (OECD) to bring more transparency into the area of intercompany profits.

The challenge of arm's length trading comes at period close, when the profit that the selling plant realized from these intercompany sales needs to be eliminated from the financial results because from a consolidation perspective that profit can only be recognized when the goods reach their final customer. In addition, any goods held in inventory by the various entities along the supply chain also will be carrying some intercompany profit that must be eliminated.

In the currency type settings shown in Figure 2.11, note the **Valuation View** column alongside the pure currency settings. The valuation view is a different way of looking at the same financial transaction. In the *legal view*, the selling plant recognizes the profit of selling goods to the buying plant as if the buying plant was an external customer. However, in the *group valuation*, the buying plant receives the goods from the selling plant at cost. A special price condition, KW00, is used to carry the costs from the first plant to the second, irrespective of intercompany markups. All transactions offer the ability to switch between the legal view and the group view, though you can use authorizations to restrict who has access to the different views.

Figure 2.14 illustrates the general approach, in which a markup is added as **Company 1** sells to **Company 2** and **Company 2** sells to **Company 3** in the legal view. In the group view, these markups are ignored and we are simply passing the costs of goods manufactured along the value chain. There is also an additional profit center valuation where one division sells to the next at a transfer price.

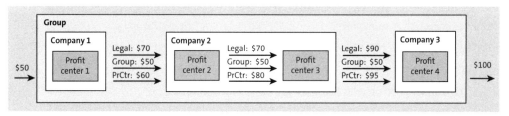

Figure 2.14 Overview of Transfer Pricing

To set up this additional valuation view (or views), you'll need to create a currency and valuation profile and assign it to the controlling area (see Figure 2.2). You can check your existing currency and valuation profiles by choosing **Controlling • General Controlling • Multiple Valuation Approaches/Transfer Prices • Basic Settings • Currency and Valuation Profile** in the IMG (see Figure 2.15). These settings continue to apply up to SAP S/4HANA 1809, but we expect that SAP will offer greater flexibility in this area in the future.

> **Group and Profit Center Valuation in SAP S/4HANA**
>
> The concept of group and profit center valuation is not new, but it was excluded from SAP S/4HANA 1503 and only added in SAP S/4HANA 1605 and 1610.
>
> The functionality hasn't changed, but the difference is that in SAP ERP, the group and profit center valuation are stored in separate versions in CO, whereas thanks to the

marriage of financial accounting and controlling data in the Universal Journal, the values are stored in a ledger. If you migrate from SAP ERP, these values are stored as currency columns in the leading ledger. If you are in a greenfield project, you can choose to keep this approach or to create dedicated ledgers for your group and profit center valuations.

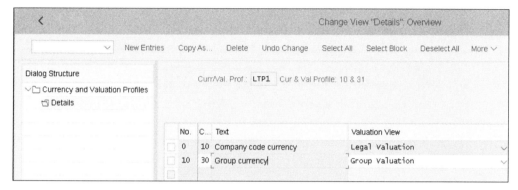

Figure 2.15 Details of Currency and Valuation Profile

You'll then need to extend your pricing schemes in sales and distribution to have them read condition KW00 at group valuation in addition to whatever intercompany prices have already been defined. To check your existing pricing procedures, choose **Sales and Distribution • Basic Functions • Pricing • Pricing Control • Define and Assign Pricing Procedures** and select a pricing procedure in the IMG. Figure 2.16 shows the entries in a sample pricing procedure, in which you can see condition type **IV01** for the **Intercompany Price** (the transfer price), condition type **KW00** for the **Group Valuation**, and condition type **PC00** for the **Profit Center Valuation**.

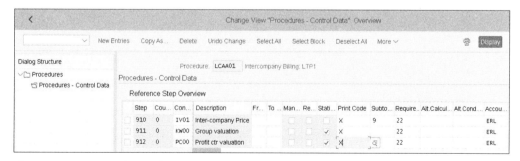

Figure 2.16 Price Conditions for Intercompany Billing

The price conditions used in the group valuation access a standard cost estimate for each of the goods moved through the supply chain. Effectively, this means that you will need two standard cost estimates for each traded item. To display the standard cost estimate, use Transaction CK13N or **Controlling • Product Cost Controlling • Product Cost Planning • Material Costing • Cost Estimate with Quantity Structure • Display** and enter a material, a plant, and a costing variant.

The first cost estimate (shown in Figure 2.17) records the material simply as a purchased good from the selling plant (or trading partner). If you look at the **Costing Structure** pane on the left side, you'll see only that the sample pot has been purchased from the selling plant (i.e., the vendor). The only hint that you're dealing with an intercompany transaction comes in the entries under **Special Procurement Data** on the **Qty. Structure** tab, where you can see that the goods are to be procured from a plant belonging to an affiliated company rather than from an external vendor. If you checked the valuation strategy, you'd find that an external price had been read for this material as if it were a raw material.

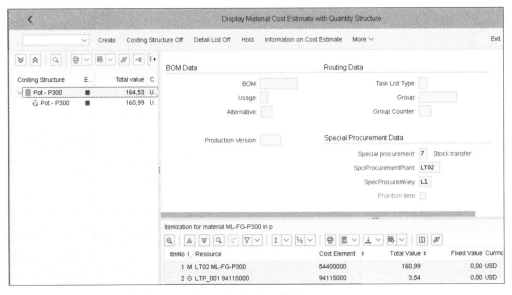

Figure 2.17 Standard Cost Estimate in the Legal View

Figure 2.18 shows the cost estimate for the same product in the group view. In this case, you need to choose a costing variant that supports group valuation. Now the

Costing Structure pane shows the entire bill of material (BOM) for one legal entity (**LT02**) and provides full transparency into the costs across the supply chain. Again, the cost estimate uses the *special procurement key* in each material master to establish the bridges that link the plants and, consequently, the legal entities in the supply chain. We noted that the settings for special procurement were the same in Figure 2.17. What has happened is that a *reference variant* was used to ensure that the BOM for the quantity structure was not exploded twice but instead simply links to the same itemization of costing items that was used to set the standard costs in the legal view. This time, the valuation strategy for the material item has been ignored and the costs of goods manufactured have been rolled up from the previous plants.

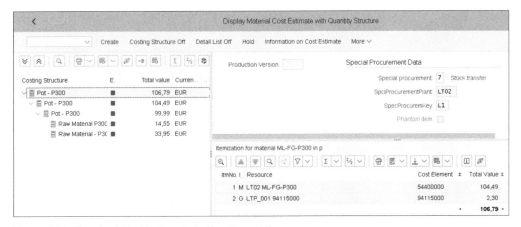

Figure 2.18 Standard Cost Estimate in the Group View

The other difference between the group and the legal view is that the cost component split shown in Figure 2.19 provides complete transparency into the cost structure across the whole supply chain. To access this view, choose the **Costs** tab and switch from the itemization to the cost component view. The raw material and conversion costs for the plant in India are effectively being rolled up and shown in the EU and US plants that consumed the material prior to sale.

If you perform actual costing, you'll see the same double view in **Material Price Analysis**. You can display this using Transaction CKM3N or by following the menu path **Controlling • Product Cost Controlling • Actual Costing/Material Ledger • Material Ledger • Material Price Analysis**.

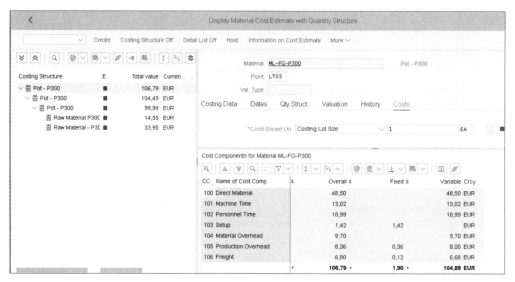

Figure 2.19 Cost Components in Group View

Figure 2.20 shows the legal view, in which the purchase of the pots again is simply treated as material usage with all the associated costs and shown in the **Direct Material** column. To the right, an additional column for intercompany profit (**I/C Profit**) captures the difference between the inventory values on the sender side and the receiver side. As the goods move from the first legal entity to the second legal entity in the supply chain, the intercompany profit between buyer and seller is recorded in this special cost component.

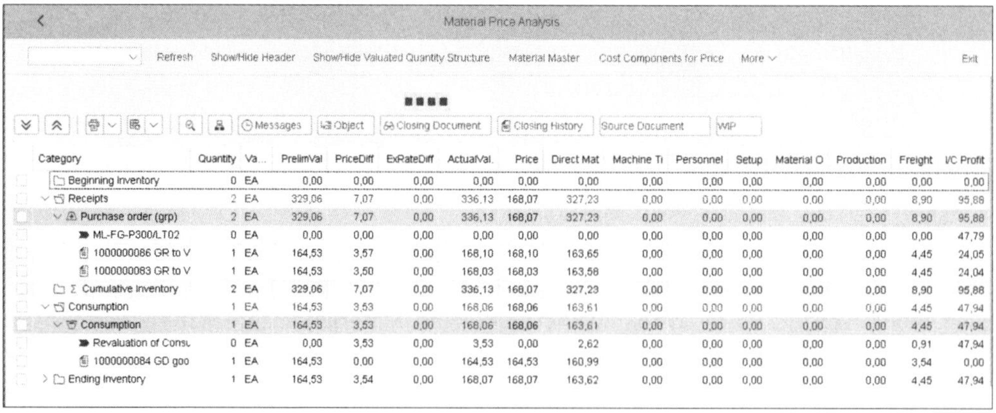

Figure 2.20 Legal View for Actual Costing

If you now look at the same transaction flows from a group perspective (see Figure 2.21), you can see that the **I/C Profit** column is empty. The **Direct Material** costs have now been split into the actual cost components so that you see the cumulated cost components for the whole supply chain, with separate figures for **Direct Material** (now containing only the costs for the original purchased components), **Machine**, **Personnel**, **Setup**, **Material Overhead**, and **Production Overhead**.

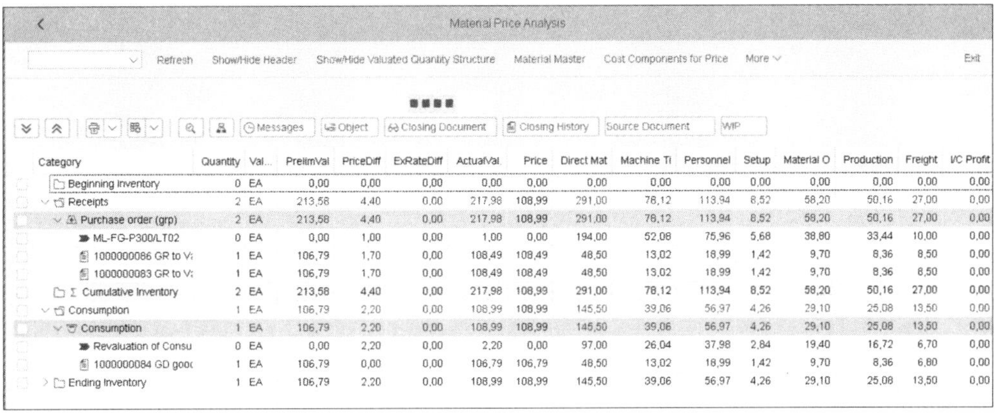

Category	Quantity	Val..	PrelimVal	PriceDiff	ExRateDiff	ActualVal	Price	Direct Mat.	Machine Ti	Personnel	Setup	Material O	Production	Freight	I/C Profit
Beginning Inventory	0	EA	0,00	0,00	0,00	0,00	0,00	0,00	0,00	0,00	0,00	0,00	0,00	0,00	0,00
Receipts	2	EA	213,58	4,40	0,00	217,98	108,99	291,00	78,12	113,94	8,52	58,20	50,16	27,00	0,00
Purchase order (grp)	2	EA	213,58	4,40	0,00	217,98	108,99	291,00	78,12	113,94	8,52	58,20	50,16	27,00	0,00
ML-FG-P300/LT02	0	EA	0,00	1,00	0,00	1,00	0,00	194,00	52,08	75,96	5,68	38,80	33,44	10,00	0,00
1000000086 GR to V:	1	EA	106,79	1,70	0,00	108,49	108,49	48,50	13,02	18,99	1,42	9,70	8,36	8,50	0,00
1000000083 GR to V:	1	EA	106,79	1,70	0,00	108,49	108,49	48,50	13,02	18,99	1,42	9,70	8,36	8,50	0,00
∑ Cumulative Inventory	2	EA	213,58	4,40	0,00	217,98	108,99	291,00	78,12	113,94	8,52	58,20	50,16	27,00	0,00
Consumption	1	EA	106,79	2,20	0,00	108,99	108,99	145,50	39,06	56,97	4,26	29,10	25,08	13,50	0,00
Consumption	1	EA	106,79	2,20	0,00	108,99	108,99	145,50	39,06	56,97	4,26	29,10	25,08	13,50	0,00
Revaluation of Consu	0	EA	0,00	2,20	0,00	2,20	0,00	97,00	26,04	37,98	2,84	19,40	16,72	6,70	0,00
1000000084 GD goo(	1	EA	106,79	0,00	0,00	106,79	106,79	48,50	13,02	18,99	1,42	9,70	8,36	6,80	0,00
Ending Inventory	1	EA	106,79	2,20	0,00	108,99	108,99	145,50	39,06	56,97	4,26	29,10	25,08	13,50	0,00

Figure 2.21 Group Valuation for Actual Costing

The columns in Figure 2.20 and Figure 2.21 are defined in the **Cost Component Structure**, the details of which are shown in Figure 2.22. This cost component differs from the usual cost components in that there are no cost elements assigned. It's used quite simply to record the difference between (a) the costs coming from below in the costing structure for the standard costs and the transfer price and (b) the actual costs from the sender and the transfer price for the receiver in actual costing. To check whether your organization has created an intercompany profit cost component (the **Company Code** flag in **Delta Profit for Group Costing**), choose **Controlling • Product Cost Controlling • Product Cost Planning • Basic Settings for Material Costing • Define Cost Component Structure**, select a cost component structure, then select the details of an individual cost component in the IMG.

Adding New Valuation Views in SAP S/4HANA

It's possible to migrate financial data from multiple valuation views to SAP S/4HANA and to configure a new system to accommodate several valuation views. However, it isn't possible to add an additional valuation view to an existing SAP S/4HANA system at the time of publication (spring 2019).

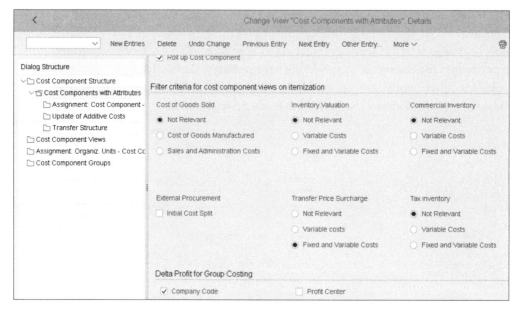

Figure 2.22 Details of Cost Component for Intercompany Profit

If your divisions also operate at an arm's length, it's also possible to set up a third valuation view that handles the pricing of goods sold between profit centers, as shown in Figure 2.14. You'll need to set up these transfer prices manually, so not all organizations choose to use this view. However, those that do effectively add an additional dimension to their global reporting. Plans are afoot to provide additional options for a group view of divisions and business units that will eliminate intercompany profit within the relevant divisions and business units.

2.3.2   Keeping Track of Stock in Transit

One of the challenges of group reporting with a physical supply chain is that at any time there will be many thousands of dollars' worth of goods moving between legal entities, or *in transit*.

Until Enhancement Package 5 of SAP ERP, such goods were not valuated as inventory, and most organizations had a manual process in place to create accrual postings for the goods on planes, boats, and trucks between their various plants. In SAP S/4HANA, business function `LOG_MM_SIT` allows organizations to treat those goods as a special stock type for in-transit stock and value them as they move about the world.

Figure 2.23 shows the material price analysis for an intercompany stock transfer, with the special stock type `T` for goods in transit. Once the business function is active, you can set up movement types that determine which entity owns the goods in transit and when the transfer of ownership takes place. From a financial perspective, what's important is that the stock in transit no longer vanishes in accounting terms but is visible in material price analysis and in logistics by using Transaction MB5T or **Logistics • Materials Management • Inventory Management • Environment • Stock • Stock in Transit** and selecting special stock type **T**.

Category	Quantity	ValQtyUnit	PrelimVal	PriceDiff	ExRateDiff	ActualVal.	Price	Direct Mat	Machine Ti	Personnel
☐ Beginning Inventory	0	EA	0,00	0,00	0,00	0,00	0,00	0,00	0,00	0,00
☐ > ☐ Receipts	20	EA	135.607,20	0,00	0,00	135.607,20	6.780,36	65.400,00	17.799,60	25.961,00
☐ ☐ Σ Cumulative Inventory	20	EA	135.607,20	0,00	0,00	135.607,20	6.780,36	65.400,00	17.799,60	25.961,00
☐ ∨ ☐ Consumption	3	EA	20.341,08	0,00	0,00	20.341,08	6.780,36	9.810,00	2.669,94	3.894,15
☐ ∨ ☐ Purchase order (grp)	3	EA	20.341,08	0,00	0,00	20.341,08	6.780,36	9.810,00	2.669,94	3.894,15
☐ ∨ ☐ ML-FG-P300 LT02	3	EA	20.341,08	0,00	0,00	20.341,08	6.780,36	9.810,00	2.669,94	3.894,15
☐ ≫ Revaluation of Consumption	0	EA	0,00	0,00	0,00	0,00	0,00	9.810,00	2.669,94	3.894,15
☐ ≫ ML-FG-P300/LT02	0	EA	0,00	0,00	0,00	0,00	0,00	0,00	0,00	0,00
☐ ☐ 1000000087 TF to Rec. Val. CST 4500014338/10	1	EA	6.780,36	0,00	0,00	6.780,36	6.780,36	0,00	0,00	0,00
☐ ☐ 1000000085 TF to Rec. Val. CST 4500014172/10	1	EA	6.780,36	0,00	0,00	6.780,36	6.780,36	0,00	0,00	0,00
☐ ☐ 1000000082 TF to Rec. Val. CST 4500013808/10	1	EA	6.780,36	0,00	0,00	6.780,36	6.780,36	0,00	0,00	0,00
☐ > ☐ Ending Inventory	17	EA	115.266,12	0,00	0,00	115.266,12	6.780,36	55.590,00	15.129,66	22.066,85

Figure 2.23 Transfer Posting to Stock in Transit in Material Price Analysis

Stock in transit also can be used in the context of revenue recognition to delay the recognition of revenue until proof of delivery has been received from the final customer.

2.4   Summary

This chapter explained how SAP S/4HANA is evolving to meet organizations' corporate reporting needs alongside their local reporting needs. We introduced the key settings that will help you to achieve a global view from within your accounting system.

In the next chapter, we'll look at how operational requirements are changing as organizations move from being product-driven to being service-driven. We'll look at the details of the consolidation process when we explore group reporting in Chapter 12.

Chapter 3

From Products to Services: Unifying Approaches to Controlling and Financial Operations

Approaches to financial accounting generally are similar across industries, but approaches to controlling and financial operations are almost inevitably different depending on the type of products sold and customers served. In this chapter, we'll look at the availability of the various industry solutions with SAP S/4HANA and the impact of industry shifts on accounting requirements.

When we told the story of SAP's first customer in the introduction to this book, it was a tale of a product-related industry: the company manufactured nylon, which other companies would buy to turn into clothing and other products for the consumer market. For this early customer, controlling was all about optimizing the resources used to manufacture the nylon, and financial operations were about collecting receivables from the companies that bought the nylon.

With the introduction of the industry solutions in SAP R/3 and SAP ERP, the first distinction was between product-related industries (e.g., chemicals, mill products, automotive, and consumer products) and service industries (e.g., banking, financial services, insurance, professional services, and so on). The first group is generally asset-heavy with large capital investments in production facilities, whereas the second is more people-focused.

Of course, it was never quite so black and white. A company selling industrial machinery generally also provides technical support for this machinery, and a company selling tractors might also offer banking services to allow farmers to finance their purchases. However, it was not uncommon to have each of the industry solutions running on separate ERP instances, to separate, for example, the manufacturing activities from the retail side of the business.

Twenty years after the introduction of separate industry solutions, we find that the traditional borders between industries are blurring even further. Although you can still buy a tractor, it's becoming increasingly common to lease the vehicle or even buy the right to use it when you need it. This new business model affects the requirements for controlling: you're still calculating the production costs for the tractor as before, but need a completely different way of handling the service rights and the invoicing of those services.

This chapter explains that these shifts change the way organizations calculate profitability and manage billing in SAP S/4HANA. We'll begin by looking at the various industry solutions available in SAP S/4HANA in Section 3.1. We'll then examine their corresponding controlling requirements in Section 3.2. Finally, we'll look at the changing face of financial operations in Section 3.3.

3.1   Industry Solutions and SAP S/4HANA

From a development point of view, some of the very early industry solutions, such as chemicals, are at the core of SAP R/3, SAP ERP, and SAP S/4HANA, so you'll find all the relevant functions in the menus and IMG whether you use them or not. Others—such as public sector, utilities, retail, or banking—are only available if the relevant industry switch is activated. This means that you will only see the menus and IMG sections designed for the retail industry solution, for example, if the retail switch is active.

As you consider a move to SAP S/4HANA, it makes sense to check the simplification list to see when your industry solution was released for SAP S/4HANA and whether there are any limitations or features that are no longer supported.

Starting with version 1511, the on-premise edition of SAP S/4HANA supports the following industries:

- Aerospace and defense (A&D)
- Automotive
- Banking
- Chemicals
- Consumer products
- Contract accounts receivable and payable (FI-CA)
- Engineering, construction, and operations (EC&O)
- High-tech
- Industrial machinery and components (IM&C)
- Insurance
- Life sciences

- Mill products
- Mining
- Professional services
- Public sector
- Sports and entertainment
- Telecommunication

- Transportation and logistics
- Utilities
- Wholesale
- Higher education and research (as of FPS 01)
- Defense and security (as of FPS 01)

Industry-specific functionality was added for the following industries in SAP S/4HANA 1610:

- Catchweight management
- Oil and gas
- Retail

Industry-specific functionality for media became available in SAP S/4HANA 1709.

New Industry Functionality

Go-to-market activities continue to take place by industry, and the easiest way to check for changes is to visit the SAP Innovation Discovery website (*https://go.support.sap.com/innovationdiscovery/#/innovations*) and search by industry to find out about the latest innovations, as shown in Figure 3.1.

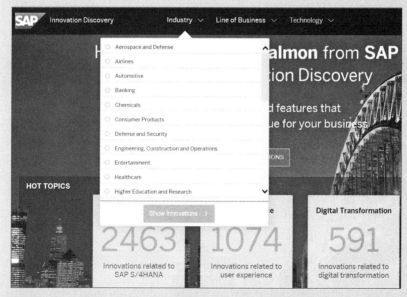

Figure 3.1 Innovation Discovery and Industry Assignment

For example, Figure 3.2 shows the first two innovations delivered for the chemicals industry: an SAP Fiori app for managing risk assessments, and the simplified management of enterprise asset management functions.

Figure 3.2 Innovations in the Chemicals Industry (Selection)

One of the key principles driving development of SAP S/4HANA is the notion of *industry to core*, which means that functions that were previously only available for one or two industries become available for everyone.

A prominent example is the use of the **Material Number** field, which was originally available only for the automotive and mill product industries. With SAP S/4HANA 1511, the digit limits for material numbers increased from eighteen to forty and became available for all industries; conversion takes place automatically when you convert to SAP S/4HANA. To find out more about the technical impact of this change, refer to SAP Note 2267140 (S4TWL: Material Number Field Length Extension).

Another example is the **Amount** field length extension to support twenty-three digits beginning in SAP S/4HANA 1809. This feature was originally available only for banking but is now available for all industries that choose to activate it by going to **Cross-Application Components • General Application Functions • Field Length Extension • Activate Extended Fields** in the IMG. To find out more about the technical impact of this change, refer to SAP Note 2628654 (S4TWL: Amount Field Length Extension).

3.2   Controlling

We'll look at controlling first in the product-related industries, then in the service-related industries, and then at the impact on controlling when the two approaches merge. We'll discuss the changes to the customer/vendor master data and the changing requirements in financial operations as industries merge.

3.2.1   Product-Related Industries

To get a feel for the controlling functions in a product-related industry, we'll start by looking at the SAP Fiori launchpads that present applications to end users in SAP S/4HANA. SAP delivers two roles containing the SAP Fiori applications for the product-related industries:

- Inventory accountant
- Production accountant

The SAP Fiori launchpad for the inventory accountant is shown in Figure 3.3. The tiles provide access to all tasks associated with setting the standard costs for the material, along with the balance sheet valuations to be performed at period close. We'll look at details of these applications in Chapter 11. Notice that we're still using a cost estimate to set the standard costs and costing runs to calculate both standard costs and actual costs (if used). The contents of these tiles will look very familiar to users of SAP ERP.

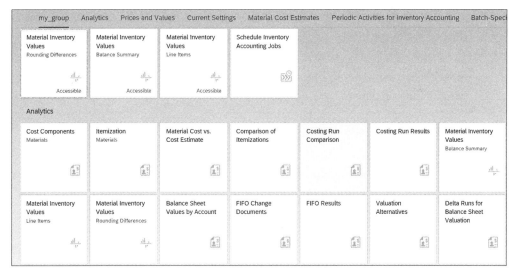

Figure 3.3 SAP Fiori Launchpad for an Inventory Accountant

The SAP Fiori launchpad for the production accountant is shown in Figure 3.4. These tiles provide access to all tasks associated with monitoring production costs and variances. Again, we'll come back to these apps in Chapter 11, but notice for the moment that the focus is largely on calculating and explaining production variances in a given plant. The controlling focus is very local.

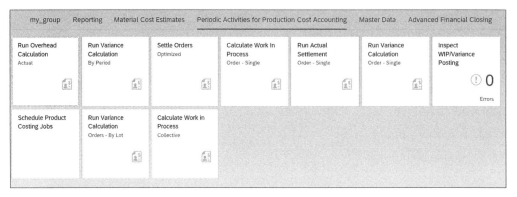

Figure 3.4 SAP Fiori Launchpad for a Production Accountant

One trend in manufacturing in recent years has been the move toward a lot size of one, whether for customized running shoes or furniture made on demand. The idea is that instead of the company amassing large amounts of inventory by trying to anticipate customer demand, manufacturing only begins when the customer places an order, usually by choosing from a range of options in a configurable BOM to shape the product to his needs.

From a manufacturing point of view, this sales order may be fulfilled as assemble-to-order using components held in stock, or it might involve purchasing individual components on demand and completing as make-to-order. This trend predates SAP S/4HANA, but it typically changes the pattern of production orders, resulting in more orders for smaller lot sizes.

In traditional make-to-stock industries, the combination of the revenue, sales quantity, standard COGS, and any production variances can be analyzed in apps such as the Product Profitability app (SAP Fiori ID F2765), shown in Figure 3.5. In the same column, you'll also notice key figures for allocated costs (**Admin Overhead**, **Sales Overhead**, **Marketing Overhead**, and **R&D Overhead**) in this view. In this example, these key figures are based on classic allocations at period close, but in Chapter 7 we'll look at new options that can allow you to derive these key figures immediately as other costs are posted.

Let's consider the simple example of a bicycle business, shown in Figure 3.5. Many organizations find that they have a gap between the product profitability for manufacturing the bicycle and any service activities related to the bicycle once it has been sold. These service activities may be performed in SAP ERP if the organization is using customer service orders. If your organization is using a CRM system, these service activities may be triggered externally, resulting in a break in the integration chain that makes it hard to paint a complete picture of the profit earned by selling and then repairing bicycles, unless you use a data warehouse to combine the costs of the production activities with the costs of the service activities; even then, there is the challenge of using the warranty arrangement to identify the customer and link the consumer purchase with the sale to the stores in which the goods were bought.

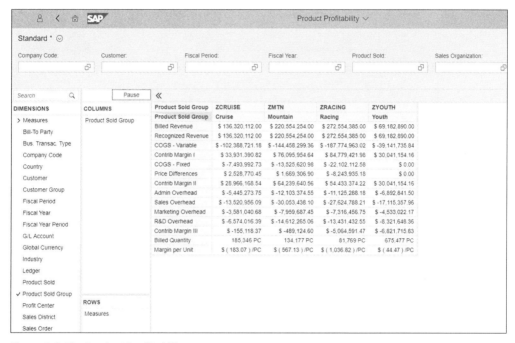

Figure 3.5 The Product Profitability App

Before we take this example further, let's look at controlling in service-related industries.

3.2.2   Service-Related Industries

We'll start by looking at changes in profitability analysis for the service industry and explain what changes when we focus on the sale of services rather than the sale of tangible goods.

Figure 3.6 shows the SAP Fiori launchpad for the sales accountant, which includes tiles for the analysis of the various market segments, as well as the analysis of revenue, costs, and work in process by project. What we see here is a move from the product profitability analysis approach that we looked at in Figure 3.5 to the monitoring of activities associated with delivering a commercial project and the valuation of these services along with their impact on work in process and accrued revenue. Profitability analysis is going deeper into the service activities associated with delivering a commercial project.

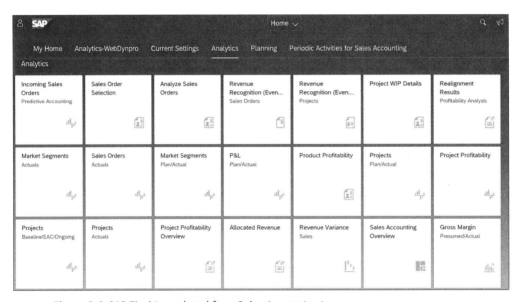

Figure 3.6 SAP Fiori Launchpad for a Sales Accountant

Figure 3.7 shows the Project Profitability app (SAP Fiori ID F2764), which shows the combined view of the project, the product sold, and the associated key figures, as well as drilldowns to associated material groups, customers, and so on. We'll look at how the key figures for recognized revenue and the like are calculated in more detail in Chapter 7, but you can already see that there is a fundamental change in the approach to profitability from Figure 3.5; we're moving from a more detailed breakdown of the P&L statement to one that includes work in process (a balance sheet key figure). We'll explain the implications of this shift in more detail in Chapter 6.

Although the use of profitability analysis is well established in the product-related industries, some industries did not use CO-PA in SAP ERP. In the retail sector, CO-PA implementations were unusual because of the huge number of different product variants being sold; in the financial services and banking industry, it was unusual because of the huge number of different retail customers (consumers) and the many different financial products that they purchased.

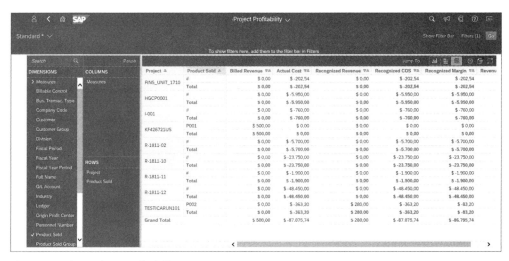

Figure 3.7 The Project Profitability App

When SAP customers consider the promise of big data and SAP HANA, they often ask us how granular profitability analysis can become in SAP S/4HANA. Figure 3.8 shows a high-level overview for a financial service organization, for which SAP S/4HANA handles the general ledger, accounts payable, accounts receivable, fixed assets, and project accounting (on the right), but separate industry-specific applications are used for accounting for financial instruments and profitability management (on the left).

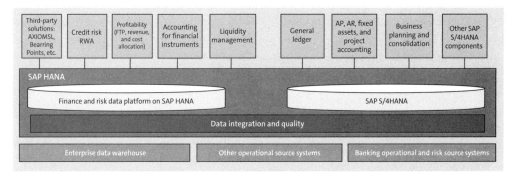

Figure 3.8 Finance and Risk Architecture

This doesn't mean that in these industries there can be no profitability analysis in SAP S/4HANA, but rather that it may be at a higher granularity simply because of the sheer volume of data involved. We'll discuss other options for the assignment of costs to profitability segments in these industries in Chapter 15.

Twenty years ago, when SAP introduced most of the industry solutions, it was assumed that most companies could be slotted neatly into one industry. As it turns out, that was already unfeasible even then and is becoming increasingly unusual now as new business models force organizations to adopt different approaches. So let's look at what happens when product-focused companies start to offer services as well. This combination is important not just from a controlling perspective but also because it has implications for IFRS 15 (which covers revenue from contracts).

3.2.3   Products and Services

Returning to the bicycle example in Section 3.2.1, let's imagine what happens if the bicycle is sold to a wholesaler and then to the end consumer.

In terms of accounts receivable and collections management, the customer is the wholesaler who bought the bicycle for resale, but often the organization will want to understand if additional revenue is earned on that bicycle from service activities for the end customer. One action that can reestablish the connection to the original bicycle is the customer signing a warranty agreement once he takes delivery of the bicycle. This has revenue implications under IFRS 15 because the value of the contract must be recognized in its entirety, and we now have a performance obligation on the selling organization for the subsequent provision of the service. Perhaps the first service activities are performed while the bicycle is under warranty; in this case, the costs and revenues for these activities would be included in the lifecycle costs for the bicycle. Often these won't be pure service activities but a mixture of spare parts (which may have been manufactured by the company offering the service) and service. Later service activities may be performed once the bicycle is out of warranty and thus in a different phase of its lifecycle.

Of course, these product-plus-service agreements are not limited to this example. Probably the best example of this kind of agreement are those offered by cell phone companies, from which a consumer buys a smartphone and the right to use a telephone network. From an accounting point of view, the whole contract (smartphone and network usage) must be considered; the organization's first performance obligation begins when the customer activates the phone on purchase. (On this note, be aware that revenue recognition from the SAP ERP Sales and Distribution component is no longer supported in SAP S/4HANA and that you will be obliged to use the SAP Revenue Accounting and Reporting [RAR] add-on.)

In our example, the bicycle is owned by the end customer, as is the case with many consumer goods (e.g., larger items like household appliances that are somewhat expensive but, unlike items such as cars, don't usually justify a capital investment) and similar products. With other products, we already observe customers changing their purchasing behavior to enter into a leasing agreement or a pure service agreement to use rather than own the product. We see this for trucks, tractors, and so on, where the capital investment is significant, but we also see these changes in the household sphere. Where once customers would buy tools to perform work in the house, it's now common to lease such tools for the weekend and return them when the job is complete.

In these cases, we'll see traditional product costing approaches such as we saw in Section 3.2.1 being used during the manufacture of the tools, but we need a totally different controlling approach later because the tools are not sold once to the hardware store but managed as a service to end consumers. In accounting terms, the tools will generally be managed as *assets* that are used by the consumer for a fee. There is nothing fundamentally new in this approach; telephone companies and utilities have been setting up infrastructure and charging customers for the use of this infrastructure for years. This shift often will bring a change in billing and payment behaviors, necessitating a move from classic accounts receivable, in which billing is triggered on delivery of the goods to the wholesaler, to contract accounting, which is more traditionally used by utilities and telecommunications companies that establish a contract with their customers, bill them for services used, and handle payments from millions of customers.

Fleet management provided by the company that originally built a car, truck, aircraft, ship, or railcar takes the idea further. Manufacturing is performed as before, but the object to be managed becomes an asset. You might think that this process is covered by enterprise asset management, but Controlling comes into play here to manage fuel costs, work by technicians, the proper handling of maintenance schedules, and so on, to ensure that costs are properly handled.

Another example of this shift comes with the provision of fertilizer as a service. Twenty years ago, a company making fertilizer would be considered a classic chemicals customer that produces bags of fertilizer, sells them via a wholesaler, and has almost no direct contact with the farmers and their fields. Now we find the same organization still making fertilizer but selling directly to farmers. This isn't merely a question of cutting out the wholesaler in the middle, but of offering service arrangements to analyze the fields the farmer manages, calculate the fertilizer requirements for each field and when the fertilizer must be made available for each crop, and then help the farmer apply the fertilizer to his fields. Again, the farmer enters into a contract with the fertilizer company and is billed for the services used (i.e., the delivery of the fertilizer at the appropriate time). In some cases, the services will go beyond simply providing fertilizer and will include the right to use machinery to spread the fertilizer on the fields.

This story illustrates the change in data volumes between the classic chemicals company using SAP ERP to the new fertilizer-as-a-service approach, in which each farmer is a customer with his own contract to be managed in SAP S/4HANA. The organization must focus on managing that contract properly and understanding the services used and the costs to provide them. New trigger data comes into play here. Perhaps sensors are being used to capture the fertilizer needed on each field and to monitor how many units of fertilizer have been delivered, for example. This sensor information is used as a basis for billing the customer, just like the usage-based billing that we might normally expect in the media industry.

With both the bicycle and the fertilizer, we still have the notion of the manufactured product and the service offering being something separate, but today we also find services being embedded into products. One example is in the automotive industry. The cost estimate for the physical components is created as before by looking at the BOM and the routing. But many cars nowadays include digital services, ranging from navigation apps to rescue services and more. The cost of developing such applications may be compared to the project-related costs of any investment project, as a combination of development effort and the purchasing of external services and the like. However, the app goes into the car not as a physical component, but as a right to call a rescue service and incur the associated costs; suddenly we have a situation that is more like claims management in the insurance industry. Many drivers will never need to be rescued, but a few will. The fact that a rescue service is included in the service BOM gives no indication of how often that service will be called. Of course, we can look at the costs of individual rescue operations, but these will give little indication of how often a service will be required in the future. For this, we need to employ the statistical models common in the insurance industry.

If controlling always has an industry flavor, so too do billing and payments, depending on whether we are in the business-to-business (B2B) or business-to-consumer (B2C) world. We'll look at the differences in financial operations in the next section.

3.3 Financial Operations

Let's return to the story of SAP's first customer, the nylon factory. Its initial focus was on purchasing, accounts payable, and accounts receivable, and sales and distribution was only introduced later. Nowadays, organizations that sell directly to end consumers find themselves dealing not just with external customers, but also with affiliated customers within their own group and with private persons. This has implications not just on their controlling processes, but also on their billing and payment processes. It also necessitates a change from the simple idea of a customer to a multi-faceted view of a business partner.

Let's start by looking at the compulsory shift to the use of the business partner rather than separate vendors and customers in SAP S/4HANA. We'll then look at what has changed in receivables management and contract accounting with SAP S/4HANA.

3.3.1 Customer/Vendor Integration

One of the key changes in SAP S/4HANA is the compulsory use of the *business partner* as the single master data entry point for all customers and suppliers/vendors. The process of harmonizing the customer and vendor data is known as *customer/vendor integration* (CVI), because this component ensures the synchronization between the business partner and the associated customers and vendors.

For many organizations, the idea of a business partner will not be new: it's already used in SAP Customer Relationship Management, SAP Supplier Relationship Management, and SAP Global Trade Services; in treasury and collections management applications in SAP ERP; and in industry solutions that use contract accounting. However, recall the master data for vendors and customers in SAP R/3 and SAP ERP, in which there were many separate transactions:

- Transaction FD01-03 was used to manage customers in accounts receivable.
- Transaction XD01-03 was used to manage customers from a sales perspective.
- Transaction VD01-03 was used to manage customers in sales for which there was no link to finance.
- Transaction FK01-03 was used to manage vendors in accounts payable.
- Transaction XK01-03 was used to manage vendors from a purchasing perspective.
- Transaction MK01-03 was used to manage vendors in purchasing for which there was no link to finance.

These transactions merged in SAP S/4HANA 1511 to be handled in a single transaction: Transaction BP. The old transactions are still in the menus, but if you select, say, Transaction FD03 (the old transaction to display customer master data), you'll be redirected to Transaction BP, as shown in Figure 3.9.

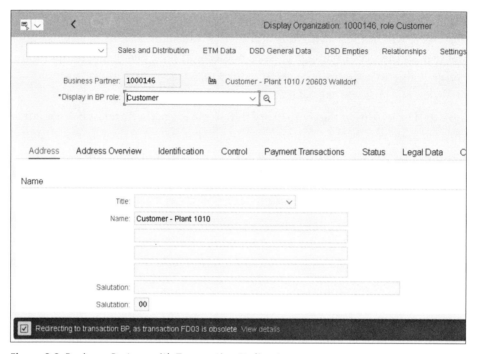

Figure 3.9 Business Partner with Transaction Redirect

The guiding principle behind the change is the *principle of one*. There should be only one way to perform certain tasks, not several. By comparison, in SAP ERP the treasury application works with the central business partner, but whenever a posting is made to the Financial Accounting component, then only the reconciliation account entered in the customer or vendor master is updated. The new architecture behind the business partner is tidier, with the shared data stored in one place.

One of the reasons for the change is that the old customer/vendor master records in SAP ERP had limitations that would periodically cause problems in the modern world, such as the following:

- Only supporting one address
- No relationship between customer and vendor in the same real-world entity
- No time dependency

By contrast, in the new business partner model, new capabilities arise:

- General data is shared across the different roles.
- One business partner can perform multiple roles, acting as both a customer and a vendor (supplier).
- One business partner can have multiple addresses.
- Time-dependency is supported for object attributes and relationships, so an organization or person might begin as a prospect and evolve into a customer.

Behind the scenes, the separate master data tables continue to exist; the business partner transaction simply provides a shell offering a unified view of the customer and vendor master data. The separate views represent using roles within the business partner transaction. Figure 3.9 shows the master data for the business partner, but with the BP role **Customer**. The following standard roles for business partners map back to the old structures:

- FLCU00: Customer (Fin. Accounting)
- FLCU01: Customer
- FLVN00: Supplier (Fin. Accounting)
- FLVN01: Supplier

You can see from the tabs in Figure 3.9 that the information needed for billing, payment, and so on is still available, even though the initial access has changed. When you convert to SAP S/4HANA, you will be forced to use the business partner as the central access point for customer and vendor data, but you won't have to change your billing and payment programs because they can work with the same master data tables as before.

The main thing to check as part of the conversion project is where number ranges for customers and vendors overlap, because they were previously stored in separate tables. SAP recommends using the same business partner number and adding the customer and vendor roles if the business partner represents the same legal person. However, while you are converting, it makes sense to take the opportunity to weed out master data that is no longer used and fix master data issues, such as incorrect postal codes or email addresses.

To help explain the how the business partner acts as a shell that is extended as different roles are added, we'll look at the various roles associated with a business partner in SAP S/4HANA.

Figure 3.10 shows the general business partner information for the organization **USSU-VSF61**. We have selected the **Business Partner (Gen.)** business partner role. The information in the general business partner role is stored in table BUT000. With this shell, you can't work with the business partner but must first assign it to the relevant roles.

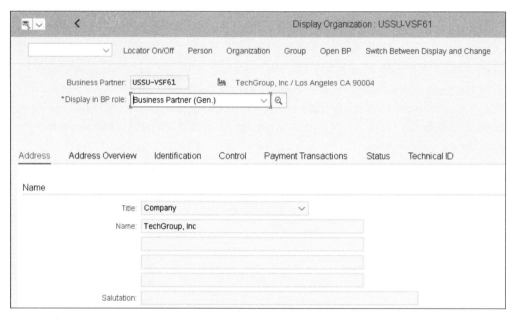

Figure 3.10 General Business Partner Data Information for a Vendor

Before you can post invoices in accounts payable for your business partner, you must extend it by creating the **Supplier (Fin. Accounting)** business partner role and making the link to a company code and reconciliation account. Figure 3.11 displays the supplier in financial accounting (formerly Transaction FK03). The vendor-related information is stored in the vendor master tables LFA1 and LFB1. You can use this master data in combination with accounts payable transactions such as Transaction FB60 for your business partner.

Although you can now work in accounts payable, you can't create a purchase order until you assign the business partner to the **Supplier** business partner role and assign it to a purchasing organization. Figure 3.12 shows the supplier in purchasing (formerly Transaction XK03). The supplier-related information is stored in table LFM1. You can use this data as part of purchasing activities, such as creating a purchase requisition or a purchase order for your business partner.

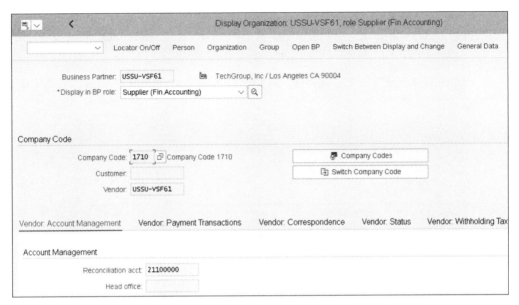

Figure 3.11 Supplier in Financial Accounting with Company Code

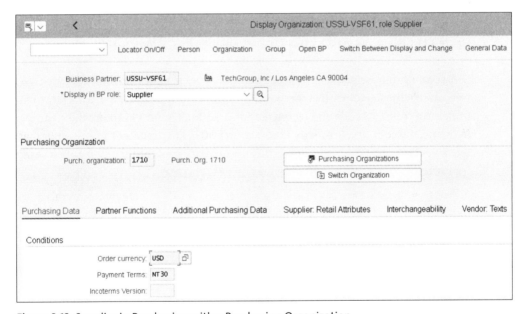

Figure 3.12 Supplier in Purchasing with a Purchasing Organization

Now let's look at the process in reverse, with the business partner as a customer. Figure 3.13 shows the general business partner information for customer **17100003**. Again, this is simply a shell containing a link to general information.

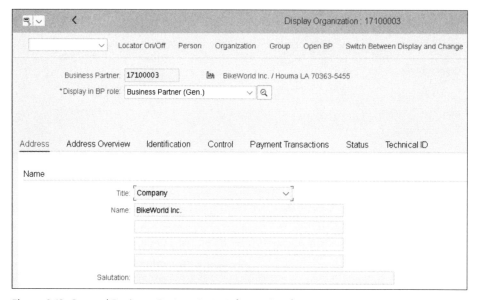

Figure 3.13 General Business Partner Data Information for Customer

Before you can post invoices in accounts receivable for your business partner, you must assign the **Customer (Fin. Accounting)** business partner role and assign the customer to a company code and reconciliation account. Figure 3.14 shows the customer in financial accounting (formerly Transaction FD03). This updates the customer master tables KNA1 and KNB1. You can use this master data in accounts receivable transactions such as Transaction FB70 for your business partner.

Although you can now work in accounts receivable, you can't create a sales order until you assign the business partner to the **Customer** business partner role and assign it to a sales organization, a distribution channel, and a division. Figure 3.15 shows the customer in sales and distribution (formerly Transaction XD03). This updates table KNVV with the assignment to a sales area. The customer can now be used in sales and distribution.

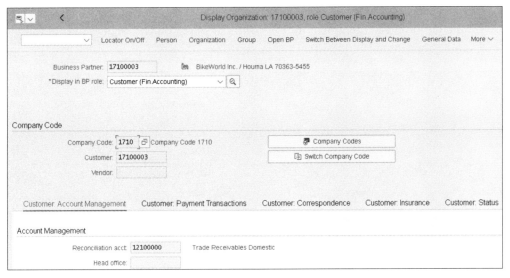

Figure 3.14 Customer in Financial Accounting

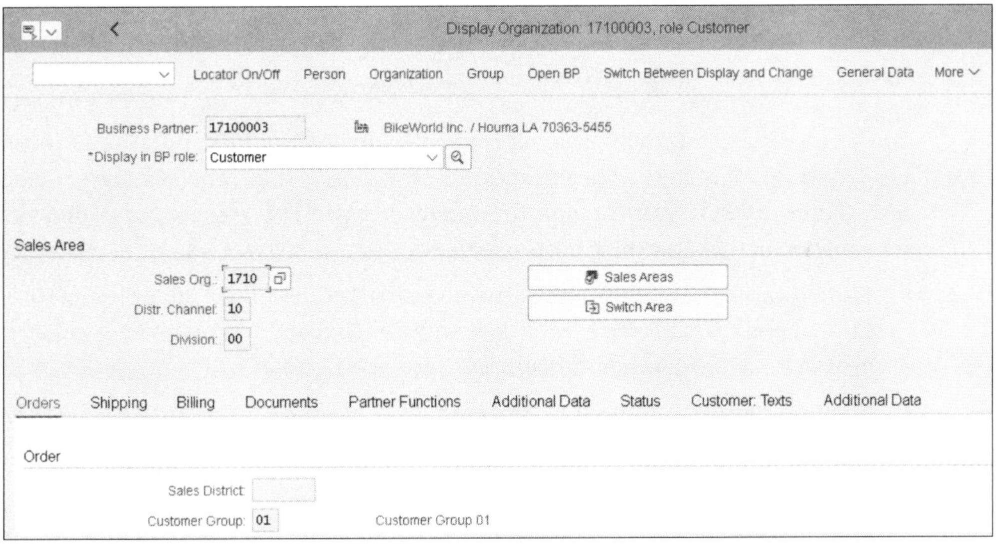

Figure 3.15 Customer in Sales and Distribution

In the SAP Receivables Management (formerly SAP Financial Supply Chain Management) components Collections Management, Credit Management, and Dispute Management, the business partner was always used. Figure 3.16 shows the same customer from a collections management perspective, together with the ability to assign a collection profile and segment for the customer once you've assigned the **Collections Management** business partner role.

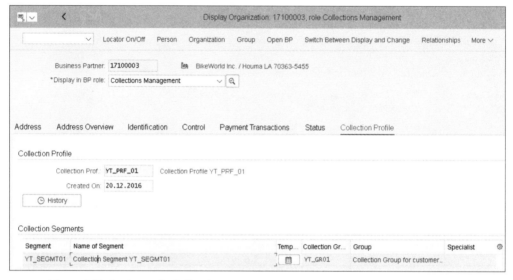

Figure 3.16 Customer in Collections Management

You'll find general information about conversion in SAP Note 2265093 (S4TWL: Business Partner). This SAP Note includes an attachment that provides step-by-step instructions to walk you through the conversion process. You may also find the information in these two blog posts useful:

- "Simplification Item: Business Partner Approach/Customer-Vendor Integration (CVI)" at *https://blogs.sap.com/2016/04/29/simplification-item-business-partner-approach-customer-vendor-integration-cvi/*
- "Business Partner Approach in SAP S/4HANA" at *https://blogs.sap.com/2018/01/18/business-partner-approach-in-sap-s4hana/*

Now that we've looked at customer/vendor integration, we'll look at changes in receivables management, which you may already have encountered in the SAP Business Suite world as in SAP Receivables Management.

3.3.2   Receivables Management

One of the biggest changes in receivables management is the new user interface delivered with SAP S/4HANA. Figure 3.17 shows the SAP Fiori launchpad for the receivables manager. It provides the key performance indicators for the collections process, including total receivables, days sales outstanding, overdue receivables, future receivables, and so on. Behind each tile is a dedicated SAP Fiori application that allows the accounts receivables manager to analyze the information in more detail.

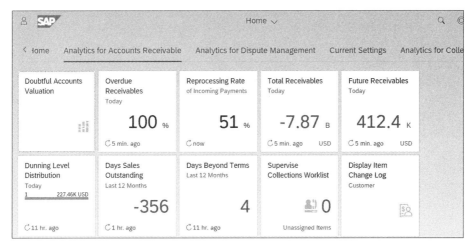

Figure 3.17 SAP Fiori Launchpad for an Accounts Receivable Manager

Figure 3.18 shows an SAP Fiori app called Overdue Receivables (SAP Fiori ID F1747), which assigns the overdue receivables to time buckets depending on by how much each open item has exceeded its due date. The views used in this app are based on the virtual data model and are pulling information directly from the accounts receivable tables.

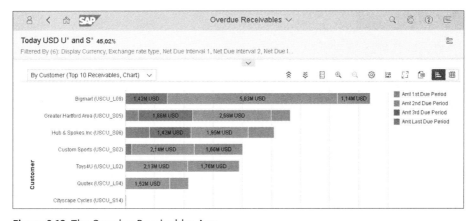

Figure 3.18 The Overdue Receivables App

There are also more classic views showing lists of customer line items, such as the Manage Customer Line Items app (SAP Fiori ID F0711) shown in Figure 3.19. Once you have selected a line item, you can edit it, create correspondence, and block line items for dunning by selecting the appropriate function.

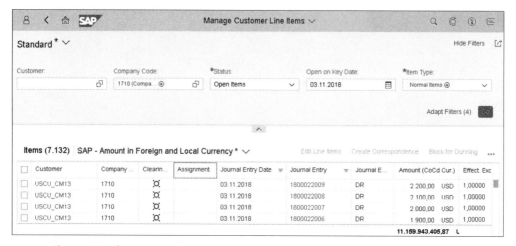

Figure 3.19 The Manage Customer Line Items App

Of course, receivables management also includes operational tasks. Figure 3.20 shows the SAP Fiori launchpad for the accounts receivable accountant, with apps for processing collections, handling disputes, creating promises to pay, and so on. On the right side, you can see sales orders that have exceeded the credit limit and require checking. We'll discuss this type of proactive alerting in Chapter 4.

Although these applications are based on classic accounts receivable functions, SAP S/4HANA also includes applications for credit management, collections management, and dispute management.

The Credit Management subcomponent in SAP ERP (FI-AR-CR) is no longer supported and must be migrated to SAP Credit Management (FIN-FSCM-CR) in SAP S/4HANA. You'll find full details of the impact of this change in SAP Note 22070544 (S4TWL: Credit Management).

Figure 3.20 SAP Fiori Launchpad for an Accounts Receivable Accountant

From the alerts shown in Figure 3.20 you can access quick activities. Figure 3.21 shows the quick activity option to check a credit limit. Notice the buttons along the bottom of the screen that show the **Approve**, **Reject**, **Claim**, **Forward**, **Suspend**, and other actions, which allow the accountant to react to the credit limit.

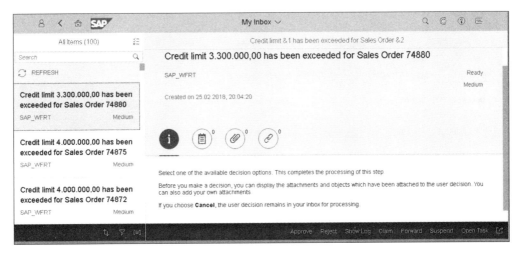

Figure 3.21 The Credit Management Inbox

Figure 3.22 shows the Supervise Collections Worklist app (SAP Fiori ID F2375), which is designed to provide an overview of the value of the open items and assign the open items to a collection specialist, a collection group, and a priority. From this list, the supervisor can assign items to a specialist.

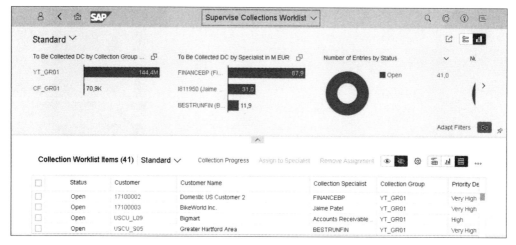

Figure 3.22 The Supervise Collections Worklist App

Figure 3.23 shows the Process Collections Worklist app (SAP Fiori ID F0380), which is designed to allow the collection specialist to work through the list of open items, prioritize processing of these items, and document the status of the receivables process.

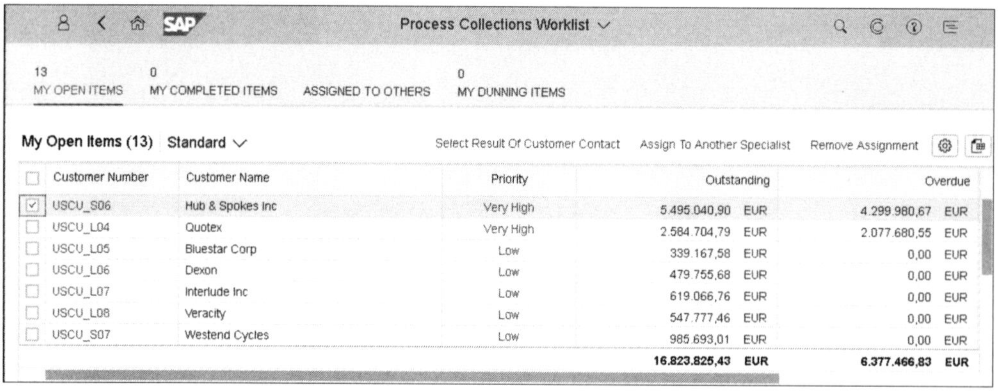

Figure 3.23 The Process Collections Worklist App

The collection specialist then can contact the customer about the missing payment. Figure 3.24 shows how to use this app to document the progress of the collections process.

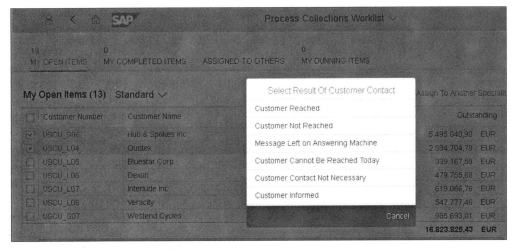

Figure 3.24 Document Result of Customer Contact

In some cases, the next step will be to record the fact that there is a dispute concerning the open invoice. Figure 3.25 shows the Manage Dispute Cases app (SAP Fiori ID FO702), which follows the same basic pattern as the Process Collections Worklist app.

Figure 3.25 The Manage Dispute Cases App

The accountant can access details of the dispute by choosing the arrow on the right of the screen. Figure 3.26 shows details of the dispute case and provides access to both the disputed invoices and documentation of any discussions between the collections specialist and the customer. It is the ability to add texts and document the progress of the dispute and collections process that distinguishes receivables management in

SAP S/4HANA from the classic accounts receivable process and that helps to reduce days sales outstanding and the level of bad debt.

Figure 3.26 Details of Dispute Case

Accounts receivable manages open items for a more classic order-related fulfilment process, but the idea of contract accounting, which we'll discuss next, is that a long-term contract is in place and that regular billing takes place with reference to that contract.

3.3.3   Contract Accounting

The Contract Accounts Receivable and Payable subledger (often shortened to contract accounting) is designed for processing the large document volumes that occur in industries characterized by a high volume of the data to be handled (e.g., insurance, utilities, telecommunications, and the public sector). They are generally highly regulated, with complex statutory requirements. From an integration point of view, this subledger cumulates the data and updates the Universal Journal. This subledger worked with the business partner from the start, so there is no need to convert it when you move to SAP S/4HANA.

This solution also is used commonly for high-volume consumption billing and invoicing by organizations that want to monetize internet of things (IoT), cloud services, or digital content that gets paid for immediately. This approach is covered by SAP Convergent Charging, which is used to create billable items (generally via an external system) that are transferred to SAP Convergent Invoicing. SAP Convergent Invoicing creates invoices and credit memos, which are managed as receivables or payables in contract accounting.

To get a sense of the difference between the tasks of an invoice manager working with SAP Convergent Invoicing and the accounts receivables manager that we looked at in Figure 3.17, look at Figure 3.27. You'll see a completely different set of KPIs, with the focus now on unbilled items and unrated items. This is because the process is designed to be run in a highly automated manner with no human intervention. Of course, the invoicing manager can access details by selecting individual billable items, billing documents, or invoicing documents.

Figure 3.27 SAP Fiori Launchpad for an Invoicing Manager (SAP Convergent Invoicing)

Figure 3.28 shows the Display Invoicing Documents app (SAP Fiori ID F2048). The invoicing manager can select any invoicing document in this list and navigate to the full document details.

Finally, Figure 3.29 shows the Analyze Unbilled Items app (SAP Fiori ID F1427), which allows you to track items that have reached their billing date but were ignored during billing or are not yet due. This kind of application is becoming more prevalent as organizations move away from their classic business models.

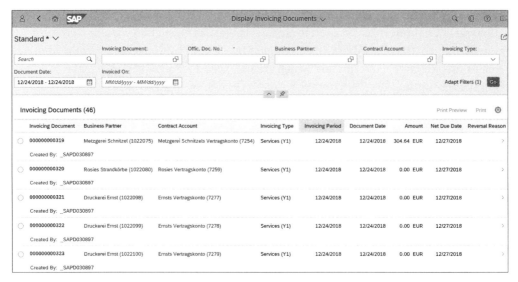

Figure 3.28 The Display Invoicing Documents App

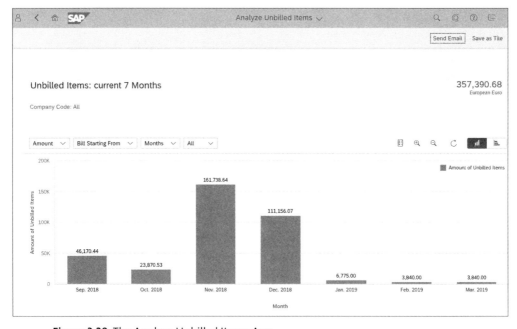

Figure 3.29 The Analyze Unbilled Items App

3.4 Summary

We've now looked at how the industry solutions became part of SAP S/4HANA and at general business trends that result in a shift from a pure product focus to a combination of products and services from a controlling perspective. We discussed the impact of the compulsory use of the business partner in SAP S/4HANA, and evaluated changes to receivables management and contract accounting thanks to the introduction of SAP Fiori as the new user interface in SAP S/4HANA.

Next, let's look at more general process improvements and how they can be automated with SAP S/4HANA.

Chapter 4

Financial Process Optimization: Standardizing and Automating Processes

This chapter explains why organizations are standardizing and automating finance processes, and where SAP S/4HANA comes in. We'll discuss the impact of an increased reliance on shared service centers and why IT is moving away from custom-designed solutions and toward standard ones to reduce financial department costs. With SAP S/4HANA, SAP is designing for simplicity as it reworks existing finance applications.

When comparing the agenda of finance with the strategic business partner role that finance is expected to fulfill in an organization, we see that there is still a high discrepancy between what is expected and what happens.

The majority of the time on the finance agenda is still consumed by executing operational tasks. Of course, you can't simply abandon operational tasks to free up time; they still need to be executed. But you can make changes to spend as little time as possible and reduce the cost of finance. To execute these operational finance tasks more efficiently, you must rethink your business processes.

On top, there is the ever-increasing demand to have access to up-to-date finance information at any moment—instead of just after the period-end close—a demand that is clearly connected to the role of finance as a strategic business partner that delivers insights for decision support.

In Section 4.1 of this chapter, we'll look at the key elements of rethinking operational (and, more specifically, financial) business processes. In Section 4.2, we'll discuss how specific processes such as cash management, goods and invoice receipt reconciliation, and accrual management have been completely revisited by SAP and now can be automated in a fundamentally different way that makes use of new technologies. Finally, in Section 4.3 we'll see how the Universal Journal brings all legal and management finance data together and how it has opened doors to redesigning applications across these two fields.

4.1   Rethinking Business Processes

There are two main reasons to redesign operational finance tasks: to reduce the cost of finance (and free up time for more tasks that add value and support the organization's steering model), and to achieve the continuous close. A *continuous close* gives an organization information throughout the month rather than only at close—but it means that closing tasks must be executed more efficiently. (Otherwise it's practically impossible to run tasks such as goods receipt/invoice receipt reconciliation multiple times in one period.)

To rethink business processes, the shift toward "intelligent" applications plays a role. But what does this mean? In short, intelligent enterprise software enables companies to automate routine work and augment humans with decision support and suggestions. The following functionality makes a system appear intelligent to an end user:

- The system automates routine work and explains what it has done and why.
- The system is proactive or guides the user through the process by looking at the data and making recommendations or predictions.
- The system can adapt its interaction with the user through the most relevant information and communication channel.
- The system's natural language processing capabilities facilitate a "conversation" with the user via voice or keyboard input, understand what the user is after, offer suggestions for further relevant actions, and so on.

Translating these functionalities into more technical terms brings us to the conclusion that redesigning finance processes is based on a couple of fundamental principles:

- Simplifying operational tasks, which also helps to automate them more easily
- Adding process guidance and enhanced collaboration capabilities within the finance department and across the organization
- Centralizing and standardizing tasks across the organization

In the following subsections, we'll dive into more detail on each of these redesign principles.

4.1.1   Simplification, Automation, Guidance, and Collaboration

The first element to focus on is the actual process itself and how it's designed and automated. With process efficiency in mind, the starting point is to make the process design as simple as possible; we can automate simple processes more easily than complex processes. Once the process steps are designed, we can start connecting them and focus on process guidance and collaboration between different stakeholders within the process.

Simplification

Everyone knows that the simpler a specific process is, the more efficiently it can be executed.

Unfortunately, rarely is process simplification so easy; in fact, many finance processes are still designed in a very complex way today. Often, we see that process redesign initiatives are taken on an individual company basis—an approach that surely makes sense for areas that help the organization distinguish itself from its competitors. But what about depreciating assets, matching open items, posting general ledger postings, and treating incoming bank statements, for instance? These aren't often considered market differentiators, but they must be done.

There are several drivers for simplification:

- Many basic finance processes are common across organizations, and it's easier for everyone to correctly follow a simpler process than a complicated one.
- Recent technical improvements like in-memory databases have removed inefficiencies from previous eras, and simplification is now possible.
- Cloud computing offers organizations new possibilities for faster deployment and continuous innovation. With cloud computing comes standard, simpler processes based on best practices.

It's a challenge for individual departments to redesign these processes and stay on top of functional and technical breakthroughs, so it's critical that organizations as a whole undertake this task.

Automation

This brings us to the second principle: *automation*.

Even today, many tasks are executed using a spreadsheet solution. Some of these spreadsheets are very flexible, but in addition to prompting data quality concerns, they are also burdened by a lack of process guidance. Therefore, organizations have been moving in the direction of automated processes, and SAP has been investing in this area from the beginning, as a cornerstone of its ERP systems.

But classic automation is rule-based. Think of the reconciliation between open items and incoming payments. This is a simple process, but even when it is automated based on a set of rules that check the amount, invoice number, business partner ID, and so on, many items remain unmatched. Therefore, the accounts receivable clerk needs to find the matching items manually over and over again.

With technological evolution comes the ability to use machine learning. In addition to the performance of a rule-based engine, machine learning-based application can "notice" manually matched items, derive matching logic, and apply that logic to future unmatched items. We'll look at how machine learning capabilities already influence finance processes today in Section 4.1.4 and Section 4.2.1.

Process Guidance

The third principle of business process redesign is *process guidance*, or a system's ability to execute one step and then automatically guide the user to the potential next steps. Let's look at an example of process guidance in SAP S/4HANA. Figure 4.1 shows a cash forecast discount, highlighting the planned payment dates for incoming invoices.

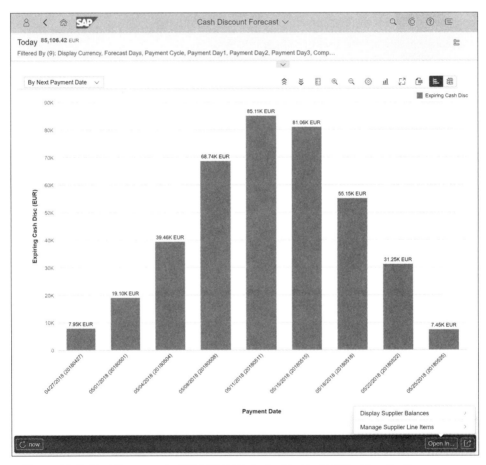

Figure 4.1 Guided Processes in SAP S/4HANA Embedded in SAP Fiori Applications

Imagine looking at your organization's cash situation. Based on the information in SAP S/4HANA, you conclude that free cash is available, and you decide to put it to good use. Having access to an overview of planned payments like the one in Figure 4.1 helps you consider whether the free cash could be used to pay some invoices earlier than planned, thereby taking advantage of some early payment discounts.

Take a closer look at the bottom-right corner of Figure 4.1. This is where the process guidance in the SAP Fiori user experience comes in: it proposes that users open the Manage Supplier Line Items app (SAP Fiori ID FO712) as a next step. From here, the discount information (and even direct access to execute the payment) becomes available, as shown in Figure 4.2.

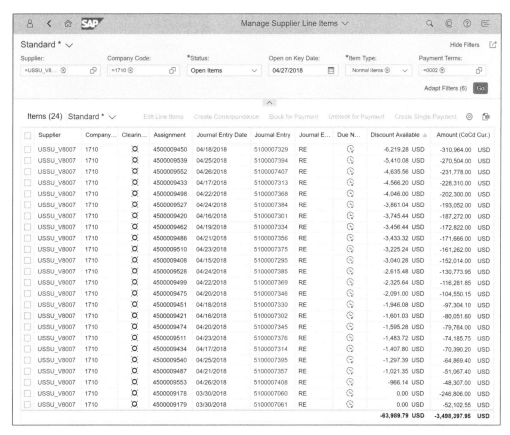

Figure 4.2 The Manage Supplier Line Items App with Discounting Information

Another variation of process guidance occurs when the system helps users determine what topic to focus on at a specific moment in time. Imagine, for instance, that you are the responsible for receivables management. Realizing that days sales outstanding (DSO) is relatively high would be a trigger to start analyzing your receivables. If, on the other hand, you notice that DSO is low, you wouldn't need to start such an analysis. By simply including this information on your home screen, your system could guide you in the right direction, helping ensure that no time is wasted by looking into finance areas that are under control.

SAP S/4HANA does this by embedding KPIs into the transactional environment. Based on all transactions in the SAP S/4HANA environment, following our example, the days sales outstanding or an alternative, like the percentage of overdue receivables KPI (in Figure 4.3, this is **61.53%**), is calculated on the fly when a user logs on to the SAP Fiori launchpad. The information is presented in such a way that it's clear what the user should focus on.

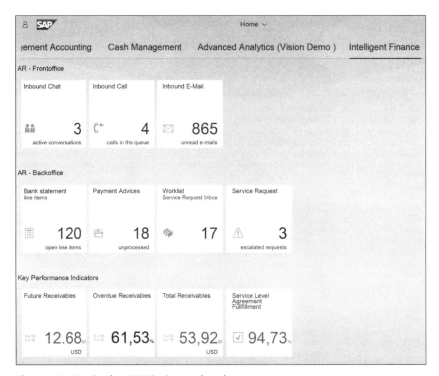

Figure 4.3 KPIs in the SAP Fiori Launchpad

This is possible thanks to the embedded analytics capabilities in SAP S/4HANA and more specifically in the SAP Fiori user experience (which we'll come back to in more detail in Chapter 5).

Flexible Collaboration

Process guidance and the identification of key focus areas through embedded analytics capabilities both focus on guiding a specific user. However, many processes also require the involvement of multiple users.

To streamline these types of processes, two options are available: either use a specific process-monitoring application that is already available (e.g., for financial closing on the entity and group levels, described in Chapter 7) or use a predesigned workflow to guide different users through a specific structured process approach. Independent of the process, it's crucial to support flexible collaboration between different users. This principle was typically missing from both spreadsheet-based solutions and many classic ERP environments.

An important new digital assistant, SAP CoPilot, supports not only collaboration but also multiple ways of interacting with the system: users can type or click as always—but now they also can use voice commands thanks to natural language processing. Consider the following key elements that are part of SAP CoPilot:

- SAP CoPilot includes so-called business context awareness, meaning that it can understand the business situation it's activated in and proactively suggest solutions based on "skills" it develops. SAP CoPilot selects the right skill based on keywords and synonyms. For example, while using the Show Me skill, if a user asks SAP Co-Pilot to show available requests for quotation (maybe the user says, "Show me requests for quotation!"), then SAP CoPilot returns a list of available quotations. No transaction codes or navigation is needed.

- It is a self-learning system that uses machine learning functionality to gain knowledge based on historic data and experience.

- SAP CoPilot logically acts across all SAP applications with one personality and one memory. So no matter what SAP Fiori application is being used, the user can always interact with the system or systems in the same way using SAP CoPilot.

- It's open and extensible for integration with non-SAP solutions, enabling anyone to extend SAP CoPilot skills through bots, agents, and APIs.

We'll see another practical example of the integration of SAP CoPilot when analyzing how the SAP S/4HANA for goods and invoice receipt reconciliation application works in Section 4.2.2.

4.1.2   Centralization

It's one thing to redesign business processes using newly available technological elements, as described in Section 4.1.1. But organizations also have been working on centralizing repetitive processes (in finance or elsewhere) by organizing them in a shared service center. In this section, we'll look at two centralization tools for finance: the SAP Shared Service Framework and Central Finance.

SAP Shared Service Framework

Independent from the finance domain, there is an evolution in the way global business services are organized. Let's consider the different types of shared service organizations:

- The most basic one is what is referred to as *singular shared services*, in which fragmented processes with local process responsibilities are still in place. This is limited mainly to a grouping of employees in a specific location.
- The next level is the move to a *global organization*, in which standardized processes are defined with regional process responsibilities, which is a leaner approach than the singular shared service.
- The next level is what we refer to as *process-driven shared services*, in which there is a focus on global process ownership and global end-to-end process standards are in place, resulting in high economies of scale.

The SAP Shared Service Framework can be applied in the different cases, but most benefits are achieved when choosing the third one. From a technology perspective, its core capabilities are related to service management (including service routing and delivery), communication management, and analytics to ensure the following elements of an effective shared services model are in place:

- A broad set of communication channels
- Sophisticated case management
- Transparency into service level agreements
- Clear responsibilities for efficient service execution and delivery
- Transparency via embedded service analytics

Because the SAP Shared Service Framework is now directly integrated into the SAP S/4HANA environment, you get direct access to the SAP automation engines—including, for instance, direct integration to several important tools:

- The collections and dispute worklist and the full SAP Receivables Management solution, shown in Figure 4.4
- The SAP Financial Closing cockpit, allowing for simplified communication and automated execution of the closing process

Figure 4.4 Processing Receivables from within the SAP Shared Service Framework

You can also incorporate intelligent automation through machine learning. Consider the benefits of using machine learning to improve the handling of service tickets through automating service ticket classification. Customer interaction centers face increased volume and speed of customer interactions. As a result, service agents must manage more interactions simultaneously while meeting customer demands for accelerated response times and a seamless handover across interaction channels. With SAP Service Ticketing, incoming customers' service tickets are classified automatically and routed to the right agent. Agents receive suggested solutions to improve operational efficiency. As shown in Figure 4.5, these items end up in a user's worklist based on the included machine learning logic.

SAP Service Ticketing leverages deep learning neural networks trained on large amounts of historical data. The model understands the semantics of unstructured ticket messages, assigns the ticket to the most likely category, and recommends solutions or articles from the knowledge base to help the agent. These recommendations are based on information from similar tickets that have been answered recently in the system. The model improves over time as more service tickets are processed and as users provide feedback.

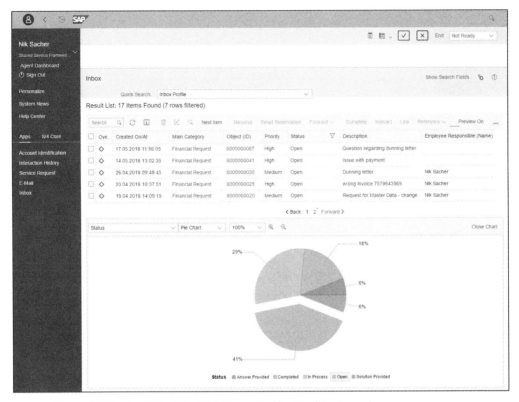

Figure 4.5 Service Ticket Worklist Generated by Machine Learning

Central Finance

Outside of developing a shared service center, another way to centralize finance processing is to execute a specific process step in a harmonized way, ideally from within a single technical environment.

Assuming an organization runs a single ERP environment, this can work. However, many organizations run different parts of their business on different ERP environments, perhaps because they have grown through mergers and acquisitions. In this case, even if you set up a shared service organization, a single accounts receivables clerk would still need to log on to different underlying ERP systems to match and clear open items with incoming payments.

SAP S/4HANA offers a new way to centralize the execution of this and other finance processes, without having to log on to different applications: the Central Finance deployment model.

In Chapter 12 on group reporting, you'll see that SAP S/4HANA deployed as a Central Finance instance enables organizations to centralize all data from different parts of the organization into a single source of truth by reposting all individual financial postings in a Central Finance environment. But this is not where the use case for Central Finance ends. Based on these centralized finance postings, an additional use case involves the central execution of follow-on finance transactions from the Central Finance system itself. Because it's a normal SAP S/4HANA system at its core, running finance transactions is part of its standard capabilities (provided that the necessary data to run the transaction is available, of course).

Table 4.1 lists the primary and secondary focus areas within finance that are typical candidates for centralization in Central Finance. Operational finance transactions related to general ledger accounting, accounts payable, and accounts receivable are possible already. Additional functionality, including production variance splitting to enrich margin reporting, is possible in Central Finance; this is because cost estimate data is transferred to the Central Finance system from the source ERP application alongside the financial postings in a package known as a *backpack*. This functionality has been added specifically with the SAP S/4HANA 1809 release.

	Financial Planning and Analysis	Accounting and Financial Close	Treasury and Financial Risk Management	Finance Operations	Enterprise Risk and Compliance Management
Primary focus area	■ Planning, budgeting, and forecasting ■ Profitability and cost management ■ Monitoring and reporting	■ Accounting ■ Entity close ■ Corporate close	■ Payments and bank communications	■ Receivables management	
Secondary focus area		■ Reporting and disclosure ■ Financial close governance	■ Cash and liquidity management	■ Invoice management ■ Financial shared services	■ Fraud management

Table 4.1 Primary and Secondary Process Candidates for Centralized Process Execution in Central Finance

Let's focus on one of these core candidates: centralized receivables management. When a sales order is billed, an open item is generated on the finance side; at the same time, the sent invoice impacts the organization's P&L sheet. In the case of a Central Finance setup, the posting that is initially posted in the source ERP system is then posted again in the Central Finance environment. Consequently, we find two open items for the same transaction: one in the source ERP system and one in the Central Finance system. When the customer pays the invoice, the incoming payment is matched with the open item. But of course, there's only one payment. So how can we match and clear the two open items without performing this task twice?

Technically, three different options exist, as shown in Figure 4.6:

- In option A, the open item in Central Finance technically gets cleared immediately and the source system remains the leading system. This is not the preferred approach because the organization cannot get a central view of all open items.

- In option B, the clearing of the open item happens in Central Finance, and then it's sent back to the source using a classical interface like ALE. But this means that until the clearing is done, the open item exists on both sides. This adds interface complexity.

- The preferred option is option C, in which the open item, when replicated from the source system to Central Finance, technically is cleared in the source. Open item management is centralized in Central Finance, which is the single source of truth for the entire organization from which all reporting is done.

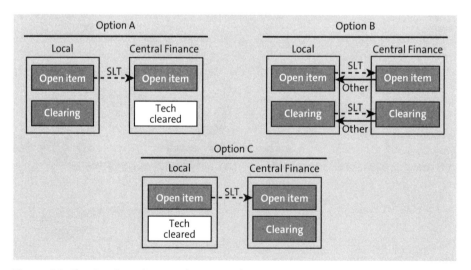

Figure 4.6 Clearing Open Items Using Central Open Item Management in Central Finance

As of SAP S/4HANA 1809, payments can be posted back to the source system, which is particularly important for down payments.

4.1.3 Standardization

Another key aspect to redesign (and thereby optimize) business processes and make finance cost effective is to standardize.

Organizations have tried to apply standardized processes for years. In fact, the purpose of SAP ERP was to apply standardized processes for non-differentiating areas like financial accounting. In the end, though, many organizations have customized their processes, evolving away from the standard processes as originally delivered with SAP ERP.

Today, many organizations are going through a finance transformation exercise, with the goal of rethinking their business processes to make them more efficient but reduce costs at the same time. As a part of this transformation, standardized processes are back on the agenda. These are conceived of in such a way that multiple organizations are running their processes based on the same technical environment. This means that the same standard processes are used and thus cannot be adapted.

This is where the evolution from on-premise systems to SAP S/4HANA in the cloud—especially multitenant cloud solutions—offers an advantage: deploying an SAP S/4HANA Cloud solution drives organizations in the direction of standard processes. Moreover, any deviations from the standard become very visible within the organization. Similarly, another advantage of adopting a cloud-based solution instead of an on-premise solution is an IT culture shift away from the practice of heavy customization that potentially blocks organizations from adopting innovations easily. Cloud solutions are designed to enable organizations to be able to adopt new innovations rapidly that add value for the organization (e.g., from an external accounting perspective, keeping up with regulatory changes), but to implement these innovations, standardization is key.

4.1.4 Machine Learning

Recall from Section 4.1.1 that in addition to classic rule-based automation, there is another way in which processes can be automated: through machine learning. Before we look at some specific examples, let's consider how machine learning works as a principle.

Machine learning is a general approach whereby a specific algorithm is programmed and then "trained" by feeding it historical data or past experiences prepared in the right format. This training data can take different forms depending on the specific machine learning application focused on. It can be structured data, plain text, video material, images, speech, and more.

As illustrated in Figure 4.7, this training data is then loaded into the machine learning algorithm to train the application and develop a machine learning model. This model, not the training data, is what is applied to the actual information as part of the process. Depending on the type of machine learning algorithm and the process it's used in, the model can be applied to automate a specific process or a process step that lacks clear rules based on the intelligence of the model itself, which is itself based on the training data.

Machine learning use cases are not limited to automating finance processes and can include the following:

- Detect and rank information in a big data set.

- Derive knowledge from historical information to increase the accuracy of predictive scenarios—especially applicable because of the feedback loop that's part of the machine learning process. The outcome of the machine learning model then can be fed back to the model as additional training data to ensure it also learns from this result.

- Provide proactive, context-sensitive support in tools such as SAP CoPilot.

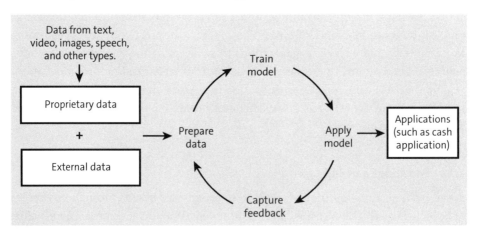

Figure 4.7 Machine Learning Sequence

This all may sound quite theoretical, so let's look at an example of how machine learning brings the human way of learning into systems. Consider passing through security controls at an airport. Laptops must be taken out, toiletries must be stored in small units in a transparent bag, belts and jackets must to be removed, and so on. The first time you passed through security, it probably took a while—and you might have had to dump a too-large bottle of shampoo in the process. But through experience, this *process* of passing through security gets better and better, faster and faster—in other words, more efficient. (Now you know to pack slightly differently the next time you take a trip.) So though you surely read the instructions on what was allowed or not the first time you traveled in the new system (the training data), your experience is what makes you pass through security more efficiently each time after.

This is similar to the way machine learning works: based on experience. Of course, if people give you unhelpful tips or if the instructions are full of errors, then you "learn" from the wrong information. Likewise, the "intelligence" of machine learning applications is based on training data, so the key to a successful application is the quality of the training data at its core.

Now that you have an overview of the key drivers behind process improvement, let's discuss how these principles have been applied in SAP S/4HANA.

4.2   Automating Finance Processes

In this section, we'll look at specific examples of how SAP has been rethinking finance processes: cash management, goods receipt and invoice receipt reconciliation, accruals management, and smart alerts. After introducing the finance process itself, we shall focus especially on how the functional design principles and technological capabilities to automate and apply process guidance are practically applied. We'll close each section with a discussion of the added value this brings to the organization.

4.2.1   SAP Cash Application with Machine Learning

One example of how SAP is rethinking business processes is related to the process of matching incoming payments with open receivables items.

SAP Cash Application is an example in which process redesign is based on adding a machine learning component. In other words, the matching between incoming payments and open items is not based on a set of rules (e.g., checking the business partner name, the amount, date, etc.) but based on an algorithm that has learned from historical matching data. This way, the model can take into consideration the impact of different currencies, discounts, potential lump-sum payments, information collected from a customer call, and so on.

The historical matching data used as training data for this machine learning model isn't necessarily restricted to the historical data sitting in the SAP S/4HANA environment in which the current items to be matched are stored. Because SAP machine learning applications are set up in the SAP Cloud Platform, it's possible to feed the model with training data from different sources to learn from a greater sample size. When open items and incoming payments are matched, SAP Cash Application is called from within the SAP S/4HANA environment in which the unmatched data is stored.

As a user working with the application shown in Figure 4.8, you won't necessarily notice a drastic change in the process steps. You still access an open item list, and then run a matching step and check whether there are remaining unmatched items that need to be handled manually.

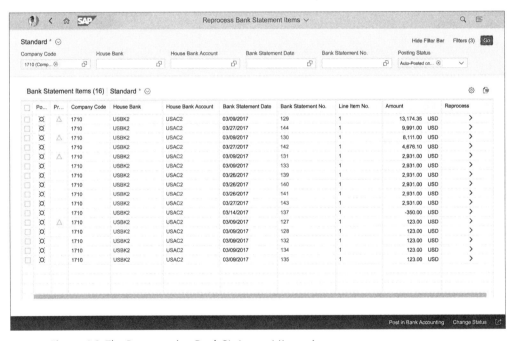

Figure 4.8 The Reprocessing Bank Statement Items App

The difference, however, is that because the matching logic has changed, the number of items in the exception list that require manual intervention will decrease over time, offering a higher level of automation and therefore a more efficient process.

Apart from the efficiency of automation, bear in mind that the quality of the outcome of the process is also critical—and directly impacts your users' trust in the cash application.

Because the machine learning model in SAP Cash Application acts as kind of a black box, users can't see which ruleset it uses to propose a specific match between a payment and an open item. Therefore, a confidence rating that expresses the level of certainty (expressed as a percentage) of a correct proposed match has been included. Based on this confidence rating, as shown at the bottom of Figure 4.9, a user can decide whether proposed matches need to be investigated manually again (by including them in the exception list) or whether the proposed match can be converted automatically into a clearing. Over time, users who have checked proposed matches manually and have seen that the application's proposals are accurate will have more confidence in the application.

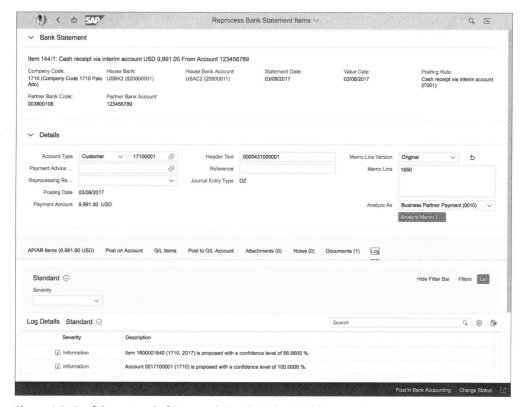

Figure 4.9 Confidence Level of Proposed Match in the Machine Learning App

As with all machine learning-based processes that rely on intelligence based on train-ing data, a key requirement for this type of process automation is to start with high-quality data. If low-quality or even wrong training data is input into the model, the machine learning algorithm behind it will be miseducated, which will lead to unhelp-ful automation in the end. This is an additional reason that it's important to have a type of check (e.g., the confidence level) available to users.

4.2.2   Goods and Invoice Receipt Reconciliation

Let's consider another example of operational processes being remodeled by combin-ing multiple techniques: the reconciliation between good receipts and related invoice receipts, which historically has been considered a cumbersome closing activity.

Many companies that deal with large amounts of purchase orders are familiar with exception handling. As part of their monthly, quarterly, or yearly closing activities, accountants have to check the GR/IR accounts and to make sure they balance out on the purchase order line item level. For example, there might be a discrepancy between the quantities listed in the goods receipts and the quantities in the corre-sponding invoice receipt.

To resolve the exception, accountants need to collaborate with different stakeholders such as accounting, procurement, warehousing, and the supplier. This is often a very time-consuming activity: the accountant manually gathers the relevant information from different transactions, merges them into a combined spreadsheet, and then starts to contact the different stakeholders individually in a manual way.

To reduce the time spent on and the data that results from this process, a new ap-proach to GR/IR reconciliation more efficiently gathers all relevant information, im-proves collaboration between all involved stakeholders, enhances the logic used for checking the items to be reconciled, and proposes how to resolve the reconciliation differences.

This has resulted in the new SAP S/4HANA for goods and invoice receipt reconciliation app. As shown in Figure 4.10, the goods receipts and invoice receipts are merged. From here, a rule-based clearing starts. If there's a match, the balance can be cleared. If there's no match, the GR/IR reconciliation app makes an intelligent recommendation for resolving the clearing issue, resulting in the end in a write-off or a GR/IR posting.

The analytical capabilities available within the SAP S/4HANA environment are used to bring together all relevant information on a single screen, including the status of the reconciliation accounts. Furthermore, it's possible to drill down into the details, thereby identifying the root cause of the problem. Smart filters help focus the atten-tion of the user on the most relevant deviations.

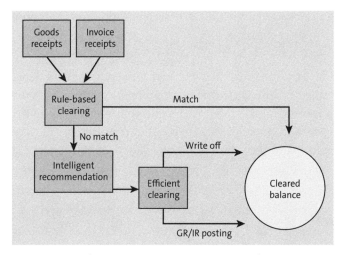

Figure 4.10 GR/IR Reconciliation Process in SAP S/4HANA

The GR/IR reconciliation app also addresses the issue of collaboration among different stakeholders. SAP CoPilot is embedded within the SAP Fiori user experience; this way, as shown in Figure 4.11, the accountant can involve other stakeholders in the discussion directly, chat with them, or forward objects for review to resolve any reconciliation issues.

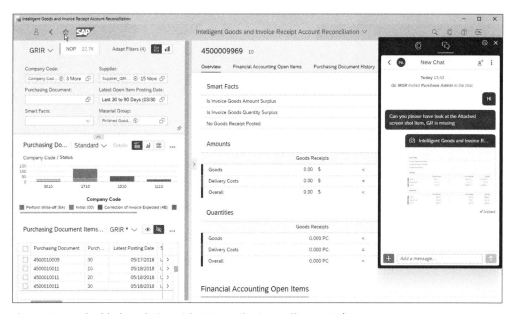

Figure 4.11 Embedded Analytics with SAP CoPilot in Intelligent GR/IR App

Finally, machine learning also plays a part in the GR/IR reconciliation app to propose a recommended approach to solve the issue.

As with the classic reconciliation approach via rule-based clearing, everything is fine if the goods receipt and invoice receipt match. But if there is no match, accountants previously needed to investigate manually to find the appropriate solution. With the introduction of machine learning, if the rule-based execution cannot finalize the clearing, then the Intelligent Recommendation Engine shown in Figure 4.12 runs. This machine learning-based engine provides a recommendation for how to proceed based on historical decisions. With specifically tailored business analytics and proactive user assistance, a user can clear the account efficiently.

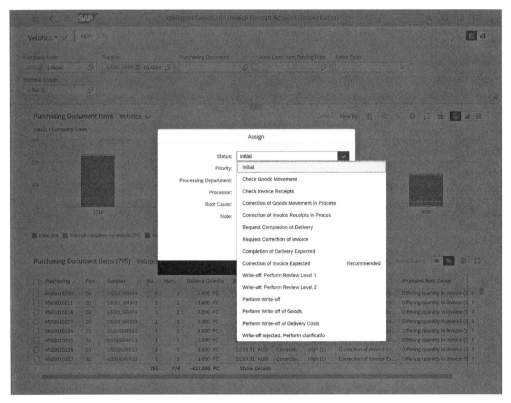

Figure 4.12 Intelligent Recommendation with the GR/IR Process

These intelligent recommendations simplify and accelerate the reconciliation process by helping automate the accountant's decisions. Fewer human interactions reduce the effort for non-value-adding activities, which in turn enables organizations to achieve a faster period-end closing with higher accuracy.

4.2.3   Accruals Management

Another example of operational process remodeling that makes use of modern technology can be found when looking at closing activity—specifically, accruals management.

This process is mostly manual and time-consuming (accountants typically need to obtain their original data, calculate accruals, post the related documents, and reverse documents) and error-prone (accountants must deal not only with these different data sources, but various calculation and logic methodologies as well). On top of this, organizations often lack transparency into how accruals are calculated, the status of the process, and the influence on overall KPIs. In other words, accruals management is another financials process with substantial room for improvement.

For accruals management, SAP S/4HANA is designed to support customers throughout the entire process of accruals: collecting inputs, calculating the correct amounts, allowing accountants to review the proposed postings, and posting the accruals as journal entries in the Universal Journal.

What does a typical input for the calculation of accruals look like? Typically, we would see contract-like data and precalculated amounts as two different sources for input. As of on-premise SAP S/4HANA 1809, accruals management covers purchase orders that are not yet fully delivered, plus the necessary accruals; manual accruals and their integration into the review and posting process; and input from spreadsheets.

SAP S/4HANA creates accrual objects from the various inputs and unifies the accrual data into one structure. For example, for purchase orders that have not yet been fully delivered, accrual objects are created automatically based on the purchase order data and its percentage of completion. The planned costs in the purchase order serve to calculate the accrual amount.

The system also displays the entire case to let an accountant review and then approve or adjust the proposed amounts as an optional step.

Throughout the entire process, accountants work in one unified environment. Embedded analytics give them full transparency and auditability. As illustrated in Figure 4.13, all the newly created accruals are shown on the left-hand side in a type of inbox. In the details of these objects, you can view the basic data (including information about the planned costs from the purchase order), the actual costs, and the calcula-tion logic (in this example, with the percentage of completion calculation). Based on this proposal, the accountant can decide to confirm or adjust the proposed data and then post it accordingly.

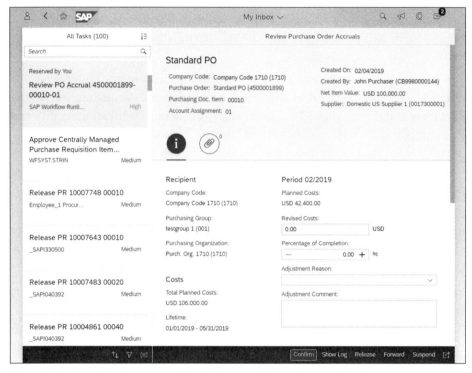

Figure 4.13 Accruals Management, Including Analytics and Central Review

A high level of automation is incorporated into the accruals process overall. When focusing on the review process, as illustrated in Figure 4.14, machine learning-driven recommendations about whether and how to adjust the values of the accrual propos-als based on similar decisions in the past add to existing rules-based proposals to fur-ther drive efficiency and accuracy (available from SAP S/4HANA Cloud 1902).

So by combining embedded analytics and machine learning in the accruals process, SAP S/4HANA drives cost-efficient process execution, from collecting the right data from the purchase orders to calculating the correct amounts and posting to the right accounts. Fully relying on automated calculations also means avoiding costly miscal-culations or delays.

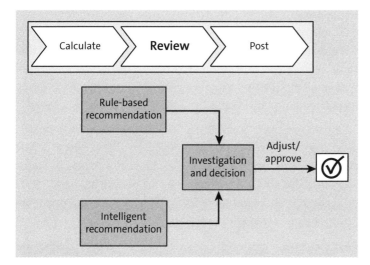

Figure 4.14 Combined Rule-Based and Machine Learning-Based Accrual Review Process

4.2.4 Smart Alerting

So far in this chapter, our focus has been on efficiency gains made during the execution of operational processes. This is important, of course—but reporting is also a source of a lot of manual work. (We'll cover flexible hierarchies as a way to optimize report definitions in Chapter 5!)

Now let's turn our attention to how machine learning can help us analyze data more efficiently. Although many finance professionals love to work with spreadsheet applications like Microsoft Excel to analyze data and drill down to find the specific product, customer, and channel that's causing margin leakage, this classic way of reporting also is very time-consuming. Another way to capitalize on machine learning is in the area of data analysis. Automatically detecting root causes for specific trends, market leakage, increased costs, or any other fluctuation is what we call *smart alerting*.

Let's look at a specific example of how this can work. Figure 4.15 shows SAP RealSpend, an SAP Cloud Platform–based cloud application that reads and interprets financial information from the Universal Journal. We'll discuss cloud extensions like SAP Real-Spend from a technical perspective in Chapter 15; for now, focus on the smart alerting functionality. For SAP RealSpend, this functionality is known as *anomaly detection*.

In this example, we're analyzing financial performance from the point of view of a single cost center in a bicycle company's e-bike production department. As the production manager, you see that there is an overspending of the approved production cost budget of $1 million allocated to the production of e-bikes. If you wanted to understand the root cause of this 13% overspending in the classic approach, you could start your analysis by slicing and dicing through a pivot table. But there is another way.

Once anomaly detection has been activated, SAP RealSpend shows the probable cause of the unexpected overspend (indicated using exclamation marks in Figure 4.15) without you needing to spend unnecessary time slicing and dicing data. Figure 4.16 shows that two batteries (**Bosch PowerPack 300 Battery** and **Bosch PowerPack 500 Battery**) were added to the produced e-bike instead of just one.

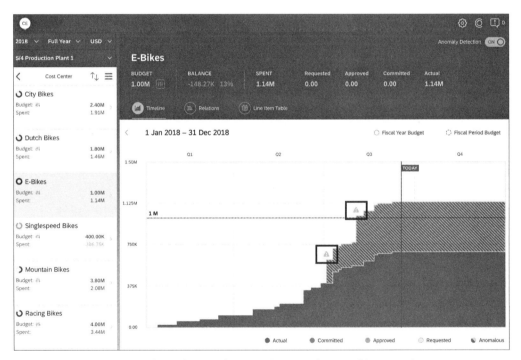

Figure 4.15 SAP RealSpend Anomaly Detection Based on Machine Learning

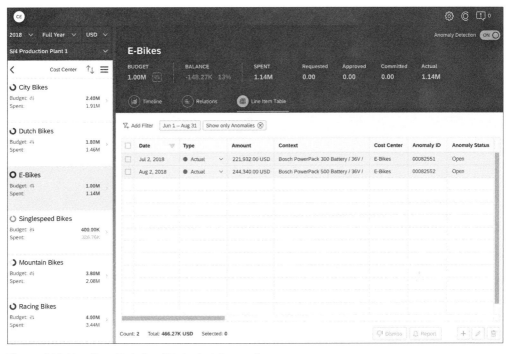

Figure 4.16 Line Item Details of Detected Anomalies

This specific application of machine learning nicely illustrates the element of continuous learning. By indicating which line item (here, which battery) is correctly added to the bill of material of the produced bicycle (by clicking the **Dismiss** button on the screen) and which one was in error (by clicking the **Report** button), this additional information is fed back into the machine learning algorithm to increase the alert quality in the next iteration.

Let's consider a second root cause-related application. SAP Financial Statement Insights focuses on analyzing a P&L using a predefined reporting view by consuming Universal Journal information. Like SAP RealSpend, it also runs on the SAP Cloud Platform. In Figure 4.17, note the serious deviation of the domestic revenue in April compared to the plan (represented by the dotted line in the chart). On the left, you can see which customer, profit center, and a series of other dimension members are causing this deviation. Thirty million are being caused by a specific area. By scrolling down the left pane, more specific data slices are automatically detected by the embedded machine learning algorithm, automatically showing the results of the root cause analysis.

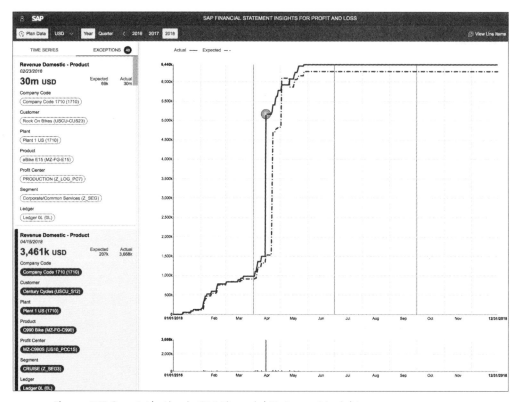

Figure 4.17 Smart Alerting in SAP Financial Statement Insights

4.3   Redesigning Applications

Earlier sections of this chapter focused on how business processes can be redesigned, offering both operational and analytics process examples. But you already know that finance processes within SAP S/4HANA run on top of the Universal Journal, meaning that, when we think about finance process optimization, an additional architectural component has yet to be addressed.

Because the Universal Journal is the single source for all financial data, all financial information across any business dimension is available for reporting centrally. So beyond optimizing specific finance processes on legal and management accounting sides separately, SAP S/4HANA also harmonizes and standardizes processes that span both disciplines. This allows us to apply common procedures and processes across the organization more widely.

This is an interesting principle, based on which a lot of future enhancements can be potentially expected. Two interesting areas in which SAP is starting to apply this principle are the harmonization of allocation logic and the reconciliation of intercompany movements. Let's look at both.

4.3.1   Universal Allocations

In this section, we'll explore the result of harmonizing data from the former FI and CO components for the purpose of allocation costs. In SAP ERP, cost allocations were available for different specific use cases in many different areas:

- General ledger–based allocations
- Allocations in cost center accounting
- Allocations on orders
- Profit center accounting–related allocations
- Project-based allocations
- Allocation logic within profitability analysis
- Allocations in special ledger and joint venture accounting scenarios
- Intercompany scenarios
- Specific logic for activity-based costing models

This complexity of different types of setups and different ways of running allocation models made allocations nontransparent, difficult to maintain, and inflexible in case of a change in the organizational structure. This non-harmonized approach introduced several disadvantages:

- **A lack of transparency into allocation logic**
  It was difficult for an organization to understand its allocation process and logic from end to end. The more complex an organizational structure becomes, the more views are required (e.g., by business unit vs. functional area of responsibility). This potentially becomes even more complex due to legal or industry-specific challenges. All this often results in a high number of allocation cycles and subcycles, known as *segments*.

  As a result, business unit managers or other responsible people within the organization often are unable to answer questions related to indirect costs that are allocated. Remarks like, "How did this cost get allocated to my area of responsibility?" are sometimes linked to a lack of traceability; more fundamentally, this confusion also can mean there is no clear view of how amounts flow across the chain of cycles, can suggest that there is doubt about the reliability of the tracing factors (drivers) used as a basis for the allocation logic, or even start discussions about which drivers are controllable or not.

- **Limited visualization of the result once the allocation models are being executed**
  It's often difficult to visualize the results after the allocation model has been executed. Especially in case of a multistep allocation, it's not easy to follow the entire flow of a cost from initial sender to final receiver of a particular cost. Similar to the lack of transparency into the allocation model, this also leads to lack of traceability of the allocated amounts.

- **Lack of simulation capabilities**
  We already discussed the growing need for forward-looking insights to improve business steering, and how organizations want to understand and identify the financial effects of changed allocation rules on their financial data. For example, perhaps an organization seeks to understand how financial performance would be impacted by the merging of two legal entities. When having to deal with complex and non-harmonized allocation models, this is difficult or even impossible to do.

However, because the Universal Journal contains all relevant information and necessary dimensionality, it's now possible to rethink the way allocations are modeled and executed. The basic idea of *universal allocations* is to provide one allocation setup for most different allocation use cases that combines actual and plan allocations, including simulation capabilities and currency breakdown. (Note that *activity allocations* and *settlements* of internal orders and work breakdown structure [WBS] elements are not planned as part of the scope.)

The first universal allocation modeling applications made available with SAP S/4HANA 1809 focus on cost center plan data scenarios only:

- **Manage Plan Overhead Allocation Cycles (SAP Fiori ID FINS_ONEALLOC_A8)**
  This SAP Fiori application is built to manage overhead allocation cycles, specifying the rules and settings by which the system is to allocate planned overhead amounts and quantities from one cost center to other cost centers or projects.

- **Manage Plan Distribution Cycles (SAP Fiori ID FINS_ONEALLOC_D8)**
  Similar to the previous app focusing on allocations, this SAP Fiori application manages distribution cycles to specify the rules and settings by which the system is to allocate planned overhead amounts and quantities from one cost center to other cost centers or projects.

Based on the modeled allocation and distribution logic, these then need to be executed. This is where the following apps come into play:

- **Run Plan Overhead Allocation (SAP Fiori ID FINS_ONEALLOC_AB)**
  This SAP Fiori application is responsible for performing allocations of planned overhead costs from cost centers to other cost centers or projects.

- **Run Plan Distribution (SAP Fiori ID FINS_ONEALLOC_DB)**
  Similar to the previous application focusing on allocations, this SAP Fiori application performs distributions of planned amounts from cost centers to other cost centers or projects.

We anticipate that SAP will release additional apps for allocations and distributions in the coming SAP S/4HANA releases, starting with the ones focusing on cost center actual data as of SAP S/4HANA Cloud 1811. The end goal is to model and run allocations harmonized from end to end, providing both transparency and traceability upon execution of these models.

Figure 4.18 shows one of the modeling steps of an allocation model, in this case showing sender and receiver information (i.e., the items from and to which costs which will be allocated).

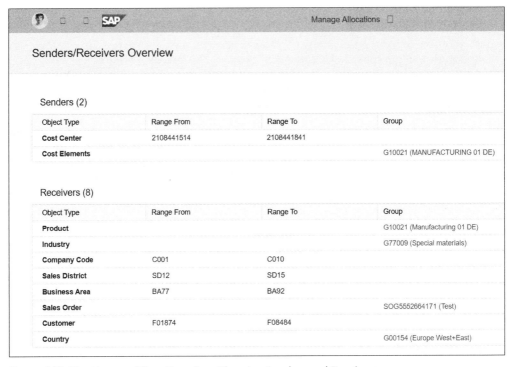

Figure 4.18 The Manage Allocations App, Showing Senders and Receivers

Figure 4.19 shows the result of a specific allocation run that was executed from a receiver's perspective.

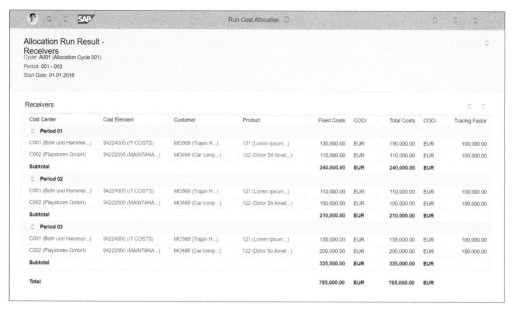

Figure 4.19 The Run Cost Allocation App, Showing the Receiver's Results

The delivered SAP Fiori applications for modeling and executing allocations and distributions are first steps in the direction of fully harmonized and transparent allocations, but SAP hopes to take the model transparency and cost allocation traceability to the next level. Figure 4.20 shows the Manage Overhead Allocations app (available as of SAP S/4HANA Cloud 1811), which displays the different segments of the allocation cycle and its status, along with the ability to drill down into the details.

Cost center responsibles are especially interested in traceability after an allocation cycle has been executed. Figure 4.21 shows a prototype for the Cost Object Analysis app. With this app, these types of questions could be answered more easily than with the classical tabular overview shown in Figure 4.19. The app shows data in a flow:

- On the left, you see the original cost centers sending costs to your area of responsibility via allocations (e.g., cafeteria, IT infrastructure, and so on).

- On the right, you see to which receivers costs are sent from your area of responsibility.

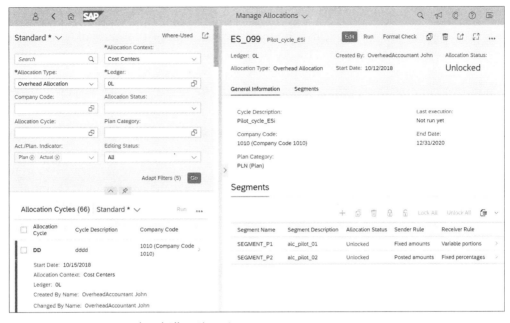

Figure 4.20 Manage Overhead Allocations App

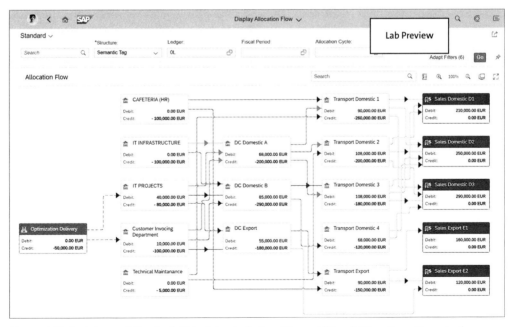

Figure 4.21 Prototype of the Cost Object Analysis App (Traceability of Allocations Executed)

4.3.2   Intercompany Reconciliation

The intercompany reconciliation process provides another example of how finance processes can be simplified via the Universal Journal. In the past, intercompany reconciliation was a highly manual process that involved matching open items for payables and receivables between companies in the same group so that these items could be excluded from the consolidated financial statements.

The first intercompany reconciliation solution was introduced with SAP R/3 and was designed to reconcile group payables and receivables across multiple systems. It was therefore built using a special ledger that would collect the relevant open items from the various systems and then allow the user to have the system reconcile them automatically. If one of the postings needed to be corrected, the system would provide a user interface via which the user could reconcile the items manually.

The next version of the intercompany reconciliation solution was introduced in SAP Business Suite powered by SAP HANA; this version worked directly on the accounting documents rather than waiting for them to be replicated into a special ledger. This provided a leaner process: any document posted in accounting was available for reconciliation immediately.

Figure 4.22 shows the Intercompany Reconciliation: Open Items application and a list of company code pairs (**1010** to **1710**, and so on) for which the open items should be matched. For each pair, you can see the open items, receivables, and payables to be reconciled.

Figure 4.23 shows a list of the documents that the system was unable to assign for intercompany trading between company codes **1010** and **1710**. The documents at the bottom have been reconciled, whereas the two columns at the top are awaiting reconciliation. The system makes proposals for the potential source of the problem; users can then navigate between company code pairs and the open items, receivables, and payables to be matched using the tree on the left.

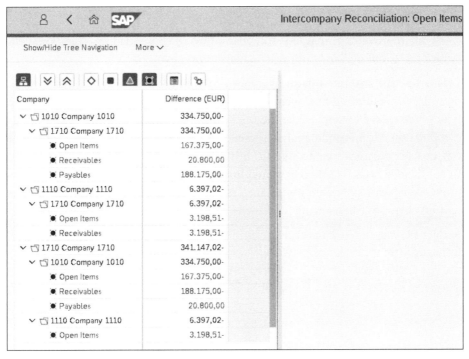

Figure 4.22 Intercompany Reconciliation: Open Items

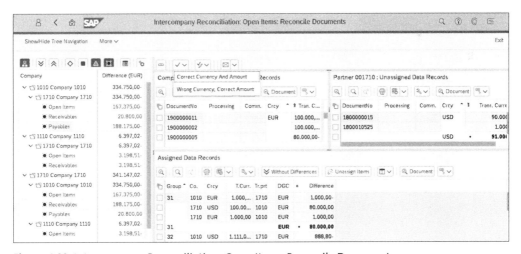

Figure 4.23 Intercompany Reconciliation: Open Items Reconcile Documents

4.4   Summary

One core improvement that SAP S/4HANA offers in comparison to traditional ERP systems is to redesign and optimize financial processes.

We started this chapter with an overview of the principles behind finance process optimization, outlining how technology helps put process optimization into practice. We discussed examples like the GR/IR reconciliation app to illustrate how the combination of embedded analytics, machine learning, and collaboration technology enables organizations to significantly reduce time and effort spent on operational finance tasks. We then explored how harmonized finance processes such as universal allocations across the finance function enable us to even become more cost-efficient while benefitting from increased transparency and traceability.

In the next chapter, we'll take a deep dive into the user experience behind these evolutions: SAP Fiori.

Chapter 5

SAP Fiori and Live Data: Merging Transactional and Analytics Data

In Chapters 3 and 4, we showed a few SAP Fiori applications—but in this chapter, we'll explain in more detail what SAP Fiori is and how live data is used in its applications as we merge transactional and analytics data in SAP S/4HANA.

SAP Fiori was introduced in 2013 as a new approach to user interface design; its applications could run not only on the desktop, but also on tablets and smartphones to deliver key information quickly to users on the move. The first finance application delivered was My Spend, which provided budget information to managers; other apps allowed employees to submit shopping carts, travel requests, leave requests, and so on for approval by their managers. These apps predate SAP S/4HANA and provided support for simple use cases with a focus on the mobile user experience.

SAP S/4HANA marks a shift in user interface design. Now, SAP Fiori is offered for *all* users, with role-based user interfaces for the asset accountant, the inventory accountant, the cost accountant, the collections specialist, and so on to support the more complex tasks and day-to-day challenges in finance. With SAP S/4HANA Cloud, all applications are delivered via SAP Fiori rather than the classic SAP GUI.

Nevertheless, opinions about SAP Fiori in the SAP community remain divided. Some organizations migrate to SAP S/4HANA but continue to use the SAP GUI transactions, with the goal of keeping changes to a minimum; they elect to use SAP Fiori only in areas such as cash management, where SAP Fiori is the only available user interface. Other SAP customers have embraced the SAP Fiori approach from the start and are using the new applications wherever possible.

By offering *compatibility views* that bring the information in the Universal Journal back into the old structures for reporting, SAP has tried to ease organizations through the transition. However, an SAP Note in December 2017 recommended moving to the embedded analytics approach instead of SAP Report Writer/Painter (SAP Note 2579584: Recommendations for Financial Reporting in SAP S/4HANA); it makes sense to take this guidance into account for your future reporting approach.

In this chapter, we'll introduce SAP Fiori and explain what it means for your data in SAP S/4HANA. In Section 5.1, we'll walk you through the basics: the SAP Fiori launchpad, the various application types, and the bread-and-butter reports that your finance organization needs. In Section 5.2, we'll show you some sample applications to give a sense of how the new applications flow. In Section 5.3, we'll take you behind the scenes to explain the virtual data model, which transforms Universal Journal, planning, and consolidation data (tables ACDOCA, ACDOCP, and ACDOCU) that we talked about in Chapter 1 into reports to support your daily tasks. Finally, we'll look at how SAP is taking this approach further to support the intelligent enterprise with business rules and machine learning in Section 5.4.

5.1   What Is SAP Fiori?

SAP Fiori is a new approach to user interface design, but it's constantly evolving, and you'll find that many different application types coexist under the SAP Fiori umbrella.

What characterizes the user experience in SAP Fiori compared to the SAP Easy Menu offered in SAP ERP is that all applications are offered through a single point of entry, the SAP Fiori launchpad, which provides access to the applications associated with your user role. We saw a few examples of these launchpads when we looked at the roles for the inventory accountant, production accountant, sales accountant, accounts receivable manager, accounts receivable accountant, and invoicing manager in Chapter 3.

In Chapter 3, we showed how the user accesses both *analytical* applications (such as the Overdue Receivables app) and *transactional* applications (such as the Process Collections Worklist app). Because the task of converting transactions from SAP ERP into SAP Fiori applications is not complete in SAP S/4HANA 1809, you'll also find SAP GUI transactions being rendered as SAP Fiori applications, which we saw when we looked at the Material Cost Estimate and Material Price Analysis applications in Chapter 2. Over time, you'll also find configuration applications being converted to SAP Fiori, along with workflow apps, scheduling apps, and so on. This progress is important because many organizations feel that they don't want to move certain user groups to SAP Fiori until most of the applications they need are available in the new "look."

Looks aside, what makes SAP Fiori different from the user interface in SAP ERP is that SAP Fiori can run on all devices. These are *responsive* user interfaces that can recognize the need to adjust to fit your phone, your tablet, or your desktop. When an application running on your smartphone or tablet connects to an SAP S/4HANA system, it uses SAP Gateway to transfer information about your user to the system and a query to request the information that you want to see. This information is then returned from SAP S/4HANA using standard protocols. To make this work, SAP must build data services to help you to access all the information needed for financial reporting. These interfaces are not to be confused with APIs and SAP Process Integration, which share data between systems. The focus is on providing simple and guided access to business data for all end users.

SAP Fiori Library

If you haven't worked with SAP Fiori before, you'll find basic information about every delivered application in the SAP Fiori apps reference library, available at *https://fioriappslibrary.hana.ondemand.com/sap/fix/externalViewer/*. Whenever we refer to an SAP Fiori application in this book, we mention the SAP Fiori ID to help you to find more information about the application via the library.

Bear in mind that there are also country-specific versions of many of the delivered roles and applications. If the application pictured here looks different than what you see in your system, this may be due to country-specific changes to meet local reporting requirements in your country.

Now, let's look at what characterizes an SAP Fiori user interface and what types of applications are available.

5.1.1   Characteristics

In the beginning, the tenets of SAP Fiori were that an application should be role-based (i.e., designed for a specific user), responsive (i.e., adaptive to the device on which it is being run, whether this is the desktop, a tablet device, or a mobile device), simple (i.e., it follows the design paradigm 1-1-3, or one user, one use case, three screens), coherent (i.e., the applications all speak the same language), and of instant value (i.e., have a low barrier to adoption).

As more and more SAP Fiori user interfaces have been built for professional users, some things have changed, so you'll now find plenty of applications with a degree of complexity—but you'll still find a common aim to support a coherent user experience. One way of achieving this is by standardizing user interface templates, so with SAP S/4HANA you'll find the same patterns being used for overview pages, analytical list view pages, object pages, and so on across all applications, not just in finance.

The connection with SAP HANA might not seem obvious from this list, but the importance of mobile access requires a higher degree of performance. Consider that a smartphone clearly cannot wait half an hour for a report to return a result. The applications need to receive results back from the server in a few seconds or the connection will time out before the response has reached the phone. Of course, use case matters; you are more likely to be showing key figures for a manager on a smartphone than doing the heavy slicing and dicing required for detailed analysis or scheduling period close tasks. You can identify the apps that are designed for use on a phone or tablet by checking the entries in the **Form Factor** in the SAP Fiori library. Applications such as My Spend are intended for use on a smartphone, whereas it's assumed that the Manage Cost Centers app will run mainly on the desktop. To check whether your devices are compatible with SAP Fiori, refer to SAP Note 1935915 (Fiori for Business Suite: Browser/Devices/OS Information).

5.1.2   Kinds of Applications

We've already seen examples of the two main kinds of applications in the previous chapters:

- Transactional apps such as Manage Customer Line Items, Manage Supplier Line Items, Supervise Collections Worklist, Process Collections Worklist, Manage Dispute Cases, and Reprocess Bank Statement Items
- Analytical apps such as Product Profitability, Project Profitability, Overdue Receivables, and Cash Discount Forecast

The third group of applications consists of the fact sheets that are provided after you have searched in the upper part of the SAP Fiori launchpad.

What's important if you're coming from a controlling world that has been split between SAP ERP and SAP BW is that the transactional apps and analytical apps are running on the same platform. Transactional apps are used to manage profit centers, cost centers, accounts, and so on, and to update the business transactions in SAP S/4HANA; meanwhile, analytical apps use those same profit centers, cost centers, and accounts within the reports with no need to load to a data warehouse or perform complicated transformations. In other words, the system is providing insight to action from *live data*, rather than data that has been replicated to a data warehouse.

If we look at the analytical apps in more detail, we find that they can be categorized further:

- SAP Design Studio apps are designed for multidimensional analysis of the kind we promised in Chapter 1; these are characterized by the lists of dimensions on the left-hand side of the screen that offer many different drilldown options, far more than were technically feasible in SAP ERP. We'll encounter many examples in finance because this is the perfect user interface for switching dimensions in the giant pivot table that is the Universal Journal. SAP Design Studio apps are not accessible (i.e., usable by visually impaired users), so all of these apps are delivered in parallel as Web Dynpro apps to support users who need screen readers.
- SAP Smart Business apps are more rigid in their display of key performance indicators. They offer the ability to switch dimensions, but they are more commonly used in accounts receivable, accounts payable, and cash management.

When we looked at the Product Profitability (Figure 3.5) and Project Profitability (Figure 3.7) apps in Chapter 3, we were looking at SAP Design Studio apps, whereas Overdue Receivables (Figure 3.18) is an SAP Smart Business app. As you see more and more of these applications, you'll start to recognize these distinctions.

The transactional apps that we've looked at until now were all built in SAPUI5. However, you'll begin to sense that SAP is serious about translating all application types to SAP Fiori when we introduce the new application types, including Generic Configuration Framework (to replace the former IMG activities), Generic Job Scheduling and Generic Application Log Framework (which we'll look at when we look at the close activities in Chapter 7), and Manage Workflow.

In case all this sounds too technical, we'll now look at some real examples to help you understand what an SAP Fiori application feels like.

5.2 First Steps in SAP Fiori

The goal of this section is not to explain the individual applications, but rather to help you understand the patterns underlying SAP Fiori. We'll look at three application areas, beginning with cash management (Section 5.2.1), the first area of finance to embrace SAP Fiori. We'll then return to the examples from financial operations that we looked at in Chapter 3 to illustrate the SAP Fiori story (Section 5.2.2). Finally, we'll look at accounting and controlling and show how the vision of the Universal Journal from Chapter 1 translates into reports that deliver live data to the business (Section 5.2.3).

5.2.1   Cash Management

We'll look at SAP S/4HANA for cash management in detail in Chapter 13. In this section, our focus is on the use of SAP Fiori in the areas of bank account management, cash position management, and cash flow analysis, with the aim of explaining the various patterns that you'll find across the different applications.

Bank Account Management

Access to all SAP Fiori applications is granted by selecting a tile in the SAP Fiori launchpad. The tiles are delivered in *business catalogs* that are then assigned to the roles (in this case, the cash manager). The app will run through the usual authorization checks before it shows any data. Proper identity and access management is a key part of implementing SAP Fiori. Many apps use the existing authorization objects, but in some cases new authorization objects have been introduced. Use the documentation about the relevant SAP Fiori app to understand the OData service it's using to access data from SAP S/4HANA and how that data is protected.

Figure 5.1 shows the tile for the Manage Banks app (SAP Fiori ID F1574). Notice that many of the SAP Fiori applications begin with the title **Manage**. What this means is that they will give you a list of the selected objects, and from there you can edit, create, display, delete, and so on. This immediately makes the access feel less clunky than in the SAP Easy Menu.

Manage Banks -
Basic

Figure 5.1 The Manage Banks Tile

When you click the tile, the SAP S/4HANA system displays the selection parameters for the bank accounts, as shown in Figure 5.2. To display the relevant banks, fill out the selection parameters and choose **Go**. The results then will be shown in the result area directly beneath the selection screen. Compared to the SAP ERP reports, one improvement here is that you don't need to leave the application to change your selection parameters. If you need to make a change, you simply adjust the parameter in the top part of the screen and choose **Go** again without losing the context of the application. Because the area available for the selection parameters has been kept

small deliberately, you might miss a selection parameter. If this is the case, choose
Adapt Filters.

Figure 5.2 Selection Parameters for the Manage Banks App

Clicking **Adapt Filters** will take you into the dialog shown in Figure 5.3, where you see
the eight selection parameters visible in Figure 5.2 and can add further selection
parameters to the report by choosing **More Filters**. This may seem to be adding clicks
at first, but it makes the initial impression of the application less daunting than the
long selection screens in many SAP ERP reports.

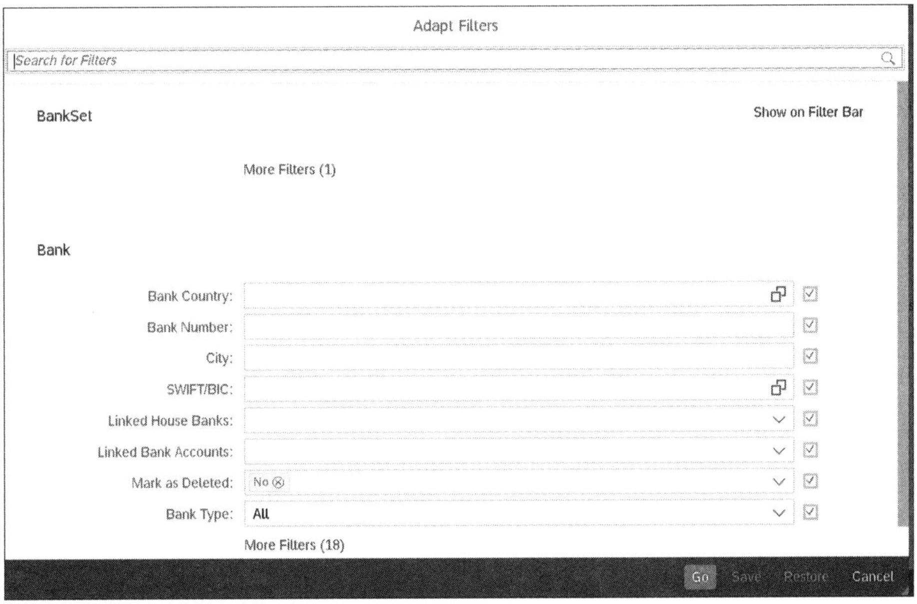

Figure 5.3 Adapting Filters for Bank Selection

Figure 5.4 shows the list of filters available to select the relevant banks. Choose any of these fields to add it to the selection screen shown in Figure 5.2. If the missing field is one that you will use regularly, save it as part of your view.

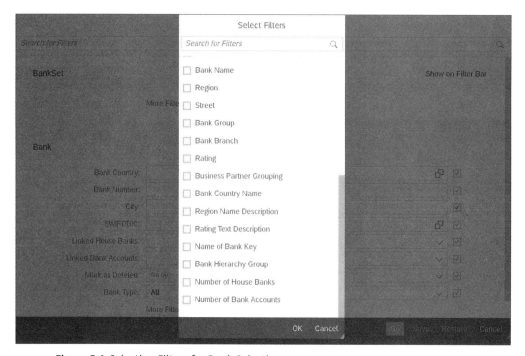

Figure 5.4 Selecting Filters for Bank Selection

Figure 5.5 shows the result of selecting the banks. We'll see this pattern throughout SAP Fiori. If the list is overwhelmingly long, use the **Search** box to enter the bank you are looking for. If you're missing a field in the results list, the chances are that it's hidden. To display additional fields, choose the wheel icon beside the **Search** box. Notice also that you can download this list to Microsoft Excel if that makes you more comfortable.

Figure 5.6 shows the **View Settings** screen for the bank results list (accessed by selecting the wheel icon on the previous screen). You can add additional fields to the results list by selecting a checkbox. You can also sort and filter the results list, using features familiar from ABAP List Viewer. Return to the screen shown in Figure 5.5 and select a line to access the master data for one of the banks, as shown in Figure 5.7.

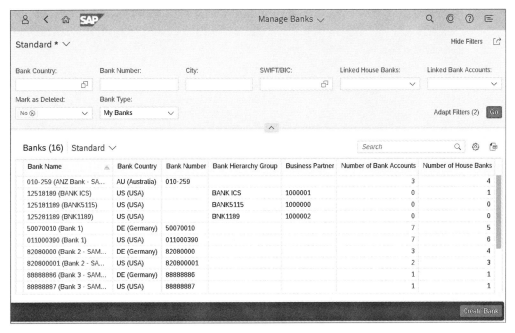

Figure 5.5 Viewing Selected Banks

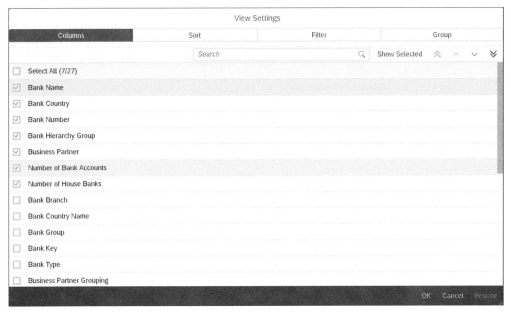

Figure 5.6 Viewing Settings for Bank Result List

Figure 5.7 shows the bank master data. Notice that the actions, such as **Edit, Save**, and **Cancel**, are at the bottom right of the screen. We have begun to edit the bank details and can tab through the bank master data by switching to **House Banks, Contact Info, Related Branches**, and **Change History**. You'll see this basic layout for many master data apps, including accounts, profit centers, cost centers, assets, and so on.

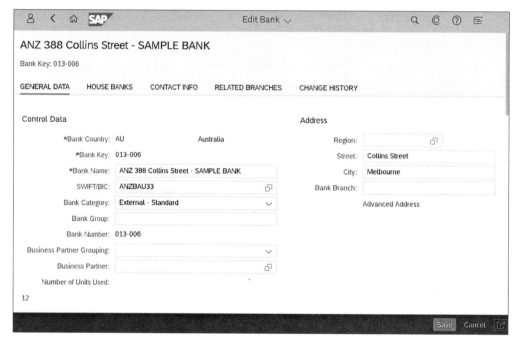

Figure 5.7 Editing Bank Master Data

We'll return to the subject of bank account management in Chapter 13. Now let's look at an example of an analytical app, the Cash Position app (SAP Fiori ID F1737).

Cash Position

If you compare Figure 5.8 with Figure 5.1, you'll see that the **Cash Position** tile shows the cash position in euros. The idea is that cash managers will recognize instinctively whether this figure is good (green) or bad (red) and know whether they need to react. Many analytical apps deliver such a key figure to the launchpad so that users can determine whether a reaction is required.

Figure 5.8 Live Figures in the Cash Position Tile

In Figure 5.9, we haven't entered any selection parameters, so we see the default selection. Clicking from the tile to the app takes you directly to the breakdown of the cash position for those bank countries that you are authorized to see. This pattern is the same as for the Overdue Receivables app shown in Chapter 3. What's happening behind the scenes is that the system has used an OData service to select the relevant cash items from SAP S/4HANA. This service will include the parameters to select by bank country in this example. To switch the view, select one of the other options from the dropdown box currently reading **By Bank Country**.

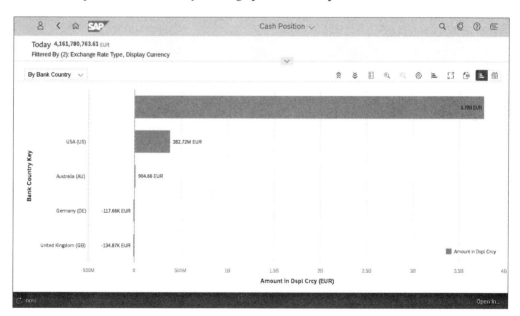

Figure 5.9 Viewing Cash Position by Bank Country

What's important is that none of these views have been precalculated. Whenever you switch views, you're triggering a new selection from the SAP HANA database. If further business transactions have taken place in the meantime, this information is immediately included and visible to you.

Figure 5.10 shows the cash position broken down by company after selecting **By Company** from the dropdown.

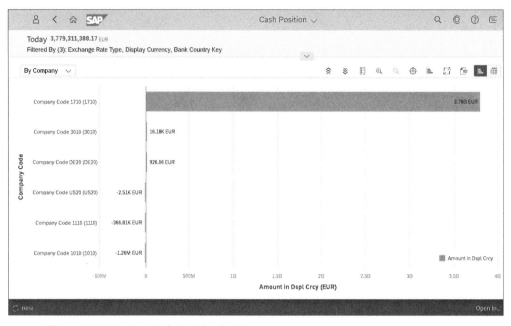

Figure 5.10 Viewing Cash Position by Company

If you prefer a different visualization, you can use the settings shown in Figure 5.11. You'll see this same basic layout in accounts receivable and accounts payable.

We'll return to the subject of managing the cash position in Chapter 13. Now let's look at a different analytical application, the Cash Flow Analyzer app.

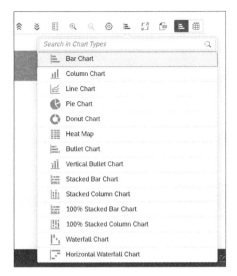

Figure 5.11 Chart Types for Cash Position

Cash Flow Analyzer

The Cash Flow Analyzer app (SAP Fiori ID F2332) is an analytical app like the one shown in Figure 5.8. However, its tile contains only an icon. This is because, like many reports in finance, the cash flow position cannot be reduced to one key figure. The cash manager needs to explore the data to understand his cash flow.

In Figure 5.12, we've filled out the selection parameters and selected **Go** to display the cash flow by currency. Again, you could extend both the selection parameters and the fields shown in the results list. Notice that a default aggregation has been set for the results list to show the flow by currency.

Figure 5.12 Viewing Results per Currency in the Cash Flow Analyzer App

From here, you can expand by bank account to see the cash flow proper in Figure 5.13. Notice the arrows representing the ins and outs of the cash flow here, something you won't see in a trial balance or financial statement.

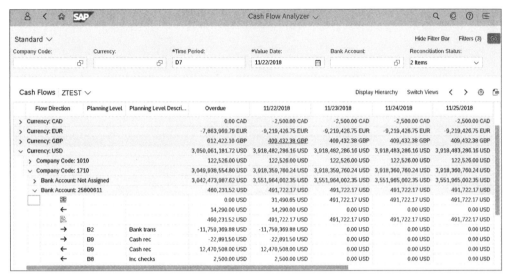

Figure 5.13 Viewing the Expanded List in the Cash Flow Analyzer App

We'll look at cash management in more detail in Chapter 13, but now we'll show how the patterns we saw in cash management repeat in financial operations.

5.2.2   Financial Operations

We discussed business changes in financial operations in Chapter 3 and explained the move to a shared service environment in Chapter 4. We'll now focus on financial operations from the user perspective.

Business Partner Management

When we looked at the changes to the business partner in SAP S/4HANA in Chapter 3, we showed the classic SAP GUI transactions to maintain the business partner. However, there is also an SAP Fiori application to manage business partners, as shown in

Figure 5.14. In this Business Partner app (SAP Fiori ID F3163), you'll notice the same approach to presenting the selection parameters as in Figure 5.2. You can again adapt the filters as in Figure 5.3 and change the fields in the result list as in Figure 5.6.

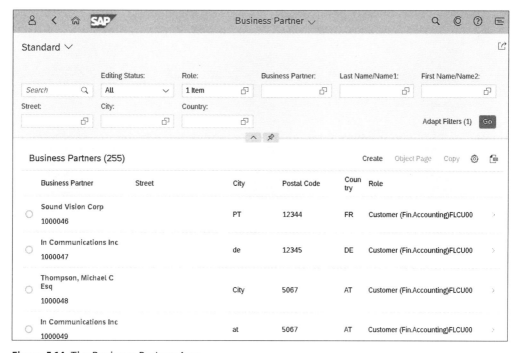

Figure 5.14 The Business Partner App

What changes slightly is that multiple actions are possible for the business partner, and the **Object Page** and **Copy** functions will only become active when you select a business partner from the results list.

Figure 5.15 shows the object page for a business partner called **In Communications Inc**. From this screen, you can access the **Roles**, **Address**, **Bank Accounts**, **Payment Cards**, **Identification**, **Contacts**, and **Attachments** tabs, in addition to the **Basic Data** tab shown on the screen.

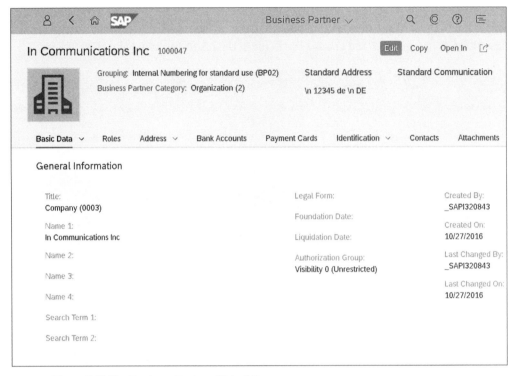

Figure 5.15 The Business Partner Object Page

Cash Discount Utilization

We looked at cash management in general, but here we'll focus on the operational part—namely, ensuring that the utilization of the cash discount is optimized for all accounts payable.

Consider the Cash Discount Utilization app (SAP Fiori ID F1736) shown in Figure 5.16, here displayed by region. Again, you can switch views and trigger a new data selection by changing the entries in the **By Region** dropdown menu.

Figure 5.17 shows a different SAP Fiori app: Days Payable Outstanding (SAP Fiori ID F1740). Our example displays the DSO from **November 2017** through **November 2018**. What's important here is that it's easy to see when the largest outstanding payables were due and react accordingly.

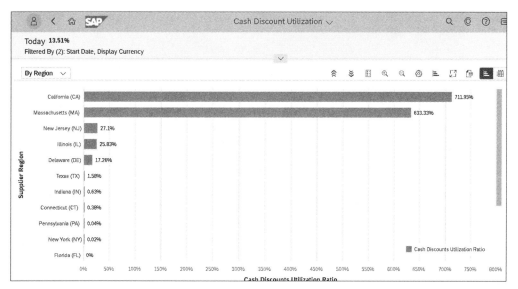

Figure 5.16 The Cash Discount Utilization App (by Region)

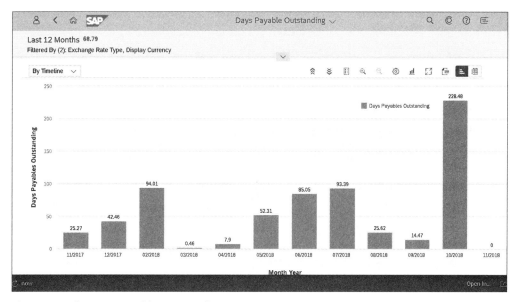

Figure 5.17 The Days Payable Outstanding App

As you explore apps like Cash Discount Utilization and Days Payable Outstanding, be aware that there was a technology shift in SAP S/4HANA 1511. In SAP S/4HANA 1503 and 1605, access to the data for these SAP Smart Business apps was provided using calculation views; your administrator had to install SAP Smart Business and SAP HANA Studio to prepare the data for display. From SAP S/4HANA 1511 onward, Core Data Services (CDS) views are used to access the data. These are part of the ABAP stack for SAP S/4HANA and do not need to be installed separately.

Supplier Line Items

Figure 5.18 shows the Manage Supplier Line Items app (SAP Fiori ID F0712). Notice that it does not simply list the open items but also provides status information. By selecting a line item, you can initiate actions such as creating correspondence, blocking a payment, and so on. The border between analytical and transactional applications is becoming blurred in SAP S/4HANA, as you saw when we discussed simplification and process guidance in Chapter 4.

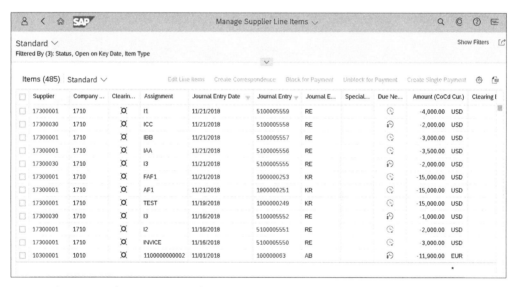

Figure 5.18 The Manage Supplier Line Items App

We'll come back to the topic of insight to action in more detail in Chapter 6. But first, we'll introduce some of the applications delivered for accounting and controlling.

5.2.3   Accounting and Controlling

We discussed the promise of improved financial reporting based on the Universal Journal in Chapter 1. Let's start to explain the reality of what you can potentially work with today.

Manage Cost Centers

Having seen the Manage Banks app in Figure 5.2 and the Business Partners app in Figure 5.14, you may find the Manage Cost Centers app (SAP Fiori ID F1443) shown in Figure 5.19 to be reassuringly familiar. One novelty is that you can use the **Standard Hierarchy Node** in the cost center master as a selection parameter rather than only in the F4 help.

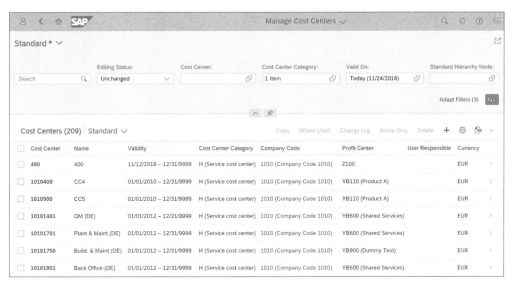

Figure 5.19 The Manage Cost Centers App

We discussed the challenges of handling organizational change and finding the connections between affected objects in Chapter 1. With this goal in mind, SAP has introduced several SAP Fiori apps to help users to visualize the connections between objects. Figure 5.20 shows the Where-Used List—Cost Centers app (SAP Fiori ID F3549), which displays all objects that are related to the selected cost center, including the assigned activity types, company codes, cost allocation cycles, cost allocation segments, fixed assets, cost center groups and hierarchies, profit centers, and splitting structures.

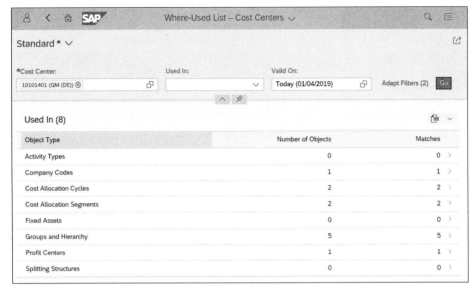

Figure 5.20 The Where-Used List—Cost Centers App

Display Financial Statement

The pattern for the Display Financial Statement app (SAP Fiori ID F0708) shown in Figure 5.21 is reminiscent of the Cash Flow Analyzer app.

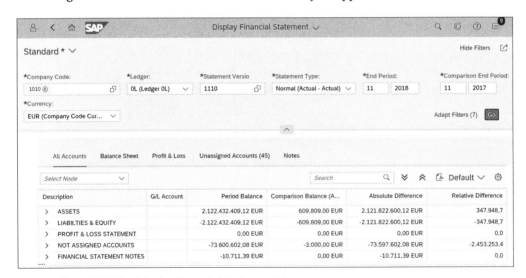

Figure 5.21 The Display Financial Statement App

Notice that you always include a ledger in the selection parameters, which we discussed in Chapter 2 when we talked about how to handle different accounting principles in reporting and that the structure of the accounts is always determined by the financial statement version. We'll return to the subject of hierarchies in Section 5.3.3.

Manage Journal Entries

Finally, Figure 5.22 shows the Manage Journal Entries app (SAP Fiori ID F0707), in which you'll recognize the design patterns from Figure 5.12 and Figure 5.18.

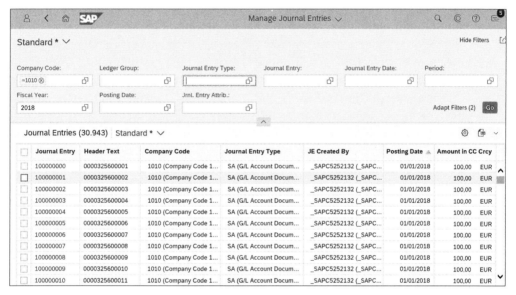

Figure 5.22 The Manage Journal Entries App

Looking at these apps, you can see what working with SAP Fiori can feel like. We'll now go behind the scenes to explain what has changed beyond the look and feel of the user interface.

5.3   Using a Virtual Data Model to Access Live Data

SAP R/3 included financial reports from the very beginning, and everybody has worked with the standard reporting in the Financial Accounting (FI), Asset Accounting, Cost Center Accounting, and other components. Most of these reports were built using Report Writer or, later, Report Painter; they provided the standard formatted reporting that we are all used to working with at month end. Most users have also worked with the drilldown reports offered for the General Ledger, special ledger, Profitability Analysis (CO-PA), Investment Management, and so on. These reports continue to work in SAP S/4HANA, meaning that you don't have to redefine your reporting strategy overnight. However, it's worth understanding what they can and can't do in SAP S/4HANA.

What these reports can do is exactly what they did before. They select the data as it was structured in SAP R/3 and SAP ERP and use the authorization objects that were available before. Behind the scenes, these reports are using compatibility views to select the data from the Universal Journal and bring it back into the old structures for reporting.

The most obvious thing you'll notice is that all the Controlling (CO) component reports continue to show cost elements, even though the cost elements and accounts have been merged into one entity, the account, as we explained in Chapter 1. If you try to perform a drilldown in the general ledger, you'll be able to use those fields that were delivered for use with the new General Ledger scenarios, but nothing more. Essentially, you'll be taking the Universal Journal with its 350-plus dimensions and chopping it back up into the old structures; consequently, you'll still have asset reports, inventory reports, cost center reports, and so on—but nothing that crosses the boundaries of the old applications unless you use the SAP Fiori applications. Because many of the classic reports used in FI and CO were based on the totals records, you'll find that they only access the sixteen fields included in table GLT0 or FAGLFLEXT in FI and table COSP or COSS in CO. You'll have what you had before, but without any of the benefits of moving to SAP S/4HANA.

Almost all the reports that were delivered in SAP ERP will continue to work with SAP S/4HANA, and you can continue to use any special ledgers that you might have defined in the past. The only time when you'll have to modernize is if you use the reports offered in the Cost Element Accounting menu, which read from the reconciliation ledger (table COFI), which is no longer available in SAP S/4HANA. However, you can easily display the same information in SAP S/4HANA by using the object type to provide a drilldown.

Figure 5.23 shows the P&L—Plan/Actual app (SAP Fiori ID F0927A). This is a sample P&L report in which we've drilled down by **Object Type** and **G/L Account** to show postings to profitability analysis (EO), to cost center/activity type (KL), to cost center (KS), and so on. You could explore the information further by pulling in the relevant profitability segments, cost centers, and activity types to determine for which account assignments revenues and costs have been incurred.

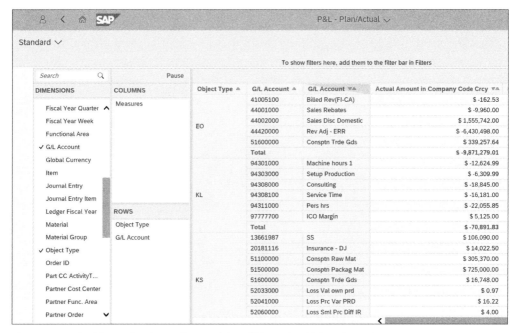

Figure 5.23 The P&L—Plan/Actual App with Drilldown by Object Type: Part 1

In Figure 5.24, we've scrolled down further in the same report to show the cumulative postings to orders (OR) and projects (PR). You could continue scrolling to see all account assignments. Finally, you would reach a # symbol (not assigned) for all those postings that did not have a CO account assignment (such as postings to balance sheet accounts and cash accounts).

Anybody who currently works with CO-PA will be familiar with this approach already, but it's new for most accountants because reporting dimensions such as company code, profit center, business area, and so on were always filled in SAP ERP.

Many organizations took their financial information and moved it to a data warehouse (e.g., SAP BW), so it's worth stopping for a moment to remember why. Many SAP customers made the move to handle performance concerns. There are often millions of data records in CO-PA and Product Cost Controlling, and it was more efficient to move them out of the operational system and into a system that was optimized for reporting. SAP S/4HANA is now fast enough to handle these volumes directly, and data warehouses or industry-specific data stores will be needed only in extreme cases.

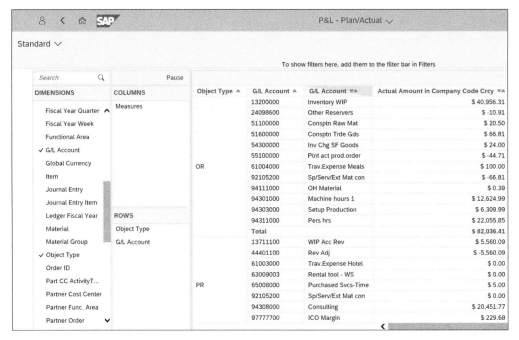

Figure 5.24 The P&L—Plan/Actual App with Drilldown by Object Type: Part 2

Other customers wanted multidimensionality and the promise of online analytical processing (OLAP). We already said that the General Ledger tables only contained limited dimensionality compared to the Universal Journal, and the same applies to Cost Center Accounting, Project Accounting, and so on. In CO-PA, the operating concern is inherently multidimensional, but performance concerns often drove organizations to move the records to a data warehouse for reporting purposes. The problem in SAP ERP was usually a *sparsely filled matrix*—in other words columns that were only partially filled with data. As we'll explain shortly, those empty cells cease to be a concern with SAP S/4HANA.

Others wanted to enrich the data to include additional attributes or data from non-SAP sources. We looked at options to enrich data when we described the extensibility options in Chapter 1. We'll look at how to include non-SAP data when we look at the options for group reporting in Chapter 12.

Of course, moving to SAP S/4HANA won't necessarily stop you from using a data warehouse. The old extractors continue to work using the same compatibility views that are supporting the legacy reports inherited from SAP ERP. There is also a new extractor, OFI_ACDOCA_10, designed specifically to extract data from the Universal

Journal and load it to SAP BW. However, we'll now explore how it's possible to report directly on large data volumes in SAP S/4HANA.

5.3.1   What Is a Column-Based Database?

You may already have heard people explain that SAP S/4HANA uses a column-based database rather than a row-based database without fully understanding what this means in finance.

In traditional databases, transactional data is organized in *rows*; in other words, each invoice and sales order in CO-PA and each material movement and order confirmation in actual costing is recorded as a row on the database. When you run a report to show the revenues for one or more regions in CO-PA, the system reads all the records in the database row by row, selects those that meet your selection criteria, and then aggregates the revenues for those invoices in the chosen region(s).

By contrast, transactional data is organized in *columns* in SAP HANA. To run the same report, the system reads only the region column and the revenue field. You get the most benefit from a column-based database compared to a traditional database when you have a high number of columns (such as the many dimensions in CO-PA or the many material-related characteristics in actual costing) and a low number of columns to be scanned for selection (only the region and revenue in our example).

The use of a column-based database also means that only those cells in the column that contain entries are relevant. Any cells that are empty are ignored during selection, and that column is displayed as # (not assigned). This means that the type of drilldowns you might perform in CO in which a cost center (KS) has charged to an order (OR) that has settled to a project (PR) that has settled to a profitability segment (EO) can be handled easily by the database.

If you're selecting an accounting document using the document number, then it won't make a whole lot of difference whether you select from a column store or a row store because every document number is different. However, if you want to select by company code, you'll only have to select from at most a few hundred in a column store, whereas you'll have to read every row in a row store. This means that the performance benefits will be largest when you're selecting by account, region, company code, and so on and then doing a huge aggregation of millions of data records.

If you've only worked with SAP ERP recently, then the chances are that you have forgotten how much information is in the line item tables because you will have almost always been working with the totals tables, which typically only contain sixteen fields. In theory, the line item table in CO (table COEP) allowed you to select by fields other than the account assignment, cost element, and period, but selecting a trading partner or an employee number would often result in a time out and most users simply learned not to try to use those fields in their selections. Similarly, the line item table in FI (table BSEG) contained many fields but was itself a cluster table combining data from several other tables and was not easy to query.

5.3.2   Embedded Analytics

The answer to live reporting in SAP S/4HANA is not just to use a column-based database. SAP has now embedded analytics into SAP S/4HANA by providing a *virtual data model* (VDM) to convert the information in the Universal Journal into a format that can be consumed by the SAP Fiori reports. The virtual data model logically combines data from the source ERP tables to provide data for consumption via frontend tools.

Figure 5.25 illustrates the idea of the VDM. At the bottom you see the physical tables that we introduced in Chapter 1: table ACDOCA for the journal entries, table ACDOCP for planning, and table ACDOCU for group reporting, along with the master data tables for the accounts, cost centers, profit centers, business partners, materials, and so on. These tables are updated whenever the business transactions taking place in finance, logistics, payroll, and so on post data.

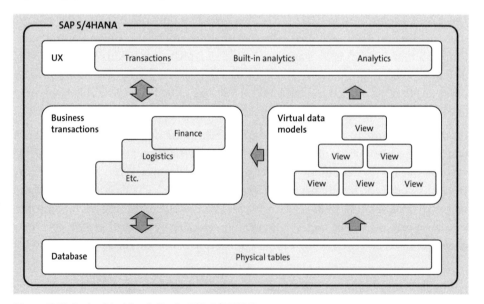

Figure 5.25 Embedded Analytics in SAP S/4HANA

The VDM, then, is simply the collection of views that allow analytical applications to select the relevant transactional data, merge it with master data, and make it part of a report. The simplest example of what a view does is to select the text for a cost center and show it in the report alongside the technical key stored in the Universal Journal. It will also select attributes (e.g., the type of cost center or the name of the cost center manager) from the master and include it in the report, along with any additional attributes if you have extended the master data tables. The views also handle the hierarchies, such as the financial statement version, cost element hierarchy, profit center hierarchy, cost center hierarchy, and so on. We'll look at these in Section 5.3.3.

Reports such as the one shown in Figure 5.26 are built using the VDM. The user interface in this case is an *analytical list page*. What this means is that there is a visual selection area at the top, a graphic showing the selected data in the middle, and a list of the selected line items at the bottom.

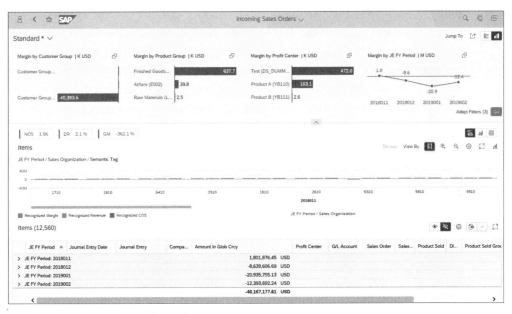

Figure 5.26 The Incoming Sales Orders App

One of the advantages of using the embedded analytics approach rather than working in a separate data warehouse is that you can switch easily between key figures and the transactions behind them. Once data has been loaded to a data warehouse, it has often been cleansed and aggregated, making it difficult to tie back to the underlying data. If you use the report shown in Figure 5.26, you can immediately access the relevant document. This helps you to trust the data, because you're seeing the documents behind the aggregated key data, but also to perform actions on these documents, such as initiating a correction. Here you're looking at what is essentially a reporting application, but in Chapter 3, Figure 3.22 you saw the same pattern used as an entry point for the Supervise Collections Worklist app to assign collection tasks to users.

You'll see other examples of this type of report when we look at event-based revenue recognition in Chapter 7 and predictive accounting in Chapter 8.

Although aggregating documents and delivering the relevant key figures sounds easy enough, one of the challenges is making such information consumable. Many users like the idea that in the Universal Journal the revenues in profitability analysis are simply different aggregations of the revenues in profit center accounting and financial accounting (see Chapter 1), but they don't always find it helpful to analyze profitability by looking at a list of accounts; looking at a chart of accounts that contains several thousand accounts can feel overwhelming. When we examined the Product Profitability app in Chapter 3, we were looking at key figures that aggregated those accounts to deliver the **Revenues**, **Cost of Goods Sold**, **Price Differences**, and other key figures. In Figure 5.27, we're using the same report but have pulled in the general ledger account as a drilldown to show how the various accounts aggregate to give the **Billed Revenue** and **Sales Deduction** key figures.

Similarly, when we looked at Project Profitability in Chapter 3, Figure 3.7 you saw the key figures for event-based revenue recognition. In Figure 5.28, we have again included the general ledger account in the drilldown to show how the accounts roll up into the **Billed Revenue**, **Actual Cost**, **Recognized Revenue**, and other key figures.

What's happening behind the scenes in these two reports is that we're using semantic tags to define the key figures, and these semantic tags are linked with general ledger accounts in the financial statement version to provide the aggregated reporting. The idea behind semantic tags is that SAP can deliver applications and key figures for which the structure remains stable. So the Product Profitability app (see Figure 5.27) and Project Profitability app (see Figure 5.28) can be used out of the box by simply mapping your own accounts/cost elements to these tags.

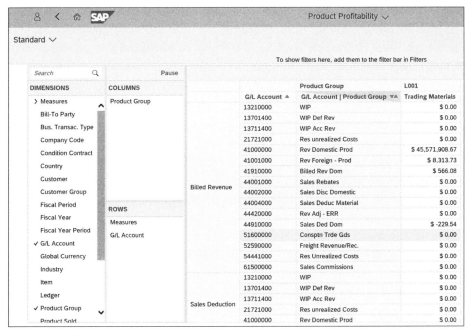

Figure 5.27 The Product Profitability App with Drilldown to General Ledger Account

Figure 5.28 The Project Profitability App with Drilldown to General Ledger Account

SAP delivers more than fifty semantic tags for cash reporting and profitability reporting, so start your journey in the IMG under **General Ledger Accounting (New) • Master**

Data • G/L Accounts • Define Semantic Tags for Balance Sheet and Profit and Loss Structures to see whether the delivered semantic tags match the value fields that you use for reporting today. You can create further tags as required. If you create new semantic tags, you'll need to extend the CDS query to reference them. To find out more about this approach, refer to SAP Note 2538634 (Semantic Tagging for FSV and CDS Query Extension).

To use the delivered tags, you need to assign your own accounts in the IMG under **General Ledger Accounting (New) • Master Data • G/L Accounts • Assign Semantic Tags for Balance Sheet and Profit and Loss Structures**. The idea is that the tags themselves should remain stable, so if you use different revenue accounts in the United States and in Brazil, you should keep one revenue tag but assign the different accounts in dependency from your financial statement version (Transaction OB58). The assignment uses the nodes of the financial statement version, but you can also assign individual accounts or combinations of accounts and functional areas to the delivered tags.

Return to Chapter 3, Figure 3.5 and notice that we're showing the fixed and variable parts of the cost of goods sold (COGS) as separate key figures, even though there is only one COGS account (see Chapter 1). What's happening here is that we're using logic in the custom analytical query to separate the fixed part of the COGS from the variable part. Note that this is currently only possible in the group currency because the costs are only split into their fixed and variable parts in group currency in the Universal Journal. SAP is expected to make this function available in company code currency in a future edition.

As you work through the delivered apps, it's often difficult to understand how the reports you use today differ from the new reports. Applications such as the Display Financial Statement app shown in Figure 5.21 should deliver the same results as its equivalent in SAP ERP. However, the report shown in Figure 5.27 shows the typical dilemma faced by project teams. If you work with the semantic tags, you can achieve something like what you had in costing-based CO-PA and Transaction KE30. As soon as you pull the general ledger account in, you have something more like what you might have built using account-based CO-PA. If you then look at Figure 5.28, you see a report that would not have been possible at all in SAP ERP because we're showing both the project as an account assignment and the product sold as part of the profitability segment. The classic reports that used Transaction KE30 could only show those characteristics included in the operating concern. Now we can build links between the account assignments and the profitability segments and consequently can build completely different reports.

5.3.3   Hierarchies in Financials

One of the challenges of financial reporting is that we commonly work with hierarchies, such as the financial statement version, cost element groups, profit center groups, cost center groups, or the freely definable hierarchies that could be set up in Report Writer.

Most of these hierarchies were built on a common technology, called *sets* in SAP ERP, but this approach needed an overhaul. (When the set maintenance tools were built in the early 1990s, nobody was asking for time dependency, versioning, and other features!) We find sets being used in SAP ERP for cost element groups, cost center groups, profit center groups, and so on and to create company code hierarchies, custom hierarchies, and so on for use with the Report Writer. Other hierarchies, such as the financial statement versions that we looked at in Chapter 2, product hierarchies and customer hierarchies for profitability analysis, and work breakdown structures for projects were built using different technologies.

SAP's approach is to introduce a new global accounting hierarchy with SAP S/4HANA. The idea is that it provides a common framework for hierarchy maintenance, including the option to make them time-dependent.

Now hierarchies are maintained using the Manage Global Accounting Hierarchies app (SAP Fiori ID F2918), shown in Figure 5.29. In SAP S/4HANA 1809, you can use this app to maintain financial statement versions, company code hierarchies, profit center hierarchies, cost center hierarchies, account groups, and custom characteristics, with more hierarchy types planned. Note that because of the link to the controlling area and the associated master data, at the time of publication (spring 2019) you cannot maintain standard profit center hierarchies and cost center hierarchies but only alternative hierarchies using the Manage Global Accounting Hierarchy app.

Instead of having separate transactions for each hierarchy type as you had in SAP ERP, you will work with one common interface. In Figure 5.29, you can choose from the different hierarchy types by choosing **Type** in the selection parameters. The same technology is also used to build hierarchies for group reporting, a process that we will return to in Chapter 12. Notice two important features not available in SAP ERP shown on this screen:

- You can maintain a validity period for your hierarchy to specify that it's valid for a fiscal year or even a quarter within that fiscal year. You can, of course, continue to define hierarchies that are valid forever (ending date 12/31/9999).

- You can maintain the hierarchy as a draft and release it when you're ready (via the **Status** field in the selection parameters).

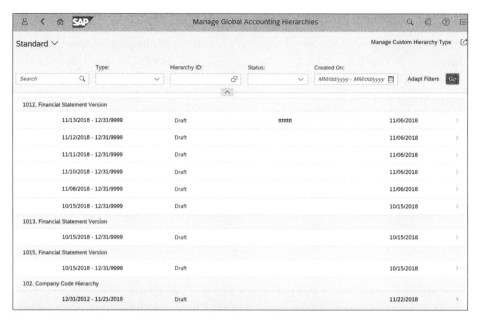

Figure 5.29 The Manage Global Accounting Hierarchies App

Figure 5.30 shows the nodes of a sample financial statement version, along with the flags that control the handling of debits, credits, and so on that are so important when aggregating financial information for use in the financial statements.

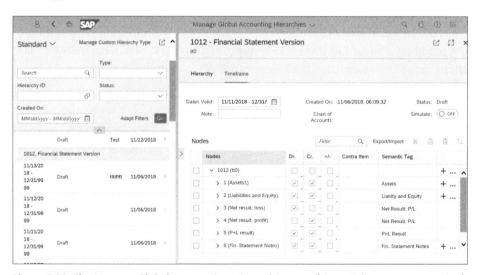

Figure 5.30 The Manage Global Accounting Hierarchies App (Financial Statement Version)

These hierarchies can be used in all SAP Fiori applications, including the Display Financial Statement app shown in Figure 5.21 or in any SAP Design Studio or Web Dynpro reporting apps, such as Figure 5.23 and Figure 5.24. They also can be read as queries for display in SAP Analysis for Microsoft Office or SAP Analytics Cloud. These hierarchies also can be extracted to SAP BW.

The hierarchies are stored in a new set of tables, so the next challenge is how to move existing hierarchies into the new world. In Figure 5.31, we've accessed and changed a financial statement version in the IMG (**General Ledger Accounting • Master Data • General Ledger Accounts • Define Financial Statement Version**), entered the transport request for the change, and received a message asking whether we want to activate the changed financial statement version. This will activate the hierarchy for the SAP Fiori applications such that the changed financial statement version will be visible on the screen from Figure 5.30 as a draft, and further processing can take place using the Manage Global Accounting Hierarchies app.

Figure 5.31 Saving and Activating a Financial Statement Version

Of course, you probably don't want to activate each hierarchy individually. The alternative is to use the Replicate Runtime Hierarchy app (SAP Fiori ID F1478) shown in Figure 5.32. This app copies the existing financial statement versions, cost center hierarchies, and profit center hierarchies into the new tables. This will not only improve the performance of your analytical apps, but also ensure that you have regular snapshots of the hierarchy structure at a given time.

Many controllers also told SAP that they struggled to keep their cost center hierarchies and profit center hierarchies in sync because they typically kept several hierarchies in parallel to provide different views of their organization, and the process of adding to or changing these hierarchies was rather cumbersome.

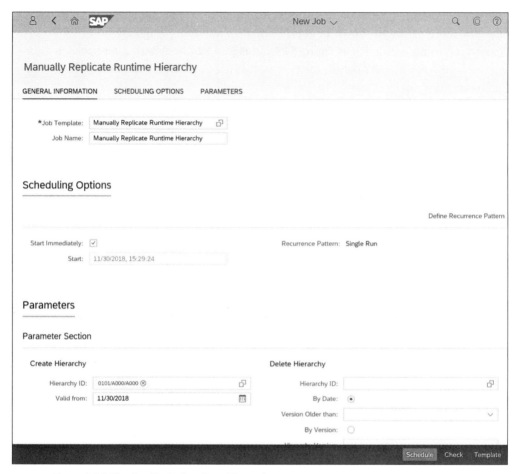

Figure 5.32 The Replicate Runtime Hierarchy App

With SAP S/4HANA 1709, SAP delivered a new app, Manage Flexible Hierarchies (SAP Fiori ID F2759), as part of the cost accountant—overhead role. It's designed to provide an alternative approach to this challenge. Figure 5.33 shows a flexible hierarchy that has been built using the cost center category as its starting point. The idea is that every cost center includes the cost center category as an attribute and you are simply using that field to build up the nodes of the hierarchy. The basic idea isn't new. If you've worked with order or project summarization in SAP ERP, you've taken the same approach to aggregation. But whereas orders and projects provide hundreds of fields that can be used to build these kind of tree structures, cost centers and profit centers offer far fewer fields.

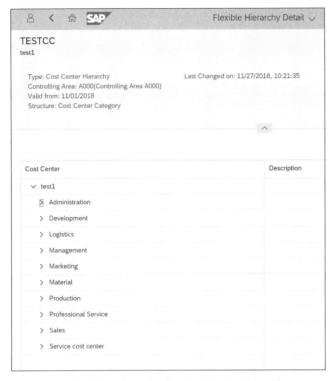

Figure 5.33 Flexible Hierarchy for Cost Center Reporting

Figure 5.34 shows the process of building up a profit center hierarchy. The hierarchy nodes are created by choosing from a list of fields at the bottom of the screen: **Line of Business**, **Product Line**, **Country Key**, **Region (State, Province, County)**, and **City**. Unlike the single-level tree shown in Figure 5.33, the hierarchy can have as many levels as you need. You simply select a field for each node and then define the sequence of the nodes. In general, to build these kinds of structures, you'll need to add new fields to the relevant master data, extending the profit center master to include custom fields that you then can use to build hierarchies.

Don't get carried away with this approach and multiply your profit centers and cost centers by all the attributes that you think you might need for reporting. Consider this a useful alternative to classic cost center and profit center hierarchies. Once you've generated a flexible hierarchy, it can be read by all the SAP Fiori reports because it's stored in the same tables as the global accounting hierarchy. If you need to delete a flexible hierarchy that you no longer need, use the **Delete Hierarchy** function shown in Figure 5.32.

Figure 5.34 Flexible Hierarchy for Profit Center Reporting

All this innovation is exciting, but if you're in the middle of a project, it can be hard to choose when to make the leap of faith to the new technology. Keep an eye on the contents of SAP Note 2349297 (S4TWL: Reporting/Analytics in Controlling), which provides details of which SAP ERP functions are supported in the SAP Fiori world and which are still pending.

So far, SAP Fiori has been all about visualizing data. We'll end this chapter by looking at how SAP plans to take this approach further.

5.4   SAP Fiori and the Intelligent Enterprise

For several years, analysts have been discussing the idea of "intelligent ERP," the basic elements of which we introduced in Chapter 4. The concept goes beyond process automation to having the system make proposals. This might be as simple as an autocomplete function that tries to complete the name of the cost center or material that you are searching for or one that proposes actions based on your previous system activities.

To illustrate this trend from a more technical angle, we'll look again at the SAP S/4HANA for goods and invoice receipt reconciliation app, whose machine learning component is delivered in the SAP Cloud Platform. This began as an analytical app that brought together key information to support the process of reconciling supplier invoices and the goods received and understanding where adjustments were needed and what had to be written off by combining information from the supplier open items, the goods receipts, invoice receipts, purchasing documents, and so on. Figure 5.35 shows the overview page for the GR/IR reconciliation app, the cards of which make it easy for a user to see the relevant key figures.

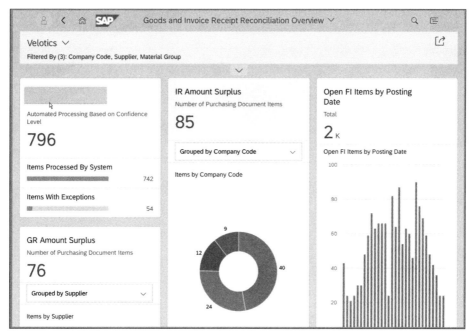

Figure 5.35 Overview Page for the SAP S/4HANA for Goods and Invoice Receipt Reconciliation App

The apps accessible from this overview page are used to identify the following situations when comparing the goods receipts against the invoice receipts:

- Goods receipt surplus amount (goods)
- Invoice surplus amount (goods)
- Goods receipt surplus amount (delivery costs)
- Goods receipt surplus quantity (goods)
- Invoice surplus quantity (goods)
- Goods receipt surplus quantity (delivery costs)
- No goods receipts posted
- No invoice receipt posted

The earliest version of the application was simply an analytical app that supported analysis of the causes of any variances. Following time spent working with users in various shared service centers, a picture emerged of what the users would do when they had made their analysis. Essentially each of these situations could be identified as a *smart fact*, and users could select all items for which the goods receipt was in excess or the invoice receipt was in excess. Smart facts describe the business situation in terms that a user can easily understand.

Figure 5.36 shows the next stage of embedding intelligence into an application, with the option to select **Smart Facts** that cover the main business reasons that can prompt the need to reconcile goods and invoice receipts.

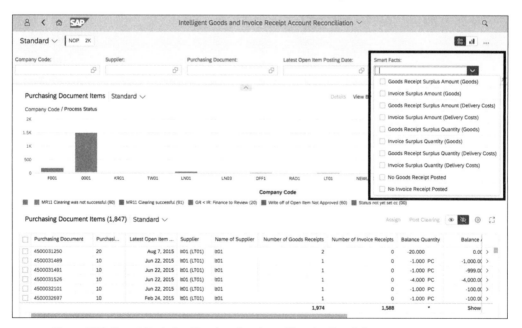

Figure 5.36 Smart Facts for Clearing Goods and Invoice Receipts

5.4.1   Business Rules

Most businesses establish business rules to define what should be done in each of the situations represented by these smart facts. It's possible to use the knowledge of the experts in a shared service center to establish business rules for the handling of these items. You saw in Chapter 4 that it's possible to set rules that try to match the goods receipt and invoice receipt items and initiate clearing postings. We can build rules based on the deep process knowledge of the users clearing goods receipts and invoice receipts and the actions that they typically perform. The challenge when we do this is that the rules are static, and it's hard to keep the business rules up to date if the business is changing or moving into new markets.

5.4.2   Machine Learning

Recall from Chapter 4 that the next level of sophistication is to watch what the processor is doing, learn the patterns, and then make suggestions. The idea is that machine learning identifies hidden patterns in knowledge-intensive processes and learns from the data without being explicitly programmed to do so.

In the first phase of machine learning, the system builds training data by recording what decisions have been made by the processors handling the goods receipts and invoice receipts. These continue to process the data as before, but each subsequent decision makes the training data more meaningful for machine learning. Once enough data has been collected, users can start to let the system propose decisions—essentially, the smart facts you saw set for each line item in Figure 5.36. Eventually, those results can be used to automate clearing.

5.5   Summary

In this chapter, we introduced SAP Fiori, the new user interface approach for SAP S/4HANA that gives users access to applications relevant for their roles within the organization on whichever device they choose. We've looked at the basic patterns behind transactional and analytical apps and explained the virtual data model that's used to translate the application tables into information that can be consumed by an end user. We've also looked at new options for hierarchy maintenance and explained how SAP is supporting the move to the intelligent enterprise with its new applications.

In the chapters that follow, we'll introduce additional SAP Fiori applications. In the next chapter, we'll start with a closer look at how to use key figures for performance management from a business perspective.

Chapter 6
Key Figures for Operational Reporting: Measuring Financial Performance

You've seen how SAP S/4HANA allows you to report on real-time data using SAP Fiori and the virtual data model. Chapter 5 essentially offered a new take on account-based reporting. Now, in this chapter, you'll see how to access key figures for your operational reporting to measure financial performance across your organization.

Think of key figures as a reference point. The idea is that they provide a way for external stakeholders to compare an organization's performance with that of other organizations operating in similar industries and regions, as well as a way for internal stakeholders to compare the performance of individual divisions and business units within the organization.

Operational key figures used in finance include return on investment, asset turnover, inventory turnover, current assets, working capital, profit margin, earnings before interest and tax, operating expenses, and so on. Key figures are interrelated, so a change in operating expenses will influence the profit margin; similarly, working capital can be broken down into inventory, accounts receivable, accounts payable, cash and cash equivalents, and so on.

There is absolutely nothing new about establishing key figures for operational management, with systems such as DuPont Analysis dating back to the 1920s. To help them steer their businesses, many organizations use balanced scorecards, strategy maps, and similar tools to present a mixture of financial and nonfinancial key figures to their management; the value driver tree, which illustrates how different metrics impact one another, has been with us for a century. After all, it's difficult to manage what you don't measure.

But calculating key figures is not a simple mathematical exercise in determining a value; rather, it involves establishing responsibility for performance within the organization. When we looked at the SAP Fiori applications for collections management in Chapter 3, we were focusing on how the applications support the user responsible for gathering outstanding payments from external customers; that user's performance is assessed through key figures such as the average days sales outstanding (DSO) in the area managed. Key figures roll up: for example, the DSO provides a view of the accounts receivable for each company code, which is the responsibility of the local CFO, but it also gives a view of the accounts receivable for divisions, business units, and so on that are the responsibility of the relevant general managers.

The need for better operational reporting in SAP's new ERP system drove one thread of SAP Fiori development. One result was the introduction of analytical applications that begin with a key figure and its status and allow the user to navigate to the details, switch dimensions, and ultimately perform certain actions.

What's changed in SAP S/4HANA is not the *idea* of a key figure, but the ease with which it can be calculated. For example, SAP Strategic Enterprise Management (SEM) included a Corporate Performance Monitor with a full management cockpit, but because SAP SEM used a data warehouse, the KPIs displayed were calculated using information loaded nightly from the operational systems. Often there was significant transformation of the data along the way, meaning that organizations were able to gain insight and track the progress of their strategies but struggled to act directly because there was a disconnect between the transactional and the analytical system. Now, SAP S/4HANA delivers *overview pages* showing the critical key figures for many roles with the aim of providing an immediate impression of performance in a given area as the user logs on.

In this chapter, we'll show how SAP S/4HANA improves financial performance measurement by offering new ways to calculate key figures for operational reporting. In Section 6.1, we'll show some simple examples of how SAP S/4HANA delivers insight that can be explored and acted upon immediately. In Section 6.2, we'll walk you through how to use semantic tags to convert the account model to the key figure model and subsequently deliver many key figure reports. We'll also explain how to extend the Universal Journal to add additional quantities above and beyond the invoice quantity for profitability reporting. Finally, in Section 6.3 we'll look at how SAP is starting to enrich the Universal Journal to support new reporting approaches.

6.1   Driving Insight to Action

When we talked about the different types of SAP Fiori applications in Chapter 5, we introduced the SAP Smart Business applications as a set of analytical applications designed to support a performance-driven working model.

Some SAP Smart Business applications, such as Overdue Receivables (Chapter 3), Days Payable Outstanding (Chapter 5), and Cash Discount Utilization (Chapter 5), provide *static* key figures, showing the current status of the relevant KPI. In terms of responsibility, these key figures are not isolated numbers, but rather a target set for the collections manager or the accounts receivable accountant related to expected performance. However, there isn't necessarily a direct action to improve a key figure, such as cash discount utilization; it merely provides an indicator of how the business is behaving.

Another key element in SAP Fiori applications is that many of the roles include an overview page that provides a mixture of key figures and *actions*. In this chapter, we'll show the overview pages for the general ledger accountant and the sales accountant, and we'll look at the overview page for the asset accountant in Chapter 10. The General Ledger Overview app (SAP Fiori ID F2445) shown in Figure 6.1 displays several different key figures as charts and offers a range of actions as **Quick Links** that allow general ledger accountants to initiate actions directly once they have clear pictures of the financial situation in their organizations.

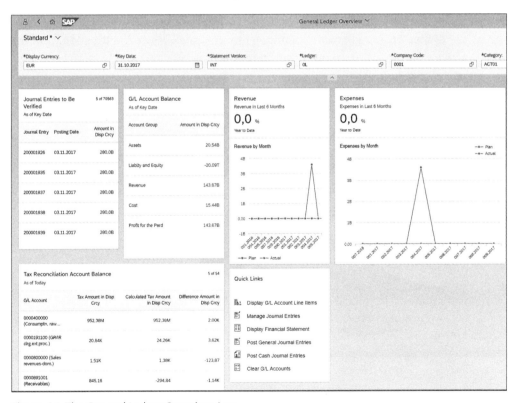

Figure 6.1 The General Ledger Overview App

We'll now look at some examples of actions being derived from the insights gained from these overview pages. Because projects are typically very dynamic in nature and often require careful monitoring of the actual costs against the budget (a topic we'll revisit when we look at planning in Chapter 9), we'll begin with the Project Financial Control Overview page. Project managers usually monitor the costs being charged to their project; the follow-on action may simply be to email an employee and ask the need for certain travel expenses. Then we look at the role of the general ledger accountant, who typically has authorization to create and reverse journal entries; we'll show how SAP Fiori helps this user find a problematic journal entry and initiate the reversal of the document. Finally, we'll explore how a cash manager with the authorization to initiate bank transfers can monitor the cash and cash equivalents within their responsibility and then initiate a bank transfer if the situation demands it.

6.1.1   Financial Control on Projects

We'll follow a simple example to show some of the actions that can be triggered within an application. Figure 6.2 shows the Status Management app (SAP Fiori ID F0779) from the Project Financial Control Overview page. This application lists the statuses of the active projects. To learn more, select one of the projects shown on the card.

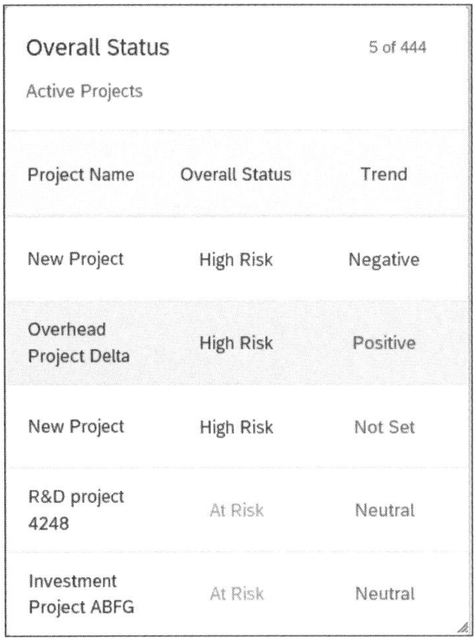

Overall Status		5 of 444
Active Projects		
Project Name	Overall Status	Trend
New Project	High Risk	Negative
Overhead Project Delta	High Risk	Positive
New Project	High Risk	Not Set
R&D project 4248	At Risk	Neutral
Investment Project ABFG	At Risk	Neutral

Figure 6.2 Project Status in the Project Financial Control Overview

Figure 6.3 shows the Project Briefs app (SAP Fiori ID F2602). This application shows the typical information that project managers pull together prior to a review meeting. Notice the **Cost** tab included in this application. As shown in Figure 6.4, this tab provides an overview of the planned and actual costs for the project. For more details, you can navigate from there to the project cost report.

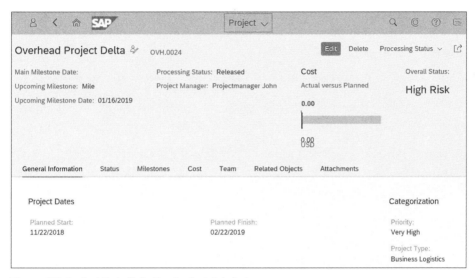

Figure 6.3 Project Details in the Project Briefs App

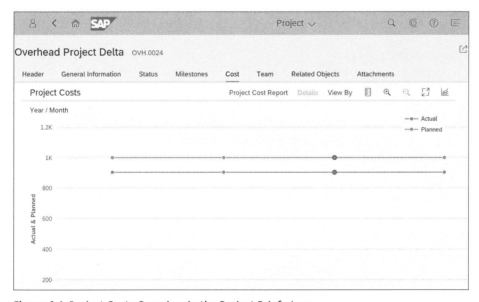

Figure 6.4 Project Costs Overview in the Project Briefs App

Project managers with appropriate authorization can edit the status information using the transactional SAP Fiori application shown in Figure 6.5. This straightforward example illustrates how easy it is to move between the analytical world (which shows the various project-related key figures) and the transactional world (in which the master data and status information resides) with only two clicks.

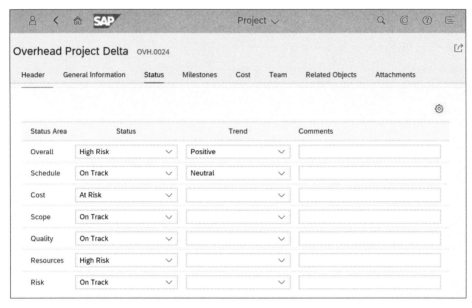

Figure 6.5 Project Status Update

6.1.2   General Ledger

The ability to update a project's status might not sound so spectacular, but we'll now look at a simple example of initiating a financial posting to see what's so exciting.

Figure 6.6 shows the Manage Journal Entries app (SAP Fiori ID FO717). We've selected all the customer invoices in **2018**. If we discover an error in these journal entries, we can simply select the document and choose the **Reverse** button in the lower right of the screen.

Figure 6.7 shows the reversal posting for the selected document. Because we made the selection in Figure 6.6, the system passes the document number and any other information needed to identify the document to the reversal application shown in Figure 6.7.

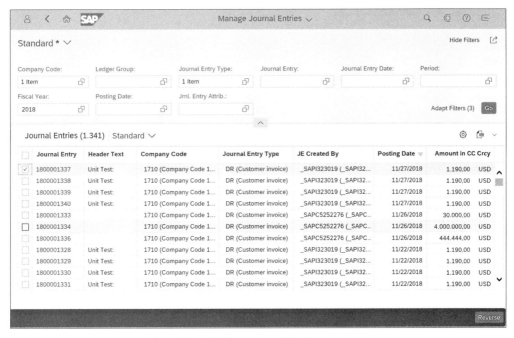

Figure 6.6 Managing Journal Entries with the Reversal Option

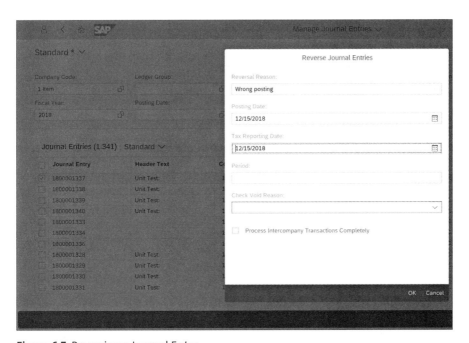

Figure 6.7 Reversing a Journal Entry

6.1.3   Cash Management

In a similar vein, the Cash Flow Analyzer app that we saw in Chapter 5 allows the user to navigate directly to applications that initiate bank transfers, as shown in Figure 6.8.

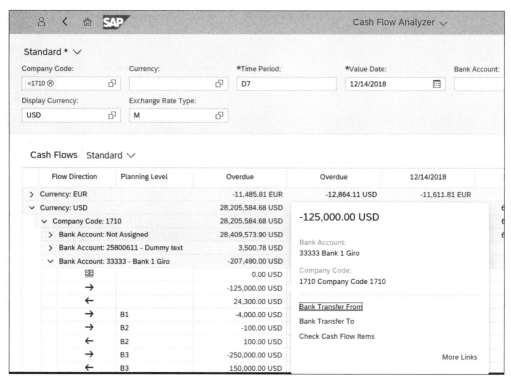

Figure 6.8 Cash Flow Analyzer with Navigation Options

For example, let's say you want to navigate to the Make Bank Transfers app (SAP Fiori ID F0691). In Figure 6.9, you can see the payment requests that make up the key figure in Figure 6.8. You can use the right-hand pane to trigger a new bank transfer and thus impact the cash key figures directly by moving money between banks.

Now that we've understood how SAP S/4HANA allows you to gain insight and drive action, we'll look behind the scenes at the semantic tags that shape the key figures.

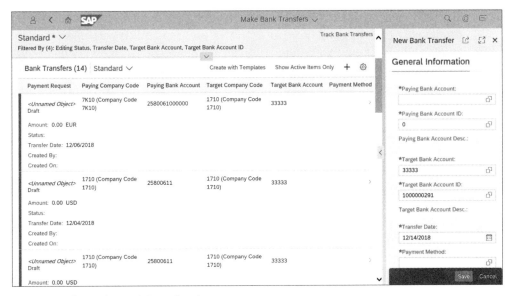

Figure 6.9 The Make Bank Transfers App

6.2   Using Semantic Tags to Link Accounts with Key Figures

In data modeling terms, there are two fundamentally different ways of looking at accounting information:

- In business terms, financial statements, trial balances, cost center reports, and so on are based on an *account model*, because the account and account groupings provide the main structure of the report. What's new for many users in SAP S/4HANA is that profitability analysis is also structured by accounts, so you can look at the sales per region or product by selecting the appropriate revenue accounts and then drilling down by profitability segment.

- While it is not the preferred way to analyze your margin in SAP S/4HANA, costing-based profitability analysis (which you may know from SAP ERP), in which all amounts are mapped to value fields, is perhaps the most obvious example of a report based on a key figure-based model. In some cases, the value fields are just a different way of looking at the same numbers; in others, there are value fields that are not directly linked with the accounts, such as the invoice quantity, delivery quantity, and so on. In this case, we need a different way of capturing the quantities and then deriving the appropriate sales volumes.

We'll now look at how to move between account models and key figure models for profitability reporting and how SAP S/4HANA uses semantic tags to make the connection between a group of accounts (e.g., all revenue accounts) and a key figure (e.g., overall revenue). We explain how SAP delivers a set of tags for the main key figures and shows how organizations can fill these key figures by linking them with their own general ledger accounts.

6.2.1 Profitability Reporting for Products and Projects

In its simplest form, looking at product profitability and project profitability involves assigning revenues and operating costs to the appropriate products and/or projects.

In Chapter 5, we looked at the Product Profitability app (SAP Fiori ID F2765) and explained how to drill down to display the appropriate revenue and cost accounts; we then looked at the Project Profitability app (SAP Fiori ID F2764) and did the same for commercial projects. We'll now dig deeper to explain how the key figures shown in the Product Profitability app are linked with the relevant income statement accounts. We'll then look more closely at the Project Profitability app to show that it also includes balance sheet accounts and explain how this changes certain basic assumptions concerning profitability analysis. Finally, we'll look at how to set up additional quantity fields for volume reporting in sales.

Sales Accounting

Figure 6.10 and Figure 6.11 show the Sales Accounting Overview app (SAP Fiori ID F3228), which uses the same approach as the previously mentioned applications to provide a more aggregated view of the same figures for the sales accountant. The idea behind these three applications is that SAP can deliver a stable set of key figure-based applications that use semantic tags to access the relevant accounts and calculate the relevant key figures accordingly.

Figure 6.12 shows a selection of the delivered semantic tags. You can check these by following **General Ledger Accounting (New)** • **Master Data** • **G/L Accounts** • **Define Semantic Tags for Balance Sheet and Profit and Loss Structures** in the IMG. You can then create further tags as required. Notice that this is a generic list that also includes tags for asset- and investment-related key figures.

Figure 6.10 Sales Accounting Overview: Part 1

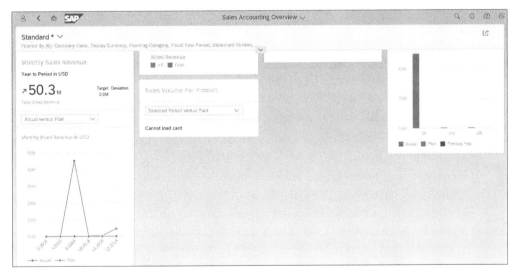

Figure 6.11 Sales Accounting Overview: Part 2

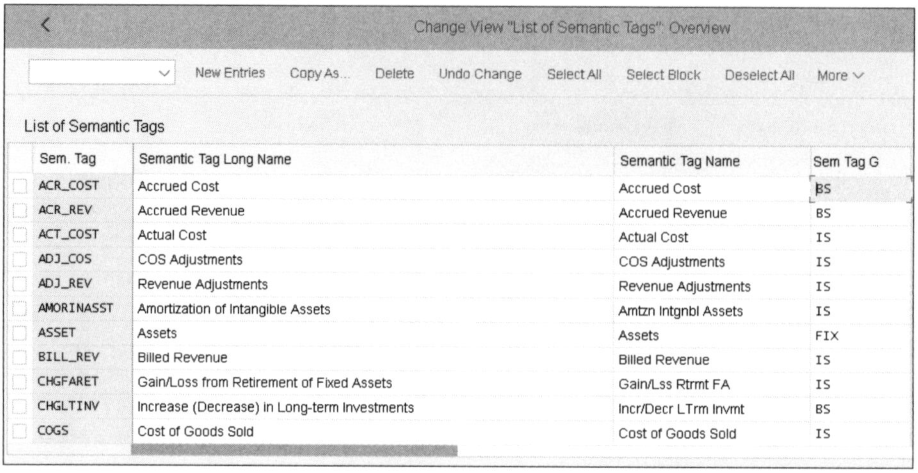

Sem. Tag	Semantic Tag Long Name	Semantic Tag Name	Sem Tag G
ACR_COST	Accrued Cost	Accrued Cost	BS
ACR_REV	Accrued Revenue	Accrued Revenue	BS
ACT_COST	Actual Cost	Actual Cost	IS
ADJ_COS	COS Adjustments	COS Adjustments	IS
ADJ_REV	Revenue Adjustments	Revenue Adjustments	IS
AMORINASST	Amortization of Intangible Assets	Amtzn Intgnbl Assets	IS
ASSET	Assets	Assets	FIX
BILL_REV	Billed Revenue	Billed Revenue	IS
CHGFARET	Gain/Loss from Retirement of Fixed Assets	Gain/Lss Rtrmt FA	IS
CHGLTINV	Increase (Decrease) in Long-term Investments	Incr/Decr LTrm Invmt	BS
COGS	Cost of Goods Sold	Cost of Goods Sold	IS

Figure 6.12 List of Semantic Tags (Selected)

To use the delivered tags, you need to assign your own accounts in the IMG under **General Ledger Accounting (New) • Master Data • G/L Accounts • Assign Semantic Tags for Balance Sheet and Profit and Loss Structures**. The assignment is always based on a financial statement version, which, as we discussed in Chapter 2, groups accounts for reporting purposes.

Balance Sheet Key Figures by Project and Profitability Segment

Notice in Figure 6.12 that the semantic tags are flagged as either IS (income statement) or BS (balance sheet).

Profitability analysis with CO-PA in SAP ERP was always focused on explaining the income statement or P&L statement, but never included balance sheet-related key figures. This changes in SAP S/4HANA with the calculation of balance sheet-related key figures for the project, including accrued costs, accrued revenue, work in process, and so on. We'll explain in detail how these are calculated in Chapter 7, but for now understand that this is a fundamental shift from the cost-of-sales method that long characterized CO-PA and the *period cost* approach, in which work in process and other key figures from the balance sheet are associated with projects and the relevant profitability characteristics.

Volume Reporting

Semantic tags work well when key figures can be derived by aggregating data assigned to a group of accounts. However, sales reporting also requires key figures that are based on *quantities* rather than amounts, as shown in the **Sales Volume per Project** card in Figure 6.11. For this reason, we'll now look at how quantities are stored in the Universal Journal. Figure 6.13 shows the include ACDOCA_SI_VALUE_DATA, which stores all quantities in the Universal Journal. Every time an invoice or delivery is recorded in profitability analysis, the system will update the quantity in the **CO Valuation Quantity** field (CO_MEGBTR).

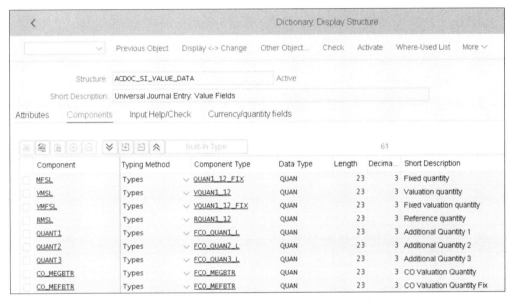

Figure 6.13 Quantity Fields in the Universal Journal

However, many organizations find that these quantities are recorded in whatever unit of measure is needed by the logistics process (e.g., blister packs of drugs, boxes of washing powder, or sacks of coffee), and then they cannot combine these items (you cannot add blister packs to pill boxes to bottles of cough syrup!) to get a reliable picture of total sales volumes. To report across the whole organization, they need to convert these quantities into a unit of measure that is consistent across the organization. For this reason, SAP has provided three extra fields in the Universal Journal: **Additional Quantity 1–3**. These quantities are whatever you define them to be, so you might, for example, convert all quantities into kilograms to be able to aggregate across the organization.

To define an additional quantity, follow **Controlling • General Controlling • Additional Amounts • Define Additional Quantity Fields** and enter your chosen quantity and unit of measure. This will activate the **Additional Quantity 1–3** fields in the Universal Journal.

235

You'll then be able to use a BAdI to fill these additional fields using whatever logic you need to fill the appropriate quantity fields. Usually these can be derived from the various units of measure in the material master.

Let's now look at how semantic tags are used in the cash flow statement.

6.2.2   Cash Flow Statement

Figure 6.14 and Figure 6.15 show the Cash Flow Statement app (SAP Fiori ID F3076). Notice that the first dimension in the navigation panel on the left is **Measures**. This generally is a sign that the report is using semantic tags.

Notice also that the **Rows** block in the middle of the figure also simply shows the word **Measures**. These are the measures or semantic tags that you saw in Figure 6.12. The report can only deliver a result if you link the measures with one or more accounts, as shown in Figure 6.16. In this example, the assignment is made using the financial statement items that make up the financial statement version that you saw in Chapter 2, but if the financial statement items don't fit your purpose, you can also use accounts and combinations of account and functional area.

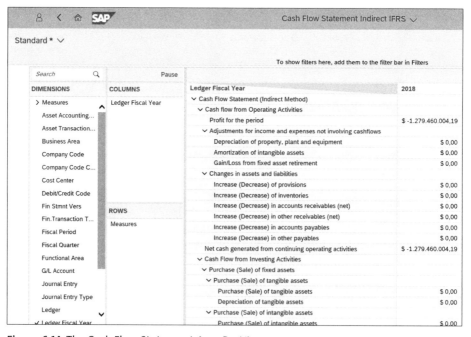

Figure 6.14 The Cash Flow Statement App: Part 1

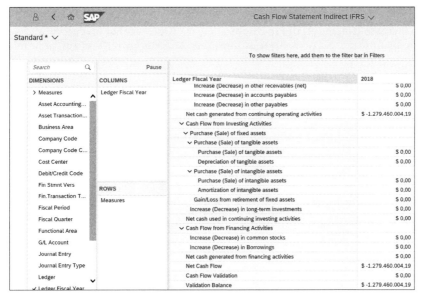

Figure 6.15 The Cash Flow Statement App: Part 2

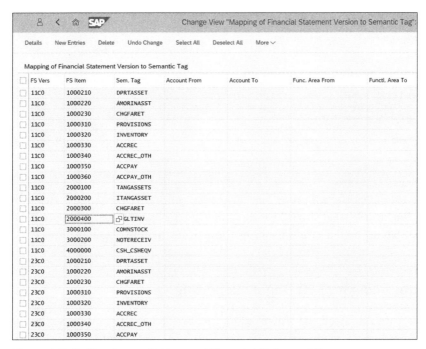

Figure 6.16 Linking Semantic Tags and Financial Statement Items

Figure 6.17 shows the details of the financial statement items—**Changes in Assets and Liabilities, Increase (Decrease) of Provisions, Increase (Decrease) of Inventory,** and so on—that make up the financial statement version we discussed in Chapter 2. A *financial statement item* represents a group of accounts for reporting purposes. Each has a numeric item that we used to make the assignment to the semantic tags in Figure 6.16. The idea is that the tags themselves should remain stable; therefore, if you use different cash accounts in the various countries that you operate in, you should keep one semantic tag but assign the different accounts contained in the various financial statement versions so that you can use the same SAP Fiori application throughout your organization.

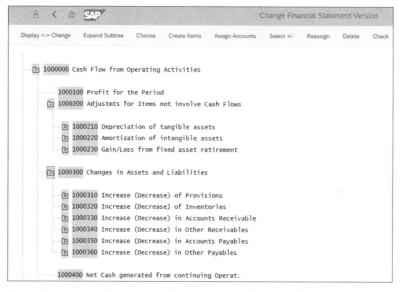

Figure 6.17 Financial Statement Items Linked to Semantic Tags

These two examples show various key figures for profitability reporting and cash reporting. We hinted in Section 6.2.1 at the provision of balance sheet-related key figures in profitability analysis; let's examine these shifts in more detail.

6.3   Redesigning for 360-Degree Reporting

In Chapter 1, we discussed the Universal Journal as the basis for the new steering model and explained how the various financial applications fold into a single journal entry to offer improved reporting.

If we think through the typical financial key figures, such as current assets and operating expenses, all are normally assigned to a company code, account, and period, but after that there is a lumpiness in the data. Some key figures can be associated with many additional dimensions, but with others the task is harder.

With the splitting rules that were introduced in SAP ERP, it's possible to assign all journal entries to a profit center by assigning the profit center to the P&L items using the CO object master data (cost center, order, project, and so on) and then applying splitting rules to derive the balance sheet items. To do this, you must set up rules that classify each account for the purposes of document splitting. If you already use document splitting in the new General Ledger, there will be no change in the logic as you move to SAP S/4HANA. If you are using an earlier version of the General Ledger, then all new documents can be split using the rules defined for document splitting. However, you will also need to split the opening balance for all accounts and all open items to have a correct key figure for the profit center balance sheet items. Tools for the subsequent activation of document splitting were introduced in SAP S/4HANA 1709; they'll walk you through this process.

In SAP ERP, you can easily use CO-PA to provide multidimensional analysis for P&L items, but not for balance sheet items. In SAP S/4HANA, your options have started to change, and this process will continue in subsequent versions. For this reason, it's worth thinking through how the various key figures you monitor relate to market segments:

- It's normally easy to assign revenues and cost of goods sold (COGS) to market segments. Both SAP ERP and SAP S/4HANA simply read the customer, the product, and the sales office from the invoice or delivery documents and use additional derivations to determine the customer group, product group, and so on.

- Overhead costs can be assigned to the market segments using allocations or settlement as in SAP ERP or, as you'll learn in Chapter 7, using real-time derivation from SAP S/4HANA. The assignments can either be very fine (e.g., product and customer) or at a higher level (e.g., product group or region), depending on the data volumes involved and the meaningfulness of the split. (It does not usually make sense to assign cents to a product, for example.)

- In SAP ERP, you couldn't assign the working capital key figures (accounts payable, accounts receivable, cash, and inventory) to market segments. With SAP S/4HANA, that situation begins to change, and it becomes possible to assign work in process (inventory) to the profitability segments.

- In the future, you can begin to assign some inventory to product-related segments, though it's generally difficult to assign raw material inventory to the final market segment. It's only possible to assign inventory to the sales-related segments if you're working in a make-to-order or engineer-to-order environment in which you know the customer throughout the process. It's rare to assign accounts payable, accounts receivable, or cash directly to market segments; such key figures typically remain at the level of the legal entity.

- Fixed assets generally are linked only with cost centers or orders/projects so that the deprecation of the fixed assets can flow into cost accounting. In truth, many fixed assets could be linked with market segments in the sense that they are used exclusively in the production of certain product groups or even products.

This changing focus is illustrated in Figure 6.18. In rows ❺ and ❻, you can see that it's possible to make a relatively fine assignment of the revenue and COGS as we just discussed. With SAP S/4HANA, we can do the same for work in process and accrued revenues for inventory transactions ❷.

For fixed assets ❶, inventory ❷, receivables ❸, and payables ❹, you can begin to provide more detail for each of the main key figures by redesigning the way the documents are posted and either enrich or split the posting to fill the gaps in SAP S/4HANA—but more is possible than is currently available. We expect that SAP will continue enriching the accounting documents to provide ever-finer key figures in the future.

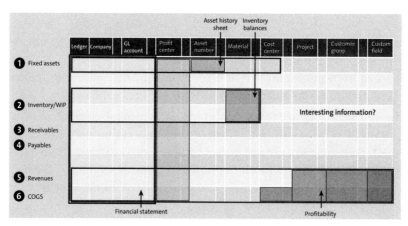

Figure 6.18 Additional Key Figures from the Universal Journal

Let's look at the process of document splitting by profit center that was introduced with the new General Ledger in SAP ERP and that has been inherited by SAP S/4HANA. We'll then look at how SAP is enriching the postings for work in process and revenue recognition, as mentioned in Section 6.2.1.

6.3.1 Assigning Profit Centers Using Document Splitting

If you look back at Figure 6.18, you can see that one challenge is to ensure that all line items in the Universal Journal are assigned to a profit center. In SAP R/3, profit centers were derived immediately for all postings to cost centers, orders, projects, and so on (the P&L items), but only at period close for accounts payable and accounts receivable (balance sheet items). Later, a new function was introduced in SAP ERP that enriched the accounts payable and accounts receivable lines with profit center information at the time of posting. We'll now look at an example that was introduced with SAP ERP and moves into SAP S/4HANA.

Figure 6.19 shows what happens when a customer invoice is posted that updates three accounts: **Receivables**, **Tax**, and **Revenues**. The revenue line can be split across several profit centers because the revenue is associated with different products. The receivables line and the tax line are initially assigned only to the company code (though the open items are available in accounts receivable).

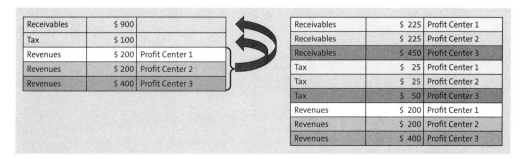

Figure 6.19 Document Splitting by Profit Center

The top left of this figure shows the entry view in the General Ledger. What happens is that all lines are assigned to profit centers. Because the P&L side is assigned to three different profit centers, splitting rules are used to split the receivables line and the tax line to the three profit centers in proportion to the relative values for the revenue lines. This results in the journal entry shown at the bottom right (the general ledger view), showing three receivables lines and three tax lines.

Figure 6.20 shows the data entry view for a customer invoice. Notice that only the revenue line is assigned to a profit center and segment, whereas the receivables line and the tax line are only assigned to the company code, because document splitting has not yet taken place.

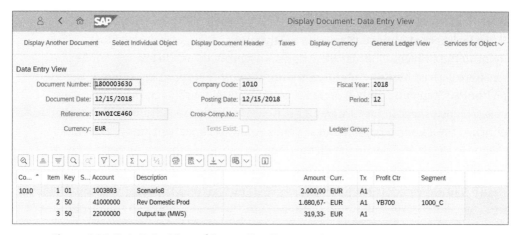

Figure 6.20 Data Entry View of Accounting Document

Figure 6.21 shows the general ledger view for the same invoice. This time, all three lines are assigned to profit centers and segments. This *enriching* of the document lines with additional reporting dimensions enables profit center reporting for both the P&L lines *and* the balance sheet lines (in this case, the receivables line). The same process applies in reverse for all vendor invoices: the accounts payable lines are enriched with the profit center and then split in proportion to the expense lines.

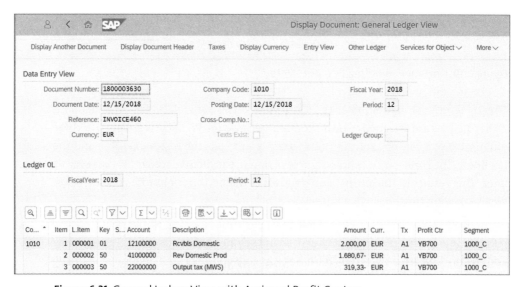

Figure 6.21 General Ledger View with Assigned Profit Centers

6.3.2   Work in Process by Profitability Segment

For many years, we explained that CO-PA in SAP ERP was simply a more granular version of the P&L statement with all items assigned to market segments. With SAP S/4HANA, the explanation is changing, as shown in Figure 6.22:

- Look at the first table in in Figure 6.22. The time confirmation continues to move costs from the cost center to the project in the P&L statement. With SAP S/4HANA, you enrich the document by deriving the market segments from the project.

- The revenue recognition document is a new document introduced with SAP S/4HANA. It's created using the planned costs and revenues to derive the revenue adjustment (P&L) and the WIP or accrued revenue (balance sheet) and assigns both items to the market segments.

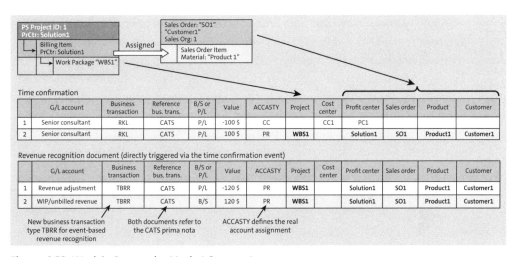

Figure 6.22 Work in Process by Market Segment

We'll explain how the revenue recognition postings are created when we look at real-time closing in Chapter 7. For now, we'll focus on the process of assigning the balance sheet items to the market segments. The sales order is found from postings on the project (the WBS element). Based on the sales order, additional information about the customer and product can be retrieved.

Figure 6.23 shows the initial assignment: travel expenses (**Trav. Expense Hotel**) have been posted to the project being assigned to the product sold (**P001**, **P002**, etc.), the customer served (**10100001**, **10100003**, etc.), and the distribution channel (**10**, etc.). Essentially, this is a simple example of what we showed for the time confirmation in Figure 6.22.

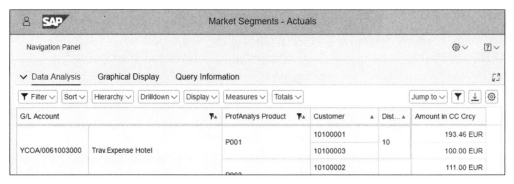

Figure 6.23 Expense Posting to Order and Profitability Segments

You can set up the derivation logic to assign these attributes by going to **Controlling •**
Profitability Analysis • Master Data • Activate Derivation for Items without Profitability
Segment in the IMG and by choosing the controlling account assignments that you
wish to associate with profitability analysis characteristics. Figure 6.24 shows the configuration for commercial projects in which we're deriving profitability analysis characteristics for both P&L accounts (e.g., the travel expenses in Figure 6.23) and balance
sheet accounts (e.g., accrued revenue and work in process). This flag represents a
huge shift in the understanding of profitability analysis as being based on the cost of
sales method: it now brings the work in process into play as an additional period cost.

Figure 6.24 Assignment of Market Segments to Projects for P&L and Balance Sheet
Accounts

Figure 6.25 shows the Project Profitability app (SAP Fiori ID F2764). In the columns
along the top you can see financial key figures for both the project and the product
sold. Notice that the key figures combine P&L items and balance sheet items for the
market segments.

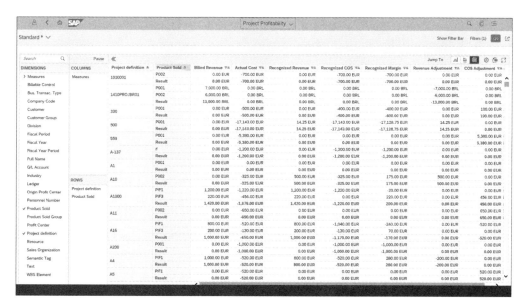

Figure 6.25 The Project Profitability App

6.3.3   Improved Project Reporting

The process of adding reporting attributes has been enhanced for project-based billing. In Figure 6.25, you can see the attributes for profitability reporting that we discussed earlier, but also that project-related attributes have been added to the Universal Journal. We would all expect to see postings to the activity type and the material on the WBS element from our experience with SAP ERP, but the journal entries are now enriched to show the work item, the personnel number, and the resource (internal or external employee) as well.

Object attributes for projects and sales orders include the following:

- Sales order, sales order item
- Customer, customer group
- Sales organization, distribution channel, division, sales district
- Product for CO-PA, material group
- Billing type
- Country key, industry key
- Bill-to party, ship-to party

Process attributes for activity allocations, expense postings, and material purchases include the following:

- Activity type
- Material (consumed)
- Work item
- Personnel number
- Resource (internal or external employee)

To include the employee number and the WBS element in the posting line, follow the IMG menu path **Controlling** • **Cost Center Accounting** • **Actual Postings** • **Additional Transaction-Related Postings** • **Derivation of Add Reporting Attributes for ICO CO Postings**. Select the **Der. Rep. At** (**Derive Reporting Attributes**) checkbox shown in Figure 6.26.

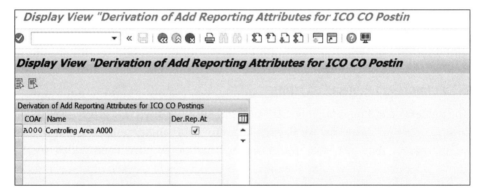

Figure 6.26 Settings for Derivation of Additional Reporting Attributes

6.4   Summary

In this chapter, we showed how operational key figures can be calculated and displayed in SAP Fiori applications using the live data in SAP S/4HANA. We explained how to create semantic tags and include additional quantities in profitability analysis, and we looked at the process of assigning balance sheet items to profit centers and market segments.

In the next chapter, we'll look at the real-time close in general and specifically how the key figures shown in profitability analysis are calculated.

Chapter 7
Real-Time Financial Close: Providing Timely Information

In this chapter, we'll explain how SAP S/4HANA can help finance departments move from a classical period-end closing process to a continuous close to both become more efficient and provide timely information to other stakeholders.

As you've learned, one of the key expectations of the finance department from business people is that it delivers reliable information that can help leadership make the right decisions.

In the early days of SAP ERP, finance departments were restricted to accessing information about the final profit margin until after the period had closed and they had performed all the necessary allocations and valuations to assign costs to the various market segments. This meant first performing an entity close for all the legal entities within the organization, then performing the group close that consolidates financial close data from the individual entities and eliminates the value of all intercompany business. For some companies, this meant scrambling to perform financial closing activities in a two- to three-day window at the end of the period; for others, this window stretched to two weeks.

This reliance on the hard close to deliver a reliable profit margin is still common for many current SAP customers, who recognize that this limitation prevents them from making margin-driven decisions with real-time data. After all, business decisions happen constantly, not only after the period-end close, so information needs may arise at any moment in time.

The good news is that recent technical advancements in SAP S/4HANA have improved the hard close for both entity and group close and have made it possible to transition to continuous accounting (sometimes called *continuous close*). This type of soft close automates repetitive tasks, such as the GR/IR clearing and intercompany reconciliation that we looked at in Chapter 4 and distributes close-related workloads throughout a period. It offers the following benefits:

- Through the continuous information flow, decision support information can be delivered at any moment in time. This enables management to better steer the business on an operational and strategic level, potentially resulting in higher profitability and/or growth thanks to earlier insight.

- Through the automation of end-to-end finance processes in a continuous manner, finance not only improves its operational efficiency, but also supports greater data integrity and improves visibility into finance processes. This results in lower effort and cost thanks to less time spent, and simultaneously produces a higher quality of work.

- Monitoring progress, quality, and financial results of the closing cycle in real time avoids bottlenecks and addresses business concerns more quickly.

The continuous close helps finance organizations position themselves as strategic business partners within their organizations. By shifting from merely processing operational transactions to delivering high-value input (e.g., real-time, early, and accurate financial insights) that actively contribute to better financial results, they can actively add value to their company.

In this chapter, we'll look at how SAP S/4HANA has changed the financial close, focusing first on the acceleration of the hard close in Section 7.1 and then on the arrival of the continuous close and its implications in Section 7.2.

7.1   Improving the Hard Close

Financial transactions for purchasing, goods movements, confirmations, and sales happen throughout the period, but some costs are always posted at period close. For example, payroll costs are typically posted to a cost center and then moved to the profitability segments either by using a simple allocation or via a more complex series of allocations and settlements that move the costs to operational cost centers, then to orders and projects, and finally to the profitability segments. Manufacturing companies must also report their work in process and the values of goods in inventory and capitalize any assets under construction. Professional service companies must report the accrued revenue and the value of unbilled work. Until all this has happened, an organization can't report on its profit margins reliably.

Every industry has a slightly different set of close tasks that it must perform in every accounting period, but the process of closing the books for a legal entity generally will involve more than one hundred tasks—some automatic, such as calculating the depreciation on fixed assets or revaluing open items for payables and receivables, and many manual, such as creating journal entries for accruals. In addition, finance organizations spend a lot of time checking the results and reconciling postings in different applications and systems.

For some organizations, financial close is a continual challenge, and it has been difficult to make the process faster and more efficient using legacy tools. Although the time needed to perform an entity close often has been reduced significantly thanks to close-related initiatives in the ERP world, many organizations struggle to perform a fast group close. The challenge here is to bring the financial statements from the local entities into a common structure, eliminate intercompany business and investments, and deliver the consolidated financial statements.

Figure 7.1 shows the financial closing process, in which *financial accounting* represents the financial transactions happening during the close (such as manual accrual postings) and *entity close* represents the tasks to be performed to close the books in each subsidiary. To perform the group close, the subsidiaries must submit their financial data to headquarters, where first it is checked and validated and then further steps are performed to prepare the consolidated financial statements that are made public in the financial reporting step.

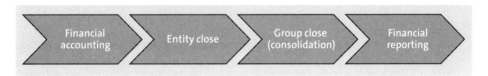

Figure 7.1 Financial Closing Sequence

In this section, we'll explore ways SAP S/4HANA has improved the hard-close process for entity close and group close, then we'll discuss two SAP S/4HANA tools for orchestrating the close process.

7.1.1   Entity Close

Let's first consider entity close. Focusing on the closing of a single entity (primarily legal entities), the key driver for a faster close is to record relevant data with minimal time and resources consumed, without errors, while ensuring compliance. Only when this step is successfully completed can organizations move on to the group close.

In terms of pure speed, SAP HANA allowed SAP to rearchitect several close steps, so there are new transactions for steps such as calculation of work in process, production variances, and settlement. You will recognize them by the addition of an *H* to the end of the transaction code; for example, instead of performing order settlement using Transaction CO88, the new transaction is CO88H in SAP S/4HANA. You'll find both the old and new transactions in the SAP Menu because they differ slightly in scope. If you work with actual costing, you'll also find that the periodic costing run has been completely rearchitected, a topic that we'll return to in Chapter 11.

There are three ways that entity close can be improved further:

- **Automation**
  Efficiencies can be gained in the entity close by automating repeated tasks like allocations and settlements, even in remote systems. It was possible to schedule such tasks as jobs in SAP ERP, but the challenge is often to understand not just whether they have run successfully but whether they have delivered reliable results. This can sometimes be achieved by building automated plausibility checks on the results and comparing against the equivalent results in the previous period or a threshold value. (Of course, not all tasks can be automated; tasks such as the creation of journal entries for accruals that require manual intervention can be accelerated through user-friendly UIs instead, as you saw in Chapter 5.)

- **Collaboration**
  The entity close process involves individuals from many different departments, including payroll, asset accounting, inventory accounting, and so on. As with any group project, collaboration between stakeholders is key because many close steps only make sense if they are performed in a certain sequence. You should only run allocations once all the costs are available on the sending cost centers, so you need first to ensure that payroll has run, asset depreciation has been posted, and so on. This can be improved through the provisioning of workflow capabilities, notifications, and so on.

- **Orchestration**
  For large organizations, financial close involves many moving parts. Companies that define a global game plan for the entity close and then apply it for the different organizational units and periodic closing cycles achieve better governance of their processes (compliance is improved through the establishment of audit trails

that log all closing activities and entries, as well as related documentation). They also gain more transparency into their closing execution and status. Again, this was possible in SAP ERP, but many organizations did not make full use of the tools available to optimize the close.

Now let's turn our attention from entity close to group close.

7.1.2   Group Close

Once all entities have closed their books, group close can occur. We'll look at this process in more detail when we look at group reporting in Chapter 12, but at a high level, group close involves several standard activities:

- **Data acquisition**
  Collect nonconsolidated data together from the financial accounting system or systems operated by the subsidiaries. In this step, local accountants submit their data to headquarters for further processing.

- **Data preparation**
  Begin by translating all financial data into the consolidation currency (group currency), running several validation checks, and ensuring intercompany information is correct so that intercompany transactions can be reconciled. These preparatory steps typically are the most time-consuming part of the entire consolidation process; they typically take place using a consolidation monitor that orders all required activities and gives a clear status report on what has been done, where errors occur, and so on. This task is a collaborative one involving both local accountants and those at headquarters.

- **Consolidation**
  Once data preparation has been finalized, the actual consolidation activities can be started. This includes eliminating intercompany movements, consolidating investments, and so on. This typically is done by executing a set of rules from a central consolidation monitor.

- **Reporting**
  When the consolidation has been executed, it's time to run a consolidated balance sheet, P&L, cash flow statement, and other relevant reports.

Traditionally, data acquisition involved duplicating unconsolidated data in a data warehouse and installing a consolidation engine on top to do data preparation and consolidation execution. Because the consolidation engine can't run until all entity close data has reached the data warehouse, an organization only has access to consolidated financial data at the very end of the process.

Unfortunately, business partners increasingly require accurate financial information at the group level during the month—not only at month end. This necessitates a fundamental shift in the consolidation approach. All consolidation tasks clearly are still required, and the actual consolidation (eliminations and the like) should not be touched, but some improvements affect the most time-consuming activities of the consolidation process: the data acquisition and preparation steps.

For example, what if you could cut out the middleman (the data warehouse and its consolidation engine) and instead collect entity close data directly from its source instead? Keeping unconsolidated data where it's originally posted would offer a monumental advantage: data preparation steps such as currency translation, validation checks, and so on can be executed at the moment the initial posting is recorded—in other words, *before* period end. As shown in Figure 7.2, the consequence is that only the core consolidation tasks need to be executed at period end. The ability to execute a shortened consolidation run multiple times a month contributes to the continuous accounting and the delivery of financial information within the month.

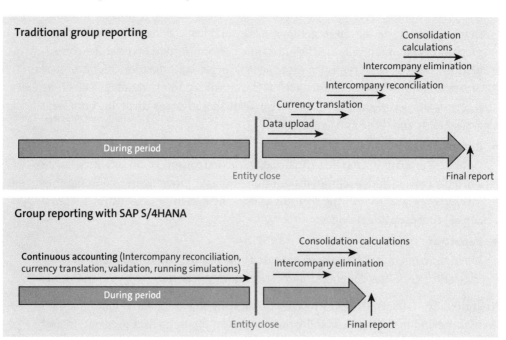

Figure 7.2 Comparing Traditional Group Close with Group Close in SAP S/4HANA

This improvement to group close is only possible if the consolidation engine can be directly integrated into the operational finance environment where the basic financial postings on the entity level are recorded. And that is exactly what has happened within SAP S/4HANA: the consolidation engine is integrated directly into the SAP S/4HANA environment.

This approach naturally raises several questions. For example, this is a possible approach in cases where all unconsolidated financials are part of the same core SAP S/4HANA application—but what if accounting for different parts of the organization is done in different systems? Executing preparatory steps at the moment of the initial finance posting can work—but what happens to the translation of the balance sheet, which usually happens at month-end?

We'll answer these questions and go into more detail about this new SAP S/4HANA solution in Chapter 12.

7.1.3   Orchestrating Close

So far in this section, we've seen where SAP S/4HANA makes improvements to entity close and group close. However, new tools are also available to orchestrate these processes in SAP S/4HANA to achieve increased efficiency, governance, and insight. Let's turn our attention to two key tools, beginning with the SAP Financial Closing cockpit.

SAP Financial Closing Cockpit for SAP S/4HANA

Organizations currently running SAP ERP might already be familiar with the SAP Financial Closing cockpit, a monitoring tool delivered as an add-on that lists the steps to be performed as part of the close as a template, creates a schedule of the tasks to be performed as part of a particular close (the *task list*), and then monitors the execution of the tasks in that close.

However, as of SAP S/4HANA 1709, this tool has been converted and integrated directly into the SAP S/4HANA environment. Because the cockpit sits directly on top of the Universal Journal, it leverages the single source of truth.

The SAP Financial Closing cockpit for SAP S/4HANA supports the planning, execution, monitoring, and analysis of financial closing tasks for the entities of your group that recur periodically (i.e., daily, monthly, and yearly), involve multiple agents, and have a fixed chronological sequence in the closing process.

It optimizes the financial close process by controlling each step of the close cycle, processing posting, and producing reports through five core capabilities:

- Highly automated, standardized functionality to manage accounting and reconciliation activities (including event-driven and remote task execution)
- Scheduling tools that help you sequence, monitor, and control workflows across your organization, so the entire close process moves along efficiently (including interpreting jobs from SAP Central Process Scheduling and other job schedulers)
- Closing templates
- Support for multiple factory calendars
- Full monitoring of the entire closing process, including flexible notifications

As an illustration, let's look at how task lists work within the SAP Financial Closing cockpit. As you can see in Figure 7.3, financial close personnel can access their task lists and closing tasks directly through the SAP Fiori launchpad.

Figure 7.3 SAP Financial Closing Cockpit in the SAP Fiori Launchpad

As shown in Figure 7.4, drilling down into the **Closing Cockpit Task List** tile produces an overview of the different tasks, their statuses, and much more information. It can also display dependencies, notes and attachments, log information, and so on.

Elements like the central storage of logs and attachments, the ability to set authorizations (e.g., on task or organizational unit level), and comprehensive audit trails and internal controls help ensure compliance and proper governance of the closing process.

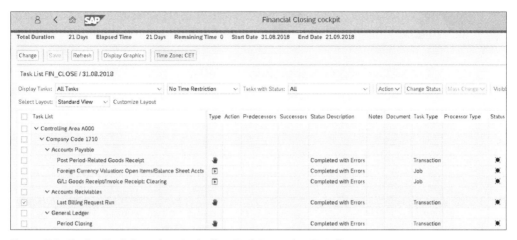

Figure 7.4 Closing Task Overview, Including Task Execution Details

To deliver complete insights throughout the entire process, predelivered KPIs like the ones in Figure 7.5 and reports (like Gantt charts) offer a clear view of closing activities across entities and close cycles.

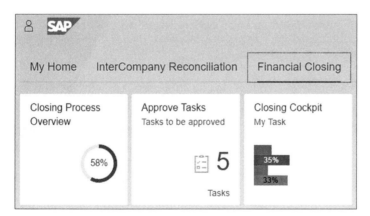

Figure 7.5 KPIs Included in the SAP Fiori Launchpad

Taken together, the SAP Financial Closing cockpit for SAP S/4HANA supports planning, executing, monitoring, and analyzing financial closing tasks for the *entities* of your group. However, remember that delivering a faster close on the level of the individual entity alone is not enough. Financial information should be made available on the (sub)consolidated level as well. Another SAP S/4HANA closing tool is on the horizon to address this gap.

SAP S/4HANA Cloud for Advanced Financial Closing

At the time of publication (spring 2019), an end-to-end closing monitor or "extended version" of the SAP Financial Closing cockpit for SAP S/4HANA is in the works at SAP.

SAP S/4HANA Cloud for advanced financial closing is a cloud-only solution that first became available with the SAP S/4HANA Cloud 1811 release. The first iteration that connects to SAP S/4HANA 1809 is available with SAP S/4HANA 1809 FSP 01, requiring SAP S/4HANA Cloud for advanced financial closing 1902. This connection to on-premise SAP S/4HANA also means that this application can be used as a closing hub, which enables you to plan, process, and monitor your financial closing for multiple on-premise systems. This first release in FSP 01 focuses on entity and group close, with financial reporting on the roadmap.

With the first release, the following capabilities are planned to be delivered and are largely in line with the classic SAP Financial Closing cockpit for SAP S/4HANA, but with a further modernized and fully SAP Fiori–based user experience:

- You can define templates to model and plan closing cycles in terms of manual and automated tasks.

- Task lists can be generated from templates for specific key dates.

- Task template sets comprise all standard closing applications and jobs with their respective sequences and interdependencies for accounts receivable, accounts payable, general ledger accounting, and cost accounting.

- You can configure the system so that notifications are automatically triggered and sent upon certain events.

- Closing tasks optionally can be subject to approval, which can be modeled in an approval workflow.

- Financial close monitoring is enabled through an overview page and an analytical list page to monitor progress and completion of your closing activities. The specific benefits of these different types of analytical SAP Fiori applications were discussed in more detail in Chapter 5. To clarify the content of these monitoring capabilities, a system example is shown in Figure 7.6 and Figure 7.7.

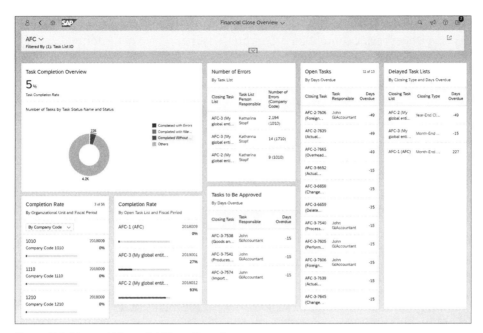

Figure 7.6 Planned Financial Close Overview

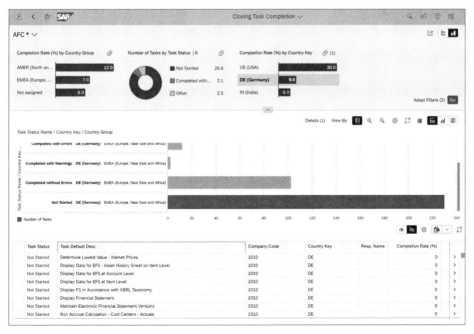

Figure 7.7 Planned Task Monitoring

Country-specific closing tasks will be supported initially for the United States and Germany, but specific content for other countries is expected in the form of extending the task templates.

We have now explained the hard close in terms of the tasks to be performed at the entity level and group level, and we introduced tools to orchestrate the steps involved. Let's now look at how SAP S/4HANA facilitates a soft close.

7.2   New Approaches for a Soft Close

In the previous section, we focused on how SAP S/4HANA helps finance organizations close their books faster. SAP has taken measures such as releasing the SAP Financial Closing cockpit and embedding a consolidation engine in the SAP S/4HANA environment to support this objective, but another approach—continuous close—offers new inroads.

At its core, *continuous accounting* springs from a belief that the structure of the record-to-report process isn't quite right and that results can be improved by organizing and scheduling work differently. The main idea is to embed automation, control, and period-end tasks within day-to-day activities, thus allowing the rigid accounting calendar to more closely mirror the broader business. It transforms the way organizations work by emphasizing automated, real-time processing, highly skilled employees, and proactive analysis. The result is more accurate financials, a more efficient close, and a more effective organization.

For example, Figure 7.8 shows how workload is distributed throughout the period in a continuous close.

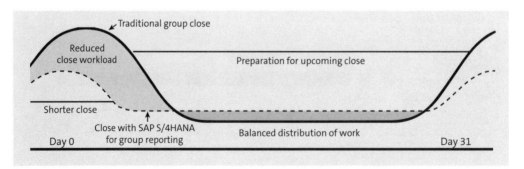

Figure 7.8 A Balanced Distribution of Work via Continuous Accounting

There are two areas that offer substantial improvements to soft close: initiatives that accelerate existing closing steps through automation, and initiatives that eliminate closing steps. Let's look at both.

7.2.1 Accelerating Closing Steps

Using software to automate manual tasks improves efficiency and speeds the completion of processes. By eliminating human intervention (and thus the potential for errors), automation can enhance financial control. End-to-end process automation is achieved when numbers are entered only once and all calculations and analyses are performed by the system. Properly configured, end-to-end automation also enforces data integrity, eliminating the need for extra checks.

Historically, process automation has been based on modeling a set of rules, which are then executed automatically by the system. Let's look at a general example, like credit control. To automate the approval of a new sales order, a credit check can be performed using a set of credit rules that typically look at the rating of the business partner, the payment behavior, and so on. Unfortunately, the complexity of the business world means that it can't always be modeled perfectly in a set of rules. (If it could, then all business partners would always comply with agreed payment terms, resulting in days sales outstanding always being equal to zero.) So though certain types of rule-based automation make a lot of sense, rules are not the answer to everything.

Hence SAP has been looking to deploy other, *intelligent* types of automation. In recent years it has sought to combine the following techniques to make a particular finance process more intelligent:

- Machine learning capabilities that enable automation
- Analytical capabilities that drive process improvements
- Flexible collaboration to connect stakeholders of a specific process
- A modern user experience that facilitates a natural way of working and user access across devices

Return to Chapter 4 for more detailed information about how SAP views optimization of finance processes. In this section, we'll focus on closing activities that have undergone this "intelligent" transformation, including the goods and invoice receipt reconciliation and accruals management.

Goods and invoice receipt reconciliation is one of the best-known examples of period-end processes that are very time-consuming and involve multiple stakeholders from different functional domains. By making use of the different innovative techniques just mentioned, the SAP S/4HANA for goods and invoice receipt reconciliation app, shown in Figure 7.9, gives you access to a 360-degree view of all relevant elements and facilitates easy collaboration with anyone that should be involved in the reconciliation process. Integrated machine learning logic delivers a recommended approach for resolving individual reconciliation issues, which further accelerates the closing process. For more information about this application, return to Chapter 4.

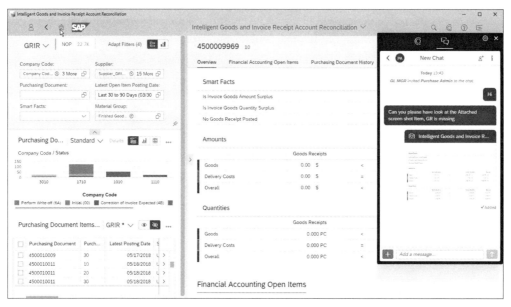

Figure 7.9 The SAP S/4HANA for Goods and Invoice Receipt Reconciliation App

7.2.2   Eliminating Closing Steps

It's one thing to increase the efficiency in executing closing tasks—and another thing entirely to eliminate them from the period-end closing process.

This might sound a little misleading. These tasks must still be performed, of course; it's just that when and how they are performed shifts from end of the period to the actual moment of the initial transaction *during the period*, as shown in Figure 7.10.

Let's look at an example in which this shift from period end to during the period is particularly impactful: margin analysis. Recall from Chapter 1 that the integration of profitability analysis data in the Universal Journal improves your margin insights overall. This technically means that all profitability segments are included in the Universal Journal and therefore are reconciled with the financial single source of truth by design. This means that organizations no longer need a separate reconciliation step to compare the profit and loss statement with the information in profitability analysis at period close.

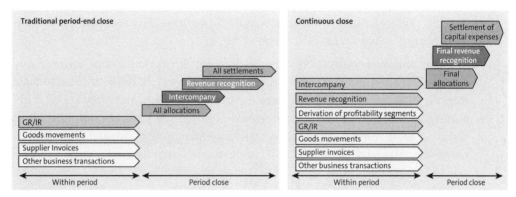

Figure 7.10 Transitioning from Traditional Period-End Close to Continuous Close

Profitability segments (or *characteristics*, as they are typically called in SAP ERP) are important market or organizational dimensions that are directly linked with financial data. You can drill down from within financial reports to details about products, customers, sales organizations, and so on, and then run multidimensional reports. Thanks to the Universal Journal–based architecture, you're no longer limited to drilling into the P&L alone; you can also drill down into additional dimensions for some balance sheet accounts. At the time of publication (spring 2019), this is provided for WIP accounts, which is particularly interesting as this is the area of the balance sheet in which a portion of the future margin sits. The assumption is that the work in process will become cost of goods sold (COGS) in a future period.

This relocation of margin analysis has two main benefits:

- Executing some of the derivation steps from month end at the time of the initial transaction brings these insights to a business's fingertips at any moment in time.
- The workload of the finance division is distributed throughout the period, lessening the bottleneck at period end.

Hence SAP is investing in this move toward a continuous delivery of margin insights across different profitability segments. In Chapter 1, we looked at the various reporting dimensions in the Universal Journal and specifically at how the sixty characteristics in the operating concern become columns in the Universal Journal, so reporting dimensions like product and customer sit alongside the company code, the profit center, and so on in the posting line. We also explained that the fundamental posting logic in SAP ERP doesn't change as you move to SAP S/4HANA. If you're posting revenues or COGS, these are associated with a cost element and must be associated with an account assignment—in this case, the multidimensional profitability segment. In Chapter 5, Figure 5.23, we saw that all postings to a profitability segment can be identified using the object type EO.

Although this availability of margin by different dimension can be immediately delivered for revenues and COGS, organizations have to wait for period end to have access to other key figures determined by profitability segments. They are typically waiting for assessment cycles to move marketing costs, sales and administration costs, and so on from the cost centers to the profitability segments and settlement to move research and development costs to the profitability segments. Again, you'll be able to identify these postings using the object type EO.

Now let's look at some simple examples of how we can change this logic to avoid the need to run allocations and settlement at period close and instead work with attributed profitability segments:

- If we charge costs to a commercial project, we know from the assigned sales order which customer will be billed for the work, which region they are assigned to, and so on. Instead of waiting for period close to move the costs from the commercial project to the profitability segments, we can derive the customer, the region, and so on immediately.

- If we charge costs to an internal order, we may be able to derive the profitability segments from the settlement rule immediately rather than waiting for the period close to move the costs to the profitability segments.

- If we charge costs to certain cost centers, we may be able to derive some profitability segments, such as the region, from the company code assigned to the cost center.

In the following subsections, we'll look into the areas where the real-time derivation of the profitability segments is available today (provided that profitability analysis integrated in the Universal Journal is set up in SAP S/4HANA).

Using Attributed Profitability Segments instead of Allocations and Settlements

The principle of immediately deriving profitability segments at the time of each primary document (i.e., the initial transaction posting) is known as *attributed profitability segments*. This approach differs from the existing accounting approach in that we've enriched the posting document so that costs are assigned to both the original account assignment (the cost center, project, order, and so on) and the attributed profitability segment. When you look at such posting lines in reporting, the object type continues to be KS (cost center), PR (project), OR (order), and so on, but the profitability segments will also be filled in. To see these profitability segments in reporting, you'll have to use either the SAP Fiori reports or Transaction KE24N (Display CO-PA Line Items), because the classic reports, including Transactions KE24 (Display CO-PA Line Items) and KE30 (Run Profitability Report) only select those postings with account assignment EO (profitability segment).

By applying this approach, you can start analyzing expenses (e.g., travel expenses) by customer or product as they occur, without waiting for the closing process and settlements to happen. Likewise, it enables you to drill down into your unbilled revenue (also known as *work in progress*) and find out more about related projects and products.

Let's look at an example to illustrate how this works. Consider the classic (i.e., SAP ERP) approach of determining profitability information based on settlements. In the flow in Figure 7.11, we have the classic split between finance and profitability postings, with table COSB being used to store the data for revenue recognition and the settlement transaction then moving the values into the balance sheet.

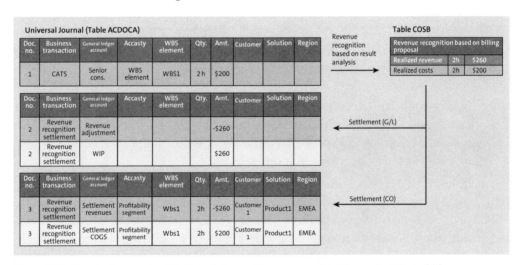

Figure 7.11 Classic Approach with Calculation of Revenue and Settlement at Period Close

Let's consider how the attributed profitability segments method is handled for customer projects that use project-based billing. The market segment information (i.e., the additional dimension values by which you want to analyze your margin) can be provided with the primary posting to the project because we know the connection between the project and the sales order. When we make the primary account assignment to the project, we use the information in the assigned sales order to enrich the posting line with the profitability segments. As shown in Figure 7.12, no settlement is required anymore, and there is no reconciliation between different tables because the posting line contains the assignment to both a WBS element and the profitability segment.

Universal Journal (Table ACDOCA)

Doc. no.	Business transaction	General ledger account	Accasty	WBS element	Qty.	Amt.	Customer	Solution	Region
1a	CATS	Senior cons.	WBS element	WBS1	2h	$200	Customer 1	Product1	EMEA

Market segment provided for every posting (assignment of sales order item is a pre-requisite)

Doc. no.	Business transaction	General ledger account	Accasty	WBS element	Qty.	Amt.	Customer	Solution	Region
1b	TBBR	Revenue adjustment	WBS element	WBS 1		-$260	Customer 1	Product1	EMEA
1b	TBBR	Unbilled revenue	WBS element	WBS1		$260	Customer 1	Product1	EMEA

WIP drilldown by project and market segment

Doc. no.	Business transaction	General ledger account	Accasty	WBS element	Qty.	Amt.	Customer	Solution	Region
3	Revenue recognition settlement	Settlement revenues	Profitability segment		2h	-$260	Customer 1	Product1	EMEA
3	Revenue recognition settlement	Settlement COGS	Profitability segment		2h	$200	Customer 1	Product1	EMEA

Figure 7.12 The Attributed Profitability Segments Approach

In this approach, derivation of the attributed profitability segments is activated in Customizing; characteristics are determined at the time the income statement item is created according to a specific derivation logic (either automated derivation logic or manually preconfigured derivation logic).

It should be clear that these attributed profitability segments are enriching the document because they are shown alongside the real account assignment to profitability segments, where the profitability segment is determined in the sending application (e.g., sales) or manually entered in the general ledger accounting posting.

Examples of this approach include the following:

- A goods issue item or billing document item in a sell-from-stock scenario
- A manual FI posting to a profitability segment
- A settlement of a cost object to profitability analysis

Both real and attributed profitability segments can be reported on, as illustrated in Figure 7.13. In this example, the **Prof. Anlys. Product** column and the **Customer** column contain attributed profitability segments, and the real account assignment is shown in the **Project Definition** column.

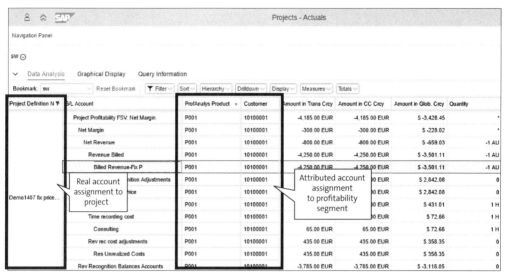

Figure 7.13 Real Account Assignments and Attributed Profitability Segments in the Project—Actuals App

You can set up the derivation logic to assign these attributes by following the menu path **Controlling • Profitability Analysis • Master Data • Activate Derivation for Items without Profitability Segment** in the IMG and choosing the controlling account assignments that you wish to associate with profitability analysis characteristics. The objective is to select those controlling account assignments that make a single-level settlement to profitability analysis. In the example in Figure 7.13, we selected **Items Assigned to Projects**. You then need to decide whether you're only deriving profitability segments for P&L accounts or whether you also want to derive profitability analysis characteristics for balance sheet accounts, such as work in process. Usually it doesn't make sense to activate the derivation for all project types, since capital expense projects don't settle to profitability. You can select your commercial projects by entering the appropriate project profile.

Using derivation doesn't prevent you from settling or performing an allocation at period close if required. In the example in Figure 7.14, the posting logic is as follows:

❶ Costs posted to internal order with automatically derived profitability characteristics (debit posting). Real account assignment in first two posting lines is internal order (object type OR) and other account assignments are attributed.

❷ Settlement of internal order to profitability segment during month end, if required due to complex settlement rules (credit posting to order). Real account assignment in third posting line is internal order.

❸ Settlement of internal order to profitability segment (debit) with real account assignment to profitability segment (object type EO in posting line item).

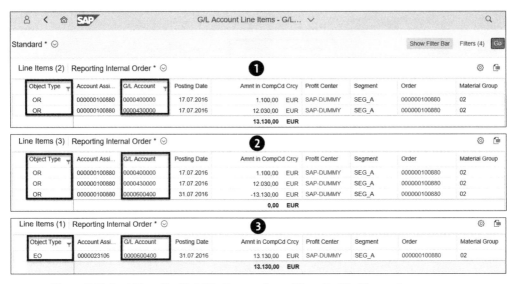

Figure 7.14 Real-Time Profitability Segments and Result of Settlement

If you don't need to settle, then you should adjust your settlement profiles for the commercial projects and flag them as **Not for Settlement**.

In the case of allocations using assessment cycles, derivation often allows you to make a high-level assignment of the costs to a region or a market unit, but you will usually need to run a classic assessment cycle to break the costs down to products, customers, and so on. There is often a business reason for this: you will need to wait for the system to collect the driver values to be used as a basis for the allocation (such as the relative invoice quantities for each product).

Now that we've shown how to enrich a posting to a project with profitability information, we'll take this idea further to show how to create additional postings to account for accrued revenues.

Real-Time Revenue Recognition for Project-Based Services

Back in Figure 7.13, you can see that the journal entries shown are not just for billed revenue and the costs associated with the project, but that they also include revenue adjustments and reserves for unrealized costs.

SAP S/4HANA allows you to create additional documents for the revenue adjustments and reserves for unrealized costs that you would normally associate with the period close. With SAP S/4HANA, every time a consultant makes a time recording to the WBS element, the revenue can be accrued *immediately*. As shown in Figure 7.15, this results in two postings being made to the WBS element based on a common reference document:

- Time recording in SAP ERP via the Cross-Application Time Sheet (CATS) would produce the first document, in which the cost center **CC1** is credited and the WBS element **WBS1** is debited for one hour of consulting work. You can identify these postings by the **RKL** business transaction in the line item in Figure 7.16.
- The second document is new in SAP S/4HANA. It uses the planned profit for the contract to calculate the revenue adjustment and unbilled revenue on the contract. You can identify these postings by the new **TBRR** business transaction in the line item in Figure 7.16.

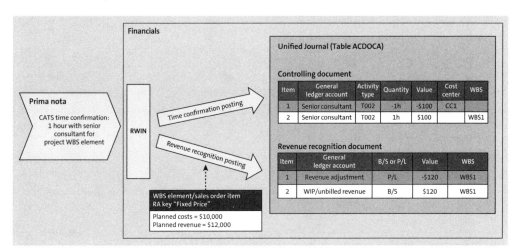

Figure 7.15 Postings for Event-Based Revenue Recognition

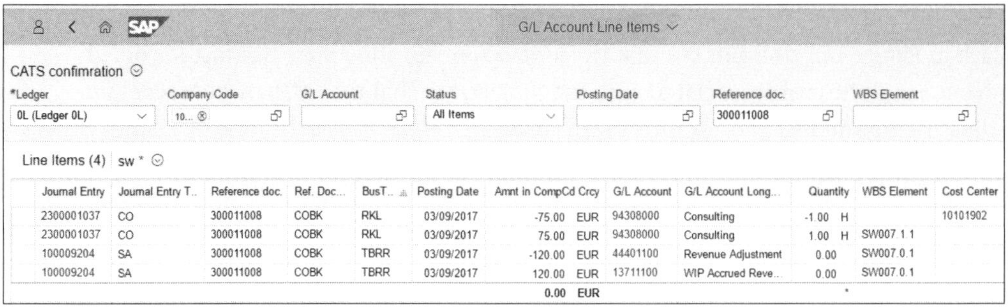

Figure 7.16 Line Items for Real-Time Revenue Recognition

Figure 7.16 shows the process in terms of the line items triggered by the time recording in the G/L Account Line Item app (SAP Fiori ID F0706), but SAP S/4HANA also includes new applications designed to help the project manager monitor the process. The Event-Based Revenue Recognition—Projects app (SAP Fiori ID F2129) shown in Figure 7.17 shows the three WBS elements that are flagged as billing elements and have a revenue recognition key (this is the trigger for event-based revenue recognition). You can then see the recognized revenue, COGS, and margin. This is useful to get an overview of all the commercial projects being handled by the manager, but more detail may be needed. To access details of the calculation, select the arrow for each posting line.

Figure 7.17 The Event-Based Revenue Recognition—Projects App: Initial Screen

Figure 7.18 shows the details for the selected line, with the billed revenue (**0 Euros**) and actual cost (**1,575 Euros**) that have been posted directly to the billing element. You can see the revenue adjustment (**3,494.12 Euros**) and accrued revenue (**-3,494.12 Euros**)

that were in Figure 7.16 and the recognized revenue (**3,494.12 Euros**), recognized COS (**1,575 Euros**), and the recognized margin (**1,919.12 Euros**) from Figure 7.17.

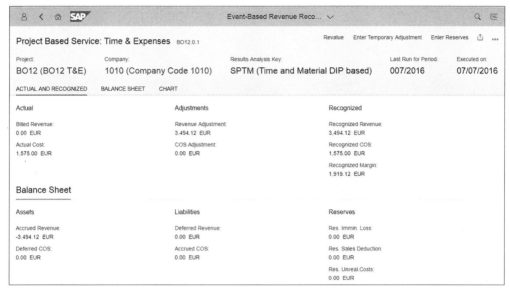

Figure 7.18 The Event-Based Revenue Recognition—Projects App: Details

You can use event-based revenue recognition for three types of commercial project:

- Fixed-price billing
- Periodic service billing
- Time and expense (T&E) billing

Let's look at journal entries for each, starting in Figure 7.19 with the journal entries for fixed-price billing like we used to post the journal entries in Figure 7.16, Figure 7.17, and Figure 7.18. There are two things to note here. First, the percentage of completion is used to realize the revenue in proportion to the costs posted; second, the accrued revenue is offset against unbilled receivables, as shown in Figure 7.19.

In this example, we are assuming planned costs of **USD $1,000** and planned revenue of **USD $2,000** with a profit margin of **100%**. With the time confirmation, we have recorded activity worth **USD $500** (posting 1). This results in a percentage of completion of **50%**, which is used to calculate revenue adjustments of **USD $1,000** (also posting 1). As the customer is invoiced, the billed revenue and receivables are recorded (posting 2) and the accrued revenues are canceled in proportion to the level of the billed revenue. At period close, we cancel the accrued and deferred revenue (posting 3).

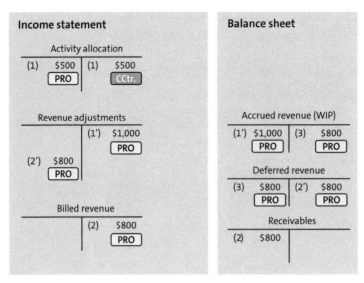

Figure 7.19 Revenue Recognition with Fixed-Price Billing

Figure 7.20 shows the journal entries if we bill the customer for time and expenses instead of charging a fixed price. In this scenario, the costs rather than the revenue lead. We don't need to plan costs or revenue in this scenario but will instead simulate the impact of SD pricing.

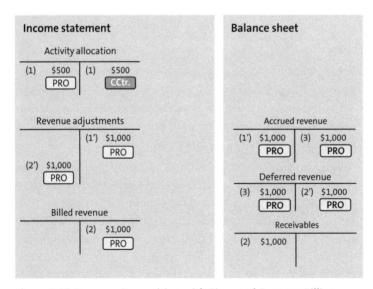

Figure 7.20 Revenue Recognition with Time and Expense Billing

In this example, the sales price for a senior consultant is **USD $200** per hour. We have recorded a time confirmation of five hours, resulting in senior consulting costs of **USD $500** (posting 1), and this triggers a revenue adjustment of **USD $1,000** (also posting 1). We then invoice the customer and record billed revenue and receivables of **USD $1,000** (posting 2) and cancel the revenue adjustment. At period close, we cancel the accrued and deferred revenue (posting 3). The same mechanisms would apply for expense postings related to a consultant traveling to the customer site and billing for those expenses.

Figure 7.21 shows the journal entries when the customer is billed periodically for services. Again, the time confirmation is made, resulting in senior consulting costs of **USD $600** (posting 1), and this is immediately recorded as work in progress (also posting 1). We invoice for **USD $1,200** per year, resulting in billed revenue and receivables (posting 2) and work in process (also posting 2). Finally, we record a periodic revenue recognition run that recognizes **USD $100** in each period (posting 3).

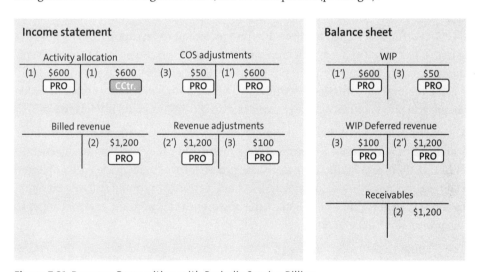

Figure 7.21 Revenue Recognition with Periodic Service Billing

We've focused on the accounting entries in this section, but if you compare Figure 7.13 with Figure 7.22, you'll notice the assignment to the **Customer**, **Customer Group**, **PA Product**, **Sales Order**, and **Sales Organization** as a result of derivation, alongside the new journal entries for revenue adjustments and accrued revenues.

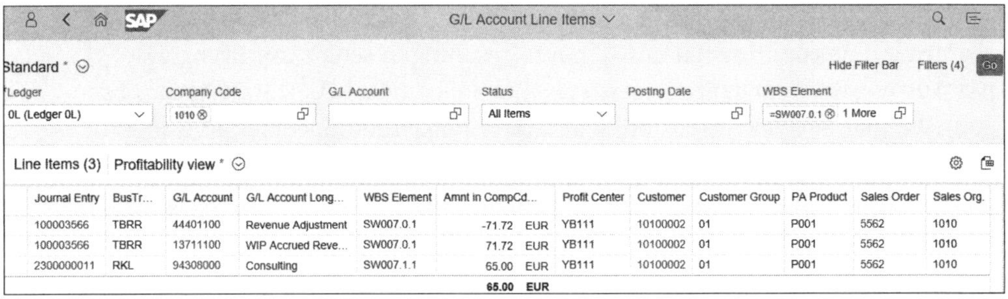

Figure 7.22 Revenue Recognition with Attributed Profitability Segments

One concern with event-based revenue recognition is that consultants may be unable to record their time if their SAP S/4HANA system is not able to generate the additional postings shown in Figure 7.15 and Figure 7.22—perhaps because there is no planned data to calculate the planned profit or because there's no revenue recognition key in the project.

SAP S/4HANA is designed to allow the time recording to be captured even if it isn't possible to create the second document. At period close, you should use the Event-Based Revenue Recognition app (SAP Fiori ID REV_REC_COL_PRO) shown in Figure 7.23 to generate any missing postings. This application will list any errors in which the second posting to recognize the revenue on the project could not be created.

The postings generated thanks to event-based revenue recognition represent a huge leap forward in the move toward real-time finance, but they can't handle all eventualities. If there is a status change to the project or the percentage of completion changes, the postings are not adjusted. At period close, you should still run the application shown in Figure 7.23 to update the postings to take account of any changes to the project during the period.

The settings to control event-based revenue recognition are in the IMG under **Controlling • Product Cost Controlling • Product Cost by Sales Order • Period-End Closing • Event-Based Revenue Recognition • Maintain Settings for Revenue Recognition**. Revenue recognition is performed only if the relevant WBS element includes a recognition key (see Figure 7.17). Figure 7.24 shows a sample revenue recognition key using the cost-based percentage of completion method.

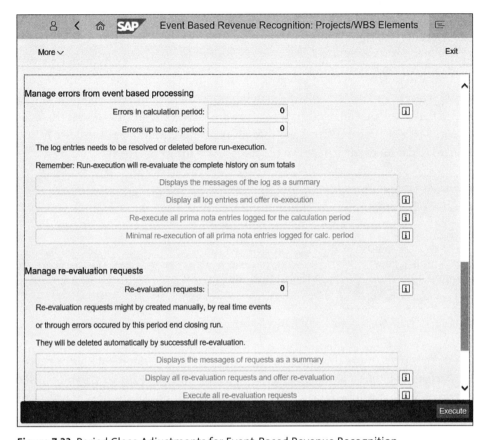

Figure 7.23 Period Close Adjustments for Event-Based Revenue Recognition

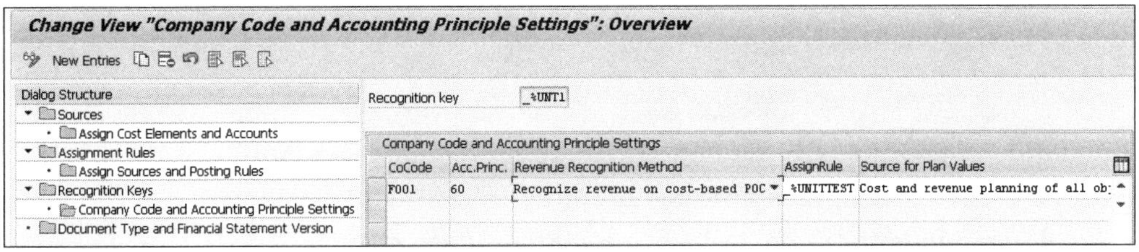

Figure 7.24 Settings for Revenue Recognition Key

The revenue recognition key alone is just the starting point for this process. (If you are familiar with results analysis, then you probably recognize the same behavior in the results analysis key!) You also need to assign the relevant accounts/cost elements for revenue recognition by defining a source under **Sources • Assign Cost Elements and Accounts** (see Figure 7.24).

In Figure 7.25, we grouped all relevant cost line items under the **Costs** debit type, but you can also use cost element categories, cost element groups, accounts, or the condition types from sales and distribution billing to make your selection. Just as you had to make sure that all relevant accounts were assigned to line IDs for results analysis in SAP ERP, you must ensure that all relevant accounts are included in the **Sources** folder for event-based revenue recognition in SAP S/4HANA.

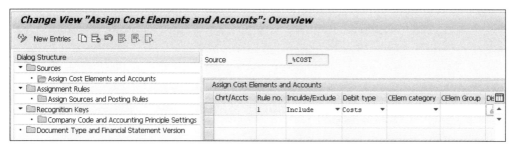

Figure 7.25 Source Assignment for Event-Based Revenue Recognition

The next step is to make this assignment source part of an **Assignment Rule** by choosing **Assignment Rules • Assign Sources and Posting Rules**. In Figure 7.26, you can see the accounts that will be updated for revenue recognition. This is the equivalent of the old posting rules for results analysis in SAP ERP; the difference in SAP S/4HANA is that the postings will be made immediately rather than on settlement.

Change View "Assign Sources and Posting Rules": Overview

Dialog Structure					
▼ ☐ Sources			Assignment Rule	_%UNITTEST	
• ☐ Assign Cost Elements and Accounts					
▼ ☐ Assignment Rules			Assign Sources and Posting Rules		

Chrt/Ac...	Sequence	Source	Usage	Deferrals (...	Accruals (...	Cost Eler
	1	%REVENUE	Revenue for Revenue Recognition Processing	▾ 791004	791003	892001
	2	%COST	Cost capitalizable and POC relevant for recognizing reven...	▾ 792003	792002	892004
	3	%NEUTRAL	Value without Revenue Recognition Processing	▾		

Figure 7.26 Posting Rules for Event-Based Revenue Recognition

Finally, you can define a separate document type for the revenue recognition postings, as shown under the **Document Type and Financial Statement Version** setting in Figure 7.27.

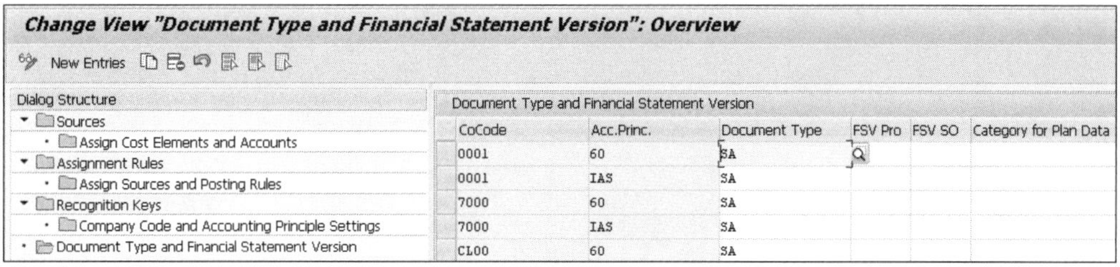

Figure 7.27 Document Types and Financial Statement Versions for Event Based-Revenue Recognition

The idea of accruing revenues whenever time is recorded to a project works well within a single legal entity. We'll now look what happens when the project is performing work across legal entities.

Intercompany Postings for Project-Based Services

As organizations become more global, time recording may no longer be between a cost center and a project in the same legal entity. It's increasingly common for the consultants performing the work on a project to be assigned to a different company code than the project itself. This results in a *cross-company time recording*, as shown in Figure 7.28. The consultant's costs are being incurred in the company code on the left (the delivering company) and the revenue billed by the company code on the right (the selling company).

❶ Time recording takes place as before, with the delivering company charging costs to the selling company. What changes in SAP S/4HANA is that we can create a markup in the delivering company that will result in a second document being created alongside the document for the time recording.

❷ The markup is used to provide a proposal for the intercompany billing process and move the costs from the delivering company code to the selling company code.

❸ These costs will then be billed to the final customer using resource-related billing.

To use this approach, you will have to activate the FINS_CO_ICO_PROC_ENH_101 business function (Intercompany Process Enhancements 1), available from SAP S/4HANA 1610.

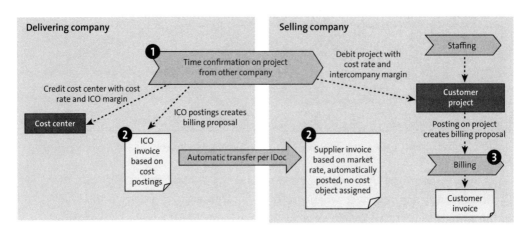

Figure 7.28 Postings for Resource-Related Intercompany Billing

If you compare the line items shown in Figure 7.29 with those shown in Figure 7.16, you'll see the same initial posting for the time recording under the business transaction **RKL**. This is the journal entry for the consulting work. This time, however, you'll see additional lines for the intercompany margin being recorded under the business transaction **KAMV** and intercompany clearing documents in both company codes.

Company Code	Journal Entry	Bus...	Reference document	G/L Account	G/L Account Long...	Amount in Tran...	Amount in CC Crcy	Quantity	Activity Type	Part. Cost C...	WBS Element
Company Code: 1710 - Company Code 1710 (AE)											
1710	2400000037	RKL	300001000	94308000	Consulting	-75.00 USD	-75.00 USD	-1.000 H	T003		SW007.1.1
1710	2400000037	RKL	300001000	99999900	ICO Clearing Acco...	75.00 USD	75.00 USD	0.000			SW007.1.1
1710	2400000038	KAMV	300001000	97777700	ICO Margin	-15.00 USD	-15.00 USD	0.000 H	T003		SW007.1.1
1710	2400000038	KAMV	300001000	98888800	ICO Clearing Acco...	15.00 USD	15.00 USD	0.000			SW007.1.1
1710						0.00 USD	0.00 USD	*			
Company Code: 1010 - ABC Ltd.											
1010	2400000038	RKL	300001000	94308000	Consulting	75.00 USD	60.00 EUR	1.000 H		T003	SW007.1.1
1010	2400000038	RKL	300001000	99999900	ICO Clearing Acco...	-75.00 USD	-60.00 EUR	0.000			
1010	2400000039	KAMV	300001000	97777700	ICO Margin	15.00 USD	12.00 EUR	0.000 H		T003	SW007.1.1
1010	2400000039	KAMV	300001000	98888800	ICO Clearing Acco...	-15.00 USD	-12.00 EUR	0.000			
1010						0.00 USD	0.00 EUR	*			
						0.00 USD	*	*			

Figure 7.29 Postings for Intercompany Billing

The postings shown in Figure 7.16 use activity rates for receivers in the same legal entity, but in SAP S/4HANA we can also define activity rates that depend on the legal entity of the receiving cost object.

Figure 7.30 shows the Maintain Activity Cost Rates app (SAP Fiori ID CMACA02), with different activity rates depending on whether the activity is performed for company code **1010** or company code **1710**. This results in the two lines shown in Figure 7.29, in which you see a charge of **USD $75** plus an intercompany charge of **USD $15**. When the time recording is posted, it triggers a second posting using Transaction KB15N that records the intercompany markup (the posting lines with business transaction **KAMV**).

You can use the same mechanisms to trigger a markup when other expenses (e.g., travel) are charged to the project. The invoicing of the consulting work to the customer continues to take place at period close using Transaction DP93.

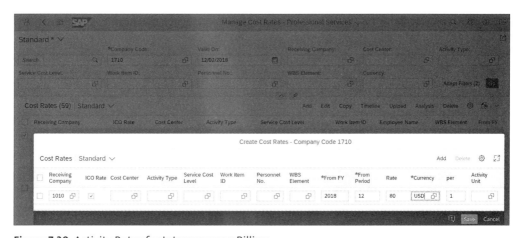

Figure 7.30 Activity Rates for Intercompany Billing

To configure this process, you'll need to set up intercompany margin accounts to be updated whenever a cross-company time recording is made by following menu path **Controlling • Cost Center Accounting • Actual Postings • Additional Transaction-Related Postings • Intercompany Margins for Activity Allocations • Assign Intercompany Margin Accounts** in the IMG. Figure 7.31 shows the intercompany margin account to be posted to whenever an activity allocation is posted using account **94308000**.

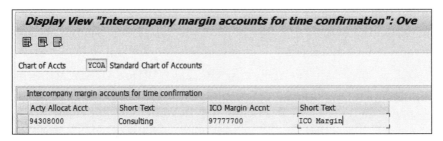

Figure 7.31 Intercompany Margin Accounts for Cross-Company Activities

You'll also need to enter intercompany clearing accounts for other expense accounts by following the menu path **Controlling • Cost Center Accounting • Actual Postings • Additional Transaction-Related Postings • Assign Intercompany Clearing Accounts** in the IMG. Figure 7.32 shows the intercompany clearing accounts to be posted to whenever one of the expense accounts (on the left) is updated.

Figure 7.32 Intercompany Margin Accounts for Cross-Company Expenses

Real-Time Overhead and Work in Process

Real-time revenue recognition was introduced for commercial projects in SAP S/4HANA, but the ability to calculate overhead immediately as a follow-on document for secondary postings was introduced for secondary costs as early as Enhancement Package 4 for SAP ERP 6.0; it was then extended in SAP S/4HANA to cover primary postings. Work continues on these transactions, which don't yet have an error-correction mechanism like that shown for event-based revenue recognition in Figure 7.23.

Over the next versions, we expect that SAP will rework the calculation of work in process and the calculation of scrap and variances to provide real-time information for production controlling as soon as the relevant material document or confirmation is posted. This way, people on the shop floor can act immediately as soon as variances become apparent instead of waiting until period close.

Figure 7.33 shows the Real-Time Work in Process app (SAP Fiori ID F1757). This shows work in process created when materials are issued to a production order, work is confirmed, or overhead charged to the order.

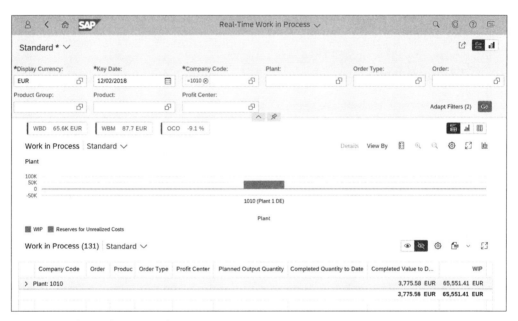

Figure 7.33 The Real-Time Work in Process App

As you saw with event-based revenue recognition, it's essential to ensure that the goods movements and confirmations can continue to be posted in logistics, even if it isn't possible to calculate work in process because of errors in configuration. For this reason, the Inspect WIP/Variance Posting app shown in Figure 7.34 displays the errors in account assignment that prevented the system from calculating work in process for some orders.

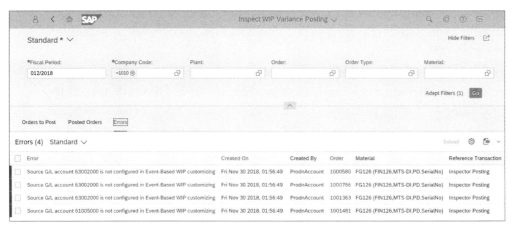

Figure 7.34 The Inspect WIP/Variance Posting App

7.3   Summary

In this chapter, we began to explore the idea of continuous accounting, showing not only how to use the SAP Financial Closing cockpit to improve the hard close, but also how to create new journal entries to provide a soft close.

In the next chapter, we'll take this idea further and look at the idea of predictive accounting and how to use contractual information already in the SAP S/4HANA system to simulate the close.

Chapter 8

Predictive Accounting:
Providing Forward-Looking Insights

This chapter introduces predictive accounting and explains how journal entries can be created in SAP S/4HANA to reflect anticipated revenue and costs, using contractual information already in the system to provide forward-looking information to steer the business.

In the previous chapter on the financial close, we discussed how the time when decision-makers could content themselves with periodic information delivered after the month-end close is well behind us. Finance can no longer afford to keep looking backward. These days, continuous delivery of relevant information is the minimum requirement—and insight into what the future will or might bring is often requested.

Nevertheless, accountants are naturally cautious as a profession, so the idea of accounting entries that aren't yet GAAP-relevant appearing in the books is likely to raise a few eyebrows. If you work in the public sector, then you are probably already familiar with the idea of *commitment accounting*; this approach ensures that committed (or encumbered) funds are recorded and can't be used for another purpose, to ensure that organizations stay within budget.

The idea of accounting for commitments is nothing new for controllers. What changes is that in *predictive accounting*, we are treating these anticipated costs as early (or predictive) accounting documents, even though they are not yet GAAP-relevant, and showing them in *all* reports that reference the ledger rather than just in the controlling reports. This will allow us to view actual costs, commitments, and budgeted or planned costs in a single report based on the Universal Journal.

But as you'll see in this chapter, this is not the only way in which forward-looking insights can be generated. We can use the same approach to look at the predicted revenues associated with a sales order. These revenues and the associated cost of goods sold (COGS) are determined based on the incoming sales orders and used together with the planned delivery data to predict what will happen and better prepare for that outcome.

Predictive accounting uses the data already available in contractual information, such as sales orders and purchase orders, to predict when these orders will be fulfilled and create journal entries in accounting. Concerned accountants can rest assured that such predictive documents are kept separate from the real accounting documents in a separate extension ledger. Any documents posted to this extension ledger are ignored in all reports to be delivered to external stakeholders. This kind of practice is a natural extension of the continuous accounting concept from Chapter 7 and another related practice, predictive analytics.

In the past, predictive tools like SAP Predictive Analytics were often in the hands of dedicated data scientists, who reviewed historic information to understand what has happened to the organization in the past and applied statistical methods to quantify the trends in the data and establish relationships in these past events. As shown in Figure 8.1, predictive analytics uses top-down information and mathematical tools to predict, for a range of outcomes, which is most likely to happen and how an organization can best prepare for the future.

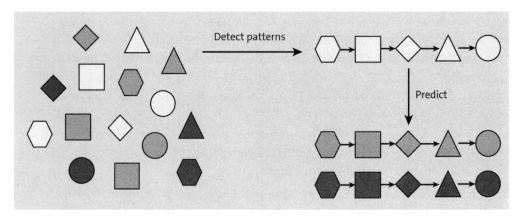

Figure 8.1 Top-Down Predictive Analytics

By contrast, predictive accounting is considered *bottom-up* because it is based on transactional line-item information already available within the SAP S/4HANA environment. As shown in Figure 8.2, it uses the sales orders from the order-to-cash process and the purchase orders from the purchase-to-pay process to create predictive journal entries—even if the orders haven't yet been fulfilled. These predictions naturally will lead to GAAP-relevant journal entries when the orders are fulfilled and invoices sent or received. At that point, the predictive journal entries get reversed by the system to avoid double counting in reporting.

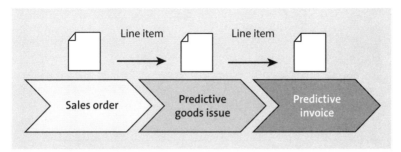

Figure 8.2 Bottom-Up Predictive Accounting

Figure 8.3 illustrates the vision for predictive accounting, which puts predictive capabilities in the hands of all business users. The first column, **Actuals**, contains all GAAP-relevant information already captured for the period (just under **$30,000,000** in this example). In a classic accounting report, this is all that a user would see midmonth.

The next column is **Costs and Revenue from Running Operations**. Here you see that the system is pretranslating costs and revenues from running operations to include information already captured as purchase orders (costs) and sales orders (revenues) in profitability calculations. In this example, this amounts to an additional **$25,000** or so for costs from the purchase orders that will be incurred within the period based on the delivery date, and revenues from the sales orders that will be fulfilled within the period. In SAP ERP, we would have needed to look at dedicated controlling reports to see this information.

The remaining columns reflect the vision of predictive accounting, in which ever-more postings will be reflected in the calculations. In the future, SAP plans to deliver predictive accounting documents that represent the recurring entries for depreciation, payroll, and so on and to simulate the impact of various closing steps, including currency remeasurement on the P&L statement. The first step in this journey is to enrich the documents with information that classify them as relating to depreciation, payroll, and so on, making it easy to identify the relevant documents and predict their impact going forward.

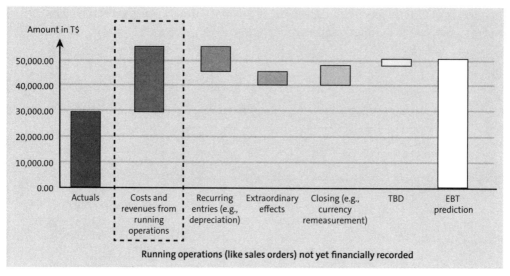

Figure 8.3 Predictive KPIs, Composed from Several Building Blocks

This kind of predictive accounting makes it possible to provide a clearer picture regarding where the organization will be at the end of the month. It is not simply a matter of capturing costs and revenues but also of recognizing *when* these postings will become accounting-relevant. The purchase order and sales order both include a planned delivery date, and it is this date that determines in which period the predicted costs or revenues will be included.

This approach allows organizations to create predictive journal entries and transform any financial measure from a real-time measure into one that includes predictive information without a major effort, while staying inherently consistent and reconciled with other information in the related document flow. This way, organizations can use predictive accounting to extend the transactional reach of accounting beyond GAAP-relevant postings while ensuring all information is still consistently stored in a single source of truth—the Universal Journal.

Now let's look at the three use cases for predictive accounting currently covered in SAP S/4HANA 1809. In the upcoming sections, we'll explain these different scenarios, detailing further how predictive accounting works technically and how predictive information is stored within SAP S/4HANA. In Section 8.1, we'll look at how to perform predictive accounting to handle incoming sales orders. In Section 8.2, we'll look at how to handle statistical sales conditions. Finally, in Section 8.3 we'll look at the new approach to handling commitments for purchase orders.

In Chapter 1 we explained that financial and controlling information is now combined in the Universal Journal and introduced the idea of an extension ledger as a way of separating any management adjustments needed for operational reporting from the figures that have been reported externally. In predictive accounting, we use a special kind of extension ledger that allows us to combine GAAP-relevant and non-GAAP-relevant information in the same data structure. In each of the sections that follow, we'll explain how the extension ledger is used to handle each specific use case.

8.1 Accounting for Incoming Sales Orders

The first predictive accounting scenario delivered in SAP S/4HANA predicts the financial impact (more specifically, the revenue, COGS, and gross margin) based on the incoming sales orders. Of course, taking corresponding actions rather than just reviewing the reported predicted margin is what will help an organization improve its accounting, but as a first step, reporting is key.

Let's look at the process in Figure 8.4. When analyzing the classic order-to-cash process flow, the key starting point is the quotation, followed by the sales order. At the time the sales order is captured, there is no financial information available. The system therefore makes two predictions:

❶ The first prediction simulates the goods delivery and determines the COGS and how this will be split into its cost components. (We'll look at how this cost splitting works in detail in Chapter 11.) It can also simulate the accrued revenue that will be associated with these costs.

❷ The next prediction simulates the invoice and determines the revenue associated with the sales order and can apply overhead and perform revenue recognition based on this information.

The first GAAP-relevant posting in this process flow is the goods issue, which credits inventory and debits COGS following the delivery. At this point, the predictive COGS is reversed.

When the sales order is billed (following the goods issue), the billing document generates an open item on the accounts receivables side and a revenue item on the P&L. The simulated revenue will be reversed when the invoice is posted and generates revenue.

In Section 8.1.1, we'll explore the impact of the incoming sales orders on product profitability, showing how they can give an earlier view of the expected revenue and costs. In Section 8.1.2, we'll explain how to create the journal entries for predictive accounting and ensure that they are kept separate from the GAAP-relevant journal entries in a dedicated extension ledger.

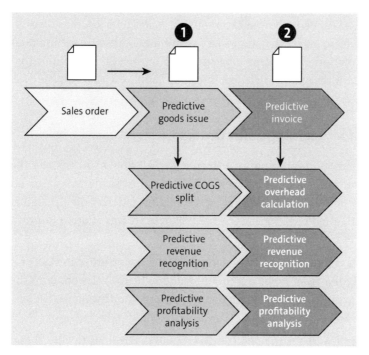

Figure 8.4 Predictive Accounting for an Incoming Sales Order

8.1.1   Including Incoming Sales Orders in Product Profitability

Sales accountants will be able to see the incoming sales orders in a dedicated SAP Fiori application, but they can also view this information in any application that can select a ledger (including the financial statements and product profitability). You can include the predictive documents by selecting the appropriate extension ledger.

Let's begin by looking at the Product Profitability app (SAP Fiori ID F2765), which shows the actual and predicted margin by product and period. The bar chart shown in Figure 8.5 displays the actual revenue, COGS (fixed and variable portions), and the resulting margin for the current period (here, fiscal period **5**, on the left side of the bar chart and the first column of the tabular report). Notice that the GAAP-relevant postings are based on the valuation principles in the leading ledger (0L), and the commitment/order entry view extends this information with the predictions associated with this ledger.

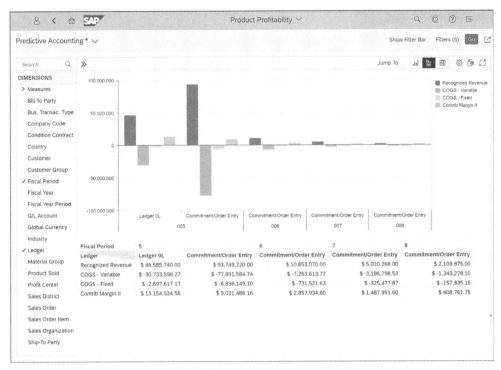

Figure 8.5 Actual and Predicted Profitability by Period

In the second column of the table and the corresponding part in the graph, the report displays the total of the actual financial results (from the first column) combined with the predicted contribution margin (and the revenue and COGS components building it). These predicted amounts are available both for the current period and for future periods as well, depending on the planned delivery dates. The reason there are predicted amounts for future periods in this example is because there are sales orders related to these periods registered in the system already. (Note that for future periods, only predicted amounts are shown because no actuals are available yet.)

The idea behind this application is not completely new. If you've worked with costing-based CO-PA in SAP ERP, you know that it was already possible to create records for incoming sales orders. These had a separate record type (A) and could thus be separated from the billing documents, which were reported as record type F. These documents used the valuation function to include both the revenue postings and the COGS postings derived from the standard cost estimate. The difference was that these records were never canceled. They provided a view of the future for comparison with the reports built to show the billing documents and associated COGS.

As a side note, we want to mention that predictive accounting helps detect some of the company's business dynamics. In this case, the example company is in a business with mainly short-term sales cycles (you can see only limited sales orders in the longer term). This is common in many high-volume sales businesses, such as consumer products and component manufacturing. For an engineer-to-order company such as an airplane construction company, this may look completely different: sales orders remain open for much longer, and there's a bigger gap between the time an order is placed and delivery of the goods.

Based on how the predictive accounting for incoming sales orders works, the basis of the predicted margin information shown in Figure 8.6 is the sales order information. The Incoming Sales Orders app (SAP Fiori ID F2964) delivers full information about the sales orders for the example company. This tabular report displays all relevant sales order information (e.g., the product sold, the sales organization, etc.). From here, it's possible to drill down to an individual sales order, from which the entire document flow can be displayed. This is where the insights get actionable.

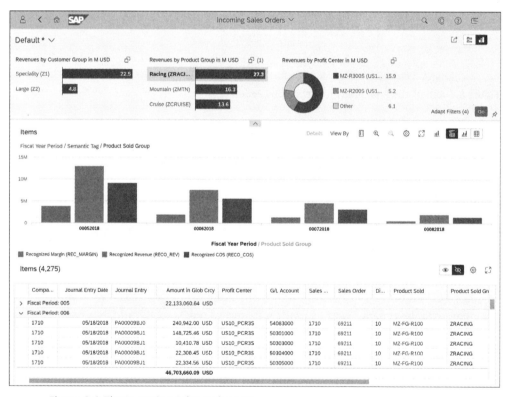

Figure 8.6 The Incoming Sales Order App

In the example shown in Figure 8.7, the requested delivery of the selected sales order (**69211**) is for **May 2018**, but the planned delivery is for the following month (**June 2018**). Hence it isn't billed yet, and no actual revenue and related COGS are posted.

From here, further analysis is possible. By understanding why this sales order hasn't been billed yet, you can act to optimize the organization's revenue streams (and related incoming cash). For example, you could check whether it's possible to move the delivery to the current month (in Figure 8.7, this is **May**), which would increase sales and pull the customer's payment due date forward.

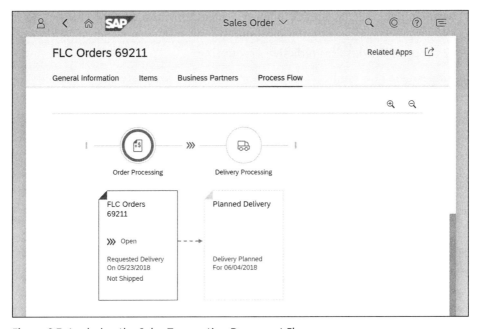

Figure 8.7 Analyzing the Sales Transaction Document Flow

At the time of publication (spring 2019), the predictive logic related to sales orders is available for the following traditional sales processes:

- Sales orders
- Returns
- Free-of-charge orders
- Credit memo requests
- Debit memo requests

It's *not* yet available for the following sales processes:

- Project-related sales processes
- Intercompany sales processes
- Third-party direct shipments
- Service sales

You've seen how the journal entries created using the predictive accounting approach appear in reporting. Now let's look at the system settings needed to activate the creation of these documents.

8.1.2   Journal Entries for Predictive Accounting

To understand how predictive accounting documents are posted, let's return to Figure 8.6 and focus on the posting documents in the **Journal Entry** column.

The predicted document numbers start with "PA" as a prefix. This nomenclature makes it easy to identify the predictive accounting postings as distinct from regular GAAP-relevant accounting documents. When the actual invoicing is executed, an actual (GAAP-relevant) posting takes place. This results in the proper recognition of the revenue in the company P&L and the creation of an open item on accounts receivable side. At that moment, the predictive posting must be cancelled automatically to prevent a double entry of the transaction.

Remembering our cautious accountants who would never include predicted information in legal reporting, we must make sure the predictive document stays separate from the actuals. By storing all predictive accounting postings in a specific extension ledger, these postings are always isolated from the legal reporting. In Figure 8.8, the GAAP-relevant postings (i.e., actuals) are recorded in the leading group ledger, whereas the predictive entries are recorded in the separate prediction extension ledger.

To view actual *and* predictive results for internal reporting, simply add the predictions to the documents in the base ledger by selecting the appropriate extension ledger. The combination of the figures in the base ledger and the prediction ledger delivers the presumed profit shown in Figure 8.8.

We'll now explain how to activate an extension ledger specifically for use in predictive accounting. Note that in SAP S/4HANA Cloud, incoming sales orders are always updated in ledger OE (Commitment/Order Entry), and all the settings described here are delivered as best practices, so you will automatically have access to this functionality.

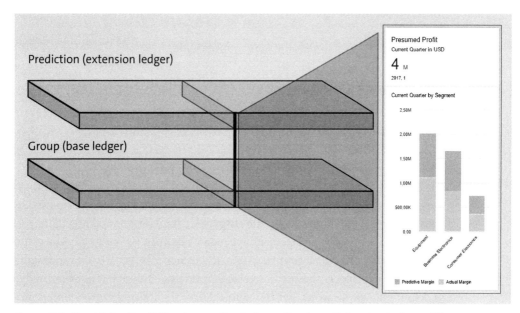

Figure 8.8 Combining Predictive Accounting Information in an Extension Ledger with GAAP-Relevant Information in the Base Ledger

To create journal entries for incoming sales orders in on-premise SAP S/4HANA, you'll have to create and activate an extension ledger, and then activate predictive accounting for both profitability analysis and sales and distribution to see the extra journal entries. Follow these steps:

1. First create your own extension ledger, in which you will store the incoming sales orders, commitments, and so on, as shown in Figure 8.9.

   You can access the ledger settings by choosing **Financial Accounting • Financial Accounting Global Settings • Ledgers • Ledger • Define Settings for Ledgers and Currency Types** in the IMG. In this example, we created a new ledger, **OE (Commitment/Order Entry)**, to separate the predictive journal entries from other GAAP-relevant journal entries. Notice that this ledger is linked with the underlying ledger **OL**, the leading ledger. All reports work by combining the contents of the extension ledger and ledger **OL**. This extension ledger differs from the ledgers for management adjustments that we discussed in Chapter 1 in that it has extension ledger type **Prediction and Simulation**.

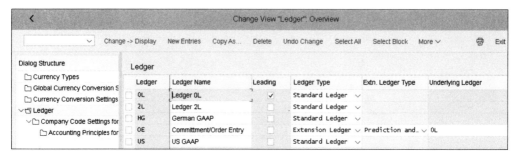

Figure 8.9 Ledger Settings for Standard and Extension Ledgers

This ledger can be accessed by any report that selects data by ledger. Figure 8.10 shows the selection parameters for the Display Financial Statement app (SAP Fiori ID F0708), in which you can select all five ledgers defined in Figure 8.9. The other four ledgers only contain accounting data. If you select ledger **OE (Commitment/ Order Entry)**, you access the predictive accounting documents. However, predictive documents alone won't tell the whole story; the journal entries only make sense in combination with the journal entries in the underlying ledger (see Figure 8.9) that contains the GAAP-relevant postings.

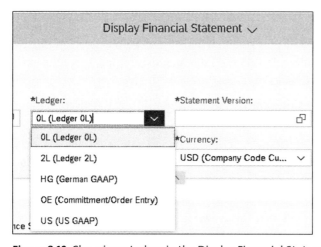

Figure 8.10 Choosing a Ledger in the Display Financial Statement App

2. To activate this extension ledger for predictions, run Transaction SM30 to update the FINSV_PRED_RLDNR view (**Ledgers for Predictive Accounting**) for your chosen ledger, as shown in Figure 8.11.

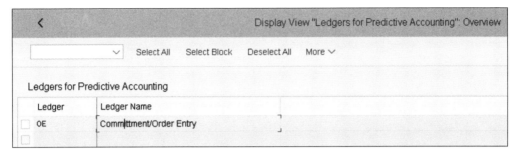

Figure 8.11 Activating a Ledger for Predictive Accounting

3. To activate predictive accounting in profitability analysis in the Universal Journal, use the IMG steps previously associated with transferring incoming sales orders to costing-based CO-PA in SAP ERP. Follow **Controlling • Profitability Analysis • Transfer of Incoming Sales Orders • Activate Predictive Accounting for Incoming Sales Orders** in the IMG, create an entry for your controlling area and the latest fiscal year, and add the **Active with Date of Entry** flag, as shown in Figure 8.12.

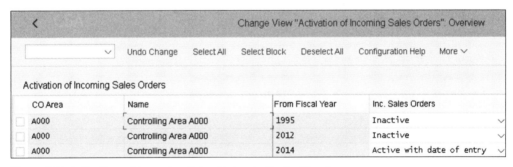

Figure 8.12 Activation of Incoming Sales Orders in Controlling Area

4. To activate predictive accounting in sales and distribution, you'll need to make some additional settings. First, use Transaction SM30 to access the FINSV_PRED_FKART view (**Assignment of Billing Type for Predictive Accounting**) and list all the billing types for which you want to create predictive journal entries. In the simple example shown in Figure 8.13, we've selected the sales document type (**SaTy**) **OR** and the billing type **F2**.

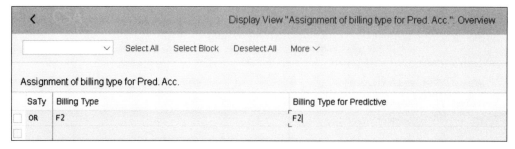

Figure 8.13 Activation of Predictive Accounting by Billing Type

5. Then use Transaction SM30 to access the `FINSV_PRED_FKREL` view (**Assignment Order-Related Billing Relevance for Predictive Accounting**) and list all the item categories for which you want to create predictive documents. Specify the desired time point in the **Relevant for Billing** column; in Figure 8.14, we chose **Relevant for Order-Related Billing—Status According to Target Quantity**.

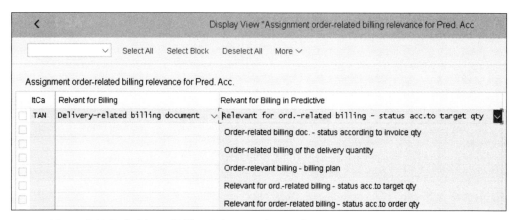

Figure 8.14 Definition of Billing Relevance for Predictive Accounting

This procedure ensures that incoming sales orders are captured as predictive accounting documents. Customers who are currently using costing-based CO-PA generally work not just with incoming sales orders, but also with statistical sales conditions. A statistical sales condition is also a kind of prediction in that it can be used to anticipate future sales bonuses, freight costs, warranty costs, and so on that have not yet been incurred as costs but do have a causal relationship with the sales order. For this reason, we'll look at how to create journal entries for these conditions in the next section.

8.2 Accounting for Statistical Sales Conditions

Let's turn our attention from predictive accounting for incoming sales orders to predictive accounting for statistical sales conditions.

Recall from Chapter 1 that all actual costs are captured in the Universal Journal and that it's possible to make statistical postings to orders and projects, with the same journal entry line being assigned to a real cost object and a statistical one that can be viewed in reporting. *Statistical sales conditions* are different again, in that they are extra lines that appear in reporting to account for future bonuses, freight costs, warranty costs, and so on.

The postings for statistical sales conditions differ from the predictive accounting we discussed in the previous section (in which the document for the entire sales order item was a prediction) in that only individual lines of the sales document are considered to be a prediction and the remainder are accounting-relevant. The assumption is always that there is a causal link between the accounting-relevant conditions in the sales order item (revenues and costs) and the expected freight costs, warranty costs, and so on and that this should therefore be captured with respect to the sales order item.

For predictive accounting of statistical sales conditions, SAP S/4HANA creates a normal journal entry for the revenues and associated receivables and an additional statistical journal entry for the planned warranty costs. In the example in Figure 8.15, we're calculating statistical warranty costs as **3%** of revenues. Note the "normal" journal entry for revenues and associated receivables (totaling **$300**) and another entry for the statistical warranty costs and reserves (totaling **$9**).

The other difference in the handling of these statistical postings is the timing of when these costs will be incurred. When we create an accounting document for an incoming sales order, we know from the planned delivery date when the COGS should be incurred and can also cancel this posting when the real COGS are captured. However, when we create an allowance for freight or warranty costs, we do *not* know at what time in the future the relevant invoices will be received. We are simply acknowledging that such costs will occur in the future and creating an accrual for them. For this reason, some companies choose to keep these items in a separate extension ledger from the incoming sales orders because there are no automatic functions to reverse these postings when the real warranty costs are incurred.

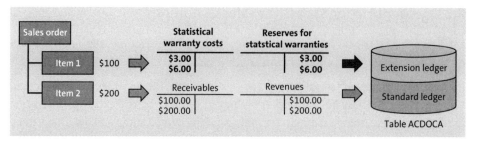

Figure 8.15 Predictive Logic for Statistical Sales Conditions

Let's now look at the settings needed to report on statistical sales conditions. In addition to creating the ledger itself, as shown in Figure 8.9, you need to activate the ledger assignment by choosing **Financial Accounting • Financial Accounting Global Settings • Ledgers • Ledger • Define Ledger Group** and selecting the **Rep. Ledger (Representative Ledger)** indicator for your ledger, as shown in Figure 8.16.

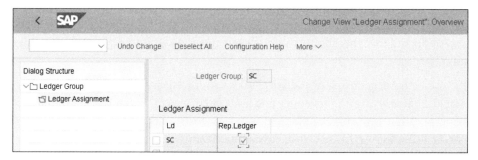

Figure 8.16 Ledger Assignment

The statistical conditions are defined as before in the pricing procedures in sales and distribution. You can access these conditions by choosing **Sales and Distribution • Basic Functions • Pricing • Pricing Control • Define and Assign Pricing Procedures** in the IMG. Normally, any price conditions that are flagged as **Statistical** won't show up in the accounting documents (remember that *statistical* in this sense means that the figures aren't relevant for accounting and are used only for statistical purposes).

Figure 8.17 shows the changed pricing conditions in SAP S/4HANA, in which we've set up a ZWAR condition to calculate statistical warranty costs. In this example, we have a **Stati... (Statistical)** statistical condition, which normally wouldn't post to accounting; however, we have set the new **Rele... (Relevant for Accounting)** flag and entered an account key in the **Account... (Account Key)** column to ensure that the values calculated for the pricing condition **Stat. Warranty Costs** will be captured as a separate journal entry in the extension ledger. If we select the extension ledger, then the values will be shown in SAP Fiori applications such as Product Profitability.

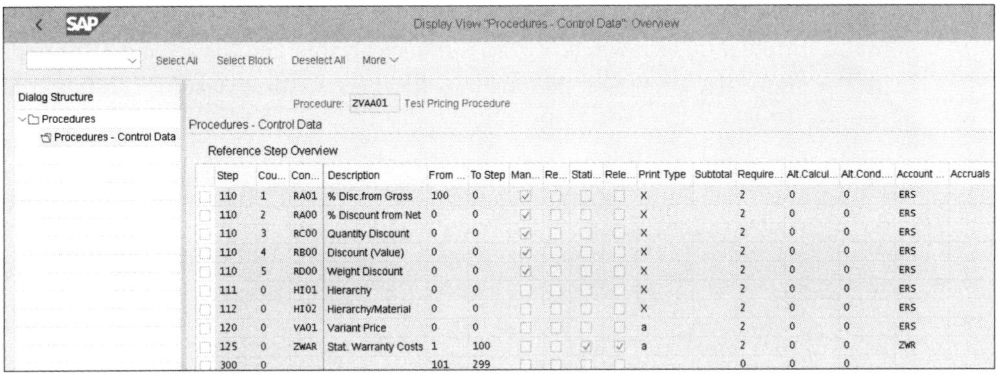

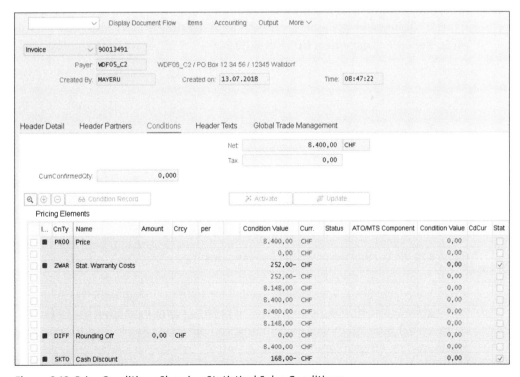

Figure 8.17 Pricing Procedures with Statistical Conditions

Figure 8.18 shows the invoice based on the price conditions configured in Figure 8.17. A **3%** warranty allowance has been included in the invoice, resulting in a reserve of **CHF 252** (Swiss francs) being set aside for the expected warranty costs (notice the flag in the **Stat.** column). This is not included in the main accounting document for the invoice but stored as a separate accounting document in the extension ledger.

Figure 8.18 Price Conditions Showing Statistical Sales Conditions

Figure 8.19 shows the accounting documents for this invoice. The first document contains the postings to revenue and accounts receivable, and the second document (with the prefix "TA") contains the postings for the statistical warranty costs in the extension ledger.

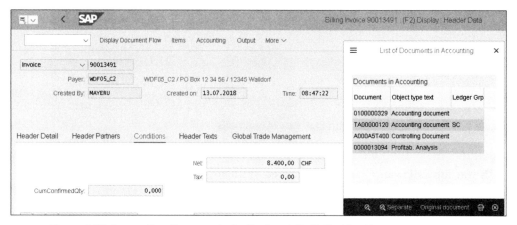

Figure 8.19 Accounting Documents for Real and Statistical Postings

Figure 8.20 shows the accounting document for the statistical warranty costs in ledger **SC** (the second document in Figure 8.19).

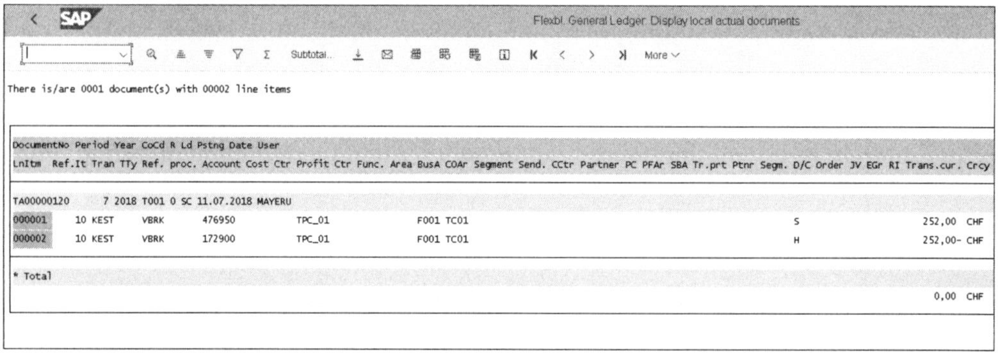

Figure 8.20 Accounting Document for Statistical Posting

So far, you've seen two types of sales-related predictions: incoming sales orders and statistical sales conditions. Now let's look at the first scenario to be delivered for purchase-related predictions and explain how commitments are created for purchase orders.

8.3   Commitment Accounting for Purchase Orders

The final use case for predictive accounting that we'll cover in this chapter can be found on the purchase order side.

There are currently two forms of commitment accounting in SAP ERP. The first is used in all industries, but especially when there is a long gap between the time that the purchase orders are created and the time of the goods receipt. The second is used only in the public sector and covers more business processes. This second option is not yet covered by the predictive accounting approach but is on the SAP S/4HANA roadmap.

Commitment accounting for non-public-sector companies in SAP ERP involves storing the commitments in a separate table (COOI) with reference to the cost center, order, or project. With this classic commitment approach, only one-sided postings in the controlling space were registered. With the harmonization of accounting and controlling, a different approach was needed that assigned the commitments to all reporting dimensions (including profit centers and the like) and considered the balance sheet and the cost sides of the posting.

With SAP S/4HANA, we can create full documents for both the cost side and the vendor side of the posting in the Universal Journal (table ACDOCA), which results in a double-sided posting. Beginning with SAP S/4HANA 1809, the predictive accounting logic is applied to capture commitments for both the balance sheet and the profit and loss statement.

From a technical perspective, the predictive postings for commitments are again isolated in an extension ledger and carry the "PA" prefix to ensure they don't appear in GAAP-relevant reports.

Commitment Accounting in SAP S/4HANA Cloud

In SAP S/4HANA Cloud, the new predictive accounting approach is the only way to capture commitments: the SAP Fiori apps read the new commitments, and you don't have access to the classic reports.

In on-premise SAP S/4HANA, the two approaches can coexist, so you can create an extension ledger and capture commitments according to the new approach but leave the existing logic running for a transition period so that your existing budget and commitment reports can continue to run. This is especially important if you work with active availability control where a new approach is in development.

Analyzing the process in some more detail, commitment accounting is similar to the predictive accounting for incoming sales orders, but in this case starts from the purchase order. A purchase order typically triggers a goods receipt, followed by an invoice receipt. As with sales orders, the commitments need to be canceled as the goods receipt and invoice receipt are recorded to ensure that the same values are not captured twice.

With the predictive accounting logic for commitments, these are simulated to enable a predictive accounting posting.

Figure 8.21 shows the Commitments by Cost Center app (SAP Fiori ID F3016), displaying the actual costs, commitments, and assigned and planned costs for each cost center. The **Commitments** column shows the predictive accounting documents. The **Assigned** column shows the sum of the actual costs and the predictive costs so that cost center managers can see the impact of this spend combination on their budget and know whether further spending is possible.

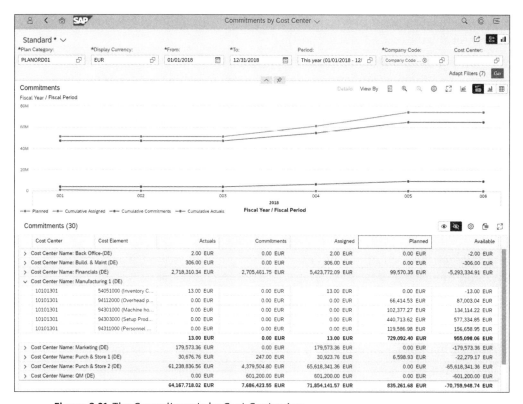

Figure 8.21 The Commitments by Cost Center App

Figure 8.22 shows the Project Cost app (SAP Fiori ID F2513), displaying the commitments and actual costs per WBS element. You'll see this report again in Chapter 9, when we look at planning and how these commitments are used to perform automatic checks against the budget to determine whether the spend can be authorized by the system.

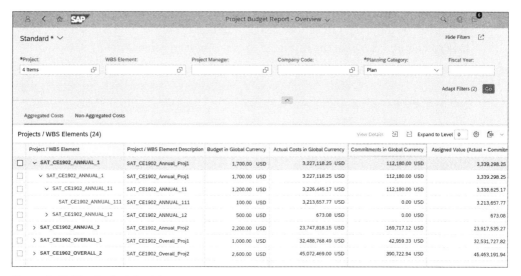

Figure 8.22 The Project Cost App

Again, the predictive accounting journey isn't yet complete. When we look at the roadmap for SAP S/4HANA in the final chapter, you'll see that further innovations are planned for commitment accounting. At the time of publication (spring 2019), predictive accounting can handle only material-related purchase orders, but not non-material-related commitments. It doesn't yet cover public sector commitment accounting, which involves scenarios beyond pure purchasing.

8.4 Summary

In this chapter, we introduced the idea of predictive accounting and explained how it builds on the contractual information already available in SAP S/4HANA to provide business steering information prior to the close. The idea is to generate journal entries in the extension ledger that can be used to predict where the business will be at the end of the next period or quarter and thus make better strategic decisions. The benefit will depend on the number of open purchase orders or sales orders you typically have at any time and the length of time between creating an order and fulfilling it. For engineer-to-order projects, in which there can be months or even years between the customer placing the order and being invoiced, the inclusion of incoming sales orders in the accounting data is essential. In faster-moving industries, such as consumer products, it's simply useful.

Whatever the industry, predictions reflect business events as they happen. We'll now look to how you can plan the future of your business in general in SAP S/4HANA.

Chapter 9
Unified Planning Model: Moving from Financial Budgeting to Driver-Based Forecasting

Now that we've examined predictive accounting within the Universal Journal, in this chapter we'll look at how to build a plan for your organization and explain how the new finance model will affect your planning options in SAP S/4HANA.

Financial planning is the process of determining how a business will meet its strategic goals and objectives. It describes the resources, activities, equipment, and materials needed to achieve these objectives and the financial impact in terms of earnings and expense and of revenue and cost.

You'll hear people refer to this process as *budgeting*, typically for a single financial year, but many organizations prepare a longer-term plan to cover long-running projects or to secure bank loans or other forms of funding. Normally there isn't just one plan, but many plans for different parts of the business: a sales plan, a production plan, an investment plan, a cash plan, and so on, each driven by a different set of stakeholders. These plans combine to give a financial plan for the whole business. And of course, there will be several versions of this overall plan to allow for different assumptions about the direction that the market is expected to take.

Forecasting is a more short-term view that involves looking at trends in actual data and predictions to derive a plan. Whereas budgeting is often undertaken from the top down, with goals being set and then cascaded down through the organization, forecasting is often bottom-up, looking at the business drivers for the actual data.

A simple example of a business driver might be the impact of the weather on sales of gardening equipment or of certain sporting events on sales of sports clothing. These external factors *drive* the plan within the organization. To get the gardening equipment or sports clothing to the stores in time to meet predicted demand, a production plan is needed; this in turn requires machine capacity, people capacity, and so on. Recall from Chapter 1 that you can only steer a business effectively if you set targets to measure whether performance is meeting expectations. These targets will cover each area of the business: sales, production, transport, investment, and so on.

Before we think about individual planning applications, let's take a moment to consider the fundamental differences between planning approaches. If you ask finance users how they plan, many will describe the structures of their spreadsheets. The advantages of planning with Microsoft Excel include its ease of use and flexibility. On the other hand, there is no integration, and data quality can become questionable—or even compromised—when various users build complex macros, the logic of which becomes difficult to unravel as it grows with each iteration of the planning process. What seemed easy can rapidly lead to dangerous assumptions about the future that can lead your business off course.

Others finance users will tell you that they work with dedicated planning applications. These combine the flexibility of the spreadsheet with the ability to build models, but integration between applications remains a challenge, and reference data must be sourced from the accounting system to provide a point of reference for the plan. Planning applications are generally more robust than spreadsheets and provide a more reliable picture of where future business is expected to be heading, but they result in a higher cost of ownership because of the required IT infrastructure.

Still others run planning in SAP ERP. This brings the advantage of tight integration with the accounting system but the challenges of limited flexibility and a set of transactions with an outdated user interface and disparate data stores. In SAP ERP, planning had the same silos as the underlying applications, meaning that cost center planning, project planning, market segment planning, profit center planning, and so on had separate planning transactions to support the collection of data in each of these applications—and yet more transactions to move data between applications. The result was a fragmented planning model that could be difficult to manage as organizations planned and replanned to reach their targets.

In the last decade, many organizations began moving their planning tasks out of SAP ERP and into data warehouses. SAP has offered multiple planning solutions in recent years, all based on SAP Business Warehouse (SAP BW):

- SAP Strategic Enterprise Management, Business Planning and Simulation (SAP SEM-BPS)
- SAP Business Warehouse Integrated Planning (SAP BW-IP)
- SAP Business Planning and Consolidation, SAP NetWeaver version (SAP BPC)

These options use SAP BW as a standalone data warehouse to store both the reference data to support planning and the data collected and calculated during the planning process. You can, of course, continue to use SAP BW as the base layer for your planning applications, but more recently a new approach has been added that does *not* require a separate data warehouse but instead uses the SAP BW instance embedded in SAP S/4HANA. This option uses a version of SAP BPC that is optimized to run on SAP S/4HANA: SAP Business Planning and Consolidation for SAP S/4HANA.

Recent years have also seen a technology shift, with many organizations starting to look at cloud applications for at least part of their planning process. Cloud planning applications are typically highly collaborative, with modeling capabilities that can be handled easily by operational managers with minimal IT support. To address this approach, SAP has introduced SAP Analytics Cloud for planning.

Financial Planning

The availability of multiple planning options naturally results in inquiries about which option is "best." While we cannot address each individual use case in this book, where we can help is to offer our perspective of SAP's overall strategy for financial planning.

SAP Analytics Cloud is SAP's strategic solution for planning, meaning that this is the solution in which SAP is investing heavily. The focus of this book on SAP S/4HANA, but the results of this investment will become clear when we look at the SAP Analytics Cloud for planning content in Section 9.2. For organizations planning to move to or already running SAP S/4HANA who want to integrate plan data into a unified model, SAP Analytics Cloud for planning is considered the go-to solution.

This does not, however, mean that SAP S/4HANA customers should not consider SAP BPC for SAP S/4HANA. It is a mature, fully functional planning (and consolidation) solution, and SAP will continue to maintain it to ensure compatibility with underlying technology components and legal compliance. In short, SAP BPC for SAP S/4HANA is still a valid option, especially for customers seeking a standalone planning solution in an on-premise environment. Customers already using SAP BPC can also leverage enhancements from SAP Analytics Cloud via a "hybrid" integration, ensuring a path of continuous innovation.

In this chapter, we'll begin in Section 9.1 by making the case for the unified planning model in SAP S/4HANA, in contrast to the multiple planning transactions that characterize the planning process in SAP ERP. We'll introduce the planning table ACDOCP as a sister to table ACDOCA and explain how they are structurally similar. This allows you to plan and report on exactly the same dimensions (general ledger accounts, profit centers, cost centers, and so on).

In Section 9.2, we'll explore the options delivered with SAP Analytics Cloud for planning and explain how to update the planning table ACDOCP. Then in Section 9.3 we'll introduce SAP BPC for SAP S/4HANA and explain how it uses the embedded SAP BW in on-premise SAP S/4HANA as a basis for the planning applications.

We'll then look at how to capture planning data as it arises out of the operational processes in Section 9.4, such as in commercial project management, capital expense projects, and production, to understand how planning is performed in these scenarios.

9.1   Moving toward a Unified Planning Model

Before we define what the unified planning model *is*, let's think about what it *isn't*.

The thousands of structurally unique spreadsheets circulating within some organizations clearly are not unified. Every manager simply has tried to put their own ideas on paper. Although this may help individual managers to formulate their goals, it doesn't necessarily translate into a good plan for the whole organization. Dedicated planning applications can be only marginally better than a thousand disparate spreadsheets. If every part of the organization builds its own planning model that is completely unrelated to the rest of the organization, there will be no way to see whether there are holes in the plan because the parts do not interconnect. This is where we need to go back to the steering model for the business that we discussed in Chapter 1.

The *unified planning model* is interconnected and captures the many different elements within an organization. In SAP S/4HANA, SAP has taken a more prescriptive role and described the framework of that plan. Essentially, SAP has determined that there must always be connections among a plan, a prediction, and the underlying steering model (the Universal Journal). You might not plan against every element in the Universal Journal, but you should certainly be planning against the key elements of that steering model.

If we made a case in Chapter 1 for bringing the transactional line items together, then the same case can be made for bringing the planning line items into one structure. In Chapter 1, Section 1.2.3, we introduced the idea of a common planning table to provide the basis for plan/actual reporting based on a single structure that used the same reporting dimensions as for the actual line items.

If we think back to the dimensions in our steering model, this means setting targets for the various organizational units, products and services, and customers. In general, these targets won't cover every dimension for which actual data can be reported, so you may plan cost center costs rather than the costs of the individual suppliers from whom you intend to purchase goods in the course of the year, product/service costs rather than the costs of the individual manufacturing and service orders, and revenues by customer group rather than individual customer—but the idea is that the actual costs roll up and can be compared against the targets for each of these key elements. The details of the various plans vary enormously by industry; some organizations have a very clear view of their future based on past data and long-standing contractual obligations, whereas others have to bring a lot more assumptions into their plans. Whatever the industry, the plans will roll up into the group view, in which data is further consolidated by legal entity and profit center.

Figure 9.1 shows the various dimensions in a typical steering model (organizations, products and services, and customers) and how these are reflected in the reporting dimensions of the Universal Journal (the actuals) and in planning and group reporting. Notice that group reporting requires only a handful of reporting dimensions (perhaps only the trading partners, profit centers, product groups, and markets), whereas the actual line items contain many more, with planning somewhere in between in terms of the dimensions to be planned (perhaps plants, legal entities, cost centers, profit centers, products, product groups, customers, customer groups, etc.).

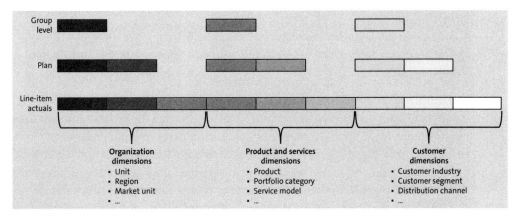

Figure 9.1 Planning and the Universal Journal

It's important to think about how you plan as an organization. Many companies set targets at group level and cascade them down, resulting in planning tasks on the group level that take place at a much higher level than the entity-level plan. Once group targets are set, each entity will perform a detailed plan that focuses on individual cost centers, projects, market segments, and so on, and roll that plan up to deliver the final entity plan. The business unit (or profit center) plan typically sits between the two, aggregating details from below and capturing high-level targets from above.

The unified planning model in SAP S/4HANA is unified in two directions: upward toward group reporting and downward towards the Universal Journal. Some fields—the company code, ledger, and account number—are common in all structures, as shown in Figure 9.2. Equally importantly, the planning table (table ACDOCP) includes the same include structures as in the Universal Journal (see Chapter 1, Figure 1.10). Four common structures are the key to planning because they contain the reporting dimensions that you will typically want to plan against:

- **General ledger fields (include structure ACDOCP_SI_GL_ACCAS)**
  These include the affiliated companies (trading partners and partner trading partners), the profit center and partner profit center, the segment and partner segment, the functional area and partner functional area, and the cost center and sender cost center.

- **Controlling fields (include structure ACDOCP_SI_CO)**
  These include the activity type and partner activity type, the WBS element and partner WBS element, the order and partner order, and so on.

- **Profitability analysis fields (include structure ACDOC_SI_COPA)**
  These are all the characteristics used in your operating concern, though you won't necessarily be able to plan against all of them.

- **Extension fields (include structure ACDOC_SI_EXT)**
  These are any fields that you have added to your steering model (see Chapter 1, Section 1.3.6).

You can visualize the planning table as a single string, just like the actuals that we discussed in Chapter 1. Any plan data captured will go through the same routines as data executed during the actual transactions. This means that if you plan salary costs for a cost center, the planning table will be updated with the affected functional area, profit center, segment, and so on; if you plan revenue for a product, the same derivations will take place in profitability analysis to fill the remaining characteristics. All this happens in one step, so you no longer need to copy plan data into the general ledger from overhead management or profitability analysis as you did in SAP ERP.

Field	Key	Initia...	Data element	Data Type	Length	Decima...	Short Description
RLDNR	☐	☐	FINS_LEDGER	CHAR	2	0	Ledger in General Ledger Accounting
RACCT	☐	☐	RACCT	CHAR	10	0	Account Number
RBUKRS	☐	☐	BUKRS	CHAR	4	0	Company Code
AWTYP	☐	☐	AWTYP	CHAR	5	0	Reference procedure
USNAM	☐	☐	USNAM	CHAR	12	0	User Name
.INCLUDE	☐	☐	ACDOCP_SI_NOTINACD..	STRU	0	0	ACDOCP: Fields which are not ion ACDOCA
.INCLUDE	☐	☐	ACDOCP_SI_00	STRU	0	0	ACDOCP: Transaction, Currencies, Units
.INCLUDE	☐	☐	ACDOC_SI_GL_ACCAS	STRU	0	0	Universal Journal Entry: G/L additional account assignments
.INCLUDE	☐	☐	ACDOCP_SI_VALUE_DA..	STRU	0	0	ACDOCP: Value Fields
.INCLUDE	☐	☐	ACDOCP_SI_FIX	STRU	0	0	ACDOCP: Mandatory fields for G/L
.INCLUDE	☐	☐	ACDOCP_SI_GEN	STRU	0	0	ACDOCP: Fields for several subledgers
.INCLUDE	☐	☐	ACDOCP_SI_CO	STRU	0	0	ACDOCP: CO fields
.INCLUDE	☐	☐	ACDOC_SI_EXT	STRU	0	0	Universal Journal Entry: Extension fields
.INCLUDE	☐	☐	ACDOC_SI_COPA	STRU	0	0	Universal Journal Entry: CO-PA fields

Figure 9.2 Planning Table in SAP S/4HANA

In Chapter 7, we looked at the various allocation and settlement processes that happen (at the latest) at period-end close to associate costs with the revenue streams. We need to go through the same process of moving costs and revenue streams in planning; consequently, we need to both capture salary costs by cost center and then plan how the people-related costs will flow into the products/services and be assigned to the market segments. This can happen very generically by using simple spreading functions to move costs from one account assignment to another or to reproduce all the allocations and settlements that will take place over several levels to move costs in the operational system at period close.

Figure 9.3 provides an overview of the financial planning process. Of course, these plans don't exist in isolation:

- The revenue plan in financials typically links with sales planning and market planning in logistics, sharing information about the sales quantities to be delivered.
- Production cost planning in financials typically links with material requirements planning (MRP) in logistics, sharing information about the production quantities to be built and the capacities required to perform these tasks.
- P&L planning in financials typically links with personnel cost planning in human resources and location planning, sharing information about headcount-related costs and facility costs.

In this section, we'll focus on the different ways of handling the financial data in the planning process in SAP S/4HANA.

These planning tasks are typically used to set targets periodically: once per year, once per quarter, or even as often as once per month. This is illustrated in Figure 9.3 by the options in the arrows at the top, each of which is represented as a separate plan category in SAP S/4HANA:

- The strategic plan generally looks far into the future but has a low granularity.
- The multiyear financial plan may be more granular and is typically used to justify funding for long-running capital expense projects or bank loans.
- The plan used to set a budget is typically focused on a single fiscal year and sets targets for each legal entity, profit center, cost center, and certain key profitability characteristics.
- As the year progresses, this budget may be revised to take into account changes in the initial budget assumptions, such as a changing market situation, changes in raw material prices, and so on.
- The forecast is usually created once a month to include actuals, predictions, and any other factors that lead to changes in the plan's original assumptions.

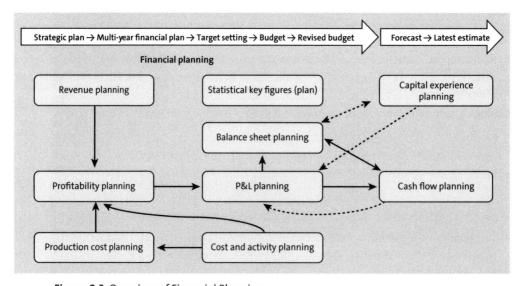

Figure 9.3 Overview of Financial Planning

In SAP S/4HANA, these periodic planning processes store data in the same table as the data captured in the operational planning processes. Figure 9.4 shows how the financial planning flow from Figure 9.3 is extended by the operational planning data. We'll look at operational planning for production processes, commercial project management, and so on in Section 9.4 because these also have a financial impact. For now, note that in SAP ERP, these processes were typically embedded in operations but became detached from the overall financial budget when the task of financial budgeting moved into dedicated planning applications. With SAP S/4HANA, they return to a common store, making it easy to roll up the plans associated with individual orders and projects and to determine how they are contributing to the overarching goals set by the organization.

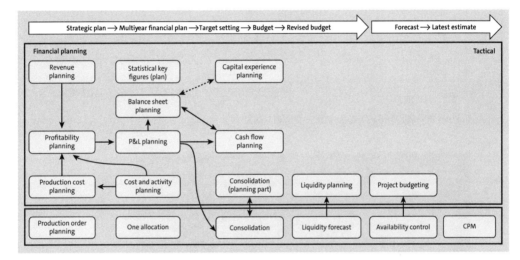

Figure 9.4 Tactical Financial Planning and Operational Planning

Figure 9.5 illustrates the two main options for financial planning using the unified planning model integrated into SAP S/4HANA. We'll look at SAP Analytics Cloud for planning in Section 9.2 and SAP BPC for SAP S/4HANA in Section 9.3. Notice that however you plan, the financial data associated with that plan will be stored in one place: table ACDOCP in the center.

In addition to these two options, it's also possible to perform a flat file upload directly into table ACDOCP. This functionality can be accessed using the Import Financial Plan Data app (SAP Fiori ID F1711) shown in Figure 9.5. For this approach, SAP delivers a range of templates for the core financial planning steps, as illustrated in Figure 9.6. This option makes sense if you're using a non-SAP planning tool or if you aren't yet ready to move to either SAP Analytics Cloud or SAP BPC for SAP S/4HANA.

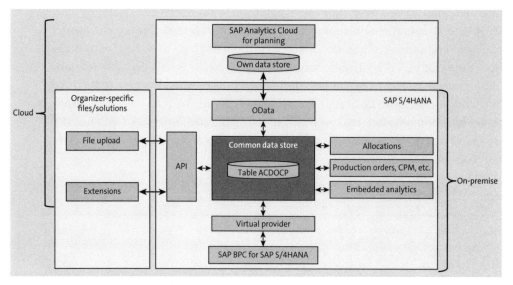

Figure 9.5 Planning Options in SAP S/4HANA

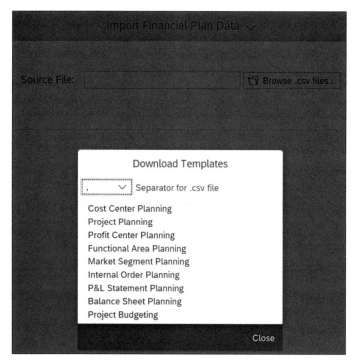

Figure 9.6 Planning Templates for Excel Upload

Moreover, the classic financial planning transactions you may know from SAP ERP continue to exist in on-premise SAP S/4HANA, even though the relevant menus have been deactivated. SAP Note 2270407 (S4TWL: Profit and Loss Planning, Profit Center Planning, Cost Center Planning, Order Planning, and Project Planning) explains how to reactivate general ledger planning and profit center planning if you want to continue using these transactions. Bear in mind that these planning transactions continue to update the totals tables that are no longer used to store actual data and that no functional enhancements are expected in this area. The idea is simply that organizations can transition to the new approach at their own speed.

9.2   SAP Analytics Cloud for Planning

Business planning is one of the first areas in financials in which we see customers moving to a cloud environment, sometimes for a couple of planning applications and sometimes for the complete corporate plan.

SAP Analytics Cloud is part of SAP's response to this demand for cloud offerings in the planning space. (Of course, SAP Analytics Cloud isn't just about planning; it's also used to deliver the digital boardroom and many dashboards that display financial data. But we'll focus on financial planning in this financials book!)

Whereas SAP Analytics Cloud for planning could already be natively connected to the SAP S/4HANA environment, which allowed users to report on data from the Universal Journal without the need for data replication, the ability to transfer planned data *from* SAP Analytics Cloud *to* SAP S/4HANA was added with SAP S/4HANA Cloud 1805 and SAP S/4HANA 1809 (SP 1). SAP Analytics Cloud can access the master data in the form of, for instance, general ledger accounts, company codes, cost centers, profit centers, functional areas, and trading partners, and it can access periodical transactional data as reference data.

Figure 9.7 shows a sample financial statement report with the option to drill down by **Company Code**, **Cost Center**, **Profit Center**, and **Functional Area** using the tabs at the top of the screen. In so doing, you are navigating through the various dimensions in the Universal Journal. Notice that you can easily switch from **Actual** to **Plan** because the structure of the data is the same in both cases.

Figure 9.8 provides a graphical overview of the **Operating Income**, **Revenue**, and **Expense** key indicators (on the left side). The application is pulling data from the Universal Journal, but now we see the strength of SAP Analytics Cloud in terms of dashboarding and making data easy for the planner to consume.

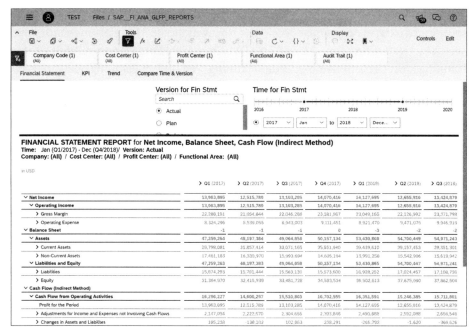

Figure 9.7 Financial Planning in SAP Analytics Cloud

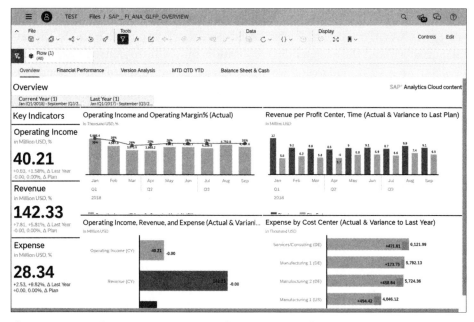

Figure 9.8 Operating Income, Revenue, and Expense Key Indicators

Planners can take a closer look at the key figures for their area. Figure 9.9 shows the breakdown of the key figures that make up the gross margin, with the option to drill down by company code, cost center, profit center, and functional area (the key dimensions for reporting and planning in the Universal Journal). Planners can also switch the time frame using the selectors at the top of the screen.

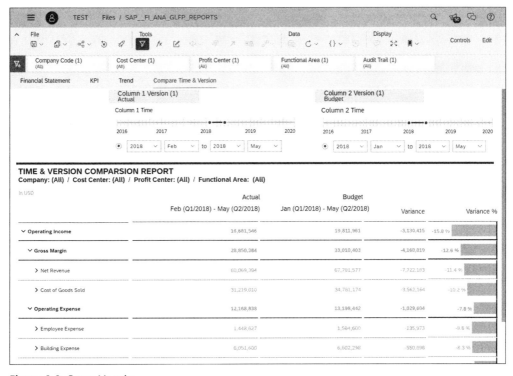

Figure 9.9 Gross Margin

Once the planner has analyzed the different views of their data, the actuals can be used to create the next plan or forecast. Figure 9.10 shows a sample input screen for the entry of figures by profit center. Once the planner has entered data, they can switch back to the previous screens to understand the impact of the data entered.

When planning is complete, the planned data is released and transferred into table ACDOCP in SAP S/4HANA using an OData service. Technically, this means that (at the time of publication) the plan data is persisted in SAP Analytics Cloud and copied over into table ACDOCP within SAP S/4HANA.

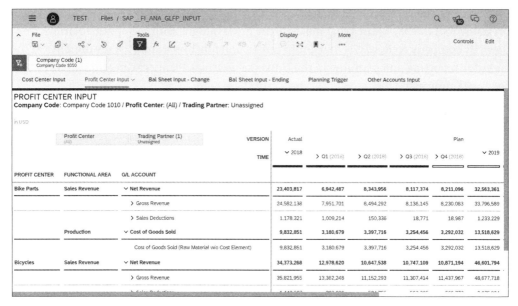

Figure 9.10 Input of Profit Center Plan

We expect that SAP will extend the integration between SAP Analytics Cloud and SAP S/4HANA by adding an option that stores plan data directly in SAP S/4HANA, removing the need for plan data persistency on the SAP Analytics Cloud side. Of course, depending on the planning scenario, it might make sense to have more plan data stored inside SAP Analytics Cloud and only transfer some to SAP S/4HANA; for example, if you're simulating multiple versions, you might settle on a single scenario for transfer to perform variance analysis.

What's typical for a cloud planning environment is the focus on collaboration and bringing the various stakeholders in the planning process together. This means going beyond the pure budget numbers to facilitating a conversation about the various planning assumptions, an approach familiar from social media but new to SAP planning transactions.

Although this is a cloud product that can be operated completely independently from SAP S/4HANA, great value has been placed on *connectivity* with SAP S/4HANA. Figure 9.11 illustrates two different approaches to cost center planning. The simple one on the left takes place entirely in SAP Analytics Cloud and only pulls actual data from SAP S/4HANA to ascertain whether the organization is delivering to plan. The extended process on the right moves data to SAP S/4HANA so that further planning tasks (e.g., allocations and activity price calculations) can be performed there and the results moved back to the SAP Analytics Cloud on completion (the dark boxes).

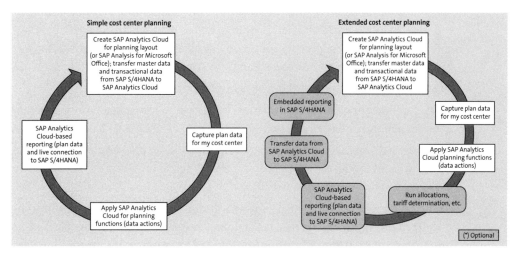

Figure 9.11 Cost Center Planning in SAP Analytics Cloud

SAP delivers business content for SAP Analytics Cloud to provide a quick and easy starting point for customer-specific planning scenarios. You can access the content library at *https://www.sapanalytics.cloud/learning/business-content/*. This sample content can be used to connect to both SAP S/4HANA Cloud and on-premise SAP S/4HANA systems. There are three sample content packages offered as SAP Best Practices:

- **The Financial Planning and Analysis for SAP S/4HANA Cloud sample content package (as shown in Figure 9.7, Figure 9.8, Figure 9.9, and Figure 9.10)**
  - The SAP Real-Time Financial Planning for SAP S/4HANA Cloud planning application enables an analyst or planner to dive into SAP S/4HANA Cloud using a real-time connector. Accelerators include a prebuilt set of live analytical dashboards, key performance indicators, and reports (scope item 1U8).
  - The SAP Financial Planning for S/4HANA Cloud component enables a planner to complete a cost center and profit center plan in SAP Analytics Cloud based on financial information sources for SAP S/4HANA Cloud. Accelerators include planning input templates, best practice allocations, and a planning process flow (scope item 2EB).
  - The SAP Financial Analysis for S/4HANA Cloud component enables an analyst or planner to analyze trends, variances, and growth rates for both actuals and

plan data in SAP Analytics Cloud. Accelerators mirror the content in Real-Time Financial Planning for SAP S/4HANA Cloud (scope item 2IJ).

- SAP delivers best practice methodologies to integrate financial results from SAP S/4HANA Cloud into SAP Analytics Cloud and to retract plan data back into SAP S/4HANA Cloud. Best practice methodology establishes SAP S/4HANA Cloud as the primary source of master data and financial structures.

- **The FI Operational Expense Planning sample content package**
  - The Overview application allows users to track operating expenses by cost center for a month, quarter, or year.
  - The Seeded Forecast application allows users to select plan and cutover data to review a rolling forecast of plan and actual values in a report that's easy to review and to enter plan values into.
  - The Account Detail worksheet provides account details by cost center for user-defined time periods. The report also calculates the variance for the plan versus actuals to make it easy to spot positive and negative contributors.
  - The Rolling Actuals worksheet provides a rolling actuals report in which users can specify cost centers they're interested in displaying and the time horizon for the report.
  - Data connectivity uses the `SAP_FI_ANA_IM_GLFP` model in SAP Analytics Cloud to show financial data from SAP S/4HANA Cloud.

- **The Project Budgeting and Planning for SAP S/4HANA Cloud sample content package**
  - SAP Project Budgeting and Planning for SAP S/4HANA Cloud enables planners to capture expense plans in the friendly, flexible, cloud-based user interface of SAP Analytics Cloud.
  - SAP customers can maintain work breakdown structures (WBS) in SAP S/4HANA Cloud but use SAP Analytics Cloud to capture project/budget expense projections. The same projections can be monitored in SAP S/4HANA Cloud and take advantage of robust project expense management features.
  - SAP delivers best practice methodologies to leverage master data structures from SAP S/4HANA Cloud in SAP Analytics Cloud, plus retract plan data back into SAP S/4HANA Cloud. Best practice methodology establishes SAP S/4HANA Cloud as the primary source of master data and financial structures.

SAP Analytics Cloud for planning is designed for a cloud environment but can be connected to SAP S/4HANA running in an on-premise environment as well. However, if you're already running on-premise SAP S/4HANA, you should consider the options available in SAP BPC for SAP S/4HANA, in which the flexible planning model is generated as part of the implementation project.

9.3 SAP BPC for SAP S/4HANA

SAP BPC has been integrated into SAP S/4HANA since the arrival of SAP S/4HANA Finance (then known as SAP Simple Finance) in 2015.

With SAP BPC for SAP S/4HANA, a set of planning scenarios and related templates bring together cost center planning, order planning, project planning, market segment planning, profit center planning, functional area planning, and P&L planning into one common planning model. Planners can capture their data in a familiar environment because workbooks are delivered for use with SAP Analysis for Microsoft Office. SAP S/4HANA customers can extend the predelivered planning scenarios using the modeling options within SAP BPC for SAP S/4HANA.

Recall from earlier in the chapter that this solution is specifically designed to work with SAP S/4HANA without necessitating a separate data warehouse. This approach uses the data warehouse inside every on-premise SAP S/4HANA system to store the planned data and run planning functions, such as copy and revaluate. Because the data load is set up differently for operational and analytics systems, you should only use the embedded SAP BW option as an *extension* of the SAP S/4HANA system and not as a generic data warehouse for significant amounts of external data.

One way of storing plan data that is entered in these workbooks or calculated using the planning logic is to save it in an *InfoProvider* (previously called a *data model* in SAP BW) within the SAP BW model embedded in the SAP S/4HANA environment. As an alternative, however, SAP S/4HANA provides the option of using a virtual InfoProvider within SAP BPC that writes the plan data records into table ACDOCP so that it's directly accessible for plan/actual reporting in SAP Fiori applications.

Before you can use these planning applications, you'll have to activate the relevant business content on SAP S/4HANA, as described in SAP Note 1972819 (Setup SAP BPC Optimized for S/4HANA Finance and Embedded BW Reporting), and define plan categories for each type of planning you wish to use. Note that the plan category replaces the plan version in SAP ERP.

To keep our focus on the content delivered by SAP BPC for SAP S/4HANA for financial planning, we'll begin in Section 9.3.1 by showing how to use the workbooks delivered with SAP BPC for SAP S/4HANA to enter P&L data, market segment data, and cost center data in different planning sheets. In Section 9.3.2, we'll describe how to go beyond this simple cost plan to plan quantities, perform simple allocations, and include product costing data for a more detailed, driver-based plan. Finally, we'll discuss what to do if you need to calculate activity prices or use other planning functions that SAP has not yet transitioned to the new planning model, in which case you can combine this solution with the classic planning transactions from SAP ERP.

9.3.1   Working with a Single Planning Model

Financial planning in SAP ERP involved many different transactions: Transaction KP06 for cost center planning, Transaction KPF6 for order planning, Transaction CJR1 for project planning, Transaction KEPM for market segment planning, and Transaction GP12N for P&L planning, to name a few. These in turn stored their data in the same tables as the aggregated actual data, so the planned data for the cost centers, orders, and projects was stored in the totals tables for controlling (COSP and COSS), the planned data for the market segments in the costing-based CO-PA tables (CE3XXXX), and the planned data for the P&L statement in the totals table for the general ledger (FAGLFLEXP). Essentially, each planning application was designed to connect with the appropriate actual data. The actual data wasn't unified, and neither was the planned data.

With SAP S/4HANA, the goal is to provide a single data store that can be accessed by multiple planners. We'll illustrate this idea with a very simple example that sets the high-level target in the P&L, performs bottom-up planning by market segment and cost centers, and shows how the two approaches interact.

Figure 9.12 shows the P&L Planning application. The account master data shown on the left is accessed directly from the master data tables in SAP S/4HANA, and the reference data for the previous year is accessed from the Universal Journal and aggregated. Behind the scenes, we're selecting and aggregating millions of lines of actual data to deliver the reference figures. It's then easy to use planning buttons such as **Copy Actual to Plan** and **Recalculate** to perform simple operations on this data and quickly arrive at a rough plan for each entity. Notice also the term **Category** in this view. In this context, the category identifies the plan, and several different categories of plan can be created for different purposes (like the old plan version in SAP ERP).

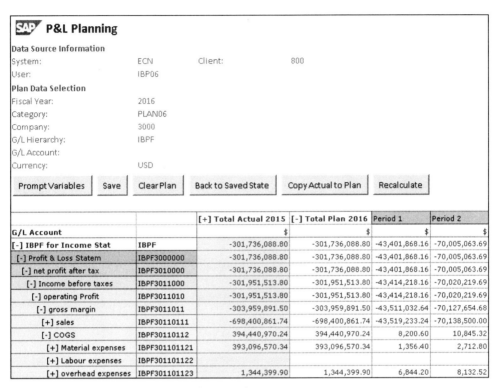

Figure 9.12 P&L Planning in SAP BPC for SAP S/4HANA

Figure 9.13 shows the same data broken down by market segment. As you start to refine the plan and change the details for these customer groups, it will be aggregated automatically into the P&L view shown in Figure 9.12, without requiring you to move data between planning applications as in SAP ERP. This makes the planning process significantly less cumbersome if you revisit your planning assumptions regularly and one plan impacts the other.

Figure 9.14 shows the same information broken down by cost center. Again, any information entered for these cost centers is immediately aggregated to fill the other views. SAP ERP transactions such as FAGL_CO_PLAN (Transfer Plan Data from Internal Orders) and KE1Z (Transfer Plan Data from Profitability Analysis) become completely obsolete with this approach.

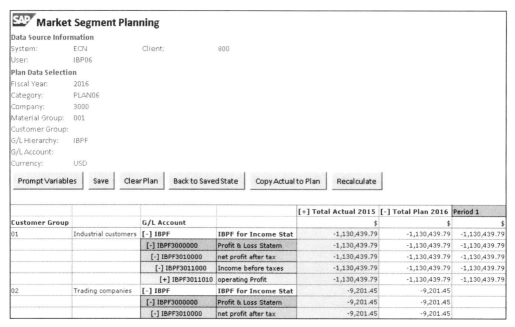

Figure 9.13 Market Segment Planning in SAP BPC for SAP S/4HANA

Cost Center	G/L Account		[+] Total Actual 2015	[-] Total Plan 2016	Period 1	Period 2
			$	$	$	$
3353	Sales Territory M3	[-] IBPF	IBPF for Income Stat	467,393.21	467,393.21	24,572.87	30,102.28
		[-] IBPF3000000	Profit & Loss Statem	467,393.21	467,393.21	24,572.87	30,102.28
		[-] IBPF3010000	net profit after tax	467,393.21	467,393.21	24,572.87	30,102.28
		[+] IBPF3011000	Income before taxes	467,393.21	467,393.21	24,572.87	30,102.28
3352	Sales Territory M2	[-] IBPF	IBPF for Income Stat	673,785.48	673,785.48	31,511.20	38,534.24
		[-] IBPF3000000	Profit & Loss Statem	673,785.48	673,785.48	31,511.20	38,534.24
		[-] IBPF3010000	net profit after tax	673,785.48	673,785.48	31,511.20	38,534.24
		[+] IBPF3011000	Income before taxes	673,785.48	673,785.48	31,511.20	38,534.24
3351	Sales Territory EvoBus	[-] IBPF	IBPF for Income Stat	757,094.54	757,094.54	37,339.61	45,730.99
		[-] IBPF3000000	Profit & Loss Statem	757,094.54	757,094.54	37,339.61	45,730.99
		[-] IBPF3010000	net profit after tax	757,094.54	757,094.54	37,339.61	45,730.99

Figure 9.14 Cost Center Planning in SAP BPC for SAP S/4HANA

By default, planned data entered in these workbooks updates the SAP S/4HANA Financials: InfoCube for Plan Data real-time InfoCube (/ERP/SFIN_R01). The delivered business content can then be extended as part of the implementation project if you need to add further market segments.

> **Switching from Cubes to Tables in Planning**
>
> SAP S/4HANA offers the SAP S/4HANA Financials: Plan Data from ACDOCP virtual InfoProvider (/ERP/SFIN_V20). This virtual InfoProvider stores the plan data records in table ACDOCP, which has almost the same structure as table ACDOCA.
>
> Before you start your planning cycle, you can choose to store your plan data in the virtual InfoProvider instead of the real-time InfoCube. You have two options:
>
> - To switch to the virtual InfoProvider centrally for all planning applications, change the default value of variable /ERP/P_0INFOPROV to /ERP/SFIN_V20.
> - To switch to the virtual InfoProvider for specific planning applications only, assign the value /ERP/SFIN_V20 directly to the 0INFOPROV characteristic in the planning filters of specific planning applications.

9.3.2   Simple Profitability Simulation

Although these three planning workbooks support a very basic planning scenario, they only cover the planning of primary costs and revenue and the roll up to the relevant accounts. Figure 9.15 shows how these planning applications were extended over time to support a driver-based approach:

❶ Instead of planning revenue as an amount, as in Figure 9.13, we can plan sales quantities, sales prices, and sales deductions, and then have the planning model bring these together. This is the simplest form of driver-based planning, with the sales quantities driving the financial plan to deliver a more detailed view of the gross sales and discounts.

❷ Instead of planning the cost of goods sold (COGS) as an amount, we can plan production quantities and use a cost estimate to determine the raw materials and activities required to deliver these goods. This is also a form of driver-based planning, this time with the production quantity driving the financial plan to deliver a more detailed view of the COGS.

❸ Instead of planning costs by cost center and leaving them as costs by nature as in Figure 9.14, we can perform allocations, either as a simple spreading of the costs to the market segments or in a two-stage spread (first to the production cost centers and then via an activity rate into the production costs).

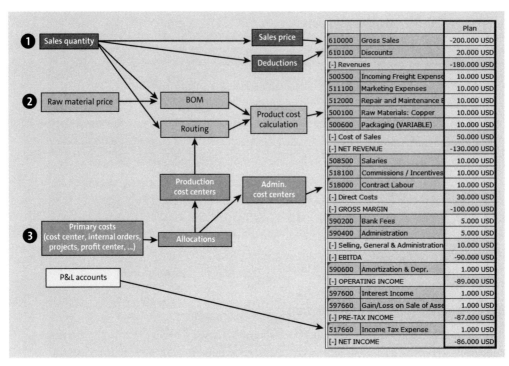

Figure 9.15 End-to-End Profitability Planning

Figure 9.16 shows a sales planning application (❶ in Figure 9.15) in which we've taken the basic idea shown in Figure 9.13 further and calculated the sales revenues using the volume of product to be sold (**Calculate Sales Amount**), instead of simply entering a dollar figure. We then included the sales deductions (**Calculate Sales Deductions**) using an additional planning layout. We then used the **Transfer Production Costs** function to access the itemization from the standard cost estimate for the products sold from SAP S/4HANA.

Figure 9.17 shows the result of transferring the lines from the product cost estimate into the planning application (❷ in Figure 9.15). Here you see figures for the material lines (derived from the bill of material), but you could scroll further to see figures for the production cost centers and the associated activity types (derived from the routing). A planner can then start to work with these basic figures to simulate the effect on the production costs (and by extension on product profitability) of changing a raw material price or an activity rate.

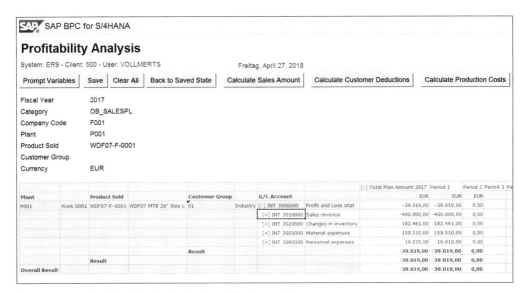

Figure 9.16 Sales Planning by Product and Customer Group

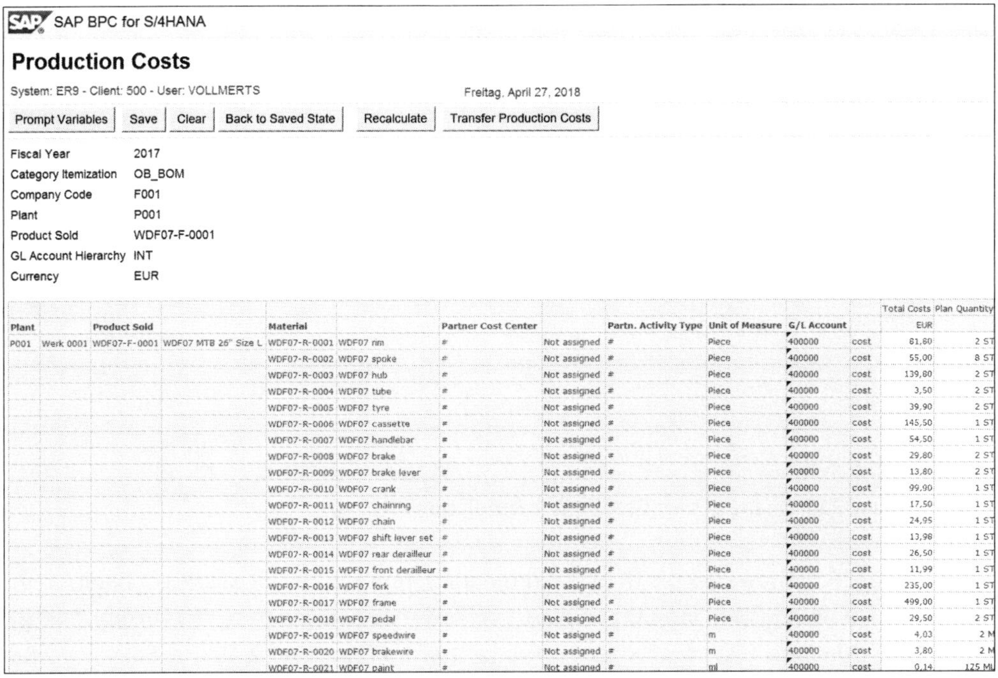

Figure 9.17 Sales Planning with Detailed Product Costs

Figure 9.18 takes the idea shown in Figure 9.14 further and shows how to plan the flow from the sender cost centers (**Cost Center** column) to the receiver cost centers (**Partner Cost Center** column; ❸ in Figure 9.15). Here we're planning the drivers for the flow in the form of quantities (hours, square footage, kilograms, and meters). These will be used to perform the simulation that will be updated under the account shown in the **Account** column.

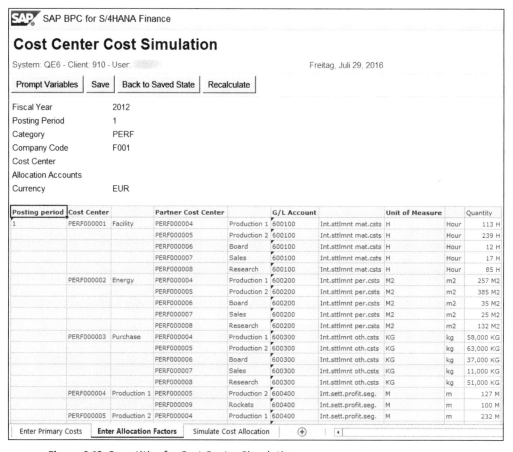

Figure 9.18 Quantities for Cost Center Simulation

Figure 9.19 shows the result of the simulation, represented by a series of debit/credit lines (see **Deb/Cred Ind CO** column). This has moved costs from the **Facility**, **Energy**, and **Purchase** cost centers to the **Production 1**, **Production 2**, **Board**, **Sales**, and **Research** cost centers.

Figure 9.19 Results of Cost Center Simulation

We've now provided a basic introduction to SAP Analytics Cloud for planning and SAP BPC for SAP S/4HANA as different options to build up plan data that can then be stored in the common planning table ACDOCP for analysis and subsequent processing. Let's now look at the operational plans and explain how to generate plan data for individual projects and orders.

9.4   Planning for the Operational Processes

The planning process that we looked at in the previous section focused on target setting for the year or period, but organizations create other plans all the time. Every time they commit to deliver a project or even release a production order, they use plan data to decide whether it makes sense to proceed or not. These plans concern the ability of the organization to deliver on a single objective (e.g., one project, one order), but they can also be rolled up in reporting to determine how the sum of all these activities reflects its ability to deliver on its more strategic goals for the period.

Although many planning tasks were moved to data warehouses in the last decade, planning for operational processes typically continued to take place in SAP ERP because planners needed access to information only available in the core system.

Let's consider an example. For production orders, the bill of material (BOM) and routing are used to calculate the planned material and activity costs. These costs in turn are used to calculate the target costs when the order is delivered to stock. In the past, the planned costs for these processes would be stored in the totals tables COSP and COSS, and the result was a loss of detail. Although it's unlikely that organizations will be able to include *every* detail from their actual cost postings in their planning, there's often a case for changing and enriching the data structures, just as we discussed when we looked at the additional fields that SAP has added to the Universal Journal to provide more transparency into the production costs in Chapter 1. The ability to include the work center and the operation is as important for planning as it is for actuals.

Although planning can be seen simply as target setting for an organization or for an individual project or order, these types of plans are not used only for plan/actual reporting. Planning data is used within the operational processes for several different purposes:

- When we looked at event-based revenue recognition in Chapter 7, we were using the planned revenues and costs for the commercial project to determine the planned profit that would be used to set the revenue to be recognized. Without a sound plan, the activities to promote a real-time close can't function because this planned data is being used to set a value for revenue recognition.

- With other types of projects, the plan represents a ceiling for spending on a project. In Chapter 8, we looked at how the system creates commitments for open purchase orders. Before we even create the purchase order, the system checks against the budget for the project to determine whether the spend is allowed or not.

Within SAP S/4HANA, the information for these planning applications is stored in table ACDOCP, but it's important to separate the different plans depending on the different assumptions by using different categories, as we discussed in Section 9.3.1, or the different types of objects for which planned data has been captured.

Figure 9.20 shows some of the delivered plan categories. SAP delivers plan categories such as **Manufacturing Order Plan Cost (PLANORD01)** and **Manufacturing Order Stan-**

dard Cost (PLANORD02) to separate the different types of planning (production orders, project management, etc.). You can create your own plan categories to separate the different planning assumptions behind the planning applications we looked at in Section 9.2 and Section 9.3.

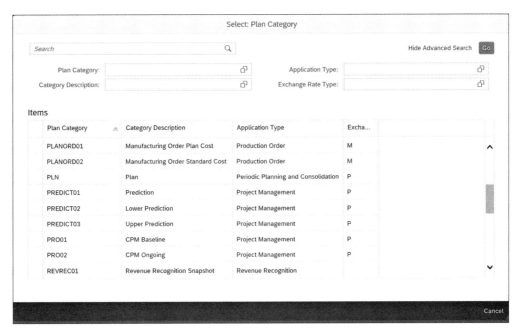

Figure 9.20 Plan Categories

Businesses typically distinguish between *commercial projects* (projects that are charged to customers, whether at a fixed price or on a cost basis) and *capital expense projects* (projects that become future assets, whether physical or intangible). In Section 9.4.1, we'll look at planning for commercial projects; in Section 9.4.2, we'll look at capital expense projects. We'll explain how the planned costs for production orders are used to set target costs and calculate variances in Section 9.4.3.

9.4.1   Planning Commercial Projects

A commercial project normally has several different sets of planned data based on different assumptions, each represented as a different plan category. Planning generally begins before the project is accepted, but the use of the plan goes beyond pure planning/analysis and is used to support event-based revenue recognition, as we discussed in Chapter 7, Section 7.2.2.

Unlike the semiautomated planning processes discussed in Section 9.1, financial planning on a commercial project is derived from entries made by project managers as they plan the tasks and staffing needed to complete the project. We'll therefore walk you through the steps to explain where the planned costs originate.

Figure 9.21 shows the Customer Projects app (SAP Fiori ID F0719), which at the time of publication (spring 2019) is currently available only in SAP S/4HANA Cloud. In the header, you can see that the project manager has planned the duration of the project (from **December 5, 2018** to **February 28, 2019**) and the effort (**200 Hours**). You can see the planned costs and planned revenue as key figures (**10,000 Euros** and **20,000 Euros**, respectively) and that the project has moved into execution.

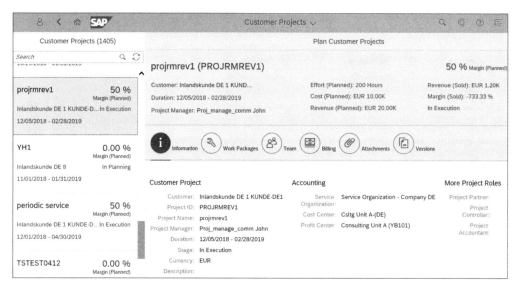

Figure 9.21 Header Information for Commercial Project Planning

Figure 9.22 shows the two work packages (**PROJMREV1** and **FIXED1**) that structure the project, together with each package's costs and revenues.

Figure 9.23 shows the staffing for the project and the costs associated with the use of these services: a senior consultant in the **PROJMREV1** work package will expend **200 Hours** of effort and cost **10,000 Euros**.

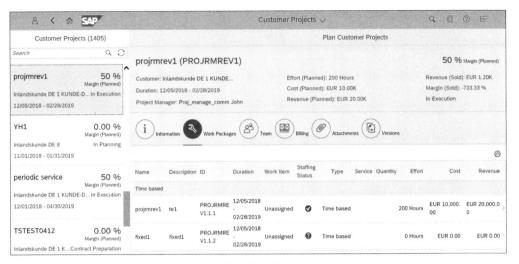

Figure 9.22 Work Packages for Commercial Project Planning

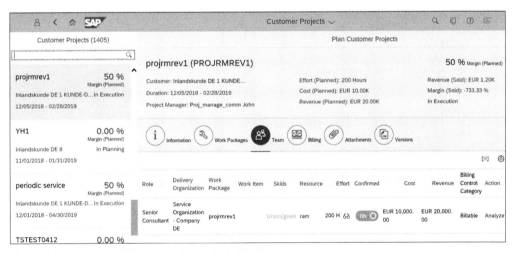

Figure 9.23 Staffing for Commercial Project Planning

Planning customer projects involves different planning estimates:

- The *baseline plan* refers to the costs originally planned to deliver the original scope in the original timeframe; this plan is typically locked before the project starts. Notice in Figure 9.20 that the baseline for the project is stored as one plan category.

331

- The *ongoing plan* includes any adjustments resulting from changes to the original project scope. Again, notice in Figure 9.20 that this is considered a different plan category.

- Project managers regularly will be asked to submit the value of the *estimate at completion* (EAC), which is the value that the project is expected to have on completion.

These various plans are compared against the actual project costs in the Projects—Baseline/EAC/Ongoing app (SAP Fiori ID F2334A), shown in Figure 9.24. These three values plus the actuals are by no means the only values available for the project. The arrow besides **Measures** in Figure 9.24 gives access to other project-related key figures, such as estimate to complete (ETC) values and various calculated values that are delivered as measures for this report.

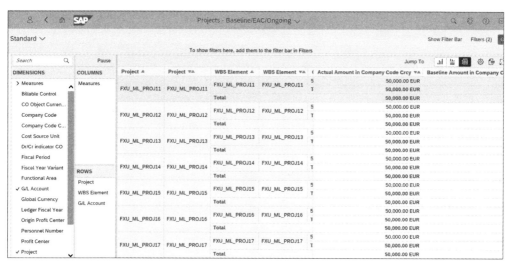

Figure 9.24 The Projects—Baseline/EAC/Ongoing App

Good planning is important to understand the success of the project, but it's also used to derive key figures for the valuation of the project. If you recall our explanation of how event-based revenue recognition worked in Chapter 7, you'll remember that we recognized revenue based on the planned costs and planned revenue. In the Project Profitability app shown in Figure 9.25, the data in the **Recognized Revenue**,

Recognized Cost of Goods Sold, and **Recognized Margin** columns is all derived from the planned costs.

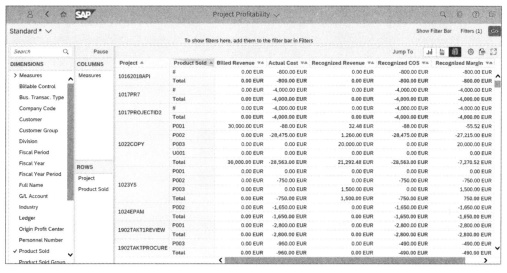

Figure 9.25 The Project Profitability App

9.4.2   Planning and Budgeting for Capital Expenses

Capital expense projects are used when assets, whether tangible or intangible, are in development. We'll look at the process of cost collection and settlement for these projects in Chapter 10, but for now note that these projects are generally considered part of a portfolio of investments within the organization, and it's the controller's job to monitor this portfolio.

SAP S/4HANA delivers the project financial controller role, which provides a set of project key figures. The focus of this overview page in Figure 9.26 and Figure 9.27 is on understanding the various costs being charged to the project and monitoring commitments (as we discussed in Chapter 8).

The planned costs shown in cards such as **Overall Budget Consumption** can be either uploaded manually using the Excel templates shown in Figure 9.6 or created using SAP Analytics Cloud or SAP BPC for SAP S/4HANA and stored in the planning table ACDOCP.

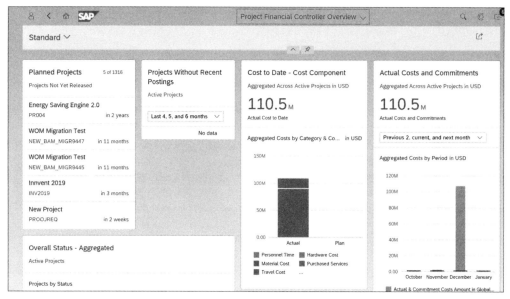

Figure 9.26 The Project Financial Controller Overview: Part 1

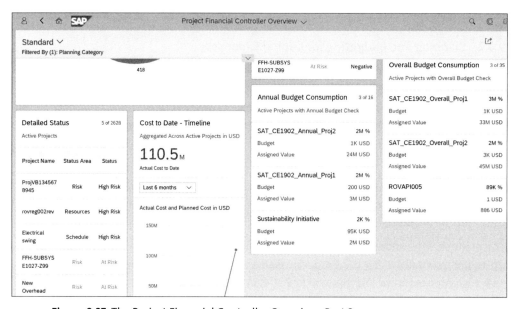

Figure 9.27 The Project Financial Controller Overview: Part 2

From these overview pages, the controller can access detailed apps, such as the Monitor Projects app (SAP Fiori F3088) shown in Figure 9.28. Here you can see how the planned costs are compared against the actual costs and used to calculate a variance. The variance is shown in red when the plan is exceeded; in this example, two variances are shown: **$12,700.00 USD** and **$11,770.00 USD**.

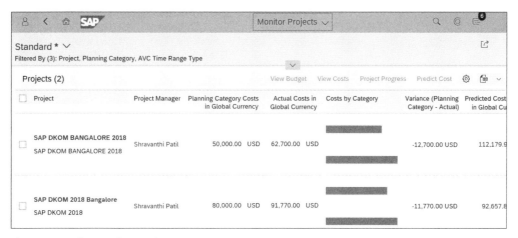

Figure 9.28 The Monitor Projects App

If you want to see more detailed reports showing how the budget is broken down for the individual WBS elements assigned to the project, you can navigate to the Project Budget Report app (SAP Fiori ID F3377) shown in Figure 9.29. This typical project report shows budget, actual costs, commitments, and assigned values. The commitments are calculated using the predictive accounting approach that we discussed in Chapter 8.

The main difference from the reports offered in SAP ERP is that it's no longer possible to assign costs to value categories. Instead, the cost breakdown is structured by the cost components shown in Figure 9.26 and Figure 9.30.

One purpose of these key figures is to provide a basis for *active availability control*. This means that before any posting is made to the project, the total costs and commitments are calculated and compared against the budget for the WBS element; an error message is issued if the posting will result in an overspend on the project. You have the same options to perform active availability control overall or by year as were available in SAP ERP. What changes in SAP S/4HANA Cloud is that the availability control is determined by checking against views that aggregate the remaining budget on the fly at the time of the availability check rather than checking against a precalculated total.

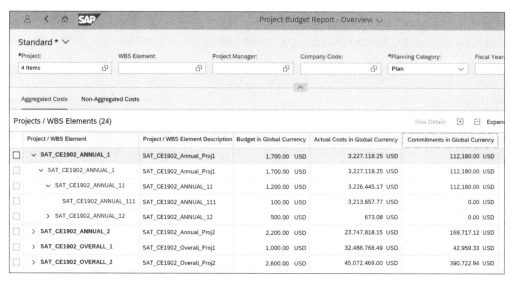

Figure 9.29 The Project Budget Report App

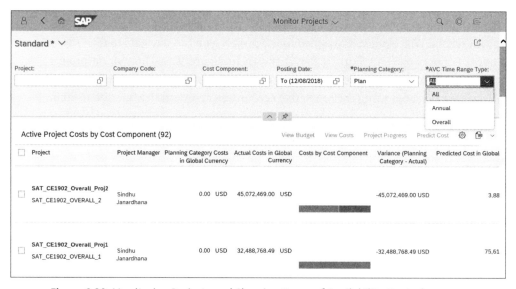

Figure 9.30 Monitoring Projects and Showing Types of Availability Control

9.4.3   Providing a Target for Production Orders

From a business point of view, the planned costs for a production order are used to determine whether the order can be released to production. Typically, the planned costs for the production order are based on the BOM, the routing, and a costing sheet—but it's common to substitute raw materials and shift to different work centers for capacity reasons. The result is that variances can be identified even before the order is released to production.

Figure 9.31 shows the selection screen for the Production Cost Analysis app (SAP Fiori ID F1780). Two plan categories are delivered for use in this context (shown on the right side):

- **Manufacturing Order Standard Cost**
  The standard costs are based on the cost estimate that was used to set the standard price for inventory valuation. These are copied into the planning table and adjusted if the order lot size and the costing lot size differ.

- **Manufacturing Order Plan Cost**
  The planned costs are calculated as the manufacturing order is created and are based on the material components and operations in the manufacturing order.

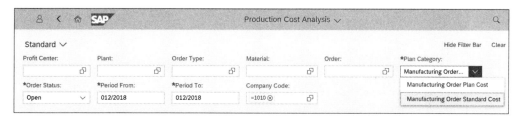

Figure 9.31 Choosing the Plan Category for Production Cost Analysis

Figure 9.32 shows the default view for order analysis. The figures shown in the **Target Debit/Actual Debit Variance** column and the **Target Cost Debit** column must be interpreted in combination with the chosen **Plan Category**. In other words, they are based on either the standard costs for the material or the planned costs for the order.

To understand how they have been calculated, access the **Order Cost Detail** screen (see Figure 9.33) by choosing the arrow on the right border. Here you can see that you're viewing the standard costs for the order, which were based on a costing lot size of five pieces. This has been adjusted to reflect the fact that two pieces (**2 Pc.**) of a planned five pieces (**5 Pc.**) have been delivered so far.

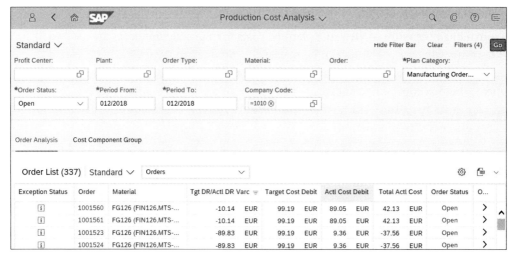

Figure 9.32 Selecting Orders for Analysis

Figure 9.33 Plan Category and Quantities for Production Order

The **Order Cost Detail** view only contains a subset of the available fields. Figure 9.34 shows the various key figures for the planned costs that are available for the production order. Normally, you won't need them (unless you're checking that values were updated correctly for the production order), but if you will use these key figures regularly, it's a good idea to create your own view to include these fields.

Figure 9.34 Creating a Layout Showing Planned Costs

In Figure 9.35, we added the **Plan Cost Debit** column to the **Order Cost Detail** layout to see the planned costs (based on a quantity of five pieces) and the target costs (based on a quantity of two pieces).

Recall from Chapter 1, Section 1.4.1 that SAP has been adding fields to the Universal Journal; these fields are also being used as part of the planning process. Figure 9.36 shows the Analyze Costs by Work Center/Operation app (SAP Fiori ID F3331). The work center and operation were included in the itemization at the time of order creation in SAP ERP but were not stored and therefore not available for subsequent reporting. In SAP S/4HANA, they are included in both the Universal Journal and the new planning table and can be used to calculate variances. We'll look at this application in more detail in Chapter 11.

We already discussed the need for planned data as a basis for real-time revenue recognition. You'll find the same situation for the calculation of work in process during production. Each time you confirm that an operation has been completed, the system uses the standard costs for that operation to determine the work in process that can be recognized for the completed operation or the value of the scrap if the operation can't be completed successfully.

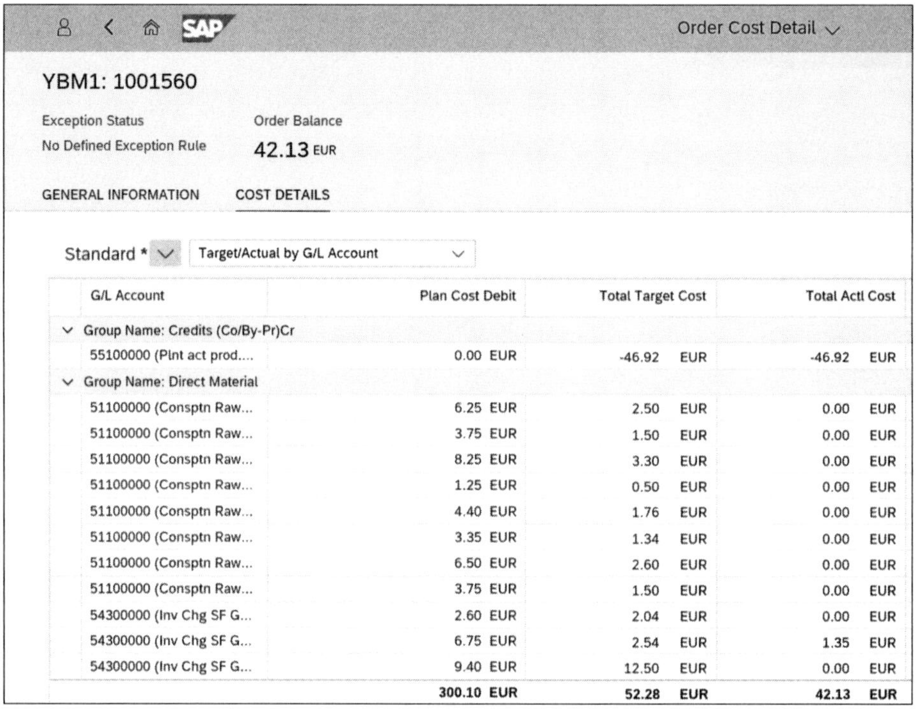

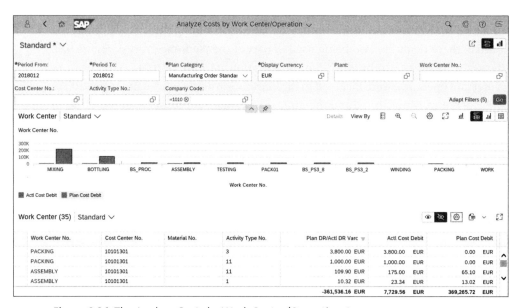

Figure 9.35 Layout Showing Planned Costs

Figure 9.36 The Analyze Costs by Work Center/Operation App

9.5 Summary

In this chapter, we discussed the fragmented approach to planning that was common before SAP S/4HANA, when data was kept in spreadsheets, dedicated planning applications, or even in the disparate tables used in SAP ERP. With SAP S/4HANA, the emphasis is on the unified planning model, which maps directly to the steering model for the business that we discussed in Chapter 1. We explored the planning capabilities in SAP Analytics Cloud and SAP BPC for SAP S/4HANA, then walked through the various operational plans that are also stored in the central planning table

We'll now move from planning and budgeting projects to focus on asset accounting in general.

9

Chapter 10

Asset Accounting: Making Real-Time Postings for Multiple Accounting Principles

So far, we've focused mainly on financial accounting and controlling. In this chapter and the next, we'll explain how two subledgers, assets and inventory, became part of the new steering model in SAP S/4HANA.

Fixed assets include land, buildings, machinery, vehicles, office equipment, furniture and fixtures, and so on, and are also known as *property, plant, and equipment* (PPE). What's important is that these are long-term assets that are required to perform normal business operations, have a useful life that spans several reporting periods, and are not easily converted into cash.

Because the costs of assets under construction and asset acquisitions are significant, budgeting for these capital expenses generally is treated separately from operating expenses, as you saw when we looked at the process of planning and budgeting capital expenses in Chapter 9. The initial cost of the asset is recorded on acquisition, and the value then is depreciated over time until the asset is disposed of either by sale or scrapping.

In terms of the steering model, fixed assets are one dimension that feeds into the asset side of the balance sheet, the value of which is gradually reduced over time by the depreciation postings at period close. The value of fixed assets represents a significant part of the balance sheet; there can be significant differences between the handling of the asset values depending on the accounting principle to be applied.

In this chapter, we'll focus on how a new approach to asset accounting has removed the need for a separate subledger for asset accounting and enabled real-time postings for multiple accounting principles. As you'll see, the new SAP S/4HANA data structure is what underlies this change, so we explore its impact and the handling of multiple accounting principles and currencies in Section 10.1. In Section 10.2, we'll pick up the key figure topic that we discussed in Chapter 6 and look at how to view the various key figures associated with asset values.

Finally, we'll consider assets from a controlling perspective in Section 10.3. Because development costs for capital expenses in the asset area are generally collected on projects or internal orders and then capitalized as assets under construction, asset accounting also has integration points with investment management; we'll look at these details in Section 10.3.1. Assets also almost always require maintenance, and we'll discuss changes to the data recorded for maintenance orders in Section 10.3.2.

10.1   New Data Structure in Asset Accounting

With SAP S/4HANA, asset accounting ceases to be a separate subledger that records the acquisition, transfer, and retirement of each asset and then rolls the information up into the general ledger. Now, each business transaction is recorded only once and updates any asset-specific fields to the universal journal, along with the general ledger accounts, the cost center to which the asset is assigned, the derived profit center, and so on.

In this section, we'll look at the results of merging the asset accounting subledger and the general ledger in the Universal Journal and discuss how depreciation works for multiple accounting principles.

10.1.1   Asset Accounting in the Universal Journal

Asset accounting has traditionally been a subledger that stores a detailed set of asset-related business transactions, the total of which roll up into the general ledger. Historically, the reporting process will start in the general ledger, and you then dig down to understand the details in the more granular, asset-specific postings. This is how asset accounting was performed in SAP ERP: the totals from the asset accounting subledger (FI-AA) rolled up to the General Ledger.

However, the notion of the subledger changes with the introduction of the new data model in SAP S/4HANA. Now there's no longer a separate set of asset-specific postings that roll up into the general ledger, but rather *a single document* that contains the asset-specific information alongside the general ledger account, cost center, profit center, and so on. Together, this data is used to steer the business in general.

To understand the merge of the ledger and subledger, we'll look at how the fields for asset accounting became part of the Universal Journal.

Figure 10.1 shows the Universal Journal (table ACDOCA) and the ACDOC_SI_FAA include structure that contains fields related to fixed assets. Notice that these fields include the **Depreciation Area** field, which controls the valuation settings, and the master data in the form of the **Group Asset Number** field, the **Asset Number** and the **Asset Subnumber** fields, the **Asset Value Data** field, and the **Asset Class** field, which controls the account determination. We then see the fields that document the value flow in asset accounting, including the **Asset Transaction Type** and **Transaction Type Category** fields. The fields of SAP ERP tables ANEK, ANEP, and ANEA have been absorbed into the Universal Journal.

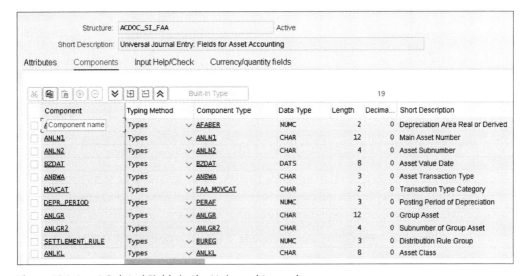

Figure 10.1 Asset-Related Fields in the Universal Journal

From an end user perspective, the shift from a separate subledger and general ledger to the Universal Journal can be seen in SAP Fiori applications such as the Trial Balance app (SAP Fiori ID F0996A). The trial balance now includes the fields from the asset subledger; you can use the navigation panel to access the asset-related fields.

Figure 10.2 shows the Trial Balance app and all postings to the **Buildings** and **Machinery & Equipment** general ledger accounts. We have drilled down by **Main Asset Number** to see how all the different asset postings roll into this single account. Notice on the left that you can also drill down by **Depreciation Area**, **Asset Subnumber**, **Asset Value Date**, **Asset Transaction Type**, **Group Asset**, and **Group Asset Subnumber**.

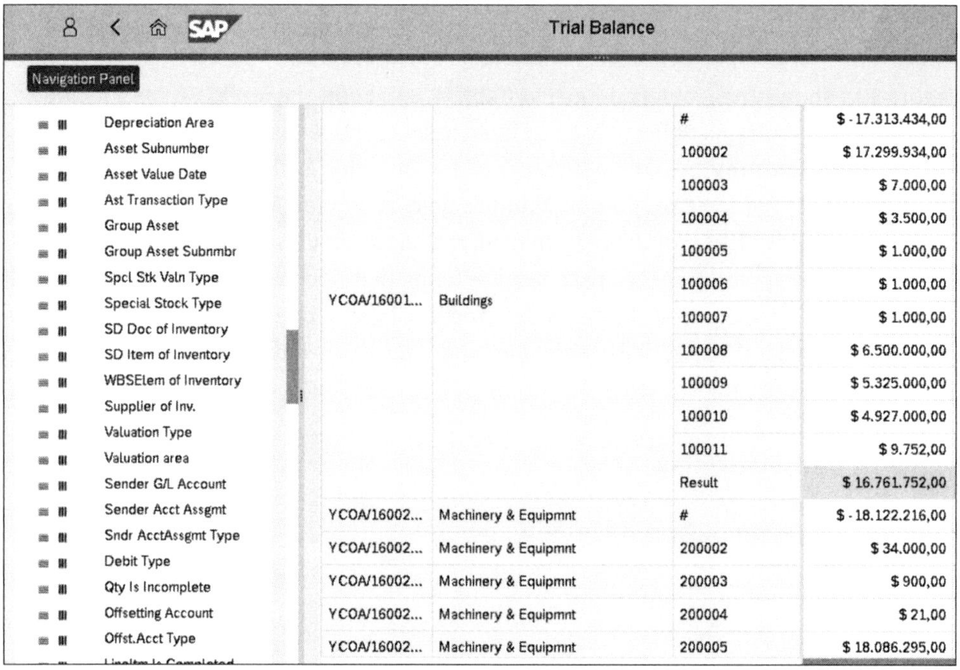

Figure 10.2 Asset-Related Fields as Drilldown Options in the Trial Balance App

With SAP S/4HANA, the posting logic changes in its granularity so that instead of multiple posting lines being created for each asset and a cumulated line in the general ledger, there is now one complete line for each asset.

You can see this most clearly when you look at the mass posting created by the depreciation run in Figure 10.3. Here you see a separate balance sheet line for each asset and the corresponding expense line that documents the asset's assignment to the cost center, functional area, profit center, and so on. In SAP ERP, this FI document would have offered only an aggregated view of the asset-related postings.

Once you have access to data in this granularity, it becomes possible to apply a substitution to each line to add, for example, the trading partner (**VBUND** field) for each asset. This wouldn't have been possible when only the asset totals were transferred to the general ledger.

This unification of asset accounting and the general ledger results in several reconciliation transactions becoming obsolete, including Transaction ABST (G/L Reconciliation), Transaction ABST2 (Account Reconciliation), and Transaction ABSTL (Reconciliation Analysis FI-AA). These are some examples of the tasks that disappear in SAP S/4HANA and no longer need to be performed during the entity close, as we discussed in Chapter 7.

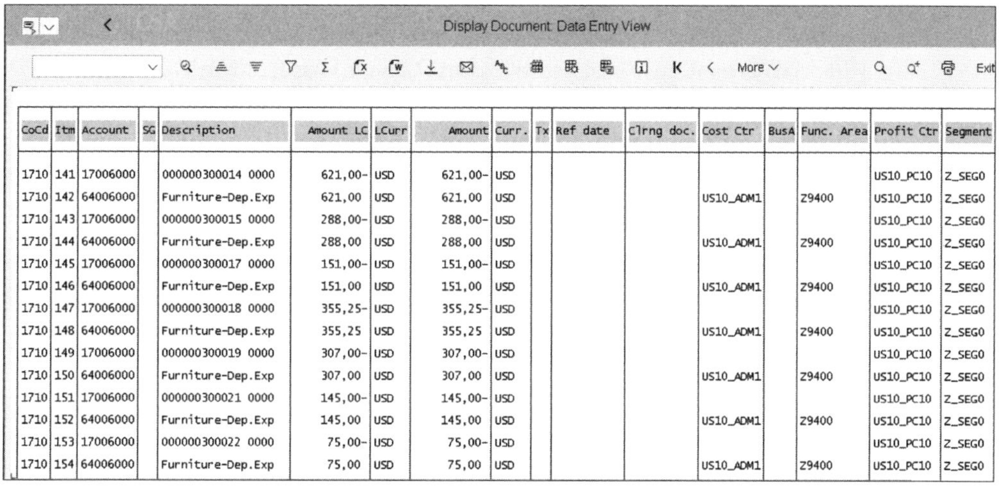

CoCd	Itm	Account	SG	Description	Amount LC	LCurr	Amount	Curr.	Tx	Ref date	Clrng doc.	Cost Ctr	BusA	Func. Area	Profit Ctr	Segment
1710	141	17006000		000000300014 0000	621,00-	USD	621,00-	USD							US10_PC10	Z_SEG0
1710	142	64006000		Furniture-Dep.Exp	621,00	USD	621,00	USD				US10_ADM1		Z9400	US10_PC10	Z_SEG0
1710	143	17006000		000000300015 0000	288,00-	USD	288,00-	USD							US10_PC10	Z_SEG0
1710	144	64006000		Furniture-Dep.Exp	288,00	USD	288,00	USD				US10_ADM1		Z9400	US10_PC10	Z_SEG0
1710	145	17006000		000000300017 0000	151,00-	USD	151,00-	USD							US10_PC10	Z_SEG0
1710	146	64006000		Furniture-Dep.Exp	151,00	USD	151,00	USD				US10_ADM1		Z9400	US10_PC10	Z_SEG0
1710	147	17006000		000000300018 0000	355,25-	USD	355,25-	USD							US10_PC10	Z_SEG0
1710	148	64006000		Furniture-Dep.Exp	355,25	USD	355,25	USD				US10_ADM1		Z9400	US10_PC10	Z_SEG0
1710	149	17006000		000000300019 0000	307,00-	USD	307,00-	USD							US10_PC10	Z_SEG0
1710	150	64006000		Furniture-Dep.Exp	307,00	USD	307,00	USD				US10_ADM1		Z9400	US10_PC10	Z_SEG0
1710	151	17006000		000000300021 0000	145,00-	USD	145,00-	USD							US10_PC10	Z_SEG0
1710	152	64006000		Furniture-Dep.Exp	145,00	USD	145,00	USD				US10_ADM1		Z9400	US10_PC10	Z_SEG0
1710	153	17006000		000000300022 0000	75,00-	USD	75,00-	USD							US10_PC10	Z_SEG0
1710	154	64006000		Furniture-Dep.Exp	75,00	USD	75,00	USD				US10_ADM1		Z9400	US10_PC10	Z_SEG0

Figure 10.3 Document Display for Depreciation Postings

Of course, it's still possible to create additional statistical postings for tax purposes and so on. These are updated to table FAAT_DOC_IT.

The asset master records haven't changed with SAP S/4HANA, but there are features that you might have missed. In SAP ERP you could assign an asset to a cost center, order, or WBS element, and the profit center would be derived on the fly at the time of posting. As shown in Figure 10.3, this assignment now forms part of the same posting line in the Universal Journal—and it's essential that the assignment is unique. The profit center is also used to derive the segment. If you haven't activated business function FIN_AA_SEGMENT_REPORTING until now, a move to SAP S/4HANA will ensure that it's activated automatically. You can then use program FAGL_ASSET_MASTERDATA_UPD to have the system assign profit centers and segments to all the assets to ensure that your master data is consistent.

To learn more about the table changes and their implications for conversion, refer to SAP Note 2270387 (S4TWL: Asset Accounting, Changes to Data Structure).

10.1.2 Depreciation with Multiple Accounting Principles and Currencies

Organizations that have assets must depreciate them based on the applicable accounting principles and in a variety of currencies.

Consequently, asset accounting in SAP ERP always has offered multiple valuations for the same asset to cover the different legal requirements that determine how the asset is depreciated. Figure 10.4 shows the assignment of a single asset to multiple depreciation areas. To check the depreciation areas used in your organization, choose **Accounting • Financial Accounting • Fixed Assets • Asset • Change • Asset** or run Transaction ASO2, enter the asset number and company code, and choose **Deprec. Areas** (depreciation areas). Here we see that the asset is assigned to six different depreciation areas. Notice the different useful lives (the estimated life span) for the same asset in the **Use. Life** column, which determine how the asset values will be depreciated over time.

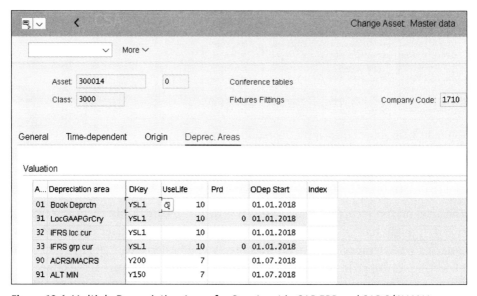

Figure 10.4 Multiple Depreciation Areas for One Asset in SAP ERP and SAP S/4HANA

The valuation of fixed assets within SAP financials solutions had already evolved before the arrival of SAP S/4HANA. In SAP R/3, only one valuation could update the general ledger in real time; all other valuations were updated at period close. With the introduction of the new General Ledger in SAP ERP, all valuations were updated simultaneously, but as *deltas* to the first posting.

Then, with the introduction of new Asset Accounting as an option in Enhancement Package 7 of SAP ERP, it became possible to update all valuations in parallel in real time. This is the approach that SAP S/4HANA has inherited.

What changes in SAP S/4HANA is the link between these depreciation areas and the general ledger. This connection is made by selecting **Financial Accounting • Asset**

Accounting • Integration with General Ledger Accounting • Define How Depreciation Areas Post to General Ledger in the IMG. Figure 10.5 shows how the depreciation areas shown in Figure 10.4 connect with the ledgers and accounting principles in accounting. Notice the **Area Posts in Real Time** setting beside areas **1** (**Book Depreciation**) and **32** (**IFRS in Local Currency**).

Chart of dep.:	1010	Chart of Depreciation 1010		

Define Depreciation Areas

	Ar.	Name of Depreciation Area	Real	Trgt Group	Acc.Princ.	G/L	
☐	1	Book Depreciation	✓	2L	LG	Area Posts in Real Time	⌄
☐	15	Local Tax in local currency	✓	2L	LG	Area Does Not Post	⌄
☐	31	Local GAAP in group currency	✓	2L	LG	Area Does Not Post	⌄
☐	32	IFRS in local currency	✓	0L	IFRS	Area Posts in Real Time	⌄
☐	33	IFRS in group currency	✓	0L	IFRS	Area Does Not Post	⌄
☐							

Figure 10.5 Link between Depreciation Areas and Accounting Principles

This coming together of the depreciation areas, the ledgers, and the accounting principles is reflected in the Asset Explorer (Transaction AW01N), shown in Figure 10.6, which illustrates how the depreciation areas are now structured by accounting principle. (The lines for IFRS and local GAAP are new in SAP S/4HANA.)

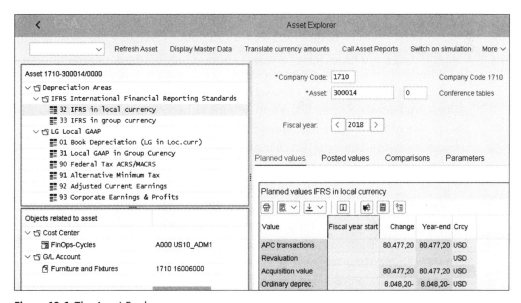

Figure 10.6 The Asset Explorer

This new focus on the accounting principle is reflected in all asset-related transactions. Figure 10.7 shows the depreciation posting run (Transaction AFAB). Notice that this run now can be started separately for each accounting principle.

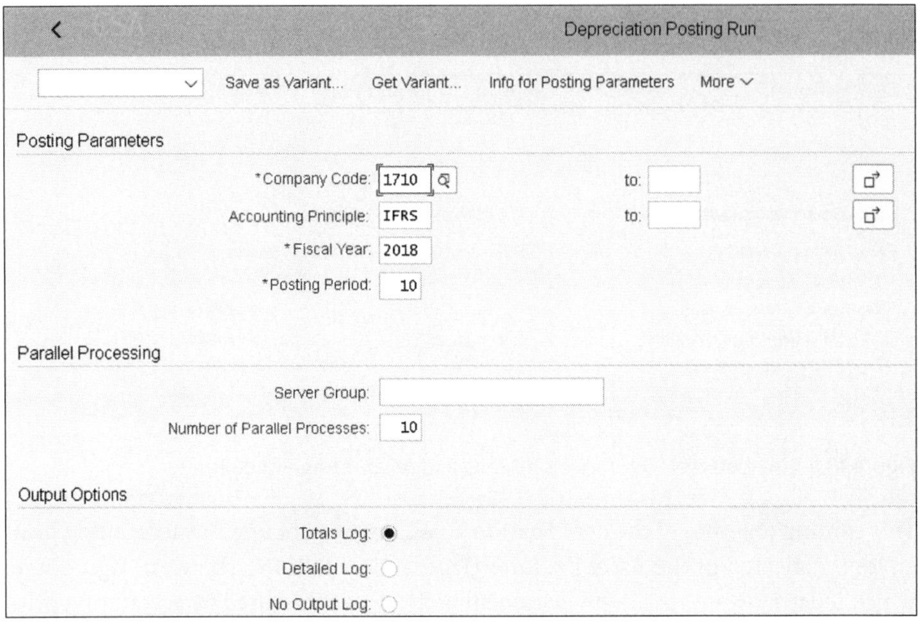

Figure 10.7 Depreciation Posting

The same changes to the posting logic to support multiple accounting principles impact all asset-related transactions in SAP S/4HANA.

To understand, let's look at a simple example of an asset acquisition. To record the acquisition, choose **Accounting • Financial Accounting • Fixed Assets • Posting • Acquisition • External Acquisition • Acquisition with Automatic Offsetting Entry** or run Transaction ABZON. Figure 10.8 shows the entry screen for the transaction with the assignment to an accounting principle and one or more depreciation areas. Note that if you were previously using new asset accounting in SAP ERP, you would see the ledger group instead of the accounting principle on this screen.

Enter the company code, the asset, the accounting principle, the depreciation area, a value, and a quantity; then choose **Simulate**. Figure 10.9 shows the document header for the asset acquisition, where you see that the purchase has been posted against a clearing account. These two lines represent the entry document. There is no change to the purchasing process, but this entry document posts to a technical clearing account (in our example, **16014100**). The introduction of the technical clearing account has allowed SAP to remove the delta depreciation areas. What changes is that the entry document posts to the clearing account, and then additional posting lines are created to update each accounting principle.

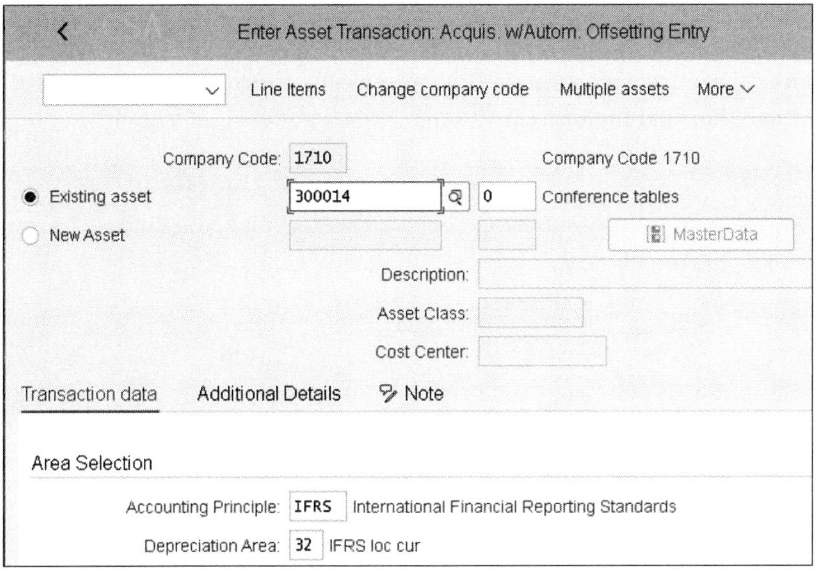

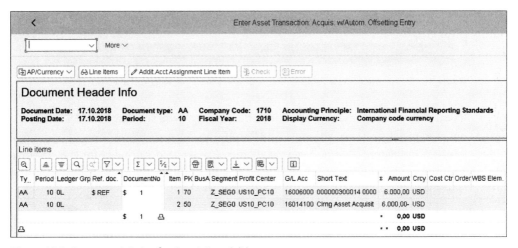

Figure 10.8 Entry Screen for Asset Transaction

Figure 10.9 Document Entry for Asset Acquisition

To set up a technical clearing account, choose **Financial Accounting • Asset Accounting • Integration with General Ledger Accounting • Technical Clearing Account for Integrated Asset Acquisition • Define Technical Clearing Account for Integrated Asset Acquisition** in the IMG. This clearing account must be a balance sheet account and always has a balance of zero.

Figure 10.10 shows what happens when you post the asset acquisition, using the information in the entry document. In this example, two documents were created: one for IFRS and the other for local GAAP (**LG**).

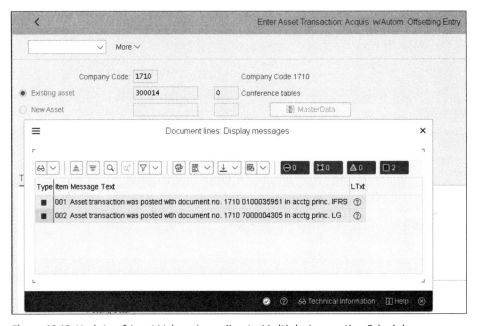

Figure 10.10 Update of Asset Values According to Multiple Accounting Principles

If you click the long text for each line in the message, you see that the IFRS values are updated in ledger **0L** and the local GAAP values in ledger **2L** (recall the settings in Figure 10.4 and Figure 10.5). Notice that there are separate documents for the postings according to each accounting principle. This substantially simplifies the process of selecting asset-related documents for reporting.

The entry document results in *identical* postings for each accounting principle, but you can use Transaction AB01L (the replacement for Transaction AB01) to adjust the values in one accounting principle to include values specific to that valuation. This might be needed if freight costs must be included in the asset acquisition costs according to one accounting principle, but not according to the other. Notice in Figure 10.11 that, as you saw in Figure 10.8, all asset transactions now include a reference to the accounting principle (**LG**). If you want to record the entry document and the valuation documents under different document types, you can set up a new document type using **Financial Accounting • Asset Accounting • Integration with General Ledger Accounting • Integrated Transactions—Specify Alternative Document Type for Accounting Principle-Specific Documents** in the IMG.

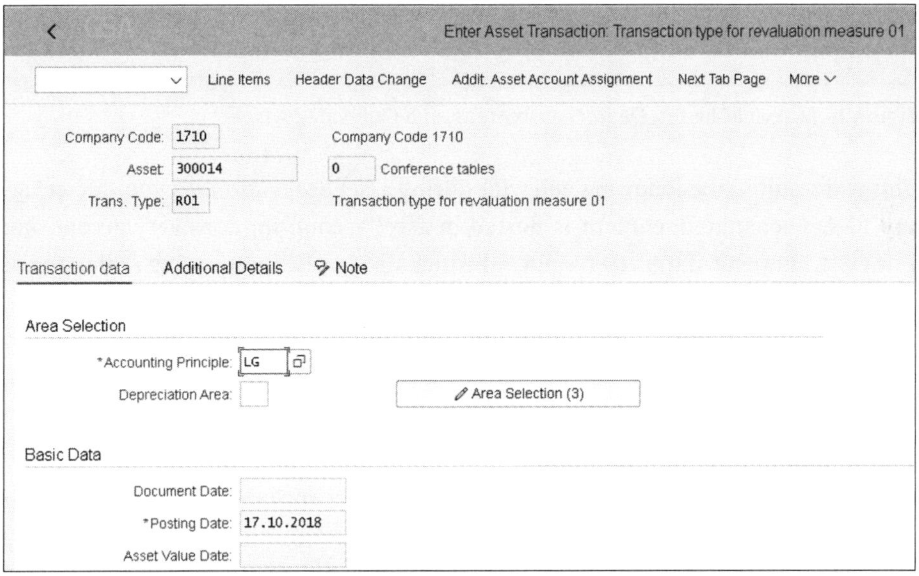

Figure 10.11 Enter Asset Transaction

One area in which organizations struggled in SAP ERP was the need to treat assets completely differently depending on the accounting principle. Under one accounting principle, the asset should be valued as an asset in the balance sheet, and in the other it's simply treated as an expense.

To handle this in SAP S/4HANA, deactivate the depreciation areas either at the asset class level or for a single asset. Figure 10.12 shows the deprecation areas for asset class **1100**. If you don't want all of these to be treated as asset postings in the general ledger, set the **Deact.** flag (**Deactivate**) for the relevant depreciation area. You can check your settings by choosing **Asset Accounting • General Valuation • Deactivate Asset Class for Chart of Depreciation** in the IMG.

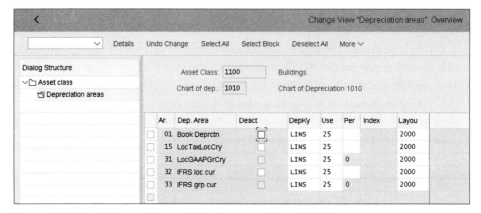

Figure 10.12 Asset Classes, Depreciation Areas, and One-Sided Assets

This will result in the following behavior during asset acquisition: As you saw in Figure 10.9, a separate document is posted in asset accounting for every accounting principle. However, if the asset is not to be included in asset accounting under one of the accounting principles, the acquisition posting will be redirected to an account for nonoperating expenses. If there are no active accounting principles, then the system will issue an error message. You can convert this to a warning message, in which case the asset value will be updated as a statistical posting only.

When an asset is retired, again a document is posted to asset accounting for every accounting principle. However, if the asset is not to be included in asset accounting under one of the accounting principles, the revenue will remain on the manually entered revenue account, from where it can be manually transferred to a different P&L account if needed. Again, if there are no active accounting principles, then the system will issue an error message.

If an asset is being treated as a P&L item during integrated acquisition, then when you create the asset, SAP S/4HANA checks that no other depreciation area in this accounting principle is posting depreciation to the general ledger to ensure that expenses are not counted twice.

We've looked so far at the implications of the new accounting data model and its impact on the postings in asset accounting. For more information, refer to SAP Note 2270388 (S4TWL: Asset Accounting: Parallel Valuation and Journal Entry). Now let's look at how these values are represented as key figures in SAP S/4HANA.

10.2   Key Figures for Asset Accounting

If Figure 10.2 looked like a typical accounting report in that it's structured by general ledger account, Figure 10.13 gives an idea of where SAP S/4HANA is heading in terms of asset reporting. The structure will look familiar if you compare the asset accountant's overview page with the pages for the general ledger accountant and sales accountant that we showed in Chapter 6.

The Asset Accounting Overview app (SAP Fiori ID F3096) shows various cards designed to give an asset accountant an immediate overview of the situation for the fixed assets in their area of responsibility. Notice that we are selecting by ledger (an entity that you might not previously have expected in asset accounting) and depreciation area.

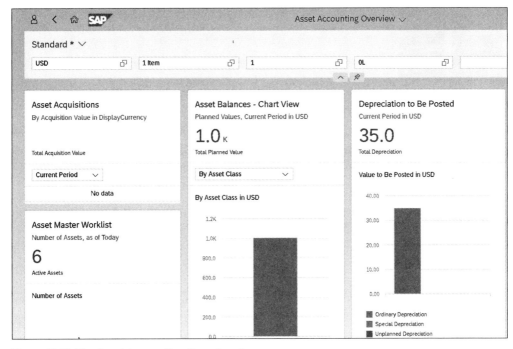

Figure 10.13 The Asset Accounting Overview App

From each of these tiles, you can access detailed reports that explain the key figures in more detail. In Figure 10.14, we've accessed the Asset Balances app (SAP Fiori ID F1617A) from the overview page in Figure 10.13. This lists the main asset-related accounts. The basic layout of the report resembles the Trial Balance app, except that this time the focus is on the fields specific to asset accounting. You can also access the assigned cost center, profit center, segment, and so on, however, by choosing the appropriate dimension.

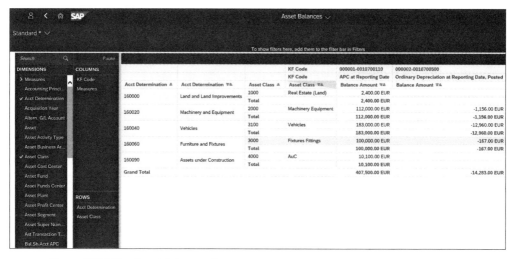

Figure 10.14 The Asset Balances App

Figure 10.15 shows the Asset Transactions app (SAP Fiori ID F1614), with a detailed list of asset transactions structured by asset transaction type. The asset transaction types structure the different types of business transaction performed for the assets and determine what follow-on processes can be performed for the asset.

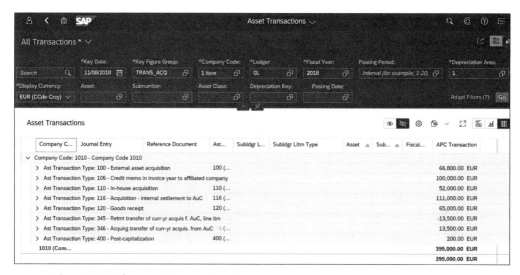

Figure 10.15 The Asset Transactions App

If you scroll down through the screen shown in Figure 10.13, you'll see additional key figures, showing the vendor and country where the asset was purchased and details of open purchase orders for assets. You'll also notice **Quick Links** taking you to familiar views, including the **Asset Transactions**, **Asset Balances**, **Asset History Sheet**, and **Display Asset** views.

Notice the **Key Figure Group** field in the selection screen in Figure 10.15 and how we're using the **TRANS_ACQ** key figure to select the acquisitions in Figure 10.16. This option makes it very easy for end users to select relevant transactions for reporting. It also provides a new technical approach to report building that replaces the logical database ADA, which was the base for most asset reporting tasks in SAP ERP.

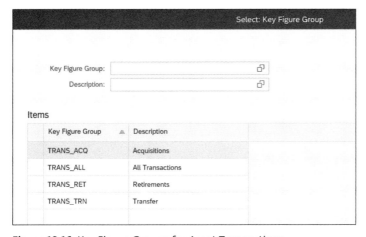

Figure 10.16 Key Figure Groups for Asset Transactions

You've seen some of the new key figures for asset accounting. Now let's look at how asset accounting integrates with controlling in SAP S/4HANA.

10.3   Asset Accounting and Controlling

So far, we've primarily considered asset accounting from the direction of financial accounting and the balance sheet, discussing how asset accounting involved both a subledger and the general ledger in SAP ERP. The other part of the equation is how asset accounting interacts with controlling to capture the costs of assets under construction. *Assets under construction* can be both physical assets (e.g., new buildings and production lines) and intangible assets (e.g., product design or movie idea). Once assets are in operation, they incur maintenance costs that also must be managed.

In the SAP ERP days, many organizations also used the Investment Management component to organize their investments into programs and classify the goals of these investments. SAP ERP offered dedicated planning and budgeting functions to monitor the expenses associated with these projects.

In this section, we'll explain how investment management changes with the move to SAP S/4HANA to increase transparency into assets under construction and maintenance orders.

10.3.1   Assets under Construction

From an asset accounting point of view, assets under construction belong to a special asset class. Their values are assigned to different accounts to separate these values from those assets that support the activities that run the business.

Apart from that, the asset balance report for assets under construction shown in Figure 10.17 resembles the Asset Balances app shown in Figure 10.14.

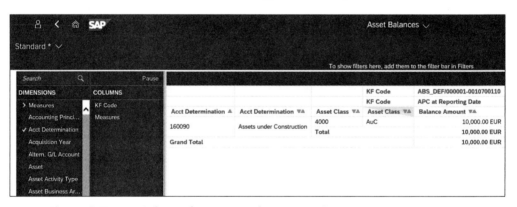

Figure 10.17 Asset Balances for Assets under Construction

What's different is that instead of the purchase order used to procure the asset being responsible for the asset costs, a project or internal order is used to capture the costs accumulated during construction. Projects used in this context have the system status **AUC** and include a link to the investment profile (see Figure 10.18). The investment profile controls whether an asset under construction is created automatically and how the costs accumulated on the project will be settled later.

When we discussed the soft close and the use of settlement for commercial projects in Chapter 7, we explained how commercial projects no longer need to settle but can assign their costs automatically to the relevant profitability segments. However, it's important to note that this process does not apply to capital expenses and that investment orders and projects continue to settle, usually to a fixed asset. It's also common in this context to have multiple distribution rules; you might settle some of the costs to a fixed asset for capitalization and some to a cost center in which they are treated as expenses. This can't be handled in the new derivation functions, which enrich the posting line rather than distributing to multiple new ones.

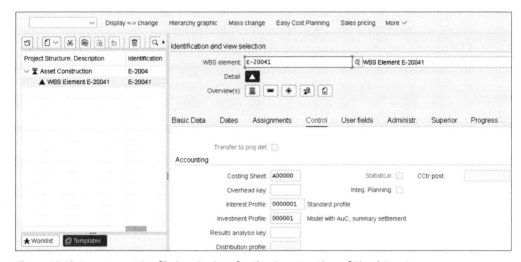

Figure 10.18 Investment Profile in a Project for the Construction of Fixed Asset

On completion, there are two ways to handle the costs. You can either do a summary settlement under a secondary cost element (the option chosen in Figure 10.18) or perform line item settlement using Transaction CJIC to define how each line item is to be settled. Once you've set up these rules, you can settle the costs, and the asset is complete.

Each project or order can be linked to an investment program that structures the capital investments within an organization. One early SAP HANA–based development led to the introduction of the following new transactions to monitor budget availability, costs, and commitments for such programs:

- Monitor Availability Control for Investment Programs (Transaction IM_AVCHANA)
- Monitor Availability Control for WBS Elements (Transaction IM_AVCHANA_WBS)
- Monitor Availability Control for Internal Orders (Transaction IM_AVCHANA_ORD)

The idea behind these new transactions is that investment controllers need to be able to check the budget for each item, the part of that budget that has already been assigned, and the part of the budget available for further spending. For large investment programs, this was typically a long-running report that would read the budget for each of the items in the program, read the assigned orders and WBS elements to determine what had already been assigned, and calculate what budget remained.

To use the new budget availability checks, choose **Accounting • Investment Management • Programs • Information System • Investment Management Reports • Programs—Current Data • Monitor Availability Control for Investment Programs** in the SAP Easy Menu or run Transaction IM_AVCHANA. Figure 10.19 shows the selection screen for the new availability control report. Enter the name of the investment program, the approval year, and whether you are looking at overall values (multiple years) or values for a single year. Don't forget to make the appropriate settings (**Report Currency**, **Warning From (%)**, and **Error From (%)**) so that the system can calculate your status.

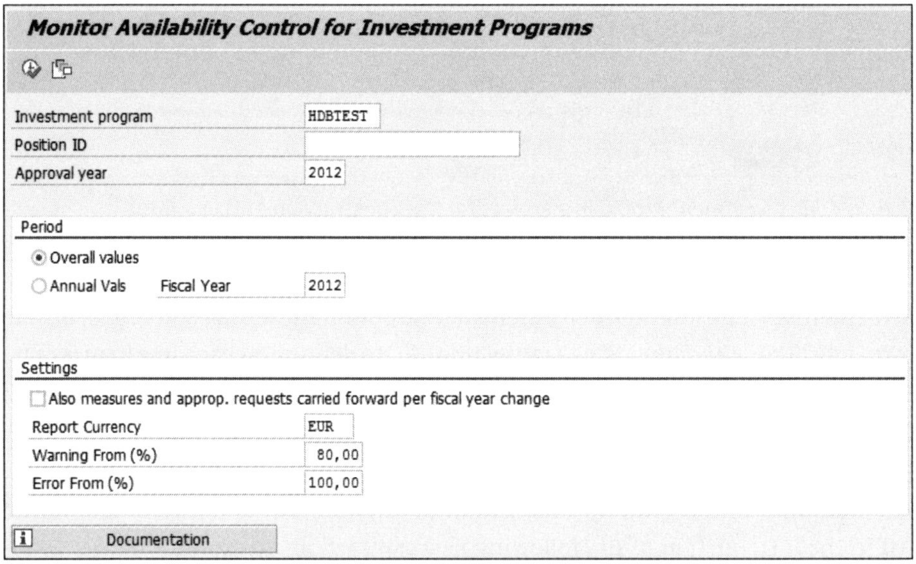

Figure 10.19 Monitor Availability Control for Investment Programs

The result of executing the transaction is shown in Figure 10.20. A status is set for each investment program item; you can expand the nodes of the investment program to understand where the budget is running short and clarification is required.

In this example, the investment programs for Berlin, Dossenheim, and Hamburg have a green status, but the investment program for Koeln has a yellow status.

Finally, you see the internal orders that are assigned to these program items. This report responds such that it can be run in dialog mode rather than in batch mode, as was common in the past. To find out more about this report, refer to SAP Note 1652021 (Monitor Availability Control for Investment Programs). For more general questions concerning Investment Management in SAP S/4HANA, refer to SAP Note 2436714 (Investment Management in SAP S/4HANA, On-Premise Edition).

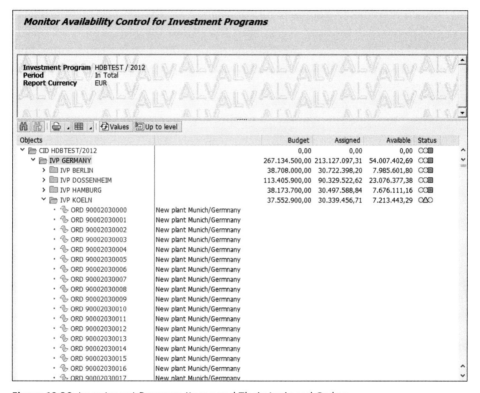

Figure 10.20 Investment Program Items and Their Assigned Orders

Investment Management in SAP S/4HANA Cloud

Investment management isn't supported in SAP S/4HANA Cloud, though you can create projects and assets under construction and settle the projects to these assets.

10.3.2   Maintenance Orders

Existing assets such as buildings, machinery, or equipment sometimes require maintenance. Asset accountants need to monitor the expenses associated with maintenance orders, even if the actual execution of maintenance orders is the purview of plant maintenance personnel.

The main functions for plant maintenance have not changed significantly in SAP S/4HANA, but an important business function, LOG_EAM_OLC, was introduced in Enhancement Package 5 for SAP ERP 6.0 and is similarly available in SAP S/4HANA.

The Operation Account Assignment function allows you to collect costs at the operation level rather than the order level. Figure 10.21 shows the costs for the two operations on maintenance order **509160**: operation **0001** that cost **110 Euros** and operation **0002** that cost **66 Euros**. You can access this report using Transaction IW33 or **Logistics • Plant Maintenance • Maintenance Processing • Order • Display** and **Extras • Cost Reports • Operation Cost Overview** in the SAP Easy Menu.

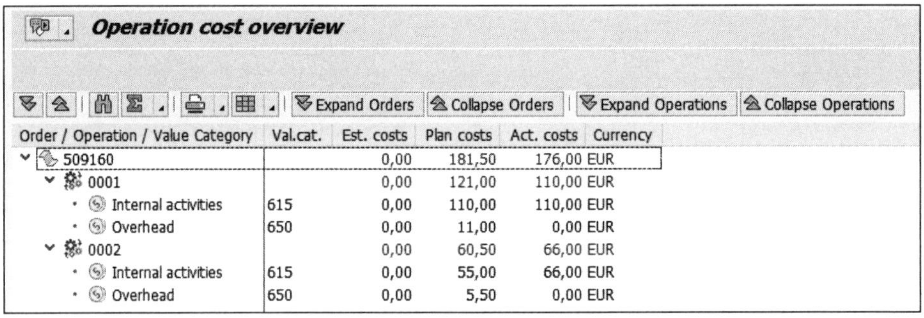

Operation cost overview

Order / Operation / Value Category	Val.cat.	Est. costs	Plan costs	Act. costs	Currency
509160		0,00	181,50	176,00	EUR
0001		0,00	121,00	110,00	EUR
• Internal activities	615	0,00	110,00	110,00	EUR
• Overhead	650	0,00	11,00	0,00	EUR
0002		0,00	60,50	66,00	EUR
• Internal activities	615	0,00	55,00	66,00	EUR
• Overhead	650	0,00	5,50	0,00	EUR

Figure 10.21 Maintenance Operations and Their Costs

You can see the costs per operation in the line item reports in controlling, as shown in Figure 10.22.

From a controlling perspective, it's also worth knowing that the Logistics Information System (LIS) is scheduled to be replaced by CDS views over the next several years as new versions of SAP S/4HANA are released. You can keep abreast of progress in this direction by referring to SAP Note 2267463 (S4TWL: LIS in EAM).

With this longer-term goal in mind, SAP has started to move key fields relevant for costing from the logistics tables and into the Universal Journal. Figure 10.23 shows the ACDOC_SI_LOG_ACT include, which includes all the fields that have been added for the purposes of reporting on maintenance and service orders. These are then consumed in the CDS views that support analytical reporting.

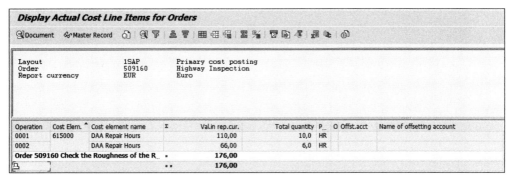

Figure 10.22 Controlling Line Item Report Showing Operation Costs

Component	Typing Method	Component Type	Data Type	Length	Decima...	Short Description
UVORN	Types	UVORN	CHAR	4	0	Suboperation
EQUNR	Types	EQUNR	CHAR	18	0	Equipment Number
TPLNR	Types	TPLNR	CHAR	30	0	Functional Location
ISTRU	Types	ISTRU	CHAR	40	0	Assembly
ILART	Types	ILA	CHAR	3	0	Maintenance activity type
PLKNZ	Types	AUF_PLKNZ	CHAR	1	0	Maintenance order planning indicator
ARTPR	Types	ARTPR	CHAR	2	0	Priority Type
PRIOK	Types	PRIOK	CHAR	1	0	Priority
MAUFNR	Types	MAUFNR	CHAR	12	0	Number of Superior Order
MATKL_MM	Types	FINS_MATKL_MM	CHAR	9	0	Material Group
PLANNED_PARTS_WORK	Types	FINS_PLANNED_PARTS.	CHAR	1	0	Planned Parts/Work

Structure: ACDOC_SI_LOG_ACT — Active

Short Description: Universal Journal Entry: Fields for Logistics - actual only

Attributes Components Input Help/Check Currency/quantity fields

Figure 10.23 Maintenance-Related Fields in the Universal Journal

10.4 Summary

In this chapter, we looked at the key changes affecting the asset subledger in SAP S/4HANA. We explained the new data structures and that the subledger is no longer separate from the general ledger. Then we looked at the valuation of fixed assets according to different accounting principles and how to view key figures for asset valuation. Finally, we looked at the handling of capital expenses and maintenance costs in controlling.

We'll now look at the changes affecting inventory valuation and the material ledger.

Chapter 11

Inventory Accounting: Simplifying Material Valuation, Production Cost Analysis, and Actual Costing

In this chapter, we'll move from asset accounting to inventory accounting and explain how this information is included in the Universal Journal. We'll then look at the changes in cost object controlling and at how actual costing has been rebuilt to simplify processing and accelerate the costing run.

Inventory accounting is the process of valuing inventories for the balance sheet, whether these are materials purchased directly for sale (as in the case of a retailer) or materials that have been manufactured in house using purchased raw materials (as in the case of the product-focused industries that we discussed in Chapter 3). From a business point of view, inventory values can be significant. Holding too much inventory can result in cash flow problems and high storage costs, whereas having too little inventory can make it difficult to fulfill some sales orders, which could result in reduced sales and lost customers.

In all industries, organizations must set a value for every unit of inventory kept in stock. In a retail environment, this value generally is driven by the purchase prices for the goods held in inventory. In the manufacturing environment, organizations must calculate the standard costs for manufacturing the product and then determine variances during the manufacturing process. Some countries and industries face a legal requirement to assign all purchase price variances and production variances to the goods in stock at period close, a process known as *actual costing*.

In this chapter on material valuation, production cost analysis, and actual costing, we'll explain how the Universal Journal table design includes product costs in the account-based model for the purposes of profitability analysis.

We'll begin by discussing the new data structures for inventory accounting in Section 11.1. With the announcement that use of the material ledger becomes compulsory beginning with SAP S/4HANA 1511, there has been a lot of confusion concerning "how much" of the material ledger organizations must use. In practice, there are two main benefits: inventory values in the material master will be available in two currencies, and inventory valuation now occurs in just one table (instead of one table in materials management and another in the material ledger) in a simplification that radically improves system performance.

In addition to the new data structures, you will find that new SAP Fiori applications make it easier to get an overview of your inventory values and make price changes. If you are a global organization, this may also be the moment to take stock of the approaches to material valuation in the various countries you operate in. If they differ radically, you might want to consider valuating inventory centrally according to your leading accounting principle (US-GAAP if you're headquartered in the United States; IFRS if you're headquartered in Europe) and locally according to the individual GAAPs followed in the different countries you operate in.

In Section 11.2, we'll explain changes to bring the production variances into the account-based model and introduce the first SAP Fiori applications for product cost controlling. We'll explain how these applications use more granular planning data and finer cost data to deliver more transparency to the shop floor.

Finally, in Section 11.3, we'll look at the impact of the redesign of actual costing beginning in SAP S/4HANA 1610 and explain what this means if you've been using actual costing in SAP ERP to date.

11.1   New Data Structure in Inventory Accounting

In Chapter 10, we looked at the changes to asset accounting that result from the merge with the general ledger. You can use that same mental model to imagine how the fields related to inventory accounting become part of the general ledger in SAP S/4HANA.

The Universal Journal is much *wider* than the general ledger table in SAP ERP with the inclusion of the many reporting dimensions. However, with inventory accounting the table generally becomes *deeper* as well because the line item limit of 999 in table BSEG meant that many organizations summarized their general ledger tables to remove the contents of the material number field. This meant that material-related lines were only visible in the costing tables and in costing-based CO-PA.

In SAP S/4HANA, the Universal Journal now contains a posting line for each material in a material document, together with either a manufacturing order (if the material is being issued to production) or a profitability segment (if the material is being issued to sales), plus the assigned material account (based on the valuation class) and profit center. Let's look at these data structures in more detail, explaining how the material ledger fields become part of the Universal Journal, how much the material ledger becomes compulsory with SAP S/4HANA 1511, and the relationships among the ledger, the accounting principles, and the various ways of valuating inventory.

11.1.1   Inventory Accounting in the Universal Journal

Let's start by looking at how the fields for inventory accounting become part of the Universal Journal. Figure 11.1 shows the Universal Journal (table ACDOCA) and the ACDOC_SI_ML include that contains the fields related to inventory accounting.

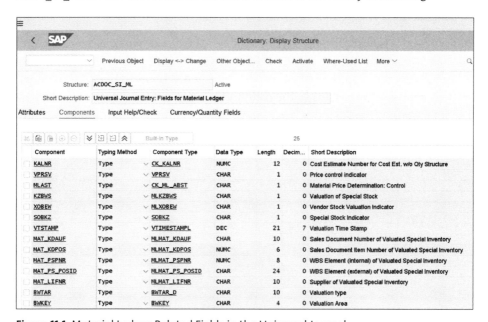

Figure 11.1 Material Ledger-Related Fields in the Universal Journal

To get a feel for the implications of the shift, we'll look at some of the key settings related to inventory valuation shown in Figure 11.1:

- The meaning of the **Price Control Indicator** setting remains unchanged and determines whether your inventory is valued at standard cost or at moving average price. Most organizations choose the moving average price for raw materials and standard cost for finished and semifinished materials; retailers set the moving average price for all materials. There is no reason to change this approach with a move to SAP S/4HANA.

- There will now be a **Material Price Determination Control** flag for all materials, but this will be set to **2** (**Transaction-Based**) unless you're already using actual costing. If you are using actual costing, then the flag will be set to **3** (**Single/Multilevel Actual Costing**) and will ensure that the materials are included in the costing run at period close. We'll come back to this in detail when we look at inventory-related accounting principles in Section 11.1.3 and actual costing in Section 11.3.

- The **Valuation Type** setting continues to be optional and is used for batch-based valuation or to distinguish by valuation type (such as origin of the material).

- Special stocks (sales order stock, project stock, vendor stock, consignment stock, stock in transit, etc.) continue to be valuated as before as a combination of the material number and the sales order, project, and so on.

To get a feel for how these fields can be used in finance, take a look at the navigation options in the Trial Balance app (SAP Fiori ID F0996A), shown in Figure 11.2. Here we've scrolled down to the inventory accounts, and you can see several material-related reporting dimensions in the column on the left of the screen, including **SD Item of Inventory**, **Special Stock Type**, and **Supplier**.

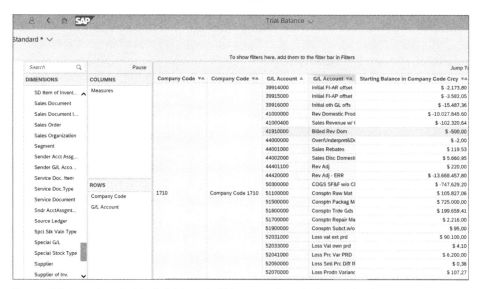

Figure 11.2 Inventory-Related Fields as Drilldown Options in the Trial Balance App

However, if it doesn't seem natural to be looking at inventory fields in the trial balance, consider using the Material Inventory Values—Balance Summary app (SAP
Fiori ID F1422A) shown in Figure 11.3 instead. Here you're still looking at inventory
values from an accounting perspective (**Company Code**, **Ledger**, and **G/L Account**), but
it's easy to drill down by those reporting dimensions that are relevant for inventory:
Valuation Area, **Valuation Class**, **Valuation Type**, and so on.

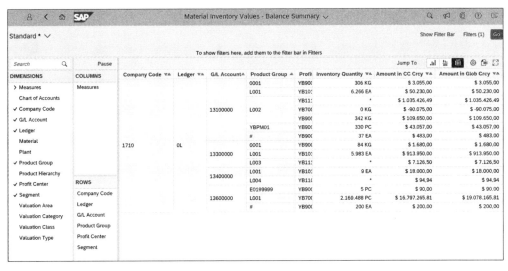

Figure 11.3 The Material Inventory Values—Balance Summary App

Behind the scenes, the contents of tables MLIT, MLPP, MLPPF, MLCR, MLCRF, MLCD, CKMI1, and
BSIM have been moved into the Universal Journal and replaced with compatibility
views.

To date, there have been no significant changes to the data structures used to store
the standard cost estimate; you'll still find the cost estimate itemization being stored
in table CKIS and the cost components in table KEKO. The main UI change is the introduction of the Manage Costing Runs—Estimated Costs app (SAP Fiori ID F1865),
shown in Figure 11.4. If you select a costing run from this screen, you'll access the
familiar costing run screens of Transaction CK40N, in which you perform the costing
steps and check the results of the costing run.

What's changed with the move to an account-based data model is how the cost com-
ponents for product costing are used in the general ledger. If you used costing-based
CO-PA in SAP ERP, then you're used to seeing the breakdown of the cost of goods sold
(COGS) as a series of value fields to which the cost component split for the product

sold are mapped. SAP S/4HANA includes a new mechanism that uses the standard cost estimate to explain the COGS by splitting them to several different *accounts* instead.

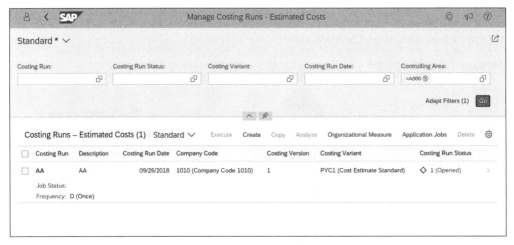

Figure 11.4 The Manage Costing Runs—Estimated Costs App

Figure 11.5 shows one of the financial documents for the delivery of a finished product to the final customer. The posting takes place in two stages:

1. In the first document, the system credits finished goods inventory and debits COGS. The main change is that both the finished goods inventory account and the COGS account must be defined as cost elements. In comparison, when using costing-based CO-PA in SAP ERP, there was no update to the account assignment for the COGS posting.

2. In the next document (shown in Figure 11.5), the COGS posting is reversed and split to form separate posting lines for the labor, material, overhead, and other charges that make up the underlying cost estimate. This function was introduced with SAP S/4HANA and is designed to explain the costs of the product sold without the need to assign them to value fields in costing-based CO-PA.

To understand what's happening in Figure 11.5, let's look at the configuration. Figure 11.6 shows the cost splitting profile that controls the process for the COGS account (**54083000**) in the first line of Figure 11.5.

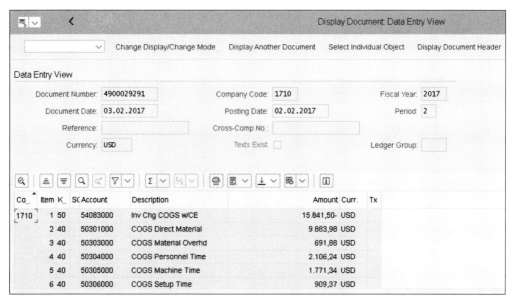

Figure 11.5 Cost of Goods Sold for Finished Goods

You can access the cost-splitting profile that controls the process by choosing **Financial Accounting • General Ledger Accounting • Periodic Processing • Integration • Materials Management • Define Accounts for Splitting Cost of Goods Sold** in the IMG. Once you've selected the cost-splitting profile, choose **Source Accounts and Valuation Views**. The system will attempt to split any postings to the COGS account (the account entered in Figure 11.6) in accordance with the detailed configuration shown in Figure 11.7.

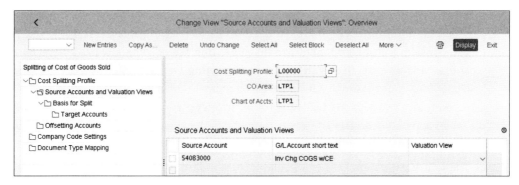

Figure 11.6 Cost Splitting for Cost of Goods Sold Account

Figure 11.7 shows the cost components for the cost component split for the product sold. Notice that you can only select one cost component structure (here we're using **L1**), rather than the main and auxiliary cost component structures; this means you'll have to choose whether the cost of goods manufactured (COGM) split or the primary cost component split will determine the split of the COGS in your organization.

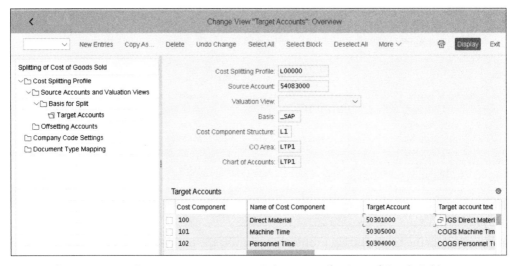

Figure 11.7 Mapping Cost Components to Subaccounts for Cost of Goods Sold

New accounts have been created for each of the components in this structure, and it's these accounts that you see in Figure 11.5. Like the COGS account, these accounts also must be flagged as cost elements. Essentially, they are refining the original posting by splitting the costs into more detailed accounts. This process will be familiar if you've been used to mapping cost components to value fields in costing-based CO-PA. The difference is simply that you're using accounts instead of value fields. However, if you consider a cost component like machine time, which generally has a fixed part and a variable part, then you might be expecting two accounts rather than one (**50305000** in our example). It's possible to separate fixed and variable costs for this account into two separate fields in group currency—you can use the Product Profitability app (SAP Fiori ID F2765), which separates the two values—but there's no split yet in the other currencies.

The splitting function has been available for standard costs since the introduction of SAP S/4HANA. The ability to update this additional split with the *actual costs* once they have been calculated using the periodic costing run was introduced with SAP

S/4HANA 1809. In that release, it's not possible to activate the cost component split if material ledger documents are already available.

Figure 11.8 shows the **Strategy Type** field, which marks which cost estimate is used to split the COGS, and the option to revalue (the **Split Revalued Consumption with Actual Cost Component Split** checkbox). You'll then have to specify that you want to update the inventory values with the actual costs using the parameters for the post-close step in actual costing (which you'll see later in Figure 11.25).

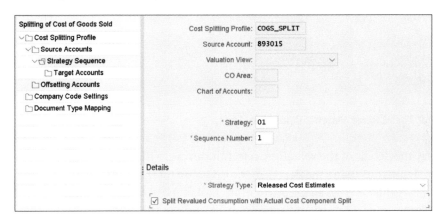

Figure 11.8 Selection of Cost Estimates for Cost of Goods Sold

11.1.2 Compulsory Use of the Material Ledger

Confusion reigned when SAP S/4HANA 1511 first was released because many customers thought that they were now obligated to do actual costing, whether they wanted to or not.

In fact, all that the change means is that all material valuations are stored in two currencies (the company code currency and the group currency), as you can see for **Material SP001** in Figure 11.9. Here we're using the Manage Material Valuations app (SAP Fiori ID F2680). Notice that in addition to the valuation information, you can access the following apps from this screen by selecting a material and choosing the corresponding tab:

- Material Price Analysis (Transaction CKM3N)
- Change Future Prices with Reference (Transaction MR21)
- Release Planned Price Changes (Transaction CKME)
- Delete Future Prices (no equivalent transaction)

Figure 11.9 The Manage Material Valuations App

To display the details of the valuation, select the arrow to the right of the **Price Unit** column. Figure 11.10 shows the details of the valuation for the selected material. This option allows you to access all the prices from the material master using the **Standard Cost Estimates**, **Costing**, **Tax and Commercial**, and **Planned Prices** tabs.

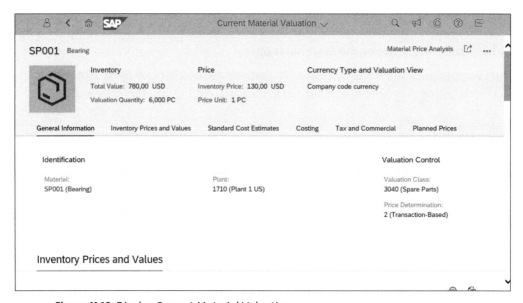

Figure 11.10 Display Current Material Valuation

After you perform the technical conversion to SAP S/4HANA, the **Accounting** view in the material master transaction will change. As shown in Figure 11.11, the **ML. Act.** flag is active for every material, and inventory values are shown in both company code currency and group currency, as you saw in Figure 11.9. You'll also find that all the material price change transactions now support both currencies.

Recall from Chapter 2 that starting with SAP S/4HANA 1610, the Universal Journal allows you to enter up to ten currencies per ledger. The material ledger tables in SAP S/4HANA only support three currencies, so you can no longer directly take the financial accounting currencies or the controlling currencies over into the material ledger. Instead you have to explicitly define the three currencies that you want to use in the material ledger. You'll find more details on these settings in SAP Note 2291076 (Message FML_CUST-010: ML Type Referencing FI or CO Is Not Allowed).

You'll still find all the familiar fields for inventory valuation under **General Valuation Data**, including the **Valuation Class** and the **Price Control** and **Price Determ.** flags that we discussed in reference to Figure 11.1. If you need more details about the impact of the conversion, refer to SAP Note 2267834 (S4TWL: Material Ledger Obligatory for Material Valuation).

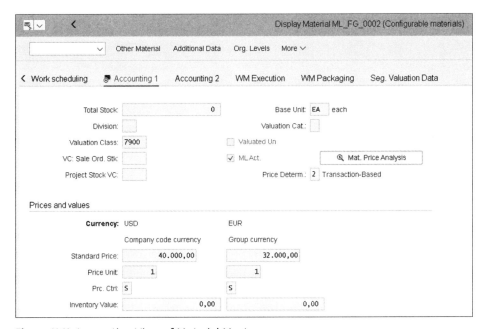

Figure 11.11 Accounting View of Material Master

As a business user, that's most of what you need to know. Behind the scenes, the totals tables have been removed from materials management. The **Total Value** fields in Figure 11.9 and Figure 11.10 and the **Inventory Value** fields in Figure 11.11 are being calculated on the fly using the data in the new table MATDOC, shown in Figure 11.12, which combines the information that used to be stored in tables MKPF and MSEG. Use of this table massively improves performance whenever material documents are captured because the system no longer needs to lock and update the inventory valuation tables (MBEW, EBEW, OBEW, QBEW, and so on, depending on the stock type) and the actual costing tables. These tables have become obsolete, along with the history tables MBEWH, EBEWH, OBEWH, and QBEWH.

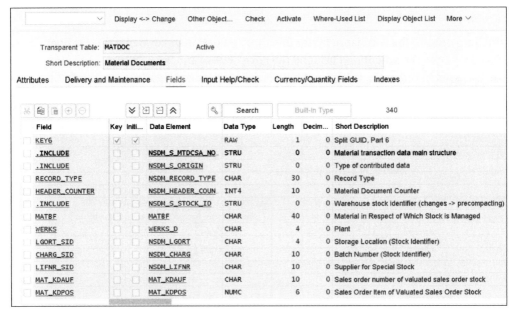

Figure 11.12 Material Document Table

If you look closely at Figure 11.11, you'll notice that it only shows the standard price, not the moving average price. You'll get the very best performance when posting material documents if you deactivate the statistical moving average price. This doesn't mean that you can't use the moving average price any longer, but if you do the system will briefly have to lock the tables to calculate the latest moving average price. You'll find more details in SAP Note 2267835 (S4TWL: Material Valuation—Statistical Moving Average Price).

11.1.3 Handling Multiple Accounting Principles

In Chapter 2, Section 2.2, we discussed the challenges faced by global organizations operating according to several different accounting principles and discussed the need to have a leading accounting principle that was consistent across all entities and local accounting principles to cover the separate needs of Brazilian GAAP, Russian GAAP, and so on.

This can be handled by setting up one ledger for the leading accounting principle and a second ledger to handle the various local accounting principles. We showed the ledger settings in Figure 2.11. In Figure 11.13, we've navigated from the view in Figure 2.11 to the **Accounting Principles for Ledger and Company Code** view to see the accounting principles that have been defined for ledger **0L** and company code **1400**.

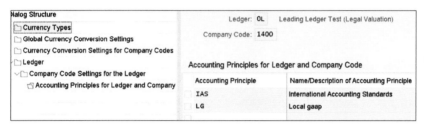

Figure 11.13 Accounting Principles for Ledger and Company Code

Figure 11.14 shows the selection screen for the Material Inventory Values—Line Items app (SAP Fiori ID 1423A). Notice the mandatory fields here: **Company Code** (here, **1710 (Company Code 1710)**), **Ledger** (here, **0L (Ledger 0L)**), and **Reporting Key Date** (here, **10/03/2018**). The results of the selection are shown in Figure 11.15.

Prompts	
Search	🔍
*Company Code:	1710 (Company Code 1710) ⊗
Plant:	
*Ledger:	0L (Ledger 0L) ⊗
G/L Account:	
Product Group:	
Material:	
*Reporting key date:	10/03/2018

Figure 11.14 Ledger Prompt in Inventory Report

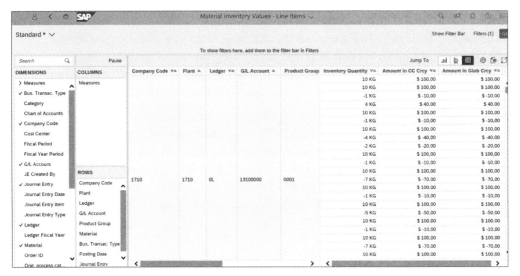

Figure 11.15 The Material Inventory Values—Line Items App

The next step is to decide—for the purposes of inventory accounting—where the accounting principles in your organization differ. The use of actual costing is common in Brazil, Russia, Turkey, and so on, whereas other countries often are happy to stick with standard costs, unless they have highly volatile raw material prices or production processes.

For countries where actual costing is used, the next question is whether the activity rates can be calculated using the same approach in all legislations, or whether there are significant differences in the depreciation of assets or payroll-related costs depending on the legislation. If this is the case, then you might wish to calculate two different activity rates and consequently two separate sets of inventory values. This will require you to activate business function FIN_CO_COGM; this function was initially deactivated in SAP S/4HANA, but it was reimplemented in SAP S/4HANA 1610 and now only works with the ledger approach. Like the group valuation and profit center valuation approaches that we looked at in Chapter 2, this will also require you to set up a currency and valuation profile and assign it to the controlling area.

However, you don't have to use actual costing in every company code; you can activate the additional accounting principles only in those company codes where you want a global accounting principle and a different local accounting principle. Figure 11.16 shows how three different accounting principles have been activated for company code **0001** and displays the different approaches to actual costing used in each case. You'll need to run two separate costing runs at period close to provide the relevant data for each accounting principle.

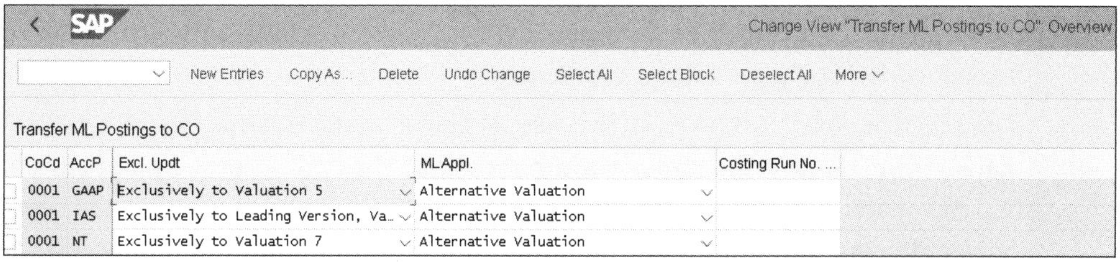

Figure 11.16 Using Different Inventory Valuation Approaches in One Company Code

Another distinction concerns the use of different balance sheet valuations to value inventory at period close. Here countries distinguish between cost-flow-based assumptions (including FIFO and LIFO) and lowest-value approaches (including range of coverage and the lower of cost or market). US-GAAP requires the lower of cost or market price, and IFRS requires the lower of cost or net realizable value. Once calculated, the write-off must be recorded as a journal entry in the appropriate ledger.

Note that SAP has begun reworking the various balance sheet valuations to improve performance and the transparency of the results. SAP S/4HANA Cloud 1811 includes a reworked range of coverage calculation.

We've now looked at the major changes affecting inventory accounting in the Universal Journal. As controllers think about the Universal Journal, their next question is how the costs flow onto production orders, process orders, product cost collectors, and so on in SAP S/4HANA—so let's now look at the major changes affecting cost object controlling.

11.2   Production Cost Analysis

In the previous section, we saw that inventory accounting is legally required to determine the value of the materials held in stock for the balance sheet and to calculate the COGS for the income statement. The next section on production cost analysis discusses more of a management than a financial accounting endeavor.

Production cost analysis is typically in the hands of plant controllers. One of the challenges these personnel faced back in the 1990s was the sheer volume of production orders being processed at any one time and the number of material movements and confirmations being made for these production orders. The result was that the controlling transactions aggregated any data that wasn't considered essential, meaning that less data was recorded than was initially captured during confirmation; this was then missing if the controller wanted to look at the costs of individual operations or being incurred at individual work centers.

If you think back to Chapter 1 and the main elements of the steering model, you'll see that all the manufacturing orders are simply variants on the order theme. You'll still find raw materials being issued to manufacturing orders and finished goods being delivered to inventory as before. You'll typically be accumulating secondary costs to the manufacturing orders in the form of confirmations and overheads. In Section 11.2.1, we'll look at the main changes that affect these manufacturing orders and how to assign the various production variances to general ledger accounts as we did the COGS. We'll then look at the SAP Fiori applications that will support production controllers when they look at manufacturing orders.

As you saw in Chapter 1, Section 1.4.1, the data structure became more granular in SAP S/4HANA, with the information captured in the confirmation being recorded with reference to the operation and the work center. In Section 11.2.2, we'll look at the new data structures in more detail. If you've been holding back on implementing an SAP Fiori project, this might be the moment to rethink that choice because you'll only see this more detailed data in the new SAP Fiori applications. The detail reports that you can access from the production order and process order will continue to show the aggregated view that contains only the cost center and the activity type.

11.2.1   Production Orders, Process Orders, and Product Cost Collectors

From the point of view of the steering model, production orders, process orders, and product cost collectors are just different types of orders that settle to inventory.

You should note, however, that cost object hierarchies and general cost objects are not supported in SAP S/4HANA and that all transactions to create master data and perform period closing tasks on these objects have been removed from the menus. If you're using one of these transactions, you'll find details about what to do going forward in SAP Note 2270411 (S4TWL: General Cost Objects and Cost Object Hierarchies).

As far as integration with production planning goes, you need to know that selection of BOMs and routings for the manufacturing orders always takes place with reference to a production version in SAP S/4HANA. You'll find more information in SAP Note 2267880 (S4TWL: BOM, Routing, Production Version).

For the cost flows themselves, the main change is to the settlement of production variances to profitability analysis. The production variances are calculated and stored as before, but SAP S/4HANA includes a new mechanism that assigns the various production variances to different accounts—just as you saw for the product cost components in Figure 11.5. Figure 11.17 shows the financial document for the settlement of the production variances from a manufacturing order to profitability analysis in the Universal Journal. Again, you'll see a two-step posting, this time in the same document:

1. The first two lines credit the production order and debit the total variance account (here, by **$2,499.30 USD**).

2. The next line reverses the posting to the variance account and splits it to general ledger accounts that represent the different variance categories (scrap, material price variances, material usage variances, activity price variances, activity usage variances, etc.). This function was introduced with SAP S/4HANA and is designed to explain production variances without needing to assign them to value fields in costing-based CO-PA.

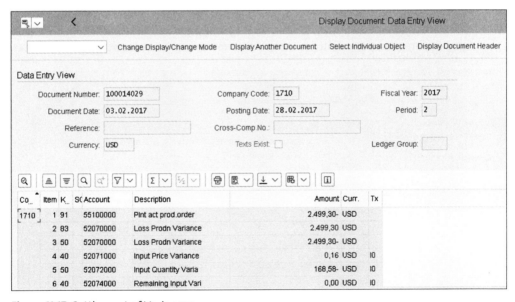

Figure 11.17 Settlement of Variances

To explain the journal entry shown in Figure 11.17, we'll now look at the configuration settings. You can access the splitting profile that controls the process by choosing

**Financial Accounting • General Ledger Accounting • Periodic Processing • Integration •
Materials Management • Define Accounts for Splitting Price Differences** in the IMG.
We're using the **L00000** price differences splitting profile in the example shown in
Figure 11.18.

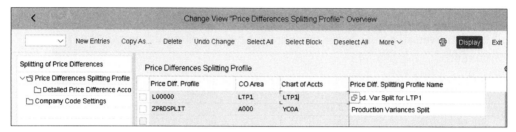

Figure 11.18 Splitting Profile

To see what happens during the split, select the **Price Differences Splitting Profile**
folder on the left side and choose the **Detailed Price Difference Accounts** subfolder.
The result, shown in Figure 11.19, shows that the various variance categories have
been linked with separate accounts. If you want to go finer still and separate the price
variances for material costs from the price variances for activity costs, for example,
you can create separate entries for the different groups of accounts.

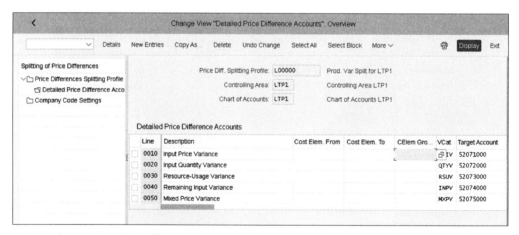

Figure 11.19 Price Difference Accounts

In addition to changing the settlement logic to break the production variances out to
separate accounts, consider using the Production Cost Analysis app (SAP Fiori ID

F1780), shown in Figure 11.20, to find manufacturing orders for analysis. This is available for production orders, process orders, product cost collectors, and rework orders; it provides an alternative to Transaction S_ALR_87013127 (menu path **Controlling • Product Cost Controlling • Product Cost by Order • Object List • Order Selection**), but you'll notice that the selection parameters also include the profit center, which wasn't available in the SAP ERP report.

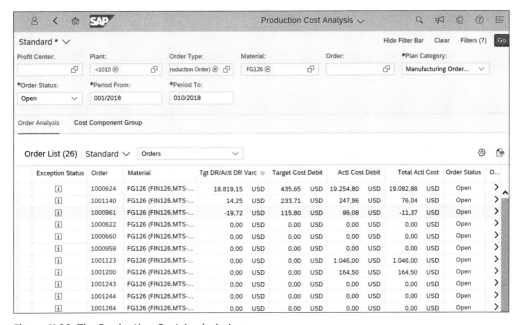

Figure 11.20 The Production Cost Analysis App

The big benefit of using the Production Cost Analysis app may not be immediately apparent, though you might wonder how the plan category relates to the target cost version in the original report. Remember that the *target costs* are calculated by taking the *planned costs* for the order and adjusting them for the delivered order quantity. In SAP ERP, calculating target costs for variance analysis was notoriously fraught with difficulty. The standard cost estimate contained all the relevant logistics information—the operation, the work center, and so on—but the order cost estimate was aggregated into the old CO structures and only included the cost element, the cost center, and the activity type. Period-close functions such as work in process at target costs, scrap at target costs, and variance calculation would call to the production planning tables to find the data they needed for the calculations. This inefficiency prompted the SAP S/4HANA redesign of the table structure for the planned and actual costs, as we discussed in Chapter 1, Section 1.3.1.

However, hiding behind the term **Plan Category** on the user interface is a new way of storing the planned costs with reference to the order. We discussed the unified planning model in Chapter 9 and explained how the planned values for the order are being recorded in full detail in the new planning table ACDOCP. We saw in Figure 9.32 that you can choose between two types of planned costs for analysis here:

- **Manufacturing Order: Standard Cost** corresponds to target cost version 0 in SAP ERP. The costs are selected from the standard cost estimate for the material and adjusted to the delivered quantity.

- **Manufacturing Order: Plan Costs** corresponds to target cost version 1 in SAP ERP. The costs are calculated for the production order and adjusted to the delivered quantity.

You'll also notice that you can select by status in the Production Cost Analysis app, though the application doesn't support linked statuses, which was previously possible using a *status profile*.

To see further details of the order costs, choose the arrow to the right of the **Order Status** column. This will bring you to the **Order Cost Detail** page, as shown in Figure 11.21. The information displayed here will be familiar if you've worked with Transaction KKBC_ORD. Again, you'll be able to scroll among four different views:

- **Target/Actual by G/L Account**
- **Target/Actual by Business Transaction**
- **Work in Process**
- **Target/Actual by Cost Component**

The CDS views used to access the data for this application offer significantly more fields than are shown on the screen. Use the wheel icon to explore the additional options, and consider creating your own views for those that you will use frequently.

The views used to calculate the cost details in Figure 11.21 aggregate data directly from the Universal Journal. The application also offers further views that assign the order costs to cost components using the cost component scheme. Figure 11.22 shows the cost component view.

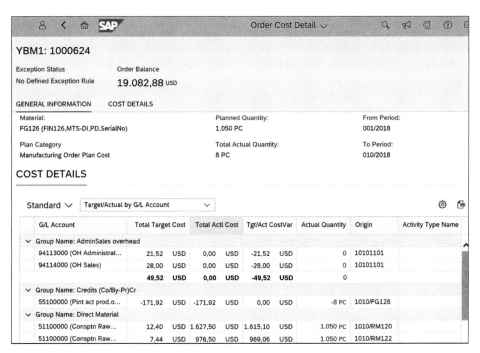

Figure 11.21 Reporting on a Manufacturing Order

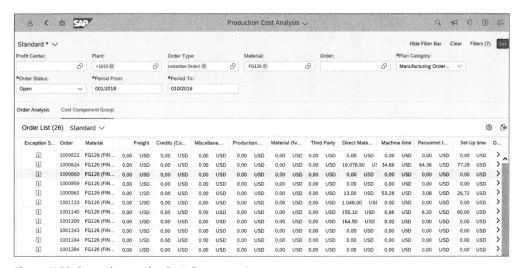

Figure 11.22 Reporting on the Cost Components

11.2.2   Work Centers

Work centers represent the places where operations are performed; they are known as *resources* in the process industry and are used for capacity requirements planning and scheduling in logistics. Every operation in a routing must be assigned to a work center.

Work centers impact finance in that each work center includes formulas that determine how each standard value in the operation is interpreted (*fixed* in the case of setup time and *varying* with the lot size in the case of machine time and labor time). Plant controllers must make decisions about the efficiency of each work center—but in SAP ERP this was somewhat difficult because the work center wasn't available as a reporting dimension in Finance.

As we discussed in Chapter 1, SAP has now added both the work center and the operation to the Universal Journal to provide increased transparency for plant controllers. If the Production Cost Analysis app looks too familiar to excite you, consider a completely different view of the same costs offered in the Analyze Costs by Work Center/Operation app (SAP Fiori ID F3331), shown in Figure 11.23. The changes introduced via the Universal Journal won't be visible in the classic transactions at all, and with the Logistics Information System scheduled for deprecation, the Analyze Costs by Work Center/Operation app could be the new way of analyzing costs for a work center.

Take a close look at Figure 11.23, and notice that **Work Center No.** is one of the selection parameters. SAP S/4HANA will select journal entries for any manufacturing orders that have been processed at that work center and display them in graphical form and in table form. What you're seeing are the costs associated with the manufacturing *activities* performed at that work center. Any other work center-related costs (e.g., maintenance) will be charged to the cost center as before and flow through the activity rate and into inventory. If the work center is idle, then this view will be empty because no production has taken place.

How useful you find this view depends on your master data definition. Manufacturing activities are always assigned to operations and work centers because the confirmation takes place at that level in production planning. Raw material usage will be assigned to the operation only if you've linked the BOM items with the relevant operation in the routing. If you do nothing, then all raw material components will be assigned to the first operation by default. But if you have significant scrap, it makes

business sense to assign the raw materials to the operations at which they are consumed; in this way, you avoid overstating losses through scrap or work in process.

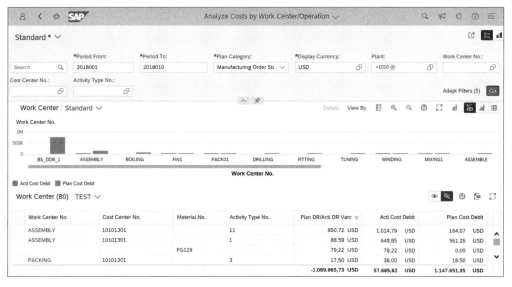

Figure 11.23 Production Costs by Work Center

You might wonder where the word *operation* in the Analyze Costs by Work Center/
Operation app comes into play. You can add both the operation number and the
operation description to the selection parameters in the top part of the screen, especially if you have operations with meaningful titles or numbering. Likewise, you can
extend the graphic in the middle and the table in the bottom part of the screen to
include the operation alongside the other columns.

In Figure 11.24, we've extended the table to display the assigned operation. Notice
how the activity lines are assigned to the work center and operation, but the material
line isn't because the BOM and routing weren't linked. Another option in this application is to enter an individual manufacturing order in the selection parameters to
see the costs for each operation in the individual order.

Production Cost Analysis in SAP S/4HANA Cloud

SAP S/4HANA Cloud allows for controlling using production orders, process orders, and
product cost collectors. The use of coproducts will be supported from SAP S/4HANA
Cloud 1902 onward.

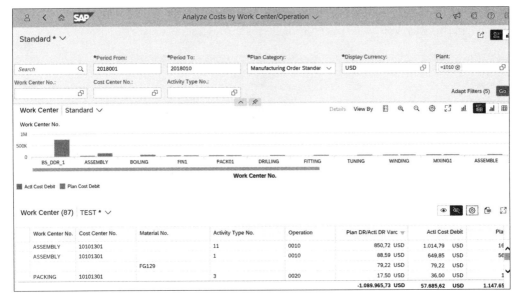

Figure 11.24 Work Center Costs with Details of Operation

To recap, remember that the changes to variance settlement and the SAP Fiori applications to analyze production costs are the main changes in cost object controlling. More significant changes took place in actual costing in SAP S/4HANA 1610, so this is what we'll look at next.

11.3   New Data Structure in Actual Costing

Since we first wrote about a new option to update the COGS with the results of the actual costing run in SAP R/3 4.7 in 2005, we've seen the conversation around actual costing evolve.

The current focus is on data quality and system performance. *Data quality* is important because actual costing depends on reliable base data and process discipline in purchasing, production, sales, and so on, but a move to SAP S/4HANA won't immediately solve data quality issues. *System performance* matters because actual costing reads every goods movement for the period to select the relevant variances and then roll them up; moving to an SAP HANA database certainly helps performance, but the larger benefit comes from the fact that the table structure has been redesigned and the costing run reimplemented in a way that wouldn't have been possible in the late 1990s, when the first customers embarked on their actual costing journeys.

SAP's motivation for reworking actual costing was to simplify processing and improve performance during the costing run.

Look at the periodic costing run, shown in Figure 11.25; from a user perspective, the changes might not look radical—but behind the scenes, the data storage and even the table used to document the status of the steps in the costing run have changed dramatically.

Let's examine the steps in the costing run in SAP S/4HANA, as shown in the actual costing cockpit in Figure 11.25:

1. **Selection**
   Here the system selects the materials for which goods movements have taken place in a period. This step was one of the first to be optimized and is available as an SAP ERP accelerator or with SAP Business Suite powered by SAP HANA. For details, refer to SAP Note 1654778 (ERP Accelerators: Material Ledger—Period-End Closing).

2. **Preparation**
   During this step, the periodic costing run determines the sequence in which materials must be costed in a multilevel structure. In the case of the alternative valuation run, this step performs the cumulation, bringing data together from multiple periods.

3. **Settlement**
   At this stage, the steps for single-level price determination, multilevel price determination, revaluation of consumption, and WIP revaluation have been combined into a single costing step. The fact that the system no longer separates single-level and multilevel price determination has implications for the account determination, making the material account determination Transactions PRV and KDV obsolete.

4. **Post-Closing**
   This step, like the first, was optimized with the first round of SAP ERP accelerators. What changes in SAP S/4HANA 1809 is that this step triggers both the inventory revaluation and the revaluation of the cost component split for the COGS. You'll also need to create a new material account determination Transaction PRL for the credit postings to the cost center.

5. **Mark Prices**
   This step remains unchanged.

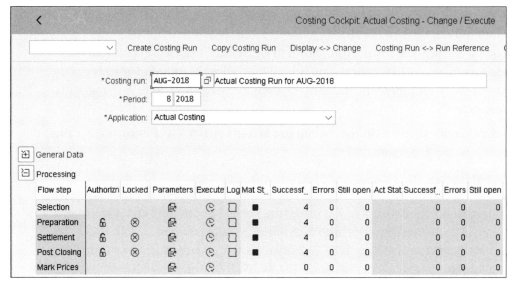

Figure 11.25 Cockpit for Actual Costing

Figure 11.26 shows the results of the actual costing run. You can see the documents for the goods movements that were used as a basis for the valuation alongside the documents that were created during actual costing to revalue consumption and update inventory. Notice that because the price determination structure and the cost components have been combined in one screen, there are significantly more columns than in the SAP ERP report.

Another significant change in the new approach is that the settlement process takes account of both the preliminary valuation and the price differences, rather than just the price differences. In the past, actual costing in SAP ERP required you to keep the preliminary valuation stable for the whole period and didn't allow for a change to the standard price. SAP S/4HANA 1610 made it possible to change the preliminary valuation during the period, if you have a strong business reason to do so. Of course, normally you will still have the idea of a standard cost and be using actual costing to assign variances compared to this standard—but if you create goods movements where there is no standard cost (as might be the case when you move goods through a distribution center), then being able to use the first goods movement to set the initial material price gives you greater flexibility to set material prices dynamically.

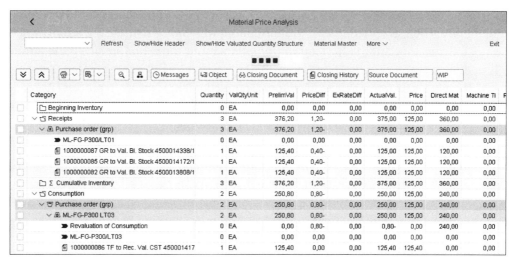

Figure 11.26 Material Price Analysis Following a Costing Run

To get a sense of what postings have been generated during the actual costing run, select a line that was generated during the close and click the **Closing Document** button. Figure 11.27 shows the settlement document created by the costing run.

Figure 11.27 Settlement Document

The main change to the posting logic is for activity price differences, for which a new transaction, Transaction PRL, was introduced with SAP S/4HANA. The activity price differences relating to the total consumption during the period are first posted from the cost center (Transaction GBB-AUI) to the new price difference account (Transaction PRL) and from there to inventory (Transaction PRY) or work in process (Transaction WPA). You'll find further details in SAP Note 2558888 (S/4HANA 1610: Post Closing Logic in Material Ledger/New Actual Costing).

All this is made possible by changes to the underlying data structure. The new document table, table MLDOC (shown in Figure 11.28), replaces many legacy tables (tables MLHD, MLIT, MLPP, MLPPF, MLCR, MLCRF, MLKEPH, CKMLPP, CKMLCR, MLCD, CKMLMV003, CKMLMV004, CKMLPPWIP, and CKMLKEPH); another new table, table MLDOCCCS, replaces the cost component tables (tables MLKEPH and CKMLKEPH). The major concern here is that unlike the shift to the Universal Journal, there are no compatibility views for actual costing. If you've written your own code to handle certain areas of actual costing and that code selects from tables no longer available in SAP S/4HANA, then that code immediately will become obsolete.

This conversion is a significant structural change, so make sure that your IT team is aware of the information in SAP Note 2352383 (S4TWL: Conversion to S/4HANA Material Ledger and Actual Costing).

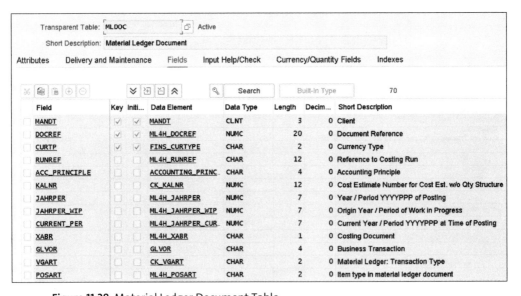

Figure 11.28 Material Ledger Document Table

> **Actual Costing in SAP S/4HANA Cloud**
>
> Actual costing is available as an optional scope item for Brazil from SAP S/4HANA Cloud 1811 onward; for the United States, Germany, and China from SAP S/4HANA Cloud 1902 onward; and as an option for other countries beginning in SAP S/4HANA Cloud 1905.

11.4 Summary

You've now seen that inventory accounting, like asset accounting, changes with the move to the Universal Journal, and we have explored cases in which inventories are valued differently depending on your local accounting principles. In this chapter, we focused on the changes in cost object controlling and in actual costing.

We'll now look at the new options for group reporting in more detail, and especially how these new functions can be incorporated in the consolidation process.

Chapter 12

Group Reporting: Producing Consolidated Financial Statements

This chapter explains the fundamental changes in SAP's approach to consolidation with SAP S/4HANA and how to leverage the data in the Universal Journal as the basis for reporting on the group level.

Any parent entity that controls several subsidiaries is required to present the cumulative assets, liabilities, equity, income, expenses, and cash flow as if they were one economic entity—in other words, to present as a consolidated set of financial statements. To do this, financial data from each subsidiary must be collected and consolidated in order to report by group.

Organizations have both external and internal motivations for conducting such a consolidation. The external motivation is to meet statutory reporting requirements. Financial data from all legal entities (organized into company codes in SAP S/4HANA) need to be brought together, the value of intercompany transactions eliminated, and a consolidated view of investments produced. From a systems perspective, the need to deliver periodic statutory consolidated statements at a fairly aggregated level can be achieved successfully using the classic approach to consolidation.

The second motivation is to develop a clear perspective for internal business-steering purposes. To eliminate transactions between management entities, the different profit centers or business units within the organization need to be consolidated. This process often takes place over several levels to deliver both a group view and a divisional view. However, monthly consolidated figures don't generally provide sufficient details to support leadership in steering the business and making the right decisions, whether for the division or business unit, or for the group as a whole.

In Chapter 7, we introduced the idea of continuous accounting as a way for finance departments to deliver insights to a business at the entity level throughout rather than after a period. Enabling these insights on the level of an individual entity is a good first step—but because many decisions are made on the level of a business unit or group, the continuous accounting principle also should be applied to the management level.

Only then can finance deliver the right information during a period to support decision-making.

While the SAP portfolio includes several consolidation tools, including SAP Business Planning and Consolidation (SAP BPC), SAP Financial Consolidation, SAP Enterprise Controlling Consolidation System (SAP EC-CS), and SAP Strategic Enterprise Management Business Consolidation (SAP SEM-BCS), SAP decided that the best way to answer these consolidation requirements was to bring the best of these different consolidation solutions together to deliver one new consolidation engine: SAP S/4HANA Finance for group reporting. This solution is designed to sit directly on top of SAP S/4HANA and leverage the single source of truth already provided, with the Universal Journal as its starting point, as we explained in Chapter 1. Technically, the group reporting solution is integrated into the SAP S/4HANA environment, but it's a separately licensed component.

To explain how the group reporting solution in SAP S/4HANA is different from the classic consolidation approach applied when using tools such as SAP Business Planning and Consolidation or SAP Financial Consolidation, in this chapter we'll first look at the classic approach and the basic principles of the group reporting solution in Section 12.1. Once this is clear, we'll discuss the key consolidation dimensions in Section 12.2, focusing on trading partners and group accounts, currencies, and intercompany information. The purpose of this section is not to deep-dive into each individual consolidation function (e.g., intercompany elimination, consolidation of investments, and all other real consolidation tasks), but to explain the integration points with operational accounting and give you a holistic view of the SAP S/4HANA capabilities for finance.

The group reporting solution runs natively in the SAP S/4HANA environment; however, not all organizations run a single SAP S/4HANA environment containing finance information for all their subsidiaries. Large multinationals often have a heterogeneous system landscape that includes SAP ERP and non-SAP systems. For this reason, we'll explore the different options to integrate nonconsolidated data from different sources into the group reporting solution in Section 12.3.

12.1   Consolidation Solutions

At a high level, we can understand the group reporting solution as a milestone in the evolution of consolidation solutions. To see the progression, let's start by looking at the "classic" approach to consolidation. This approach applies to any organization not already running SAP S/4HANA, as well as to any organization running SAP S/4HANA that uses one of the existing consolidation solutions.

12.1.1   Classic Consolidation

In the classic approach to consolidation, organizations connect their SAP and non-SAP source systems that contain nonconsolidated financial data to their consolidation solution. As shown in Figure 12.1, this means that the subsidiaries' entity data is copied into a data warehouse and then processed by the consolidation tool or transferred to the consolidation environment directly by uploading spreadsheets containing the figures for the smaller subsidiaries.

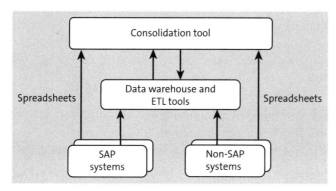

Figure 12.1 Classic Consolidation Architecture

Either route results in high effort, often requiring a lot of data transformation (e.g., to translate from local charts of accounts into a group chart and to convert all submitted values into group currency), a time delay, and an additional reconciliation effort, along with substantial validation of the submitted figures. If not correctly monitored, this process can easily result in data quality issues. Moreover, in most cases nonconsolidated data is only transferred to the consolidation tool on an aggregated level, instead of at the transactional level. This classic approach to consolidation generally provides the aggregated data by trading partner for legal consolidation or by business unit for matrix consolidation, so it focuses on the flows of values between entities at a high level.

However, from a managerial accounting perspective, the classic approach does not fulfill the need for more granular information. Organizations are interested in more detailed information so that they can steer their entire business. To do this, they need to understand the flow of goods and services between divisions and to evaluate the success of individual product groups and regions, rather than focusing solely on the affiliated companies in the value chain. This is especially true when many different legal entities are involved in manufacturing a product or delivering a service and when there is a substantial time lag involving holding profit in inventory across the value chain.

After all, steering an organization is a continuous effort! These detailed insights therefore should be available at any moment a decision needs to be made, not just at month end after the periodic consolidation process has been executed. Multinational organizations seek to understand the relative performance of their regions and product groups throughout the accounting period, not in the middle of the following month.

For organizations with a small amount of intercompany business, these classic consolidation systems and processes might be sufficient. For others, it's essential to ensure that timely information is available to manage the business.

12.1.2   Group Reporting

As we've just discussed, the classic model of consolidation can't help organizations if their business demands much faster access to group-wide decision-support information. They can't afford to wait for their data to be moved to a data warehouse, run through the various validation and transformation processes, and then consolidated.

That's why SAP set out to develop a new strategy for consolidation that combines the benefits and power of existing solutions into a single consolidation tool by working with a common data model. The single consolidation tool needed to accomplish several things:

- **Create a fully unified framework for local and group-level reporting**
  As its work on consolidation progressed, SAP developed a consolidation process that placed the SAP BPC consolidation engine on top of the Universal Journal. In theory, this approach, known as Real-Time Consolidation, offered a group closing directly on the nonconsolidated entity information, meaning that the local close and group close was already based on a single source of truth. However, because of the SAP BPC–specific user interface, Real-Time Consolidation didn't bring a fully integrated experience to the end user; a fully unified framework for local and group-level reporting was still missing.

- **Cover the entire flow from collecting, processing, and analyzing data up to the publication of reports**
  It was critical that the solution differentiate between planned, actual, simulated, and predicted data, as well as varying reporting cycles. For this reason, tight integration with SAP Analytics Cloud would be key.

- **Connect quantitative and qualitative data**
  For group-level reporting, both nonfinancial measures and notes and other qualitative data are as important as the numbers themselves. A new framework should

support not only annotations but also communication between stakeholders when preparing group reports.

- **Be deployable in the cloud**
Today, many organizations deploy a combination of on-premise and cloud applications as the source of their financial consolidation data. In the future, cloud-based consolidation may be the only preferred method, so a new solution should be deployable in the cloud or on premise to help organizations as they transition their IT and financial operations to the cloud.

To deliver a consolidation solution to customers that would meet these requirements, additional development was necessary.

Recall from Chapter 1 that a centralized, transaction-level steering model—the Universal Journal—was introduced with SAP S/4HANA. This means that if the different entities that need to be consolidated are running SAP S/4HANA, then all nonconsolidated financial data is available within this Universal Journal. (Of course, there might be situations in which not all entities are included in a single SAP S/4HANA instance, but we'll come back to combining financial information from different SAP and non-SAP systems in a single SAP S/4HANA instance in Section 12.3.) So let's assume that we have all nonconsolidated financials together. Rather than copying all data to a consolidation tool, why not bring the consolidation engine directly into the environment in which the source data already sits?

This is the idea behind the group reporting solution. As shown in Figure 12.2, the group reporting solution sits in the same environment as local accounting—resulting in real-time access to the local data from within the consolidation solution. This allows for a direct interrogation of the source data. If the delivered data exceeds certain thresholds, a group accountant can immediately view the underlying data records to understand what has caused the problem.

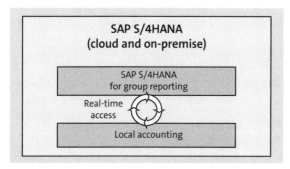

Figure 12.2 Architecture of Group Reporting in SAP S/4HANA

Let's consider the impact of running legal and management consolidation integrated in SAP S/4HANA. The first big improvement centers on data quality. You don't need to move or transform your data, which eliminates the risk of reconciliation issues. This architecture means that both entity close and group close can be based on shared master data in the form of accounts, cost centers, profit centers, and so on. But it also means that when running local accounting and group accounting in a single environment, postings can be validated immediately on release to the group reporting solution because the validation rules (which are part of the consolidation engine) are immediately available. The same logic applies to other preparatory consolidation steps, like translation into group currency. The group reporting solution uses the figures for reporting dimensions captured in the Universal Journal, but it also has its own entities, such as *consolidation units* (used to structure the various business units for the purposes of elimination), *consolidation groups* (used to bring the consolidation units into a hierarchy), and *financial statement items* (used to group the accounts).

The second improvement relates to the realization of continuous close on the consolidated level. Being able to validate entries at the source means you can translate a financial posting into group currency at the time of the initial posting. The consequence is that time-consuming preparation tasks for consolidation no longer need to be executed as part of the group closing process. Therefore, group reporting supports the move toward continuous accounting (which was discussed in Chapter 7).

Figure 12.3 shows what happens when the preparation steps for consolidation (data upload, currency translation, validation checks on the nonconsolidated figures, intercompany reconciliation) are executed in both a classic approach and the SAP S/4HANA integrated approach. As shown at the bottom of the figure, the group reporting solution moves tasks out of the period close so that only the genuine consolidation steps remain to be performed within the close. In the new workflow, because the data load is no longer needed and the currency translation is already complete, the only steps left to execute at period end are the intercompany elimination and specific consolidation calculations. Therefore, the time spent to run the consolidation process is significantly reduced.

In addition, time can be saved by performing data validations immediately to check the plausibility of the data from the subsidiaries. These might be simple checks such as whether the data for certain items exceeds a threshold compared with the previous period, or they can include more complex logic to determine whether the posting is allowed. The group reporting solution includes a new validation rules framework that makes it easy for non-expert users to set up rules and validate against these rules; this way, group accountants can be sure that they're dealing with reliable financial data in the steps that follow.

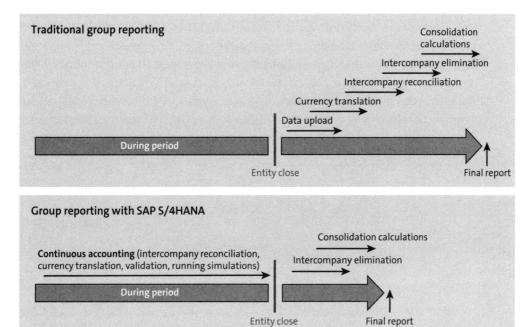

Figure 12.3 Comparing Classic Group Reporting and SAP S/4HANA for Group Reporting

Moreover, a consolidation run *within a period* becomes an option—at least when the relevant postings are available from the subsidiaries. Consequently, the principle of continuous accounting now also can be enlarged to include group financial figures as well. Do note that we don't expect SAP to provide real-time legal consolidation because some of the underlying postings will be missing during a period, such as the revaluation of open receivables and payables. Instead, we expect SAP to work on providing a *managerial view* of the situation that gives detailed insight into the income statement by delivering divisional or group-level figures.

The third improvement is that this setup provides unprecedented transparency. Organizations can drill down from consolidation items to the document line items of the entity because all data is found back in the single source of financial information: the Universal Journal. This immediately builds trust in the user community that the figures are valid and allows users to reallocate their effort from manual checks to value-adding activities.

This all ties back into the overall view to run financial reporting directly from the SAP S/4HANA environment itself by making use of the embedded reporting capabilities: no matter whether you run an entity-level report in an SAP Fiori–based analytical application or run it on the divisional or group level, the way you report is exactly the same. As you can see in the group balance sheet report in Figure 12.4 and group cash flow statement in Figure 12.5, embedded reporting capabilities are applied in the same way to deliver instant insights on the group level, as we discussed in Chapter 5. The only difference is that the account hierarchy is based on financial statement items, rather than being in a flat list. Notice also how the local reporting dimensions that we discussed in Chapter 1 are available for drill-down alongside the group reporting-specific consolidation units and consolidation groups in the left-hand **Dimensions** panel.

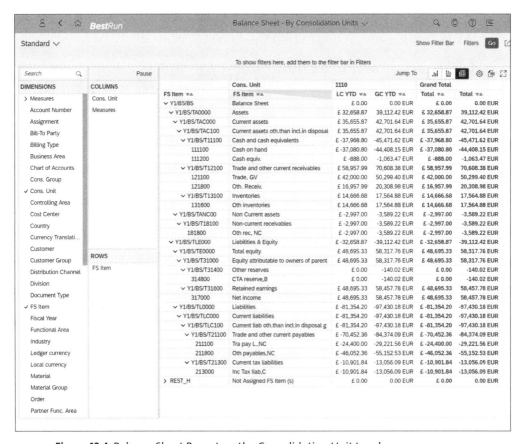

Figure 12.4 Balance Sheet Report on the Consolidation Unit Level

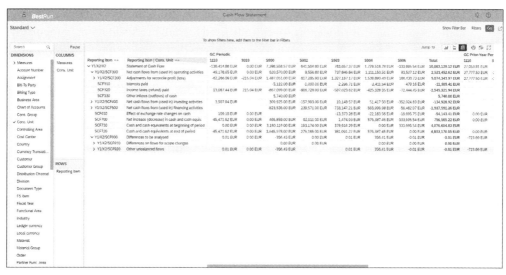

Figure 12.5 Cash Flow Statement on the Consolidation Group Level

One of SAP BPC's strengths inherited by the group reporting solution is its rule-based reporting, which classifies individual reporting lines for embedded reporting. The setup of reporting lines is illustrated in Figure 12.6, in which you can see the link between the financial statement items and the reporting lines. This means that reports can be built dynamically for a relevant version and period, but the account structure and posting logic in the underlying data remain stable.

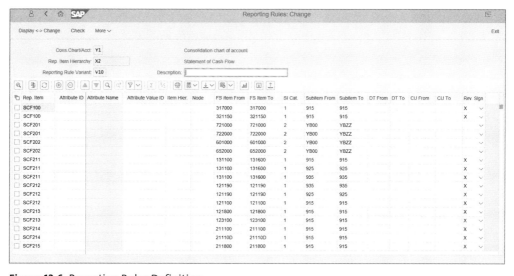

Figure 12.6 Reporting Rules Definition

Linked to this, the so-called flow principle is inherited from the SAP Financial Consolidation solution. This concept is specifically used for balance sheet items, supporting the creation of a consolidated cash flow statement that takes into consideration the correct cash movements. Notice the column **SI Cat.** (subitem category) in this context, which is used to identify the movements for the cash flow statement. These flows were visualized in the Cash Flow Analyzer app that we showed as an example of an SAP Fiori application in Chapter 5.

One of the key strengths of the SAP Enterprise Controlling Consolidation System (SAP EC-CS) and SAP Business Consolidation (SAP SEM-BCS) solutions was the accounting document principle, which means that each consolidation task results in an auditable consolidation posting. These consolidation postings cover the initial data load; automatic postings for interunit eliminations, investment eliminations, and so on; and manual postings for corrections. This is also how consolidation postings are added to the Universal Journal. The application of this document principle is illustrated in Figure 12.7, which shows an example of a reclassification item. Looking at the details, you can see the line items of each posting, including the item type that identifies the type of posting, the financial statement item posted to, and both the consolidation unit and partner.

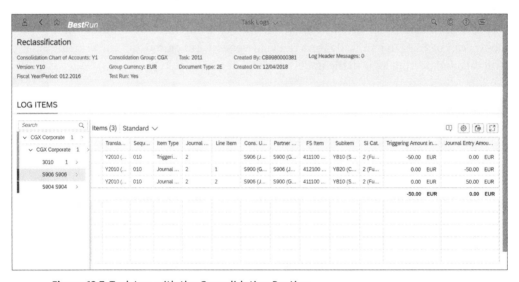

Figure 12.7 Task Log with the Consolidation Posting

The consolidation process itself is another area in which the group reporting solution leverages previous development. It uses two monitors that were previously used in the SAP EC-CS and SAP BCS solutions: the Data Monitor to track data collection and preparation tasks, and the Consolidation Monitor (shown in Figure 12.8) to follow up on the consolidation steps themselves.

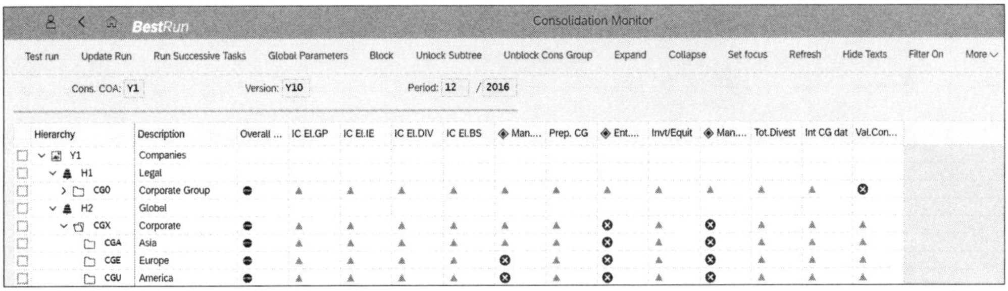

Figure 12.8 The Consolidation Monitor

Note that the Consolidation Monitor is helpful for monitoring the group closing process, but the long-term goal is to have a single process follow-up in place for both local close and group close. This is where the evolution to the advanced financial closing solution (as explained in Chapter 7) comes into play.

So far in this chapter, we've tracked the progress from classic consolidation to the group reporting solution and outlined where it offers advances for SAP S/4HANA customers. Now let's take a closer look at the reporting dimensions that are relevant for consolidation.

12.2 Group Reporting Dimensions

You've already seen that the group reporting solution runs on top of the Universal Journal and that there are multiple ways in which all nonconsolidated data can be brought together. Now let's take a deeper look at how the data model works.

Recall from our discussion of financial planning in Chapter 9 that the Universal Journal consists of different tables: actuals are stored in table ACDOCA, and plan data is stored in table ACDOCP. However, as shown in Figure 12.9, a third table becomes relevant: table ACDOCU.

Table ACDOCU contains all records created by the group reporting solution (remember that consolidation postings are made with the group reporting solution) plus any financial data from non-SAP sources that are uploaded using the applicable data acquisition logic. This applies not only to actuals, but also to other versions of data collected in this way.

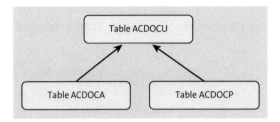

Figure 12.9 Universal Journal: Tables ACDOCA, ACDOCP, and ACDOCU

In Chapter 9, we explained that the Universal Journal contains all reporting dimensions and that planning processes use a subset of these dimensions to set and monitor targets. The group reporting solution also uses a subset of the reporting dimensions in the Universal Journal as the basis for consolidation. Figure 12.10 shows the FC07_ S_ACDOCU_ADD include (Additional Fields in Consolidation Journal Entries in SAP S/4HANA), which contains the reporting dimensions for operational reporting in the Universal Journal. The idea is that these dimensions can be consumed directly as reporting dimensions for group reporting. Notice that you have direct access to the operational chart of accounts and the accounts therein and that the next set of fields is for the general ledger account assignments that we discussed in Chapter 1.

	Structure:	FC07_S_ACDOCU_ADD		Active			
	Short Description:	Additional Fields in Consolidation Journal Entries in S/4					

Attributes   Components   Input Help/Check   Currency/quantity fields

Built-In Type   41

Component	Typing Method	Component Type	Data Type	Length	Decima...	Short Description
KTOPL	Types	KTOPL	CHAR	4	0	Chart of Accounts
RACCT	Types	RACCT	CHAR	10	0	Account Number
XBLNR	Types	XBLNR1	CHAR	16	0	Reference Document Number
ZUONR	Types	DZUONR	CHAR	18	0	Assignment number
.INCLUDE	Types	ACDOC_SI_GL_ACCAS		0	0	Universal Journal Entry: G/L additional account assignments
RCNTR	Types	KOSTL	CHAR	10	0	Cost Center
PRCTR	Types	PRCTR	CHAR	10	0	Profit Center
RFAREA	Types	FKBER	CHAR	16	0	Functional Area
RBUSA	Types	GSBER	CHAR	4	0	Business Area
KOKRS	Types	KOKRS	CHAR	4	0	Controlling Area
SEGMENT	Types	FB_SEGMENT	CHAR	10	0	Segment for Segmental Reporting

Figure 12.10 Fields from Universal Journal Used in the Consolidation Journal

It's always been possible to use fields such as **Profit Center**, **Segment**, and **Business Area** for group management reporting—but with the group reporting solution, you now can use a finer granularity and access projects and orders and all the market segments in profitability analysis. What's important here is that you ensure that all the reporting dimensions that you plan to use in group reporting are captured in the Universal Journal so that they are directly accessible without transformation.

An example of this is shown in Figure 12.11. Reading from left to right, the first columns (**Is Master Data**, **Has Hierarchy**, and **Superordinate Field**) describe the general data model for group reporting. The next fields (**Enable Inputs** and **Use as Master Data**) determine whether these fields will be used in group reporting. Notice that only a subset of the available fields has been selected here, and that we're sharing master data here. There is no transformation step to convert the operational accounts, cost centers, and so on for the purposes of consolidation. The data in the Universal Journal is being selected directly.

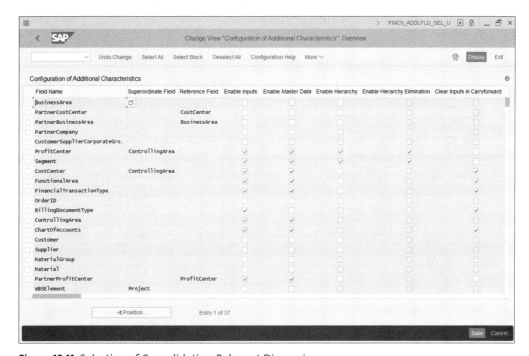

Figure 12.11 Selection of Consolidation-Relevant Dimensions

You can imagine the chosen fields in this table as the base layer for consolidation, along with the amounts in group currency. With this base layer in place, the group reporting solution can begin to perform the eliminations and reclassifications needed to provide the consolidated financial statements. These are stored as auditable documents in the group reporting solution. Going forward, the local documents could be enriched to provide the information needed for group reporting.

We have seen that hierarchy information is used in combination with many of the fields shown here. The definition of these hierarches is made using the Manage Global Accounting Hierarchies app (SAP Fiori ID F2918) that we introduced in Chapter 5. This is another example of how the entity-level accounting world and the consolidation world are coming together in SAP S/4HANA.

Now we've taken an overall look at what types of functionality are in play in terms of base consolidation logic, reporting, process monitoring, and so on, let's touch on the key dimensions in the SAP S/4HANA data model that are important to run a consolidation.

12.2.1   Trading Partners and Group Accounts

Simple consolidation systems are two-dimensional, in that they contain the trading partners (the affiliated companies) and the accounts to be used for legal consolidation.

In Chapter 1, we discussed the way that accounts and cost elements were merged in the Universal Journal so that all reporting could be based on the account. In Chapter 2, we discussed the challenge of combining local legal reporting requirements with the group reporting requirements in terms of the accounts used. Historically speaking, many organizations have worked with three charts of accounts: the group chart of accounts for group reporting, the operational chart of accounts for local reporting, and a country-specific chart of accounts that handles local requirements tied to specific account names and taxonomies.

For the purposes of consolidation, the practice of mapping tables has been used to translate the operational accounts into group accounts, working with a combination of account and functional area where needed. The big step forward in the group reporting solution is that you can work with the operational charts of accounts directly and simply map them to the relevant financial statement items; this greatly simplifies the process of merging the group and entity close because in terms of the accounts they use, both sides are "speaking" the same language. However, this pushes the requirement for a consistent chart of accounts back to the local accountants—but even so, it's clear that if the base data can be delivered in a consistent structure, huge time savings are possible in the consolidation process.

Assigning trading partners to each vendor and customer (*business partners* in SAP S/4HANA) is key to understanding which companies have traded with one another and need to be included in the intercompany elimination. This process in SAP S/4HANA remains the same as in SAP ERP. You can also assign trading partners to general ledger accounts directly as before. This is the key information for understanding which companies have traded with one another and need to be included in the intercompany elimination process. With the combination of the accounts and the trading partners, you have the starting point for consolidation in group reporting.

As we discussed earlier in the chapter, group reporting also goes beyond this two-dimensional model and allows you to directly access other account assignments in the Universal Journal, including the cost center, profit center, segment, functional area, and so on, orders and projects, and the market segments in profitability analysis (see Figure 12.10). The challenge here is to determine how fine the group reporting process should become and which reporting dimensions should be included in the data model for group reporting, since there's a chance to use finer granularity than in a classic matrix consolidation (see Figure 12.11).

Of course, group reporting also has its own entities. The *consolidation unit* is the smallest unit in the group reporting structure; consolidation units can be combined within *consolidation groups* for processing in the group reporting solution.

12.2.2 Currencies

In Chapter 2, we discussed the new options to add additional currencies to the Universal Journal. At present, the group reporting solution stores three currencies (transactional currency, local currency, and group currency).

Currency translation—in which the values submitted by the various subsidiaries in their local currency are translated into a common currency prior to consolidation—typically has been one of the first steps in traditional consolidation. With SAP S/4HANA, all accounting documents in the Universal Journal are stored in a local currency and global currency. The group reporting solution can work directly with the group currency in the Universal Journal or make its own currency conversion to enrich the data using conversion rules defined for group reporting. When a conversion is made, the new solution includes a task log that allows the group accountant to understand how the conversion has been performed and explain any translation differences.

12.2.3 Intercompany Information

Recall from Chapter 4 that intercompany reconciliation is often considered a preparatory step for group reporting. The idea here is to ensure that the value of the open item requested by one affiliated company matches the value of the open item recorded on the other side or triggers a correction process to make the related postings match.

The group reporting process goes further and eliminates the values of open items between affiliated companies based on a set of business rules, creating consolidation documents that eliminate these items from the group financial statements. Again, the new solution delivers a protocol that explains the intercompany elimination postings.

We discussed the group view for intercompany trading in Chapter 2. From a local legal perspective, the selling company applied a profit margin when it invoiced the receiving company. However, this profit margin must be eliminated from a group perspective because the profit can be realized only at the end of the value chain, when the goods reach the final customer. Again, the group reporting process creates consolidation documents that eliminate intercompany income and expenses from the group financial statements. This is different from the process of passing values "at cost" into the group view for management reporting in the Universal Journal.

Any finished goods, work in process, and stock in transit in inventory at period close generally also carry this profit markup as part of the inventory value. Again, this markup must be identified and eliminated from a group perspective because from a group perspective the profit can only be recognized when the goods reach the final customer. The group view in the Universal Journal will show only the cost view for these inventories, rather than creating elimination postings.

Another key aspect of group reporting is the consolidation of investments and the elimination of investments and equity. This is an example of a pure consolidation step that is outside the scope of the Universal Journal, which simply collects the relevant business transactions but doesn't carry any information about the investment of the parent in the subsidiary. This ownership information is entirely the domain of the group reporting solution.

12.3   Consolidation Data Sources

Given the complexity of SAP S/4HANA customers' financial and IT landscapes, not all organizations maintain a single SAP S/4HANA environment for all legal entities. Of course, the group reporting solution sits on top of the Universal Journal, so this data somehow needs to be accessed.

For such companies, there are two approaches: using either SAP Group Reporting Data Collection or a Central Finance deployment.

12.3.1   Data Collection Application

The first option is to transfer nonconsolidated figures from specific sources into the SAP S/4HANA environment in which the group reporting solution is located. This is classic data acquisition from source systems.

To support this process, including the ability to manually enter additional source data, SAP offers the cloud-based SAP Group Reporting Data Collection, which runs on SAP Cloud Platform.

SAP S/4HANA customers can use this solution to load SAP or non-SAP accounting data into the consolidation environment in multiple ways:

- Send data through a specific API.
- Upload generated or manually created files.
- Set up manual data entry forms and provide these to subsidiaries, which in turn provide the required financial data by filling in the forms.

Figure 12.12 shows an example of the manual data entry forms. On the left side, you can see a series of predefined forms for several types of data required for consolidation (**Profit and Loss, Balance Sheet Accounts Detailed by Partners, Summary Layouts**, etc.). On the right side, you can see an open P&L entry form.

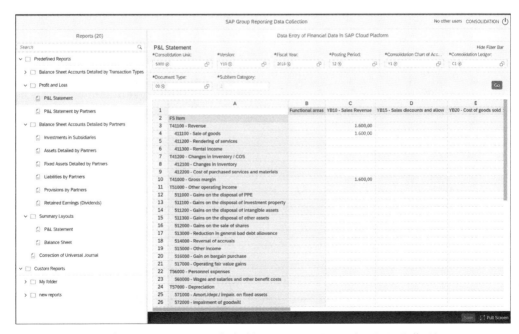

Figure 12.12 Manual Data Entry Form Included in SAP Group Reporting Data Collection

There are a few functionalities of SAP Group Reporting Data Collection to highlight. First, this manual data entry method also can be used to enrich automatically provided data with manual additions.

Second, the data acquisition application allows for more than just a single user simply entering data. Multiple concurrent users can work on data entry, and user-specific working parameters that have been integrated with group reporting can be applied. All data changes are tracked by dedicated document type, including user and time-stamping information for each entry. To lower the risk of false data entry, forbidden dimension-member combinations are pulled from the group reporting model and indicated as display-only in the data entry form, with a reason included. Users can improve data entry and transfer to/from the entry grid, clipboard, spreadsheet, and so on using a multicell copy-and-paste capability.

Finally, when using spreadsheets for data preparation, integrated templates for manual adjustments, two-sided elimination, and group-dependent adjustments are provided. Prior to importing journal entries, a precheck can be executed to validate the data.

12.3.2   Deployment Using Central Finance

Let's consider the combination of financial information from different sources in a broader context.

Imagine, for instance, that you are part of an organization that regularly acquires new companies. From a financial reporting perspective, it's of high importance to have access to a complete financial overview across the entire organization as quickly as possible, even though operational integration of the newly acquired entity might take some time.

This is one of the original use cases for a Central Finance deployment of SAP S/4HANA. This deployment method puts a specific instance of SAP S/4HANA in place and connects the different SAP or non-SAP source systems to it. Technically, this architecture means that every financial posting in the source system is replicated in the Central Finance environment—and because the Central Finance instance is a standard SAP S/4HANA setup, all the replicated financial postings that end up in Central Finance technically end up in the Universal Journal in the SAP S/4HANA Central Finance instance. (Also, because this is a standard SAP S/4HANA environment, solutions like the group reporting solution can be activated easily within the Central Finance system.)

So independent from the mergers and acquisitions use case, this architecture facilitates an interesting approach to ensuring that all financial information from different entities initially posted in different systems can be brought together in a single SAP S/4HANA environment (within which the group reporting functionality then can be applied). It should be noted that deploying an SAP S/4HANA environment as a Central Finance instance requires an additional license.

Let's consider how data flows into the Central Finance instance for consolidation purposes, as shown in Figure 12.13:

- Financial postings from an SAP source system are transferred on the fly into the Universal Journal and can be transformed into a common structure using mapping rules so that the group reporting solution can easily consume the financial data collected.

- Financial postings from non-SAP instances are not immediately transferred in real time but are *nearly real-time*. In this situation, mapping source and destination data models usually is also more complex; for this reason, SAP partners with Magnitude to add intelligence to understand data model structures from non-SAP applications.

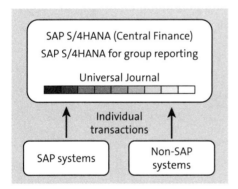

Figure 12.13 Group Reporting in a Central Finance Architecture

12.4 Summary

In this chapter, we introduced the new consolidation solution embedded in the SAP S/4HANA environment, the group reporting solution. Its first iteration was released in May 2017 as part of SAP S/4HANA Cloud; since then, with the arrival of SAP S/4HANA

Cloud 1808 and on-premise SAP S/4HANA 1809, the solution's functionality has evolved to cover regular legal and management consolidation. Although this is SAP's latest consolidation solution (and it also represents SAP's future path), it's worth noting that classic consolidation solutions remain valid, especially in standalone and non-cloud-based environments. We recommend reviewing the product availability matrix (*www.sap.com/pam*), which documents the availability of each SAP solution.

Meanwhile, more functionality for the group reporting solution will be released in the coming quarters—perhaps even weeks after the publication of this book!—so we recommend that you keep an eye out for new developments. One area of new development might center on the process of creating an annual report that includes both financial and nonfinancial as well as both structured and non-structured information. It also includes the capability of delivering officially required consolidation reports in the right electronic format eXtensible Business Reporting Language (XBRL) to governmental bodies.

Now that we've reviewed group financial reporting, in the next chapter we'll dig deeper into the cash flow report we showed in Figure 12.5 and explain how cash management changes with SAP S/4HANA.

Chapter 13
Cash Management: Improving Cash Operations

One of the key innovations of SAP S/4HANA has been the fundamental reorganization of cash data to give organizations better visibility into cash-related operations and information. This chapter introduces the "new" cash management and SAP Fiori applications for bank account management, cash operations, and liquidity forecasting and planning.

Cash management is the functional process of collecting and distributing cash. Its main purpose is to ensure an organization has access to the liquidity needed to support its activities in the short, medium, and long term.

Although many business processes have an impact on the organization's cash situation, most activities are executed under the responsibility of departments outside the cash manager's purview. Therefore, cash managers should concentrate on setting up strict rules for cash and liquidity, including appropriate approval workflows for payments and bank accounts. To keep a close grip on the cash situation, cash managers should understand the impact of any business transaction on the procure-to-pay and order-to-cash processes in real time and should be able simulate potential actions to optimize the cash situation daily.

In addition to understanding the cash situation, cash managers should keep an eye on external factors, such as regulations like Single European Payments Area (SEPA), the Sarbanes-Oxley Act (SOX), International Financial Reporting Standards (IFRS), and European Market Infrastructure Regulation (EMIR), which impact cash. They should similarly understand the impact of increased globalization by developing a clear view of cash across multiple currencies, markets, and time zones. Finally, cash managers should grasp the potential benefits of new technologies like big data, predictive analytics, and machine learning in the cash management context.

With its new SAP S/4HANA for cash management solution, which comes with a specific license, SAP has responded to cash managers' current requirements. By making cash management an integral part of SAP S/4HANA, SAP has given organizations tighter control of the end-to-end cash management and liquidity planning processes. Depending on the organizational setup, basic cash operations–related activities (including control of payments and bank communication) are also on the agenda of different finance and other business professionals. We'll focus our discussion on cash management here; though more advanced treasury-related activities are also part of this end-to-end view, core treasury activities are out of scope for this book because they would need to be addressed in much more detail.

In this chapter, we'll go over the main components of the cash management solution. The basis of cash management is bank master data. In Section 13.1, we'll explore how banks, bank accounts, house banks, and house bank accounts are all maintained centrally in specific SAP Fiori applications that are part of the Bank Account Management (BAM) component. That all these items are now master data and not configuration is a significant change from the classic approach applied in the past.

In Section 13.2, we'll explore the execution of cash operations in SAP S/4HANA for daily cash positioning. Cash position reports allow cash managers to analyze the exact source of a cash flow by drilling down to the individual line-item and even document levels.

A third component, liquidity management, focuses on planning future cash flows in different forms. As we'll cover in Section 13.3, there are different types of forward-looking views into the cash flow on a trajectory that begins with creating insights into realized cash flows and continues in the direction of forecasted cash flows. Some cash flows are already registered in the system but haven't hit the bank account yet. Looking at the longer term, future cash flow projections also can be set up. The actuals and forecasted cash flows can be used as a basis for longer-term projections (called *liquidity plans*) because all three are based on the same analytical structure.

Before we begin, we want to highlight two architectural changes for cash management in the SAP S/4HANA context. The most important evolution is that all cash management–related processes run on the *single source of cash information*. In line with the evolution within finance in SAP S/4HANA overall, in which the Universal Journal is the single source of financial truth, for cash management the single source is called the *One Exposure from operations*. This is a fundamental difference from how cash data was organized in SAP ERP, in which the liquidity planner and cash management ran on completely separate data models.

The second important difference is more generic: thanks to the in-memory technology (i.e., SAP HANA) on which SAP S/4HANA runs, there is no longer any need to store subtotals or aggregates. Now, all roll-ups of data can be executed on the fly in real time—a paradigm that applies to cash management as well.

New Cash Management

Readers who have worked with SAP ERP environments should note that the "new" cash management solution in SAP S/4HANA replaces the classic components for cash management completely. Cash position and liquidity forecast reports from the SAP ERP world have been replaced by new SAP Fiori–based reports. As far as cash planning is concerned, the former liquidity planner is replaced by a set of new SAP Fiori applications as well, as we'll discuss in Section 13.3.

Now let's look at each component in more detail.

13

13.1 Bank Account Management

Bank account management is all about the setup and maintenance of banks and bank accounts, as well as house banks (i.e., banks through which an organization runs all payment transactions) and house bank accounts. Both the bank and house bank master data elements are maintained within the BAM component. They are maintained similarly.

This may sound like a basic element, but it's crucial for an organization to have a complete view of all bank accounts, especially in more complex organizational set-ups. Bank account management enables the cash manager to own the process of maintaining bank master data.

Let's take a more detailed look at bank accounts and approval workflows.

13.1.1 Bank Accounts

In contrast to the way banks and house banks were handled in SAP ERP configuration, in SAP S/4HANA they are treated as master data.

As shown in Figure 13.1, this means the master data is created immediately in the productive system ❶ and then needs to be replicated in other systems including the development ❷ and quality assurance system ❷ₐ. Once the master data is available in the development environment, the necessary configuration settings are made and tested in the quality assurance environment ❸ ❹ ❺ before being transported to the production system ❻.

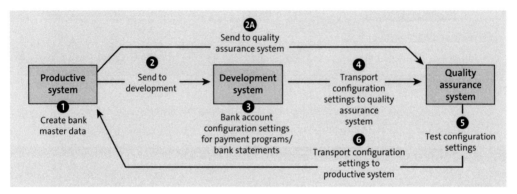

Figure 13.1 Bank Account Management Process Flow

Understanding how bank accounts are replicated within an SAP system landscape is the first step. But the core value of the BAM component is that it enables centralized management of the bank master data and the cash management system at large. Not every organization has a single productive SAP S/4HANA environment, so managing bank accounts centrally across systems is a significant step forward: all opening and changing processes can be maintained in a single BAM instance, with a potential link to satellite systems, including SAP S/4HANA environments, SAP ERP environments, and even non-SAP systems.

From an operational perspective, this means that bank master data elements are maintained using specific SAP Fiori applications accessible to end users, who might be cash managers or analysts; for example, the Manage Banks app (SAP Fiori ID F1574) is used to create banks and house banks. After the house bank is created, bank accounts can be set up for it in the Manage Bank Accounts app (SAP Fiori ID F1366A).

In addition to these basic master data elements, additional items can be set up. The Bank Hierarchy View app (SAP Fiori ID F1366) shows the hierarchical relationship of banks within a banking group, as shown in Figure 13.2. All attributes for the individual bank accounts, including a description, the bank key, and the status (whether it's active), are included. Users can alter the view as necessary.

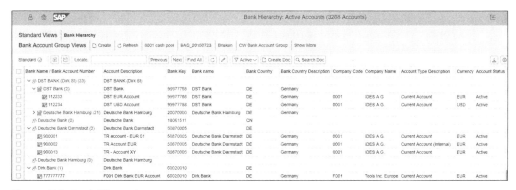

Figure 13.2 Bank Hierarchy

Note that a bank hierarchy is not the same as a bank account group. A *bank account group* is used to group bank accounts based on regions, areas of responsibility, or any other business criteria. Bank account groups are also used as the basis for defining cash pools.

As part of the bank account master data itself, general data (e.g., account number, holder, opening date, etc.), overdraft limits, and payment signatories are defined. These signatories are required to define the appropriate approval authorizations for executing payments.

In addition, documents related to the bank account management process (e.g., signed contracts, copies of signatory IDs, etc.) also can be stored within the system thanks to embedded document management system capabilities.

13.1.2 Approval Workflows

Within SAP S/4HANA, a standard workflow is available in the BAM component for designing the bank master data management process, and covers opening, closing, and changing bank master data; changing signatories; adapting specific attributes; and so on. Alternatively, organizations can set up their own specific workflows, which are centrally managed using SAP Fiori applications. For example, the My Bank Account Worklist app shows all worklist items to be executed and their statuses.

Let's discuss some of the key activities within the master data management process, starting with the opening of a new bank account. For this operation, security is crucial, and multiple stakeholders are involved. The predelivered workflow starts from the request to open a bank account; this request must be reviewed and approved

13

before negotiations with the bank start. When the account is finally opened, detailed account information is added in the BAM component. From a technical perspective, the new bank account then needs to be added in payment and bank statement processes. This means configuration in the development system.

Bank accounts need to be reviewed on a regular basis; in some cases, this is even legally required. Therefore, the review process is also supported within the BAM component; you can use the Bank Account Review Status Monitor to monitor the progress of the review process. Figure 13.3 shows the initiation of the review process.

Figure 13.3 Selecting Bank Accounts to Initiate a Review

Coming back to the signatories, a specific SAP Fiori app, Maintain Signatory (SAP Fiori ID F1372), allows organizations to perform mass maintenance of these signatory rights for users across multiple accounts.

Bank account management is the foundation of cash management. Now let's turn our attention to cash operations, another fundamental element.

13.2 Cash Operations

Once the required bank master data is set up in the BAM component, the SAP S/4HANA system is ready to support cash managers in their daily operations as they review the cash position, understand cash distribution, analyze whether there's room to invest free cash in the short term (e.g., by paying vendors earlier and thereby taking advantage of cash discounts), and so on. These activities are supported via the cash operations capabilities within SAP S/4HANA for cash management.

Let's take a more detailed look at how the cash management solution supports these typical cash manager tasks.

13.2.1   Bank Statement Management

The first task typically executed is to check whether all bank statements have been loaded and investigate any technical issues internally or with the connected bank.

For this purpose, SAP S/4HANA offers the Bank Statement Monitor KPI, which displays the percentage of successfully loaded bank statements. In Figure 13.4, this is **100%**. Cash managers can click the KPI to see more details and get a clear view into whether all further analyses and activities performed are based on up-to-date information.

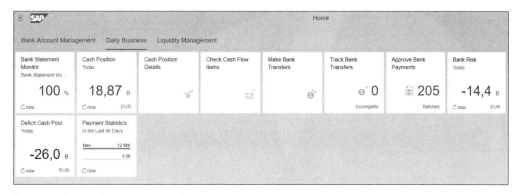

Figure 13.4 Bank Statement Monitor KPI

13.2.2   Cash Position Analysis

Once all bank statements have been loaded successfully, analysis of the short-term cash position can start.

The idea here is to understand how much cash the organization has on hand by reviewing the cash position, including insights into where cash is distributed among entities, countries, and banks. In SAP S/4HANA, you do this through the Cash Position app (SAP Fiori ID F1737), shown in Figure 13.5. The application allows you to analyze the cash position via different dimensions: bank country, bank group, company, bank and currency, currency and country, and currency.

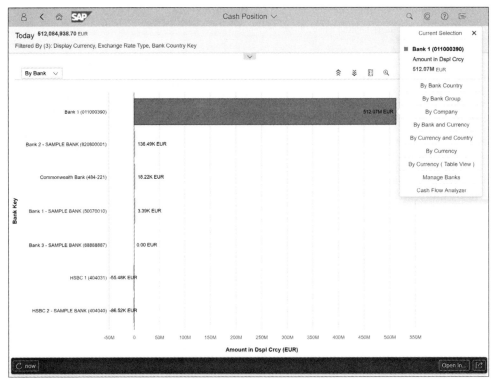

Figure 13.5 Viewing Cash Position by Bank

From this high-level analysis, you can drill down into more details via several different options—including the cash position details, which shows the daily cash position (starting with the value date), including overdue items, cash flow for various days, and so on for each bank account. For each individual date, you can check the opening balance, cash flows, and forecasted closing, with the opening balance being carried forward from the previous day's closing balance.

Forecasted cash flows are structured by planning levels, indicating the degree of certainty of the cash flow. These forecasted cash flows include both financial payments (inherited from the SAP S/4HANA payment programs) and manual payments, planned cash flows from financial instruments (inherited from the treasury management solution), and memo records. You can also display additional information beyond what's already delivered by default, like sales order, purchase requisition, purchase order, and scheduling agreements. Overdue cash flows (which have a value date in the past) are shown separately; you can analyze individual cash flow items for more details.

Figure 13.6 and Figure 13.7 illustrate how the cash position can be easily analyzed using the Cash Flow Analyzer app (SAP Fiori ID F2332). This is the central place to check cash flows from different types of sources. We want to highlight a few key elements in this application:

- **The flexibility and level of detail of the report structure**
  You can adapt the order in which you drill down by currency, company code, and bank account to fit your reporting needs.
- **The graphical indicator for the cash flow direction**
  The red and green arrows show whether cash is incoming or outgoing.
- **Planning levels**
  These indicate the level of certainty at which the forecasted cash flows may turn into actual cash flows.
- **The time period and level of granularity of the report**
  These can be changed easily by the user.

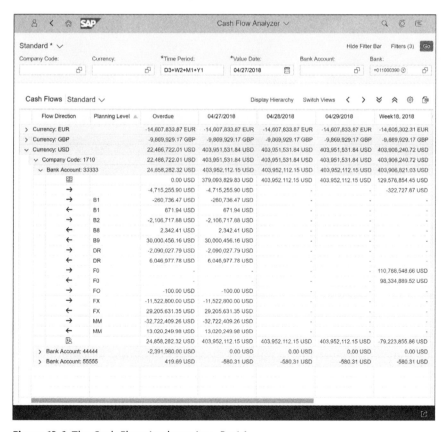

Figure 13.6 The Cash Flow Analyzer App: Part 1

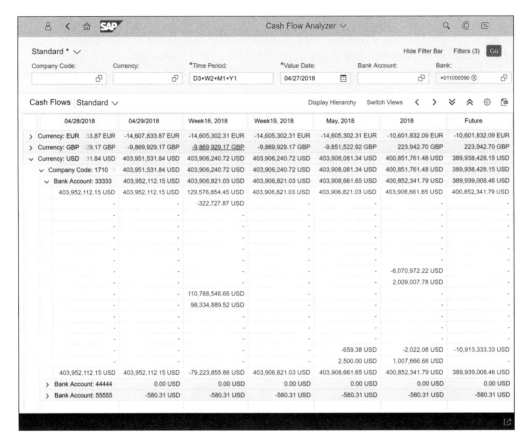

Figure 13.7 The Cash Flow Analyzer App: Part 2

Let's take a closer look at the columns in Figure 13.6. The report starts with a column for the overdue items (the **Overdue** column), followed by the structured cash flow for various days, starting with the value date and another column for cash flows with a later value date (the **04/27/2018**, **04/28/2018**, and **04/29/2018** columns). For each date, the opening balance, cash flows, and forecasted closing balance is shown; the opening balance is carried forward from the closing balance of the previous day.

In the header of the example, the **Time Period** field is defined as **D3+W2+M1+Y1**, meaning that the cash flow is presented on a daily basis for the first three days, after which a weekly total is given for the upcoming two weeks, followed by a summary on a monthly basis for the following month, and then the cash flow is aggregated at the level of the year for the first upcoming year. This becomes clear when you look at the column headers of both figures: Figure 13.7 shows the columns **Week 18, 2018**, **Week**

19, 2019, May 2018, 2018, and **Future**. By changing **W2** to **W4**, you could detail the future on a weekly basis for four weeks instead of two weeks, starting from the value date.

13.2.3   Cash Transactions

Once bank statements have been processed and managers understand the cash position, cash transactions can begin. Let's explore bank transfers and payment approvals, memo record management, and cash concentration.

Bank Transfers and Payment Approvals

The most important cash transaction is the creation of bank transfers. These can take place for different types of reasons, such as payments to third parties and intercompany transfers. However, before bank transfers can be executed, they first need to update the cash position and be approved so that managers can verify the impact on the cash position upfront.

The Make Bank Transfer app (SAP Fiori ID F0691) shows the day's forecasted closing balance for each bank account. From there, SAP S/4HANA creates a payment request and executes the payment run. To make bank transfer approvals more transparent, you can use the Approve Bank Payments app (SAP Fiori ID F0673A).

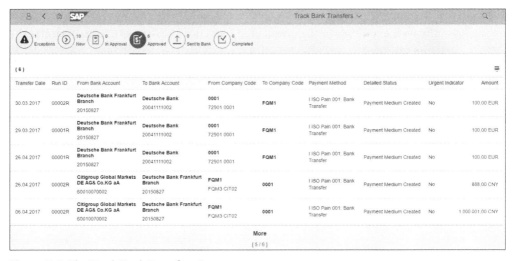

Figure 13.8 The Track Bank Transfers App

If your organization has installed Bank Communication Management, a separate component in SAP S/4HANA, then the payments are merged and the approval process is started. To give the cash department a clear view of all transfers and potential exceptions, the approval status, and the overall status (whether already sent to the bank or confirmed by the bank), the Track Bank Transfers app (SAP Fiori ID F0692) has been added in the cash management solution (see Figure 13.8).

Memo Record Management

To register *potential* cash in- and outflows that are still uncertain, cash managers can create memo records to update the cash position immediately.

This is an interesting way to see the cash position (including these types of nonconfirmed elements) and to enable cash managers to confirm whether cash is truly available or whether additional internal or external funding is required. If a transfer doesn't take place, the memo record can simply be removed.

Regarding these memo records, it's critical to understand that they only update the cash management solution reports. No accounting records are involved in any way because we're only talking about potential impacts.

Cash Concentration

Cash pooling is a centralized cash management strategy involving several related bank accounts; the objective is to reduce external debt and increase the available liquidity by maximizing both current credit and debit cash positions to optimize the use of the surplus funds of all subsidiaries in a group. In SAP S/4HANA, cash pools are based on bank account groups; you can define more than a single cash pool in one bank account group.

One of the most common use cases of cash pools is to reduce costs by consolidating cash. In some cases, *cash concentrations* (i.e., the consolidation of cash from diverse accounts) are based on bank services; however, because this is sometimes unavailable or expensive, manual cash concentration is also possible. Within the Process Cash Concentration app (SAP Fiori ID EPIC_FF73), a transfer amount is proposed automatically, based on the forecasted closing balance of the day and on the planned balance and the minimum transfer amount. Once the cash manager reviews the proposal, a payment request is created within the application; from there, the standard payment request program is activated, posting the payments to the bank clearing accounts and generating the medium file sent to the bank.

13.3 Liquidity Management

In the previous section on cash operations, we focused on actual cash flows and projected cash flows based on actuals. In addition to this view, cash departments are interested in a forward-looking view of the liquidity of the organization so that they can hedge against long-term currency fluctuations and develop financing strategies. This is where the third key component of the cash management solution, liquidity management, comes into play.

Overall, within the cash management solution, multiple views to help analyze cash flow data for different time horizons are available via different applications. As shown in Figure 13.9, some applications are meant for historical analysis, whereas others look ahead one to five days, up to 24 weeks, or beyond. Therefore, the applications offer different kinds of analysis:

- *Cash flow analysis* analyzes cash flows that have already materialized—in other words, actual cash flows that have already hit the bank account or another cash equivalent account. As we'll discuss in Section 13.3.1, this allows cash departments to understand where their cash is coming from and where it's going, which will help them compare the realized cash flow with planned cash flows.

- Whereas cash flow analysis focuses on history, *cash position analysis*, as discussed in Section 13.2.2, shows the cash balance and forecasted balance for the current day and the next few days. Both are important views for managing cash, but they're not the same.

- *Liquidity forecasting* takes a longer view, focusing on cash flow data already in the system with future value dates and creating insights into actions that have a cash impact in the future. These insights are based on information from purchase orders, sales orders, received and issued invoices, and other applications. As we'll discuss in Section 13.3.2, the liquidity forecasting application delivers a view of the short- and medium-term liquidity situation of an organization.

- The *liquidity planning* application is significantly different from these other liquidity applications because it's based on plan data from planning activities instead of data that's already in the SAP S/4HANA environment. To execute manual long-term planning, liquidity planning reuses the embedded SAP Business Planning and Consolidation (SAP BPC) planning functionality integrated in the SAP S/4HANA environment. On top of this planning engine, a predefined planning process is delivered by SAP, as we'll discuss in Section 13.3.3.

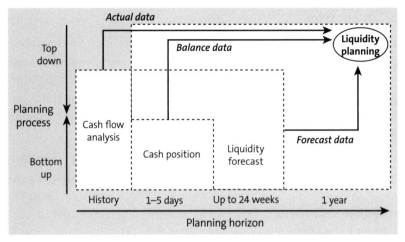

Figure 13.9 Time Horizon for Liquidity Management Applications

The SAP Fiori launchpad, shown in Figure 13.10, brings these different components together to make it easy for cash managers to combine insights.

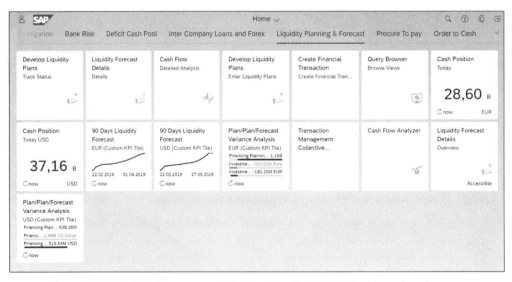

Figure 13.10 Liquidity Management Applications in the SAP Fiori Launchpad

13.3.1   Cash Flow Analysis

Whereas it's quite simple to link the cash flow to bank accounts, currencies, and other attributes based on the bank statement information, it can be harder to trace a specific cash movement back to its source. The main reason it can be difficult is that this information and the realization of the cash flow happen at different moments in time. As a simple example: the original purchase order (or another cash flow–originating action) might have been created 30 days, 60 days, or even longer before the moment the actual cash flow occurs to the bank account. Recall from Section 13.2.2 that the Cash Position app focuses on the link between cash flow and a bank account or other attributes; the Cash Flow Analyzer app (SAP Fiori ID F2332) focuses on the specific source.

In liquidity management, the liquidity item is used to indicate the source (nature) of a particular cash movement. This information about the nature of the cash flow mostly sits in the revenue and expense items of the accounting document. The document flow is analyzed by liquidity management personnel to automatically assign the correct liquidity item (e.g., purchase of goods, purchase of services, sales of good/service, other revenues or expenses, investment interest, dividends, interest payments, etc.). For reporting purposes, liquidity items can be grouped into hierarchies. This enables you to report easily on operational versus investment versus financing cash flow, for instance.

13.3.2   Liquidity Forecasting

The liquidity forecast functionality in the cash management solution creates insights into actions that have a cash impact before they hit the bank accounts; this is typically two to six months into the future.

Like the Cash Flow Analyzer app mentioned in the previous section, the SAP Smart Business Liquidity Forecast app provides an overview of the current liquidity forecast and shows a trend of the forecasted closing balances. Figure 13.11 shows the tiles for these two applications side by side; they both offer the same kind of information in the same visual format.

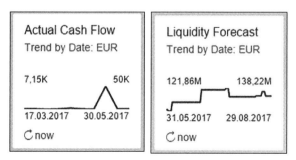

Figure 13.11 The Cash Flow Analyzer and Liquidity Forecast Apps

Drilling into the details of the Liquidity Forecast app, the cash manager can analyze the daily forecasted closing balanced and net cash flows for the next 90 days. In addition to this SAP Smart Business application, the Liquidity Forecast Details app (SAP Fiori FO741A) displays opening balance, net flow (i.e., forecasted net cash flows by future date), and closing balance, as shown in Figure 13.12. To analyze the detailed cash flows behind a net cash flow of a specific date, you can click any item in the report.

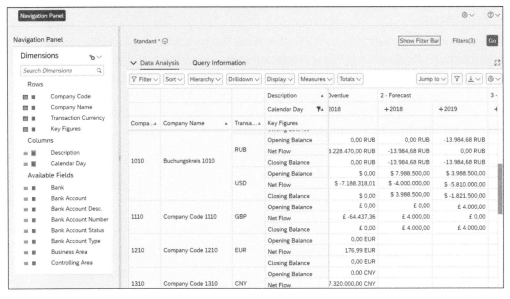

Figure 13.12 The Liquidity Forecast Details App

The details page of the Liquidity Forecast Details app doesn't contain any balance information because it focuses on forecasted cash flows. As with the actual cash flow analysis application, the structure of the report is based on the liquidity items hierarchy here (as is the case for many other reports).

13.3.3   Liquidity Planning

Now let's move beyond the insights created from actual information already available in the SAP S/4HANA environment.

Long-term liquidity plans are based on budget forecasts, sales forecasts, headcount projections, payroll plans, and potentially many other planning activities. Although transactional information already available in SAP S/4HANA *can* also be used as a basis for long-term liquidity planning, liquidity planning is mostly based on manual or automated planning activities and logic. The liquidity item represents the source and use of cash flows in an organization; along with organizational dimensions (e.g., profit center or legal entity) and cash flow characteristics (e.g., currency), it's one of the key planning dimensions in long-term liquidity planning.

Recall that the liquidity planning logic in the cash management solution is based on the SAP BPC engine integrated in SAP S/4HANA. This is in line with the broader option of organizing financial planning based on this technical architecture, as we discussed in Chapter 9. This setup not only makes it possible to support an organization's liquidity planning process from a calculation perspective via the available SAP BPC planning functions, but also enables you to streamline the liquidity planning process. It supports multiple approaches to planning, including a bottom-up approach.

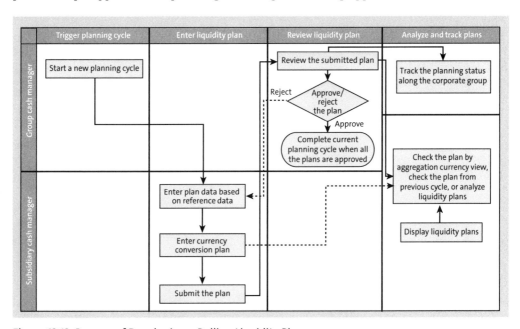

Figure 13.13 Process of Developing a Rolling Liquidity Plan

Let's focus on the template approach delivered as part of liquidity management. This template includes a 12-month rolling liquidity planning scenario that manages the planning process and monitors the status of the planning cycle. Overall responsibility sits with the group cash manager, who, as shown at the top left of Figure 13.13, typically triggers the planning cycle. From there, the subsidiaries' cash managers get an email or workflow item, from which they can click links to open the application. Individual cash managers can access different planning activities and reporting and analysis capabilities. Local cash managers can enter plan data, perhaps including suggested amounts proposed by the system for different liquidity items. Group cash managers also can look at foreign currency information to define a currency hedge plan.

When local cash managers submit their plan data to the group level for review, plan data is automatically aggregated. The last phase is to analyze and track an existing plan; thanks to built-in reporting capabilities, variance analyses can be performed to compare forecasted figures to actuals on all organizational levels.

Next, let's look briefly at how this process works in SAP S/4HANA. Group cash managers who trigger the planning cycle are using the workflow capabilities (known as *business process flows*) within the integrated SAP BPC solution. As shown in Figure 13.14, individual planning steps and screens can be linked to a specific user, period, and so on.

Figure 13.14 Triggering the Planning Process Using Business Process Flows

Based on this step, individual planning users receive a notification via SAP workflow capabilities or via email, after which planning activities start. These activities can be performed using a browser or the SAP Analysis for Microsoft Office add-on; this means that the user accesses a Microsoft Excel grid like the one shown in Figure 13.15.

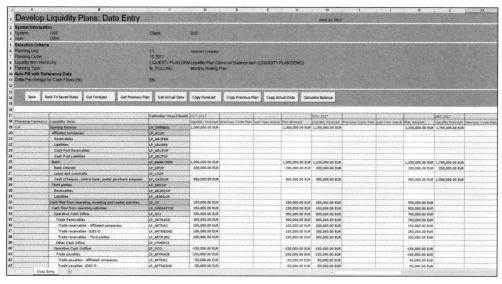

Figure 13.15 Excel-Based Frontend for Plan Data Entry

Zooming into the level at which liquidity is being planned, note the following:

- From the organizational structure perspective, the planning unit is the entity for which a separate liquidity subplan is made. Multiple planning units are rolled up using a planning unit hierarchy.

- From a data perspective, one of the important changes for planning in liquidity management (compared to the classic liquidity planner prior to SAP S/4HANA) is the option to include real-time actual and forecasted liquidity data as a basis for the planning exercise.

Once the plan entry and calculation are finalized, the plan for the individual planning unit can be submitted. At this time, the group cash planner starts the approval activity. This again is managed and monitored from the business process flows, as illustrated in Figure 13.16.

13

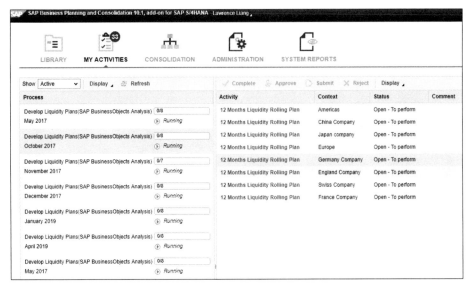

Figure 13.16 Submitting the Plan for a Specific Planning Unit

The final step is analysis to ensure the organization is making appropriate cash-related decisions based on the SAP S/4HANA reporting capabilities. SAP Fiori applications such as the Liquidity Forecast app (SAP Fiori ID FO521A) shown in Figure 13.17 are available to help draw conclusions from this cash management data.

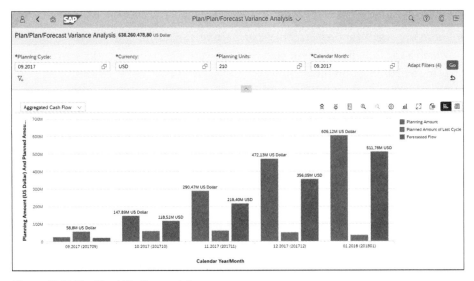

Figure 13.17 The Liquidity Forecast App

13.4   Summary

We've all heard the mantra: cash is king. Yet despite its apparent importance, cash is often pushed to a corner and handled by the cash manager alone.

However, as we explained in this chapter, the need for a clear view into cash across the business—not just within the cash department—is a key element in understanding the health of any organization. With the cash management solution in SAP S/4HANA, the entire topic of cash operations, the related master data management, and the forward-looking view that is needed by organizations have been completely reorganized to facilitate better visibility into cash operations, cash position, and overall cash flow. The new architecture for bank account management, cash operations, and liquidity management capabilities running on the SAP S/4HANA platform—with the One Exposure for operations table as the data centerpiece—impacts actuals and short-, mid-, and long-term forecasting information.

Looking ahead, the SAP Analytics Cloud solution will become increasingly important in the field of cash forecasting and liquidity planning. This is in line with the overall increased use of SAP Analytics Cloud for planning scenarios, as we discussed in Chapter 9.

Now that we've addressed the cash management topic, in the next chapter we'll look at taxes—another finance topic too often treated in isolation.

13

Chapter 14

Tax and Legal Reporting: Ensuring Compliance with Key Requirements

Facing increasing and changing tax rules and regulations, organizations need a holistic approach to determine, calculate, and report taxes. In this chapter, we'll explore indirect tax elements in the overall SAP offering and concentrate on how these solutions reduce risks and costs associated with noncompliance.

Like cash management, tax and legal reporting requirements are often neglected as organizations consider their overall finance requirements. Because these topics are typically handled by teams of tax and legal reporting specialists with expertise in meeting local and global requirements, they often fall outside the day-to-day concerns of their operational peers in the greater finance organization. However, as we'll see in this chapter, the increasing complexity of tax and legal reporting regulations are transforming tax and legal reporting from a peripheral finance topic into a genuine finance driver.

Before jumping into the evolution of legal and tax reporting requirements and the specific solutions that address them, we shouldn't overlook the basic requirement of having access to the necessary *country versions* of SAP S/4HANA, designed to allow you to run your business operations in a particular country.

Country versions do not constitute separate application components. Instead, the country-specific functions are contained in the various application components. This means that financial accounting in SAP S/4HANA, for example, contains not only generic functions, but country-specific functions as well. All the SAP-standard country versions are mutually compatible. This means, for example, that you can use the country versions for Brazil, China, and Turkey in a single physical system.

Every country version is based on the generic functions in the standard SAP S/4HANA system—that is, those functions that are shared by the majority of countries, such as general ledger accounting. In addition to the generic functions, country versions also include country-specific functions. These are functions that are only used in a particular country or region and cover needs arising from local legislation or business practices. They include the following:

- **Localized versions of generic functions**
  Some generic functions are heavily localized, such as the numerous value-added tax reports covering the needs of different countries. Other generic functions may only have to be localized for fewer countries; for example, the vendor payment history report is available in a generic form and as a Singaporean version.

- **Functions not otherwise covered by the generic functions**
  An example of this is manufacturing cost sheet used in South Korea.

Country Versions

Note that the term *country* doesn't necessarily indicate the existence of a nation state.

As of SAP S/4HANA 1809, the following country versions are available for SAP S/4HANA: Argentina, Australia, Austria, Belarus (delivered as an add-on), Belgium, Brazil, Bulgaria, Canada, Chile, China, Colombia, Croatia, Czech Republic, Denmark, Egypt, Estonia, Finland, France, Germany, Greece, Hong Kong, Hungary, India, Indonesia, Ireland, Israel, Italy, Japan, Kazakhstan, Kuwait, Latvia, Lithuania, Luxembourg, Malaysia, Mexico, Netherlands, New Zealand, Norway, Oman, Peru, Philippines, Poland, Portugal, Qatar, Romania, Russia, Saudi Arabia, Serbia, Singapore, Slovakia, Slovenia, South Africa, South Korea, Spain, Sweden, Switzerland, Taiwan, Thailand, Turkey, Ukraine, United Arab, Emirates, United Kingdom, United States, and Venezuela. Further details are also available in SAP Note 2349004.

As of SAP S/4HANA Cloud 1811, the following country versions are available for SAP S/4HANA Cloud: Australia, Austria, Belgium, Brazil, Canada, China, Denmark, Finland, France, Germany, Hong Kong, Hungary, India, Indonesia, Ireland, Italy, Japan, Luxembourg, Malaysia, Mexico, Netherlands, New Zealand, Norway, Philippines, Poland, Romania, Saudi Arabia, Singapore, Spain, South Africa, South Korea, Sweden, Switzerland, Taiwan, Turkey, United Kingdom, United Arab Emirates, and United States.

Related to country specifics, although less driven by legislation, is language support. The language in which your users operate the system is independent of your choice of country version. In general, 39 languages are supported in SAP S/4HANA. However, for multitenant SAP S/4HANA Cloud, SAP offers 22 languages at the time of publication (spring 2019).

Looking at recent evolutions, different national and international official agencies have increased their demands for transparency from the organizations they tax. Commonly known examples include the following:

- The Goods and Services Tax (GST) is applicable in different ways across several areas of the world.

- The Standard Audit File for Tax (SAF-T) is an electronic XML format for efficient transfer of accounting data from companies to tax authorities or external auditors.

- *Nota fiscale electrônica* (NFE), or *nota fiscal*, translates as *invoice* or *receipt* in English. In Brazil, this refers to an official document that proves the existence of a commercial act (i.e., the buying and selling of goods or the provision of services). It's issued to meet the requirements of Brazilian tax collection, the transit of goods, and transactions between buyers and suppliers.

- Immediate Supply of Information on VAT (SII) refers to the obligation in Spain to file VAT registry data electronically in real time.

- New regulations around e-invoicing, for example, makes it possible for tax authorities to dig into relevant transaction data to cross-check declared amounts.

Another trend is the shift away from direct taxes applied on organizations' incomes (e.g., income tax, corporate tax, wealth tax, etc.) and toward indirect taxes applied based on consumption or transactions such as the manufacturing or sales of goods and services (e.g. sales tax, service tax, excise duties). New tax practices necessitate new analysis of external requirements and implementation of corresponding software solutions.

Taken together, proper management of these tax and legal reporting requirements is critical to a company's financial well-being. Therefore, SAP offers a holistic approach to legal and tax reporting requirements. Let's focus on the following two new capabilities that come with SAP S/4HANA:

- SAP S/4HANA for advanced compliance reporting is a platform that handles all legal reporting requirements in a period so that organizations can centrally access all reports in a single solution rather than looking into different areas within the system or even a patchwork of solutions.

- From a tax calculation perspective, a multisystem landscape makes it difficult and costly to ensure accurate and harmonized tax calculation. This issue is being addressed by SAP Localization Hub, tax service, which connects tax management across cloud and on-premise applications like SAP S/4HANA and peripheral applications.

Let's now focus our discussion on SAP S/4HANA for advanced compliance reporting in Section 14.1 and the tax service in Section 14.2.

14.1   Legal Reporting with SAP S/4HANA for Advanced Compliance Reporting

In this section, we'll look into the advanced compliance reporting solution that is technically embedded in SAP S/4HANA. *Compliance* is a generic term referring to conforming to a rule, but what's really meant here is conformance with all legal and statutory reporting requirements, including tax reporting.

First, we'll look at the classic approach to legal reporting and how this is changing with the introduction of the advanced compliance reporting solution. Then we'll look at the extended capabilities of the solution, which is the main driver behind calling this *advanced* compliance reporting.

14.1.1   Legal Reporting

Let's first focus on legal reporting requirements.

Because legal reporting touches on periodic tax demands from myriad governmental bodies of companies using multiple ERP systems, the classic approach to legal reporting required a lot of manual tasks involving data extraction, collection, and report generation (as shown in Figure 14.1). Organizations had limited transparency into their end-to-end reporting compliance across this heterogeneous landscape.

Organizations that run SAP ERP already have access to many legal reports for different countries, but these are still spread across the system in different places, making it quite cumbersome to get a clear overall view. Moreover, with SAP ERP it can be difficult to extend or adapt the existing reports.

To address these pain points, SAP S/4HANA includes SAP Advanced Compliance Reporting, introducing the homogeneous legal reporting approach shown in Figure 14.2; the idea is to consume all relevant data from SAP S/4HANA, which enables organizations to centrally access all reports from a single place *and* deliver these reports in the right formats as prescribed by the relevant governmental bodies.

It covers the following reporting requirements, among others:

- VAT return
- EC sales list
- Withholding tax
- Balance of payments
- VAT sales and purchase ledger

- Standard audit files
- Asset reporting
- Foreign trade declaration
- Transport tax
- Goods and service tax

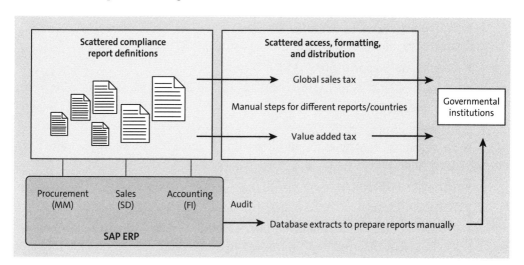

Figure 14.1 Classic Heterogeneous Approach to Legal Reporting

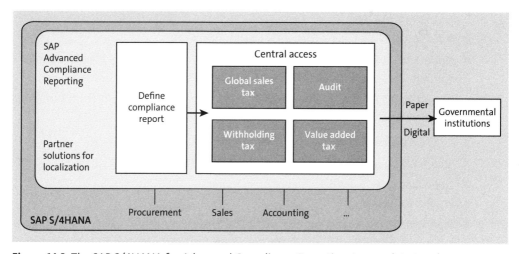

Figure 14.2 The SAP S/4HANA for Advanced Compliance Reporting Approach to Legal Reporting

As of SAP S/4HANA 1809, the advanced compliance reporting solution offers more than 120 out-of-the-box reports. The following list covers some of them, but we should note that this list is constantly evolving and that regulatory and licensing issues that might impact report timelines are outside SAP's control:

- *Argentina:* Daily VAT Reporting, Sales VAT, Purchase VAT, VAT Return
- *Australia:* VAT—BAS Reporting
- *Austria:* EC Sales List
- *Belgium:* EC Sales list, Withholding Tax Declaration 281.50, Annual Sales List, Balance of Payments—F01DGS, F01MER, F02CMS, and F02CMS
- *Canada:* GST Reporting (HST, PST, RITC, and QST)
- *China:* Input VAT Transfer, Input VAT Details, Audit Data Extraction Reports (Asset Accounting, Account Payables and Receivables, Common Information, General Ledger)
- *Colombia:* DIAN Magnetic Media Reporting (Format 1001, 1003, 1005, 1006, 1007, 1008, and 1009)
- *Denmark:* EC Sales List
- *Egypt:* VAT Return
- *France:* EC Sales List, Withholding Tax Declaration—DAS2, Balance of Payments—ECO and RTE, Deferred VAT Return, VAT Return—CA3
- *Great Britain:* VAT Return, EC Sales List, Withholding Tax Reporting—CIS 300
- *Hungary:* Domestic Sales (65M), EC Sales and Purchase List (A60), Audit Files (AEA), VAT Return—65A
- *India:* Withholding Tax—Quarterly Declaration
- *Indonesia:* VAT Summary Report, Withholding Tax Reporting—PPH 23/26, Withholding Tax Reporting (PPH 4, PPH 15, and PPH 22)
- *Ireland:* VAT 3 Return, EC Sales List—VIES, Withholding Tax—Deduction Summary
- *Israel:* VAT Return
- *Italy:* Quarterly VAT Declaration, Withholding Tax Declaration—CU
- *Japan:* Withholding Tax Reporting: Blue Returns, White Returns
- *Luxembourg:* EC Sales list, Balance of Payments STATEC Form 26, SAF-T (FAIA), VAT Return—Annual
- *Malaysia:* GST03 Reporting, GST Audit File (GAF)
- *Mexico:* DIOT Reporting, Chart of Accounts Reporting, Account Balance Reporting, VAT Declaration

- *Netherlands:* EC Sales List—ICP, VAT Return

- *Philippines:* Tax Summary List (Summary List of Importations, Sales and Purchases), Withholding Tax Reporting—BIR 2307, VAT Return—Quarterly, VAT Declaration—Monthly, Computerized Accounting System Reports (General Journal, General Ledger, Inventory Book, Purchase Journal, Sales Journal)

- *Russia:* VAT Purchase Ledger, VAT Sales Ledger, Invoice Journal, VAT Return

- *Saudi Arabia:* VAT Return

- *Singapore:* GST Return

- *South Africa:* VAT Return

- *South Korea:* Withholding Tax Reporting (Business Income/Other Income), VAT Return (Tax Invoices of Sales and Purchases)

- *Spain:* EC Sales and Purchase List—Model 349, VAT Return—Model 303, Withholding Tax—Model 190, Form 347 (Annual Transaction Statement, Incoming Cash Transaction)

- *Sweden:* EC Sales List

- *Switzerland:* National Bank Reporting (Balance of Payments)

- *Taiwan:* VAT (BAN.TXT, BAN.TO2, and BAN.TO8)

- *Thailand:* VAT Return, VAT Exceeded 6M Return

- *United Arab Emirates:* VAT Return, FAF Audit Report File for VAT line items

- *United States:* Withholding Tax Reporting: 1099 MISC, 1099 G, 1099 K,1099 INT, 1042 S

- *Venezuela:* VAT Return, Sales VAT, Purchase VAT

In addition to these out-of-the-box reports, the advanced compliance reporting solution also offers several other advantages:

- Tax and statutory reporting teams can review data prior to submission based on embedded analytics capabilities, which were discussed in earlier chapters.

- The advanced compliance reporting solution is based on SAP S/4HANA, so it benefits from real-time reporting without data replication and thus no reconciliation needs. It accesses SAP S/4HANA data directly during report preparation, which improves efficiency.

- Because all reports are centralized in one place, SAP S/4HANA for advanced compliance reporting facilitates end-to-end monitoring and complete transparency into overall reporting compliance. In Figure 14.3, the system has returned one report, which is overdue.

14

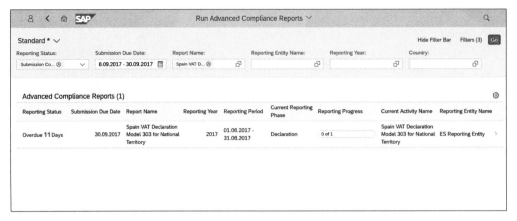

Figure 14.3 Running Advanced Compliance Reports Centrally

Statutory reporting usually involves a set of activities that needs to be carried out during the reporting process. These activities (e.g., consolidation, exception analysis, and posting of tax payables) can be carried out before or after the legal report generation. Thanks to the flexible reporting activities concept in the advanced compliance reporting solution, all these activities can be plugged in to enable end-to-end legal reporting.

Legal reporting, as mentioned briefly earlier, is also required in a specific format. To address this complexity, legal reports can be generated in the advanced compliance reporting solution in output formats such as XML, PDF, TXT, or XBRL. You can also choose to view the information in a data preview or tabular format and use the information to file your tax returns manually through the authorized government portals. The legal reports can then be submitted to the government through all available gateways of government authorities. In addition, notifications can be received from the government if the report content is accepted or rejected.

14.1.2   Extensions

The advanced compliance reporting solution includes more than one hundred out-of-the-box reports, but the endless combinations of federal, state, and provincial legal requirements mean that the standard-delivered reports might not be enough. This could be because some countries aren't localized by SAP or because a specific organization or its industry has a unique requirement.

To answer this situation, the extended version of the advanced compliance reporting solution also includes a guided platform for defining new reports and adding extensions to existing reports to support specific requirements. Once custom reports have been created, they can be reused—and even though they're custom-made, they can share the look and feel of standard reports delivered out of the box.

When designing a new report, the report developer provides the different attributes and input required to create a new report definition. The data sources for the mappings to be performed are Core Data Services (CDS) views. These views sit on top of the actual tables containing the data (like the Universal Journal), from which legal reporting data is accessed. In many cases, existing views can be used, but you can also create additional views.

In the example shown in Figure 14.4, fields for Spanish VAT reporting are selected as part of the report definition.

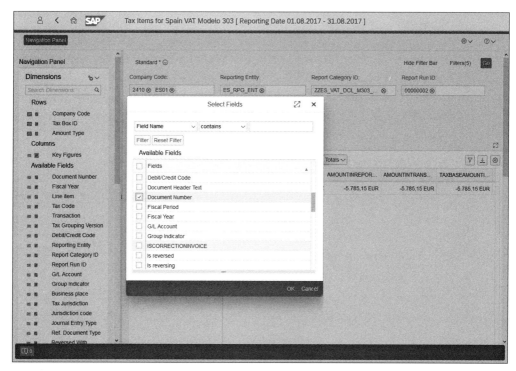

Figure 14.4 Field Selection and Mapping as Part of the Guided Process to Create a New Legal Report

The advanced compliance reporting solution can now support the incorporation of business rules to control and influence the data and formatting of legal reports. This is achieved through the app's integration with Business Rule Framework plus (BRFplus).

In summary, the advanced compliance reporting solution is a flexible platform to enable legal reporting requirements and monitor compliance uniformly across many countries. It's a homogenous, integrated, and extensible solution to generate and run legal reports while making sure everything remains auditable. This also translates into cost savings when complying with legal reporting requirements.

Now that we've looked at how SAP supports a homogeneous approach to legal reporting, let's zoom into how the relevant tax input can be calculated and delivered efficiently while ensuring compliance.

14.2   Indirect Tax Compliance with SAP Localization Hub, Tax Service

As noted at the beginning of this chapter, there's a fundamental shift happening from direct taxes toward indirect taxation based on consumption, or transaction-based taxation.

The indirect-tax-related topics can be divided roughly into two cycles:

- **The transactional cycle**
  This is when taxes are determined and calculated. Because of the multitude of rules, regulations, and calculations and the frequency with which they change in some regions, it can be hard to keep up. This becomes even more cumbersome when you take into consideration that many organizations are running multiple applications containing tax-relevant transactions.

- **The analytical cycle**
  This takes place less frequently, typically on a monthly, quarterly, or yearly basis. At these times, all tax-relevant transactions are grouped and declared to the relevant tax authorities.

These reporting requirements are also getting more and more complex to answer as some reporting requirements evolve toward intraperiod reporting. At the same time, authorities are demanding increased transparency into organizations' activities and are starting to dig into more details of the transactional data through the introduction of regulations related to e-invoicing, for instance. This makes it possible to cross-check the tax reporting that was declared. Organizations therefore see increasing workload and complexity in finding, collecting, and submitting the right information to tax authorities in the right format. This results in a cost increase. On top of that, there's a risk of additional costs because of noncompliance. Hence, providing an answer to these regulations is very high on the agenda of finance—and more specifically, tax responsibles.

With this shift in mind, let's look at how the tax service solution supports organizations to more efficiently handle indirect tax compliance in increasingly complex systems environments, across different countries, and at a time when authorities are asking for increasingly detailed information.

14.2.1   Tax Service

In reality, organizations often have a scattered solution landscape of applications. From a tax calculation perspective, such a multisystem landscape makes it difficult and costly to ensure accurate and harmonized tax calculation.

Even within SAP applications, tax determination and computation rules and logic have always been integrated in a specific product (e.g., tax determination and calculation within core SAP ERP components such as Sales and Distribution and Materials Management). Because SAP's on-premise and cloud product portfolio has increased to cover parts of the procure-to-pay and order-to-cash process in different ways, the result could be the unfortunate multiplication of maintenance efforts to ensure all these rules and logic are made available in a consistent way across these different applications.

To address this problem, SAP Localization Hub has been working on a tax service solution that aims to deliver centralized indirect tax determination and calculation in a single application as an independently consumable service. As shown at the bottom of Figure 14.5, peripheral applications such as SAP S/4HANA, SAP Ariba, and so on are connected to the tax service solution, which runs on the SAP Cloud Platform. Its open API provides a method to determine and compute applicable country-specific taxes on a given business transaction. It includes up-to-date tax content like country-specific tax types, tax rates, deductibility, and tax exemptions.

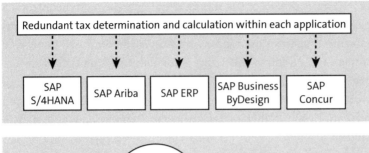

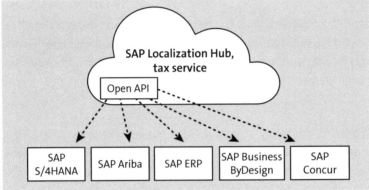

Figure 14.5 Redundant vs. Centralized Tax Determination and Calculation

To better understand how it works and connects to multiple applications, let's look at the tax service architecture in Figure 14.6. It consists of the following parts:

- On the right, you see the calculation engine and default tax content that are predelivered and maintained by SAP.

- On the left, you see the tax service API, which allows additional configuration by customers, as well as through the partner framework to connect external tax solutions from SAP partners.

The objective is to complete all tax information automatically without input from a user. Because the tax service is solution-independent, any consumer application can be connected to the tax service solution engine and content via the API. After an initial authorization setup, the consumer application will send tax-relevant data from a business transaction (e.g., an invoice) in a predefined format. This includes all tax-relevant data involved in the transaction, such as the classification as a sale or purchase, the definition of gross or net amounts, the various locations with countries or region codes, and business partner roles. Once the data is sent to the tax service solution, it's processed by the tax engine based on the configuration and the content.

As a result, the tax service solution determines data like a specific tax event and types, calculated tax amounts, and legal texts. The result is sent back to the connected application, where it will be used to complete the transaction.

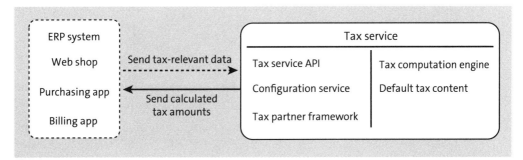

Figure 14.6 SAP Localization Hub, Tax Service Components

14.2.2 Partner Tax Applications

Organizations using the tax service solution can either use SAP's internal tax engine to determine and calculate indirect taxes or use an external partner solution. If a specific partner solution is chosen, it can be connected to the tax service and then to SAP S/4HANA through the tax partner integration framework as shown in Figure 14.7. We recommend reviewing the details of available SAP-certified partner applications at the SAP App Center (*www.sapappcenter.com*).

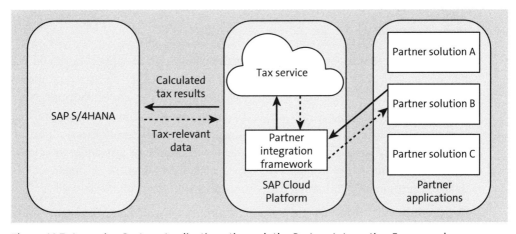

Figure 14.7 Accessing Partner Applications through the Partner Integration Framework

As an example of this approach, consider tax requirements in Brazil. For Brazil, the SAP S/4HANA solution includes the following tax-relevant localizations:

- Fiscal tax attributes, including relevant taxes sorted by business place and business partner (e.g., NCM codes, which defines the industrialized product tax rate and other elements), are included.

- Tax processing is integrated into all business transactions that are tax-relevant in Brazil (e.g., purchase orders, sales orders, and billing and invoicing transactions).

- The tax calculation and invoice information is stored in these business transactions, enabling organizations to issue a correct Brazilian invoice (*nota fiscal*).

- Through the tax partner integration framework, organizations can manage the assignment of partner tax engines to Brazil as a specific country. Cloud-based partner solutions can include Brazilian indirect taxes, including ICMS (for goods and service circulation), IPI (for industrialized products), PIS, COFINS, ISS, and CSLL—as well as the country-specific withholding taxes for legal entities (e.g., PIS/COFINS, IR, INSS, ISS dispute).

- The framework also provides legal maintenance covering rates, tax types, formulas, deductions, and related information for the tax invoice, and it makes it possible to add exemption rules for specific laws.

With consistent tax calculation results, automated processes, and less maintenance effort, there's a lower cost involved in complying with tax regulations.

14.3   Summary

We started this chapter by clarifying the general approach to support legal and tax requirements in different countries with SAP S/4HANA. We then discussed the global trend toward the digitization of compliance and indirect tax regimes. Authorities are demanding more transparency by requesting near-real-time (transactional) information like SII and NFE, and more in-depth information within period-end reporting like SAF-T. A key business driver behind the evolution of how SAP addresses global tax management is the avoidance of noncompliance by identifying incorrect tax data and automatically initiating correction and documentation measures.

Therefore, as we saw in this chapter, SAP solutions for global tax management are designed to help organizations automate tax determination, calculation, reporting, and compliance on a global scale. Both SAP S/4HANA for advanced compliance reporting and the SAP Localization Hub, tax service (when connected to SAP S/4HANA) are based on a single source of truth (for taxes) within the core business processes and are supported by the Universal Journal within SAP S/4HANA. Embedded reporting solutions and support for different digital formats are available to fulfill digital compliance obligations. All this is combined with easier maintenance of tax calculations and report definitions, enabling organizations to comply with all regulations more cost-efficiently.

14

Chapter 15

Cloud Extensions and Connectivity: Looking Beyond the Core

So far in this book, we've covered many key capabilities of SAP S/4HANA that support finance departments. Let's turn our attention to how solutions and extensions outside the SAP S/4HANA digital core support end-to-end finance process execution in real time.

Over the course of this book, we looked at how SAP S/4HANA architectural changes and key capabilities improve the way organizations proactively steer their businesses and execute their finance operations efficiently.

But running a business is about more than just finance. To be successful, organizations must evolve so that they more effectively use their data assets to achieve their desired outcomes faster and with less risk. To become what SAP calls an *intelligent enterprise*, businesses need to invest in the three key areas shown in Figure 15.1:

- **Intelligent suite**
  This ensures businesses manage their customers, supply chains, networks, employees, and core processes (like finance) in an integrated way.

- **Intelligent technologies**
  These allow for rapid and continuous innovation. Already in this book we've touched on the integration of analytics, the use of machine learning, and the inclusion of the SAP CoPilot digital assistant as examples of technological innovations that improve both decision-making and operational finance processes.

- **Digital platform**
  This allows an organization to manage data from any source, in any format, and to and rapidly develop, integrate, and extend business applications.

SAP S/4HANA is the centerpiece of SAP's intelligent suite, and it can be extended via SAP's digital platform, SAP Cloud Platform. It allows organizations to integrate end-to-end processes like procure-to-pay, order-to-cash and hire-to-retire. This is why it's also referred to as the *digital core*.

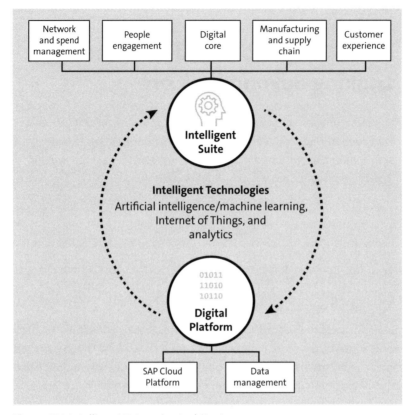

Figure 15.1 Intelligent Enterprise Architecture

As you've seen throughout this book, many finance process steps are supported within SAP S/4HANA itself. In specific cases, however, parts of the finance process become more complete by combining SAP S/4HANA with an additional solution component from the SAP portfolio, either leveraging the SAP HANA platform or building off the SAP Cloud Platform (or both!).

Solutions and Extensions

You've already seen some extensions earlier in the book! In Chapter 9, we mentioned SAP Analytics Cloud's planning capabilities. Likewise, we discussed SAP S/4HANA Cloud for advanced financial closing when tackling the closing process, which is also based on the SAP Cloud Platform. Specific solutions, including machine learning capabilities (like SAP Cash Application and the GR/IR reconciliation app addressed in Chapter 4), are also built on the SAP Cloud Platform.

In this section, we'll introduce several solutions (in Section 15.1) and extensions (in Section 15.2) that make SAP S/4HANA an even more compelling system for financial organizations. (Do note that these tend to be licensed separately from the SAP S/4HANA digital core.)

15.1 Finance Solutions

As we consider how peripheral SAP solutions can supplement core SAP S/4HANA finance processes, let's circle back to the four-step financial management process view we examined in the introduction of this book (shown again in Figure 15.2) and layer in three specific solutions: SAP Product Lifecycle Costing for COGS planning and simulation; SAP Profitability and Performance Management for complex, multi-source allocation and simulation and for transfer pricing simulation; and SAP Customer Profitability Analytics for subscription business probability.

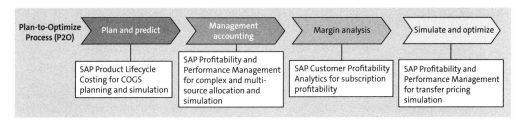

Figure 15.2 Finance Operations in SAP S/4HANA with Peripheral Finance Solutions

The first solution, connected to the planning and forecasting step within the end-to-end finance process, is related to manufacturing organizations (especially the automobile industry).

15.1.1 SAP Product Lifecycle Costing

In manufacturing industries like the automobile industry, the lifecycles of products are relatively long, so product cost planning for new products (e.g., cars) must start when a design begins in the R&D phase.

Lack of visibility into early product costs hurts profitability downstream, but legacy tools like Microsoft Excel are insufficient for managing early cost estimates and plans. Microsoft Excel is readily available and sufficient for many things—but trying to manage bills of material (BOMs) with Microsoft Excel in a collaborative environment increases the risk of hidden costs or profit losses. Microsoft Excel BOMs can be generated by exporting computer-aided design (CAD) or ERP data but cannot be shared and tracked in a controlled manner. When the BOMs are complex, control is easily lost.

Meanwhile, the competitive pressure to reduce time-to-market and improve design-for-cost metrics drives organizations to identify cost drivers and optimize the cost structure along their products' lifecycles. When structures and values are only partially available and evolve over time, an advanced solution is needed to accompany the R&D and quotation processes with accurate cost estimates. Such a solution should enable organizations to optimize costs through simulation and evaluation of production or supply costs, as well as improve the cost structure of the organization.

What's possible in SAP S/4HANA? After the start of production, all master data (e.g., BOM, materials, prices, routings, and rates) are completely defined and available in SAP S/4HANA. Powerful cost-calculation capabilities already available in this application calculate product costs. These tools are deeply integrated, for example, into logistics and controlling.

On the other hand, in the early phase of product development (i.e., before production starts), the data needed typically is incomplete. This is why there's a need for tools that allow for a cost estimate with incomplete BOMs, temporary materials, and preliminary pricing information.

This is where the SAP Product Lifecycle Costing solution comes in, offering SAP S/4HANA customers an edge in the three specific use cases shown in Figure 15.3:

❶ Preliminary cost estimate
Preliminary cost estimates are relevant for all companies that require cost information within a project for a product that either is being newly designed (i.e., new product introduction) or is planned to be the successor to or a new version of an existing product (i.e., continuous improvement). Often, a manufacturer wants to evaluate the potential cost elements, breakdowns, and drivers before manufacturing the product. This is usually done in iterations to keep an eye on target costs and other milestones in the development project.

❷ Quotation costing
The second use case is related to cost calculation based on an inquiry from a customer, for which a quote needs to be generated. This could be an inquiry for a complex, customer-specific machine; for a set of products; or even for a solution consisting of multiple products in varying quantities. The cost of these individual products or solutions can't be calculated through a market price, which makes getting insights into each cost component crucial.

❸ Lifecycle costing

The third use case also relates to a customer inquiry, but in this case the cost of the product or solution needs to be calculated over an entire future period of time and take into account varying volumes, component and raw material prices, labor rates, currency fluctuations, and so on. Typically, this use case is predominant for automotive first-tier suppliers and, to some extent, for high-tech contract manufacturers that engage in multiquarter or multiyear projects with their customers. It also applies to customers that need to add initial and future one-off costs into the cost equation to ensure they can make their projected profit margins.

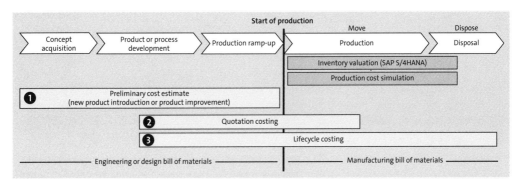

Figure 15.3 Use Cases of SAP Product Lifecycle Costing

As SAP's answer to these advanced requirements, SAP Product Lifecycle Costing leverages information from SAP S/4HANA and runs on top of the SAP HANA platform; this architecture results in high performance and makes it possible to integrate other data sources.

The integration with SAP S/4HANA enables you to replicate master data such as materials and related prices, as well as manufacturing activity types and related rates, plus other relevant costing data. BOMs and routings also can be imported from any data source to initially create or update costing structures (i.e., hierarchies that consist of items to be costed).

SAP Product Lifecycle Costing provides a cockpit view that helps users organize their work and navigate through different versions of cost calculations; in the example in Figure 15.4, five different versions are visible. The cockpit view also helps users bundle calculations of multiple products or product variants belonging to one product line. As you can see, the top node bundles all projects rather than products; this is because these cost simulations typically take place as part of the R&D phase (i.e., as development projects) before the actual production starts.

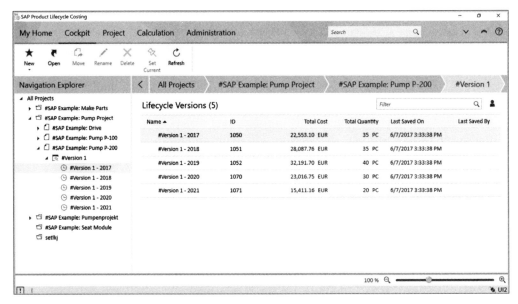

Figure 15.4 Cockpit View of SAP Product Lifecycle Costing

SAP Product Lifecycle Costing also provides a calculation view like the one shown in Figure 15.5. This view shows the costing structure in different ways. It includes a spreadsheet-like table view that enables you to create, change, or add cost estimates in a fully customized way, allowing you to add any required data field. Users can maintain different calculation versions and display KPIs in this view.

SAP Product Lifecycle Costing offers several options to help you price components and activities, including the selection of a different source for prices (e.g., coming from SAP S/4HANA), manual price determination, and price determination based on a price from the SAP ERP or SAP S/4HANA environment. You also have the option to define a price-priority strategy with confidence levels. Once the first iteration of pricing is complete, the solution highlights previous or outdated prices and recalculates whenever new price information is available, either on request or automatically.

When working on the cost structure, you can analyze the choices that have been made regarding materials, processes, activities, prices, quantities, and overheads. There are two ways of doing this:

- **Using cost component splits**
  You can analyze the breakdown of costs for each item and identify the major cost drivers. The cost component split updates automatically with every change. In

addition, you can apply any of the cost component splits that have been created in master data to any item at any time.

- **Using the costing sheet**

  This method defines how overheads are determined and how totals are calculated. The values calculated by the costing sheet are shown for every item that you select. You can select the appropriate costing sheet from a dropdown list.

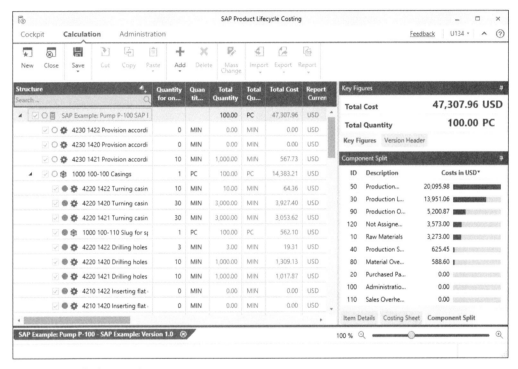

Figure 15.5 Calculation View

In addition to the predelivered analysis tools, you can use SAP HANA views to create your custom reporting. You can display reporting in different ways, including through SAP Analysis for Microsoft Office. Figure 15.6 shows an example of the total product cost split in material, activity, and overhead costs displayed in SAP Analysis for Microsoft Office, which uses Microsoft Excel as its frontend.

In summary, SAP Product Lifecycle Costing supports the R&D phase (mainly prior to production start) with detailed cost estimates when designs are evolving and master data is only partially available. Through simulation and evaluation, it helps optimize both supply and production costs, and thereby serves as input for the standard costs used later in SAP S/4HANA. Cost control throughout the entire lifecycle of a product leads to improvement of an organization's cost structure.

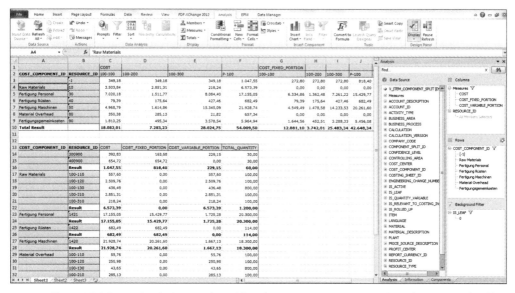

Figure 15.6 Reporting in SAP Product Lifecycle Costing Using SAP Analysis for Microsoft Office

15.1.2   SAP Profitability and Performance Management

The next solution we'll cover, SAP Profitability and Performance Management, also focuses on an organization's costing setup.

The name of the solution might suggest that profitability analysis wouldn't otherwise be available in SAP S/4HANA—but recall from Chapter 1 that the integration of margin information in the Universal Journal in SAP S/4HANA has already improved the ways the margin can be analyzed across different business dimensions. So surely the go-to solution for profitability analysis is the SAP S/4HANA solution itself.

However, there are specific cases when an additional profitability solution may be warranted:

- **Multiple ERP sources**
  What if not all relevant revenue and costing information is available in the SAP S/4HANA environment because it's instead stored in another ERP system? Although it's possible to add additional dimensions to the Universal Journal, in some cases a number of dimensions by which an organization wants to analyze its

margin—or even the financial data itself—aren't stored in the ERP environment but in additional sources.

- **Very large data volumes**
  In certain cases, very large data volumes need to be treated (e.g., individual transaction details in a retail environment). Integrating them into SAP S/4HANA for the execution of a business process wouldn't add much value.

- **Advanced costing modeling**
  For some organizations, the structure of the profit and loss statement is such that there is a high impact from overhead costs on the total margin, which requires advanced allocations of indirect costs. One example of such a situation is the calculation of the total cost to serve a customer. In these situations, advanced activity-based costing (ABC) logic is sometimes used. Although SAP S/4HANA supports basic ABC (just as SAP ERP did), more advanced ABC modeling is needed in certain cases. These advanced, fine-grained allocation models are, for instance, also used in the insurance business.

- **Driver-based modeling**
  Another case in which advanced cost modeling adds value is for calculating estimates or performing simulations and what-if scenarios. This is especially relevant in the case of driver-based modeling, in which the underlying business drivers are not necessarily available within the SAP S/4HANA environment.

- **Transfer prices**
  A specific what-if scenario or simulation related mainly to indirect costs but also to direct costs is the simulation of transfer prices for different purposes or different "views" on intercompany profit: a legal, tax, or management view. Recall from Chapter 2 that once transfer prices are defined, these different views are delivered from within the SAP S/4HANA environment. But increasingly often, questions are raised regarding the optimization (i.e., the simulation) of transfer prices. This part of the process is typically performed manually, often using a spreadsheet-based solution.

In short, though many industry-specific use cases related to margin analysis can be covered fully by the standard capabilities delivered with SAP S/4HANA, SAP Profitability and Performance Management brings additional capabilities for further detailed profitability modeling and optimization. Let's take a closer look.

SAP Profitability and Performance Management can be described technically as a calculation engine that processes high volumes of data from different sources. Of course, before you can make any calculations, the solution has to gather all relevant

15

information. This is done by SAP Profitability and Performance Management's business data aggregator, which collects data from multiple databases, SAP applications (e.g., SAP S/4HANA), web services, and other functions or files. Depending on the source, data doesn't need to be physically replicated to SAP Profitability and Performance Management. In case of SAP HANA–based applications (like SAP S/4HANA), this duplication and therefore reconciliation isn't required.

The second layer of the solution is the actual calculation engine, which has the following capabilities:

- **Profitability and allocation**
  Assessment and global recharges, top-down distribution, and activity-based costing

- **Plan and forecast modeling**
  Driver-based and deterministic models, predictive and machine learning models, and stochastic models

- **Funds transfer pricing**
  Matched maturity, net present value, and replication portfolio

- **Risk, capital, and solvency II**
  Life and nonlife risk, counterparty default risk, and market risk

- **Cash flow modelling**
  Interest currency and economic indicator models, behavior models, and cash flow processing estimations

- **Data access**
  Virtual and physical data models, adapters for files and systems, and view, join, union, and collections

- **Enrichment**
  Derivation and lookup, currency and unit conversion, and calculation and formulas

- **Process control**
  Process and assumption management, business error and event management, and report management

- **Analysis and reporting**
  Analytic queries and reports, item variance and reconciliation reports, optional Microsoft Excel frontend

- **Process extensions**
  SQL, Java, ABAP, Graph, Spark, R, Python, Scala, and more

Notice in this list that some of the predelivered calculation functions are specifically related to the banking and insurance industry (including solvency II and funds transfer pricing). This is because SAP Profitability and Performance Management was originally built for these types of organizations. However, the following areas are of high interest across industries: top-down distribution, global recharges, activity-based costing, currency and unit conversion, derivation capabilities, forecasting modeling functions supporting the simulation requirements, and more.

Figure 15.7 shows the end-to-end profitability and performance cost modeling process. Notice that most of the steps are taken by functional users within the finance department who have specific experience with selecting the appropriate option within the calculation engine to deliver the best profitability or cost insights. Consequently, it's key that functional users be able to model the solution.

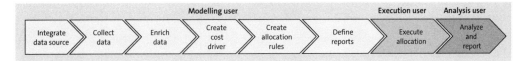

Figure 15.7 Cost Modeling and Execution Process

To streamline the modeling process and improve the user experience, SAP Fiori is used to guide the user through this process. Users can build an entire costing model from scratch, but they also can take advantage of sample content to speed up this modeling process. Sample content available includes the following use cases:

- Profitability and cost management
- IT cost management
- Funds and liquidity transfer pricing
- Allocation simulation
- Agile plan and forecast modeling
- Global transfer pricing
- Carbon footprint management
- Travel and transportation profitability
- Estimated cash flow preparation
- Telecommunications profitability and cost management
- Chemicals profitability and cost management
- Airline profitability and cost management
- Consumer product profitability and cost management

- Life sciences profitability and cost management
- High-tech profitability and cost management

Figure 15.8 shows the sample content for transfer price simulation. On the left side, the top node of the hierarchy shows the sample content name (**Global Transfer Pricing**), after which each step of the model starting from the data sources, additional data input, and the actual logic (referred to as processing) can be walked through. Details of each step are shown on the right side. This same look and feel is used when creating a new model from scratch as well.

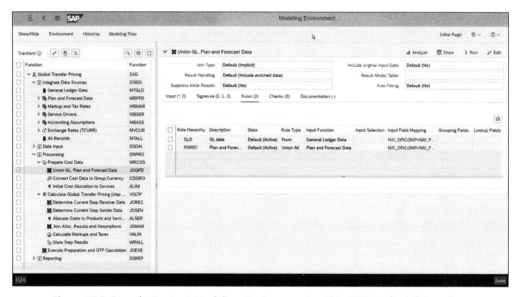

Figure 15.8 Sample Content Modeling Environment within SAP Profitability and Performance Management

Once the model is finalized, the next step is to execute the designed cost allocation logic or other model and then to analyze and report on the results.

Simulation capabilities also are available within the reporting SAP Fiori app shown in Figure 15.9. In the example, it becomes clear what part of the model, what version, and so on is being reported at the left side of the screen. This is also where simulation parameters are indicated (in this case, **Markup Increment**). Results of the executed model and simulations are shown in different formats at the right. You can easily toggle between tabular and graphical presentations and filter or drill down across available data elements. It's also possible to integrate the solution with SAP Analytics Cloud for additional reporting and analysis.

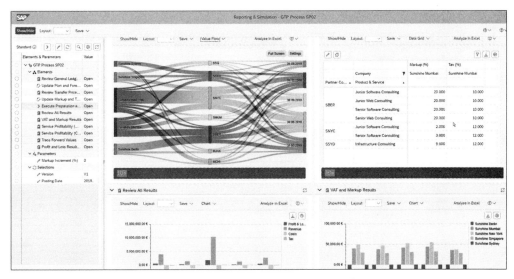

Figure 15.9 Reporting and Simulation with SAP Profitability and Performance Management

In summary, SAP Profitability and Performance Management allows for detailed profitability modeling and optimization for a high number of dimensions and a high data volume coming from different sources, including the option to simulate, thereby providing an option to model different costing scenarios.

15.1.3   SAP Customer Profitability Analytics

Recall that in SAP S/4HANA, internal and external P&L are based on transaction data (postings) from the general ledger that are centrally stored in the Universal Journal. The internal P&L integrates all data needed for the profitability views and provides all figures on the company level.

But depending on the type of business and the related business drivers, additional granularity and logic may be required. In general, the financial information shown on the left side of Figure 15.10 is typically available in SAP S/4HANA. However, non-financial information (including business drivers such as customer behavior, which impact costs and margin) isn't always available in SAP S/4HANA. It all depends on the organization-specific setup of the system landscape. A difference can be detected when comparing various types of businesses: for manufacturing organizations, all product costing information, which makes up a big part of the organization's financial contribution, is available in SAP S/4HANA. Less granular data is available on average for service-driven subscription industries (like telecommunications or utilities).

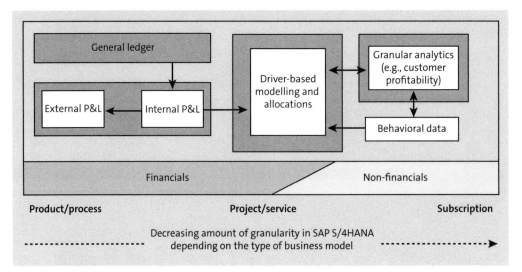

Figure 15.10 End-to-End View of Profitability Management

We already discussed the situations in which SAP Profitability and Performance Management may be of interest, mainly focusing on indirect costing and requiring the setup of a cost model. SAP Customer Profitability Analytics, on the other hand, is all about providing insights into the contribution each individual customer makes to a company's profit or loss. It started by focusing on the subscription-based industries, and a specific data model that originated in the telecommunications industry has been integrated into the solution. SAP Customer Profitability Analytics leverages data sources outside SAP S/4HANA, like billing data from standalone billing engines, customer relationship management, and metering systems.

The subscription-level profitability insights provided by SAP Customer Profitability Analytics don't require modeling from scratch but are generated by making use of intelligent technologies like data science and artificial intelligence to detect margin leakages and their root causes. Consider the practice of *discount stacking*, a common risk in the telecommunications industry. In this scenario, a single subscriber might be granted a contract with a discount because he or she is in a specific age category; the subscriber might combine that first discount with another discount because he or she is a university student, and then with another discount based on a promotion for an online subscription. It would benefit the telecommunications company to understand this individual customer's impact on its profitability. Other examples can be found in the utilities space; here, a company might want to identify low-margin subscribers that charge their electric car more often via a specific charging point-partner with unfavorable rates.

In more detail, the specific machine learning algorithms embedded in SAP Customer Profitability Analytics cover the following functionality:

- **Clustering**
  Larger sets of customers can be broken down into smaller and similar subsets by clustering customers based on KPIs and margin drivers. An example of the exploration of margin drivers by cluster is included in Figure 15.11, in which seven customer clusters shown on the far-left side are the starting point of the analysis.

- **Outlier detection**
  Detect and analyze unprofitable subscriptions or customers based on certain measures like margins, costs, and revenues.

- **Root-cause analysis**
  Provide findings of a granular structure of customer attributes, usage patterns, and customer demographics, including their impact on profitability.

- **Delta analysis**
  Detect changes in key figures (e.g., profit) that take place over time, in combination with possible reasons for the changes.

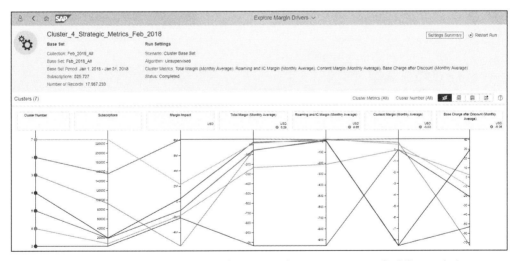

Figure 15.11 Cluster-Based Margin Driver Exploration with SAP Customer Profitability Analytics

To analyze findings, users can take advantage of the embedded dashboard as delivered and tap into the SAP Analytics Cloud environment.

15.2   Finance Extensions

Part of the beauty of SAP S/4HANA is that its financial capabilities built into the digital core can be extended through applications developed on the SAP Cloud Platform.

The idea behind the architectural approach shown in Figure 15.12 is twofold: to keep the core ERP environment stable and to enable the flexible addition of innovations for a specific business requirement. As you learned in the introduction to this chapter, SAP S/4HANA is designed to work with the SAP Cloud Platform, so financials data stored in SAP S/4HANA can be used in these applications without replication. Each application is meant for a very specific finance subprocess; because they are cloud applications built around best practices, they are "lightweight" and easy to deploy.

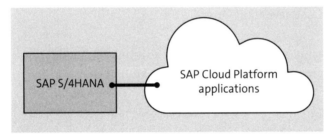

Figure 15.12 Connecting SAP Cloud Platform Apps to the SAP S/4HANA Environment

SAP Cloud Platform Applications

It's also possible for organizations or SAP partners to develop their own applications on the SAP Cloud Platform. You can browse through and in some cases demo applications available for purchase at the online SAP store: *www.sapappcenter.com*.

In this section, we'll distinguish between two categories of apps. As we'll discuss next in Section 15.2.1, some apps focus on a specific analytical capability, such as spending, whereas others look to extend a particular finance process, such as receivables management.

15.2.1   Analytics

In this section, we'll explore two analytics extensions, SAP RealSpend and SAP Financial Statement Insights, and discuss how they build off financial information from the Universal Journal.

SAP RealSpend

Every line manager (or, in financial terms, *cost center owner*) within an organization wants to conduct some kind of budget analysis. This is usually based on reports about past spending but can also extend to the future impact of past decisions.

For example, consider an organization's travel budget. For many companies, the decision to approve or reject a business travel request depends on whether the travel budget has already been consumed (assuming the purpose of the business travel has already been validated!). However, managers might be working from incomplete information: reports about travel budget consumption typically don't take into consideration existing travel plans for which costs haven't been registered in the finance system yet.

Going a step further, organizations also are increasingly interested in simulating what the budget situation will look like throughout the year. In other cases, budgets might need to be reordered between different categories, sometimes called *budget envelopes*. These types of requirements from business controllers or line managers surely are not limited to the example of travel expenses alone.

To address this more complete and flexible view of budget spending, SAP introduced the SAP RealSpend application. Because this application integrates with SAP S/4HANA, it can consume all actual and committed financial information from the Universal Journal without duplicating it. Information about approved (but not financially recorded) and requested budgets can be added. This is what sets SAP RealSpend apart: the accessibility of forward-looking insights displayed in a predefined format using different color shades.

Let's look at an example. In Figure 15.13, **Today** is marked with the vertical line and the available budget (**439,950 Euros**) is marked by the horizontal line. You can see that there is no risk of overspending yet—but by adding the approved and requested spending into the picture, you can see that we're actually close to consuming the total available budget.

Figure 15.13 also illustrates the capability of showing different areas of responsibility: the left side of the figure shows the use of tags to regroup specific analytical dimensions (e.g., cost centers, projects, products, and so on). Although SAP RealSpend surely is not to be considered as a planning or budgeting tool—a topic we addressed in Chapter 9—the pop-up in Figure 15.13 also highlights the application's ability to move budgeted amounts between two subareas for which a specific user is responsible if needed, without impacting the overall budget or plan.

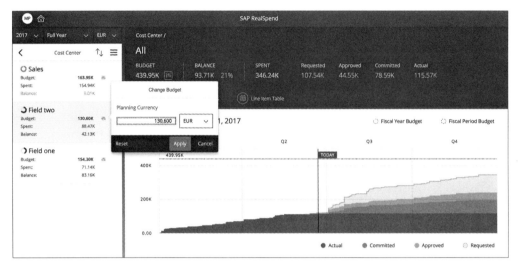

Figure 15.13 SAP RealSpend Visualization

Of course, getting forward-looking information does help users make decisions and understand the impact on the department's budget—but it's still a reactive approach based on checking reports manually.

To change this manual approach and enable organizations to automatically detect the root cause of, for instance, an increase in cost, SAP RealSpend uses machine learning logic to automate the detection of anomalies and ensure it learns every time an anomaly is detected. When this capability is activated (it's included in the application by default), potential anomalies show up accompanied by triangular exclamation marks. By drilling down into the individual line items, a user can indicate whether the automatically detected anomaly is correct or not. This additional user-driven input is then injected in the application to further increase the accuracy of the anomalies detected in the future.

Let's look at another example. In Figure 15.14, the person responsible for the e-bike production department (as shown on the left-hand side) has overspent their budget. After activating the **Anomaly Detection** switch in the upper-left corner, SAP RealSpend shows the probable cause with exclamation marks. After clicking the **Line Item Table** icon and diving into the detailed line item information, a user can further investigate and understand the cause of the unexpected high costs—without spending unnecessary time slicing and dicing data.

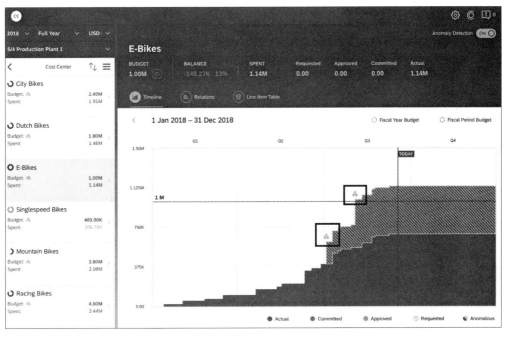

Figure 15.14 Anomaly Detection in SAP RealSpend

15

SAP Financial Statement Insights

Many available solutions can give finance professionals flexible and visually appealing representations of their financial figures, yet many professionals struggle to understand the underlying drivers of their margins. One common challenge is the fact that rigid data structures make it difficult to respond to unforeseen trends. On top of this, the kinds of analytics information that would help businesses make the right strategic decisions are evolving rapidly.

In certain cases, changing realities also require a change in organizational models, or at least the ability to simulate the impact on financial performance. For example, how would you analyze the impact of fast-emerging revenue streams that have been generated by newly developed omnichannel sales flows? This is just one example of how the digitization of the economy impacts the need for evolution and flexibility in getting insights into profitability. Many existing applications allow ad hoc analysis, of course, but these are based on the organizational structure as is.

Acting on a changing reality requires personalized ad hoc analysis of financial statements in real time, including the simulation and display of alternative organizational structures to "play" with new ideas instantly, based on up-to-date information.

SAP Financial Statement Insights is another finance extension that integrates with SAP S/4HANA; this application allows for real-time, line-item-level access to SAP S/4HANA data without data duplication. Users can tap into on-the-fly organizational model simulation through predelivered visualizations, including cross-period comparison, and drill down to underlying accounting documents in SAP S/4HANA.

The existing profit center structure from the underlying SAP S/4HANA environment is used as a foundation, but this SAP Cloud Platform application also allows you to dynamically adapt and simulate the impact of hierarchy reorganizations on the fly. Plan data sitting in the Universal Journal (table ACDOCP) can be accessed, thus enabling variance analyses.

Variance analyses, drilldowns, and so on still involve manual work from finance users. So why not automate this process by automatically alerting such users to the root causes behind a deviation from plan?

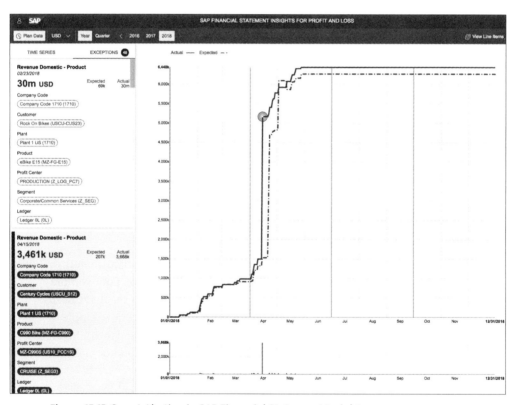

Figure 15.15 Smart Alerting in SAP Financial Statement Insights

This is what the embedded machine learning logarithm in the SAP Financial Statement Insights app does. *Smart alerts* notify users about changes in trending behavior, detect unusual increases and decreases, warn about correlations and changes between different KPIs, and automatically explore all dimensions and combinations to do so.

As shown in Figure 15.15, smart alerts automatically show the main product, sales area, or other dimension causing a deviation of the actual revenue from the plan (here, for the month of **April**). These business dimension values (the specific company code, customer, plant, product, profit center, segment, etc.) are displayed on the left side.

15.2.2   Finance Operations

Now that you've seen SAP Cloud Platform apps for finance analytics, let's shift to extensions for finance operations that add a specific subset of process capabilities to the existing end-to-end process within SAP S/4HANA.

We'll focus on the area in which most SAP Cloud Platform extensions have been developed—accounts receivable—and start by considering what's already available out of the box in SAP S/4HANA. Within the SAP S/4HANA environment, a lot is already available in terms of cross-system automation for credit, dispute, and collections processes, with the aim to reduce bad debt, as we discussed in Chapter 3. Standard-delivered analytics and workflow capabilities align sales and accounts receivable departments and business executives to reduce days sales outstanding, including the following capabilities:

- Credit checks for every business transaction
- Customer credit limits
- Dispute resolution workflow
- Automated creation of credit memos and accounting postings
- Prioritization of collections
- Synchronization among accounting, incoming payments, promised payments, and open disputes

Thus it's perfectly possible for an organization to follow up on its receivables with standard SAP S/4HANA functionality. There are, however, some elements that could further improve the receivables situation of organizations: the integration of credit information from external credit agencies, and more efficient business partner engagement for exchanging open item information and payments.

In this section, we'll look at three applications that address these more specialized requirements. Just like SAP Cash Application, which uses machine learning-based automation to get a higher level of automation for matching open items and incoming payments (as we discussed in Chapter 4), these extensions are built on the SAP Cloud Platform and fully integrate with the SAP S/4HANA environment.

SAP S/4HANA Cloud for Credit Integration

First consider how organizations use credit ratings from external agencies as inputs to improve the internal scoring model for business partners.

To monitor a particular customer's credit risk, you need a good mix of internal data (e.g., past payment behavior) and external data from credit agencies like Creditsafe, Dun & Bradstreet, and others. The catch is that different credit agencies have highly qualitative data for specific geographical regions. If an organization acts globally, this means that the information from different agencies needs to be integrated into the SAP S/4HANA environment. Historically, each of these interfaces would need to be built manually by an organization's IT department, resulting in a significant effort—especially if multiple agencies need to be linked.

But this is exactly the issue addressed by the SAP S/4HANA Cloud for credit integration solution built on top of the SAP Cloud Platform. This subscription-based app takes care of the integration component; as shown in Figure 15.16, the SAP S/4HANA Cloud for credit integration solution is the link between SAP S/4HANA (the system of record), with its SAP Credit Management add-on, and peripheral credit agencies. This means that all the data included in an agency's credit reports—literally hundreds of data fields, including financial reporting information and profitability and liquidity indicators—can be used in automated analyses of customer creditworthiness.

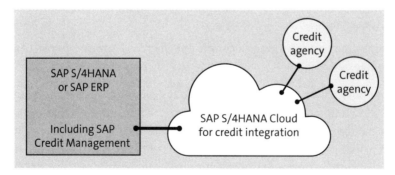

Figure 15.16 SAP S/4HANA Cloud for Credit Integration

The SAP S/4HANA Cloud for credit integration solution supports the following use cases:

- **Business partner searches**
  Once an organization sends a list of its business partners, their addresses, and other attributes to a credit agency, the credit agency can return a list of business partners that fit the search criteria, including its unique identifiers. The receivables user then selects the correct business partner. Based on this, the respective unique identifier is uploaded in the SAP Credit Management add-on.

- **Business partner credit reports**
  In this scenario, the business partner's unique identifier, product code, and reason code are sent to the credit agency, which returns the requested credit report, including credit rating, proposed credit limit, and so on. The credit report is then stored in the SAP S/4HANA Cloud for credit integration solution. Data like ratings, legal forms, and so on are updated in the SAP Credit Management add-on that runs on top of SAP ERP or SAP S/4HANA.

- **Business partner monitoring**
  The idea here is to get updates from the credit agency regarding a specific business partner and what's changed: from just an updated rating to a full new credit report.

From a data management perspective, the bulk of the data in external credit reports remains in the app. Targeted data fields (e.g., the external rating or the date a company was founded) are transferred to SAP Credit Management to enable scoring based on external and internal data. Technically, credit scoring is part of the SAP Credit Management add-on.

SAP S/4HANA Cloud for Customer Payments

Another receivables management process with room for improvement is related to the time spent interacting with business partners on very operational, receivables-related topics.

However, the invoice-to-cash process could be substantially accelerated by providing a self-service solution for customers to download invoices, access invoice duplicates, automatically make payments, or send remittances. These manual tasks often result in errors, which increase operational finance costs.

The principal idea behind the SAP S/4HANA Cloud for customer payments solution is to provide a customer-facing portal that gives business partners self-service access to their own account information. It acts as a window into your receivables data that can be viewed and acted upon by your customers—restricted to only the information relevant to each individual customer, of course.

SAP S/4HANA Cloud for customer payments allows your customers to pay their bills online at any moment (as shown in Figure 15.17). Through an email integration, customers can be informed of a new bill; clicking the bill opens the payments solution and displays the list of bills, including original invoice documents. From there, specific bills can be selected, credits can be applied, the appropriate payment method can be selected, and the payment can be executed.

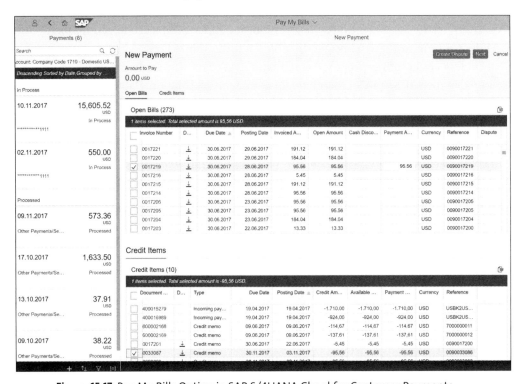

Figure 15.17 Pay My Bills Option in SAP S/4HANA Cloud for Customer Payments

Another option is the provision of remittance information. Once a payment has been selected and assigned to the relevant invoices for clearing, the payment advice then can be sent so that the accounts receivable team can apply the remittance.

Also, more basic information—like viewing the account statement or displaying customers' own master data in your SAP S/4HANA environment—is accessible through this application.

SAP Digital Payments Add-on

Another payment solution, the SAP digital payments add-on, further automates the accounts receivable process while allowing your customers to access multiple digital payment methods.

With this solution, SAP provides an alternative to complex customer-specific implementations. The SAP digital payments add-on is a cloud service that allows companies to process incoming credit card and other real-time payment methods in a secure and efficient way, significantly reducing cash reconciliation effort. This capability targets organizations running any variant of the SAP order-to-cash process (in B2B, B2C, point of sale, web shops, and other scenarios), but it focuses on organizations that need to offer their customers access to multiple digital payment methods.

As shown in Figure 15.18, the SAP digital payments add-on serves as a hub between a vendor running SAP S/4HANA who requests payment from the customer, the point-of-sale mechanism used to pay, and the payment service provider that authorizes payment.

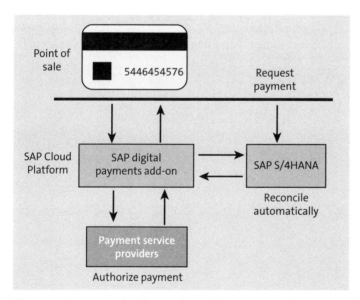

Figure 15.18 Process Flow for Credit Card Payments with SAP Digital Payments Add-On

Data storage is a sensitive topic for payment. Unlike other services that have nonstandard integration points or that store sensitive data in the ERP system (and subsequently open the ERP system up to PCI-compliance audits), with the SAP digital payments add-on, sensitive data is stored on the payment service provider side. Data remains fully secure thanks to the embedded tokenization approach. At the time of publication (spring 2019), two payment service providers, Paymetric and Stripe, are supported by this application.

15.3   Summary

As we discussed in this chapter, many finance process steps are supported by the finance functionalities included in the SAP S/4HANA solution itself—but in some cases, it's helpful to get an added boost from solutions in the SAP portfolio or extensions in the SAP Cloud Platform. We explored solutions that supplement native controlling functionality: SAP Product Lifecycle Costing, SAP Profitability and Performance Management, and SAP Customer Profitability Analytics. Because these solutions meet somewhat specialized requirements, they aren't embedded inside SAP S/4HANA, but rather are connected to it. We also considered applications built on the SAP Cloud Platform—SAP S/4HANA Cloud for credit integration, SAP S/4HANA Cloud for customer payments, and the SAP digital payments add-on—which serve an even narrower business need (including credit integration and customer payments).

Looking Ahead with SAP S/4HANA

Throughout this book, we introduced what we consider the fifteen major changes in SAP S/4HANA for finance. Now we'll end with information about the roadmap for the future and explain where to find more information.

The question often asked at the end of customer meetings is whether we're "finished" developing SAP S/4HANA Finance. It's a hard question to answer because as product managers we always know what we're working on currently, but we don't always know which additional requirements are waiting in the wings.

To help in these situations, SAP delivers a roadmap showing planned innovations and provides details of each innovation on SAP Innovation Discovery, so it's worth keeping an eye on these sources as you start to investigate the impact of a move to SAP S/4HANA for your organization. We'll look at these recent and planned innovations in the Recent Innovations section.

The roadmap also includes statements about the longer-term plan. These notes can affect timing decisions for the project as a whole or concerning a potential move to cash management or group reporting. We'll look at the product direction and vision in the Planned and Future Innovations section.

When it comes to finding more information, we can no longer simply point to the release notes and delta trainings and leave things at that. These days, there's almost too much information available, making it hard to decide which blogs you really should be reading and which you can safely ignore. In the Additional Resources section, we'll point you to some resources that will help you to understand how best to approach SAP S/4HANA, whether you're a new customer or an SAP ERP customer looking to make the move.

Recent Innovations

You can access the SAP S/4HANA roadmaps by visiting *https://www.sap.com/products/roadmaps.html* and searching for SAP S/4HANA. This will provide a general statement of direction for every area of SAP S/4HANA.

You can use the SAP Innovation Discovery page (*https://go.support.sap.com/innovationdiscovery/*) to find details of each innovation, with product features and implementation information for the key words in the lists that follow.

For example, Figure A.1 shows the entries for accounting for incoming sales orders in the cloud and on-premise editions. As you can see, the innovations described in Chapter 8 are available in SAP S/4HANA 1809 and SAP S/4HANA Cloud. An additional innovation is planned that will provide predictive journal entries for further procurement processes (not visible in Figure A.1). In the upcoming lists of important innovations in SAP S/4HANA 1809 and beyond, we've used the text shown in SAP Innovation Discovery to help you search for further details.

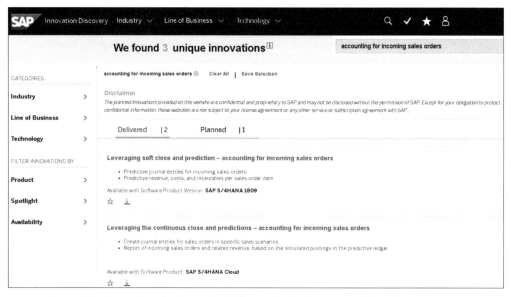

Figure A.1 Accounting for Incoming Sales Orders in SAP Innovation Discovery

These innovations were introduced with the on-premise release SAP S/4HANA 1809 in September 2018, but we'll list them here because you may not yet have the latest version of SAP S/4HANA in your organization:

- **Universal Journal (Chapter 1)**
  - Accounting for incoming sales orders
  - Statistical sales conditions
  - COGS split based on actual cost components

- **Local and global accounting (Chapter 2)**
  - Multiple currencies in follow-on processes
- **Financial process optimization (Chapter 4)**
  - Purchase order accruals
- **SAP Fiori (Chapter 5)**
  - Enhancements for flexible hierarchies
- **Predictive accounting (Chapter 8)**
  - Accounting for incoming sales orders
  - Statistical sales conditions
  - First commitment scenarios
- **Financial planning (Chapter 9)**
  - Plan data allocations reworked to update new plan data persistency
  - Connectivity of SAP Analytics Cloud with on-premise planning environment
- **Inventory accounting (Chapter 11)**
  - COGS split based on actual cost components
- **Group reporting (Chapter 12)**
  - Legal consolidation
  - Plan data consolidation
  - Increased level of detail in consolidation data
  - Intercompany reconciliation report
  - External system integration
- **Cash management (Chapter 13)**
  - Enhanced liquidity forecast through integration of real estate data
  - Snapshot of historic cash position report
  - Bank fee importing and reporting
  - Correspondence for bank account management
- **Cloud connectivity (Chapter 15)**
  - SAP RealSpend anomaly detection
  - Smart alerting in SAP Financial Statement Insights

Planned and Future Innovations

From a roadmap perspective, SAP distinguishes between those innovations that are planned over the following year (2019, in our case) and innovations that can be considered product direction or even product vision elements. For short-term innovations that are planned for release in the following year, you'll also find an entry in SAP Innovation Discovery. We've kept the text descriptions the same so that you can check information online.

Innovations planned for the medium term (part of the *product direction*) or longer term (part of the *product vision*) are shown on the roadmap but not described in detail. In many cases, SAP is still working with customers to build out these visions and understand what's needed going forward, so these topics are to be understood as a statement of direction rather than a list of planned features.

In this section, we'll give our perspective on expected developments from SAP and help connect the dots to topics already covered in this book.

The Universal Journal

The Universal Journal is clearly one of the big changes in SAP S/4HANA, and the change is largely complete. Nevertheless, two further innovations are planned for 2019.

First, top-down distribution is used to spread costs posted at a higher level (e.g., freight or bonuses) to more granular profitability segments (e.g., products or customers) in proportion to a key figure (e.g., revenue per product). We didn't cover this topic when we looked at profitability analysis because top-down distribution currently works exactly as it did when it was introduced for account-based CO-PA in SAP R/3 release 4.7 and onward.

The process currently is being redesigned to take into account that the relevant data is now in the Universal Journal and to optimize performance. Usability is also under review, with the plan to include this function in the universal allocation approach that we discussed in Chapter 4.

The product vision for profitability analysis does more than simply offer an optimized version of top-down distribution. The intent is to cover all scenarios previously only available in costing-based CO-PA so that SAP ERP customers can transition smoothly to the unified accounting model.

The second innovation centers on organizational change, which has been one of the great promises of SAP S/4HANA. The removal of the totals tables and summarization objects promises greater flexibility because it's no longer necessary to reflect an organizational change in all aggregated tables. Any change requires a toolset to determine the objects affected by the change and then implement the change. As we discussed, tools are available to adjust assignments in profitability analysis or reorganize profit centers. However, organizations continue to struggle to reorganize cost centers or change account structures. For this reason, the first step will be to provide an impact analysis that shows where a given object is used and what the impact of the change will be. You already saw the first steps in this direction when we looked at the where-used lists for cost centers in Chapter 5.

The product vision includes a change cockpit to orchestrate all changes to financial structures and the associated financial postings.

Local and Group Controlling

As local and group accounting structures continue to converge with SAP S/4HANA, there has been a lot of interest in the topics of currencies, accounting principles, and the need to see whole value chains rather than fragmented processes.

In 2019, SAP plans to enable the handling of an additional currency in applications writing data to the Universal Journal. With this topic comes a fundamental concern to get the currency set up right the first time. For this reason, the product direction includes the ability to add a new currency at a later stage and revisit the historical data to include that currency.

The product vision concerns the delivery of better value chain reporting to allow organizations to see how goods are flowing across multiple legal entities and the detailed cost breakout across the value chain. The goal is to enhance the various valuations and currencies captured in the Universal Journal to deliver the base data for the group reporting process and support the vision of a continual close.

Unified Controlling and Financial Operations

As we discuss the convergence of product-based and service-based industries, many innovations will be shown under the relevant industry, rather than in pure finance. One area in which contract accounting is to be extended concerns integration with SAP Bank Communication Management.

Financial Process Optimization

Financial process optimization is at the heart of innovations under the umbrella of the intelligent enterprise. The following innovations are planned for 2019:

- Further scenarios for universal allocation
- Machine learning for accruals management
- Application for goods receipt and invoice receipt monitor

As we discussed in Chapter 4, the first version of universal allocation is quite basic and more scenarios are planned, including the top-down distribution that we discussed earlier.

In this book, we discussed the topic of machine learning in finance, and as time progresses we'll find machine learning being used to reduce manual work and create recommendations for both accruals management and goods receipt/invoice receipt monitoring. The product direction is to deliver more scenarios for accrual management to further reduce the cost of finance and automate more accrual postings.

SAP Fiori

The SAP Fiori roadmap is organized by roles. Most roles in finance are still not completely free of SAP ERP transactions, so you should check the applications for the individual roles your organization uses to see when your users can potentially be working entirely in SAP Fiori.

Real-Time Financial Close

In Chapter 7, we showed new ways of orchestrating the entity close and demonstrated features already delivered in the cloud environment. We also discussed the idea that this approach will also be used to handle the group close going forward. Use SAP Innovation Discovery to check out the following innovations that are planned for delivery in 2019:

- Orchestrating entity close with advanced financial closing
- Integration of the group reporting solution into the advanced financial closing solution

Predictive Accounting

In Chapter 8, we looked at predictive accounting and laid out a vision for predicting the whole close. We showed how predictive accounting is used to support commitment accounting, and in SAP S/4HANA 1909 SAP plans to continue work to predict costs using the purchase order to take account of non-material-related purchase items.

The product direction concerns top-down and bottom-up prediction and the use of third-party data in these predictions. The idea is that the handling of the contractual obligations in predictive accounting will be fleshed out, with additional top-down and external data used to provide more reliable predictions concerning future financial performance.

Financial Planning

Chapter 9 focused on the need for a unified planning model and a common table that can be filled in using SAP Analytics Cloud, SAP BPC for SAP S/4HANA, spreadsheets, and so on. Clearly, we also need to be able to access this data directly. This might involve simple tasks, such as deleting all data that belongs to a plan category or copying data from one plan category to another. SAP plans to deliver a cockpit for managing planned data in 2019. In addition, keep an eye on the roadmaps for SAP Analytics Cloud for planning, which we expect to support even more financial planning scenarios that have traditionally been performed in controlling.

Group Reporting

Group reporting was introduced in SAP S/4HANA 1705 in the multitenant cloud and SAP S/4HANA 1809 in the single-tenant cloud and on-premise release. Each edition brings a lot of changes as the solution matures. The innovations planned for delivery in 2019 are intended to cover more features that organizations would expect to be available in a consolidation solution, such as matrix consolidation, the consolidation of investments, or intercompany reconciliation. Notice also the close integration (see Chapter 8) and the plan integration (see Chapter 9) and the improved data validation that is designed to accelerate the group close by identifying issues in the underlying data up front.

Moving forward, the product direction is to deliver on the real-time close story (Chapter 8) by offering continuous group reporting and to offer further consolidation-specific features, including restatement and the automated elimination of interunit profit in inventory (see Chapter 2). Additional features are also planned to support the intelligent enterprise in the way we discussed for other areas in Chapter 4.

Cash Management

Although cash management has undergone a complete changeover with SAP S/4HANA, moving forward with the solution the focus will be on end-to-end analytics for the cash and treasury manager. It will also incorporate further extensions toward the use of SAP Analytics Cloud for planning capabilities for liquidity planning, including predictive use cases.

On the level of bank account management, further automation is planned to be delivered with electronic bank account management (eBAM).

Tax and Legal Reporting

The roadmap for legal reporting for individual countries is handled by globalization, with specialists in the country monitoring changing legal requirements. The roadmap topic that is potentially of interest to all organizations is the introduction of time-dependent tax in 2019. This will allow organizations to keep the same tax codes but change the rates for a given validity period whenever tax rates are changed by the local governments.

Additional Resources

There are many different sources of information to guide you, but we've put together a list of key resources via which you can dig deeper:

- To find general information about what's in the finance solution, use the SAP Solution Explorer: *https://solutionexplorer.sap.com/solexp/ui/vlm/default/vlm/default-lob-64*.

- If you're an existing customer trying to determine your next steps based on the transactions that you use today, use SAP Business Scenario Recommendations to explore in more detail: *https://blogs.sap.com/2015/07/27/sap-s4hana-get-your-business-scenario-recommendations-today/*.

- If you're an existing customer trying to understand how to approach the digital transformation, use the SAP Transformation Navigator to chart a potential way forward: *https://support.sap.com/en/tools/upgrade-transformation-tools/transformation-navigator.html*.

- If you're a new customer, investigate the SAP Activate Methodology to understand how to approach a cloud project: *https://www.sap.com/products/activate-methodology.html*.

- If you're a new customer, use the SAP Best Practices Explorer to understand the scope of the SAP S/4HANA solution today: *https://rapid.sap.com/bp/#/browse/packageversions/BP_OP_ENTPR*.

Postscript

With our background mainly in the areas of controlling and financial planning and analysis, we've always been convinced that finance is about much more than registering accounting entries, monitoring receivables and cash, and publishing legal reports.

These operational finance tasks are essential for any organization, but they're only part of making sure a business remains healthy. We're now experiencing a shift from "pure accounting" to a management approach that has the CFO working very much alongside the CEO. Providing the right insights for decision-making and making sure you look forward (rather than just understand what happened in the past) are some of the key areas business leaders expect finance to deliver on to ensure the organization reaches its goals. These are the *value-adding* activities that have historically been dealt with in a data warehouse or even a series of spreadsheets.

When we attended a controlling conference in 2017, what struck us was the fact that many CFOs explained they were running SAP ERP—but that not a lot seemed to have changed since the 1990s in terms of how they used the system for decision support. This was especially noticeable because, by 2017, we had seen how finance professionals' mindsets change once they understand what SAP S/4HANA really can mean to them, in terms of not only automating operational tasks but also supporting strategy.

In recent years, we've talked about finance with SAP S/4HANA across the world with organizations of every shape and size, from huge multinationals that operate across the globe to local German companies that operate in a single city. We've talked with organizations that began their SAP journey with SAP R/2 and SAP R/3, and with others that are moving from legacy systems to implement SAP S/4HANA directly. We've talked indirectly with many more because we're regularly called in to handle individual queries from our own field and from partners.

And though there are a lot of SAP colleagues and knowledgeable people in the SAP ecosystem, many CFOs, heads of accounting, sales and production controllers, and others like them find themselves in situations in which they lack the "right" information to build their understanding of how technology can improve their professional lives. This is one reason we decided to take on a new challenge and write this book.

In the meantime, running finance in the cloud has become a genuine alternative to the classic on-premise implementation, even if we're only just beginning to explore the potential of the genuinely intelligent enterprise. (Let's not forget that there are still a lot of people doing mundane clerical and administrative tasks that easily could be automated, and that machine learning can help provide recommendations for accrual postings and items to be cleared, as well as the clerk's next online purchase!) Far better collaboration between teams is possible to bring value to the business.

Writing this all down helps us to realize how far we've come since the first experiments with SAP HANA and the move to get rid of totals records and work only with line items back in 2012. In this book, we've been able to illustrate many processes using SAP Fiori applications, even if the journey is by no means complete and there are still plenty of classic user interfaces out there. It's sobering to realize how much remains to be done to truly simplify the business architecture for a global enterprise and provide meaningful insights using the huge data store we collect in finance. We're only beginning to understand the potential reach of machine learning in finance, but it's exciting to see finance being innovative and to talk to organizations that have made massive changes in the last several years.

Announcements such as the release of SAP Cloud Platform Blockchain service, which aims to provide a unified view of all transactional enterprise data whether it resides in core systems or in the blockchain, offer exciting possibilities to extend the finance story further. However, this book can only describe what's available or at least known at the time of publication. We hope it has helped you pick your way between the promises and the current reality. As authors, we hate the idea that the book will become outdated, but as product and solution managers, with each revision we love being able to cross out "at the time of publication" and explain what we successfully delivered.

We hope that this book has helped you navigate your way through the finance changes that are part of SAP S/4HANA.

Janet Salmon and **Michel Haesendonckx**
April 2019

The Authors

Janet Salmon is the chief product owner for management accounting at SAP SE and has accompanied many developments to the Controlling components of SAP ERP Financials as both a product and a solution manager. She regularly works with key customers and user groups in the United States and Germany to understand their controlling challenges and requirements. Her role is to design and implement innovative controlling solutions with development teams in Germany and China.

Michel Haesendonckx is the global solution owner for financial planning and analysis at SAP SE with broad expertise in finance and performance management and a primary focus on management accounting and reporting. He is responsible for driving the go-to-market initiatives in this area for SAP, and is highly involved in key innovation topics. He has 23 years of experience in the area of financial processes and analytics, of which 20 years have been focused on SAP solutions. Michel built his functional experience as an external auditor, a controller in the oil sector, and a CFO in the port logistics industry; he extended his view in this field through his leadership position in FP&A in a globally operating consulting organization.

Index

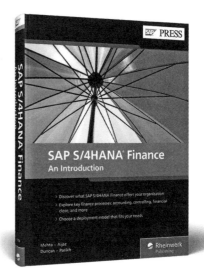

- Discover what SAP S/4HANA Finance offers your organization

- Explore key finance processes: accounting, controlling, financial close, and more

- Choose a deployment model that fits your needs

Mehta, Aijaz, Duncan, Parikh

SAP S/4HANA Finance

An Introduction

What will your financial transformation look like? This introduction to SAP S/4HANA Finance shows you next-generation finance in the new suite: financial accounting, management accounting, risk management, financial planning, and more. Consider how each process works in SAP S/4HANA, and explore the SAP Fiori apps that help you meet today's business user and reporting requirements. From previewing project planning to navigating deployment options, take your first steps toward financial transformation!

397 pages, pub. 01/2019
E-Book: $69.99 | **Print:** $79.95 | **Bundle:** $89.99
www.sap-press.com/4784

- Migrate your financials data from SAP ERP to SAP S/4HANA

- Configure the general ledger, asset accounting, cash management, and more

- Employ data migration best practices for SAP S/4HANA

Anup Maheshwari

Implementing SAP S/4HANA Finance

Ensure a smooth transition to SAP S/4HANA Finance with this system conversion guide! Follow step-by-step instructions for data migration and functional configuration. From the general ledger to asset accounting and beyond, you'll align your new system with existing Finance requirements and go live. Get the nitty-gritty details and pro tips that will make your SAP S/4HANA project a success!

570 pages, 2nd edition, pub. 11/2017
E-Book: $69.99 | **Print:** $79.95 | **Bundle:** $89.99

www.sap-press.com/4525

- See how Central Finance taps into SAP S/4HANA to improve financial processes and reporting

- Implement and set up a Central Finance landscape

- Use Central Finance to achieve your company's finance and IT transformation goals

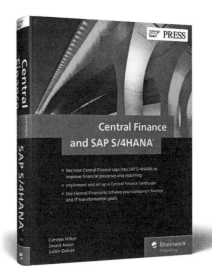

Hilker, Awan, Delvat

Central Finance and SAP S/4HANA

With Central Finance, SAP provides a lean deployment option for SAP S/4HANA. In this guide, see how Central Finance works, what it can do, and when to deploy it. Want to keep your existing ERP landscape? Learn how. Regularly undergo mergers and acquisitions? Plan ahead! Ground yourself in the system architecture and get step-by-step instructions for implementation. With details on Central Finance operations, master data management, and reporting, this is your one-stop shop for everything Central Finance!

458 pages, pub. 09/2018
E-Book: $69.99 | **Print:** $79.95 | **Bundle:** $89.99

www.sap-press.com/4667

- Learn what SAP S/4HANA offers your company

- Explore key business processes and system architecture

- Consider your deployment options and implementation paths

Bardhan, Baumgartl, Choi, Dudgeon, Lahiri, Meijerink, Worsley-Tonks

SAP S/4HANA

An Introduction

Whether you're already en route to SAP S/4HANA or taking your first look, this book is your go-to introduction to the new suite. See what SAP S/4HANA offers for your core business processes: finance, manufacturing, sales, and more. Learn about your reporting, extension, and adoption options, and consult customer case studies to learn from current customers. From the cloud to SAP Leonardo, get on the cutting edge of SAP!

647 pages, 3rd edition, pub. 12/2018
E-Book: $69.99 | **Print:** $79.95 | **Bundle:** $89.99

www.sap-press.com/4782

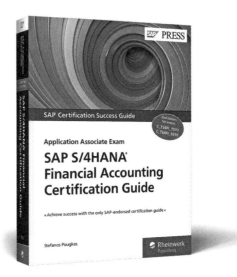

- Learn about the SAP S/4HANA Finance certification test structure and how to prepare

- Review the key topics covered in each portion of your exam

- Test your knowledge with practice questions and answers

Stefanos Pougkas

SAP S/4HANA Financial Accounting Certification Guide

Application Associate Exam

Preparing for your financial accounting exam? Make the grade with this SAP S/4HANA 1709 and 1809 certification study guide! From general ledger accounting to financial close, this guide will review the key technical and functional knowledge you need to pass with flying colors. Explore test methodology, key concepts for each topic area, and practice questions and answers. Your path to financial accounting certification begins here!

approx. 480 pp., 2nd edition, avail. 06/2019
E-Book: $69.99 | **Print:** $79.95 | **Bundle:** $89.99

www.sap-press.com/4856

- Master the profitability analysis functionality in SAP S/4HANA Finance

- Set up your value flows, reporting, and planning processes

- Learn how to migrate your profitability analysis data from SAP ERP to SAP S/4HANA

Kathrin Schmalzing

CO-PA in SAP S/4HANA Finance

Business Processes, Functionality, and Configuration

SAP S/4HANA Finance has transformed the CO-PA landscape! Learn about the updates and developments to profitability analysis in SAP S/4HANA Finance, and then configure your new system with step-by-step instructions and screenshots. Start with the basics: master data, actual value flow, and data enrichment. Then learn how to migrate your existing SAP ERP data into SAP S/4HANA Finance. The future of CO-PA with SAP is here!

337 pages, pub. 10/2017

E-Book: $79.99 | **Print:** $89.95 | **Bundle:** $99.99

www.sap-press.com/4383

Interested in reading more?

Please visit our website for all new book
and e-book releases from SAP PRESS.

www.sap-press.com